JEWISH MYSTICISM

An Introduction

J.H. Laenen

Translated by
David E. Orton

Westminster John Knox Press
LOUISVILLE
LONDON · LEIDEN

© 2001 Westminster John Knox Press

Originally published by Uitgeverij Kok – Kampen/Uitgeverij Lannoo – Tielt, as
Joodse Mystiek. Een inleiding, copyright © 1998 Uitgeverij Kok

Book design by Deo Publishing
Cover design by designpointinc.com

First edition
Published by Westminster John Knox Press
Louisville, Kentucky

A Deo title

This book is printed on acid-free paper that meets the American National
Standards Institute Z39.48 standard. ∞

PRINTED IN THE UNITED STATES OF AMERICA

01 02 03 04 05 06 07 08 09 10 — 10 9 8 7 6 5 4 3 2 1

Library of Congress Cataloging-in-Publication Data
Laenen, J. H.
    Jewish mysticism : an introduction / J. H. Laenen ; translated by David E.
    Orton.
        p. cm.
    Includes bibliographical references and index.
    ISBN 0-664-22457-1 (alk. paper)
    1. Mysticism—Judaism—History. 2. Cabala—History. I. Title.

BM723 .L24 2001
296.7′12—dc21

2001026108

Contents

Foreword

It is often assumed that the germ of Jewish mysticism was laid in the following classic rabbinic parable:

> Four entered the Garden: Ben Azzai, Ben Zoma, Aher and Rabbi Akiva.
> One cast a quick glance and died.
> One cast a quick glance and was smitten.
> One cast a quick glance and hacked the young plant down.
> And one ascended in peace and came down in peace.
> Ben Azzai cast a quick glance and died. Concerning him Scripture says: *Precious in the sight of the Lord is the death of his saints* (Ps. 116:15).
> Ben Zoma cast a quick glance and was smitten. Concerning him Scripture says: *If you have found honey, eat only enough for you ...* (Prov. 25:16).
> Elisha cast a quick glance and hacked the young plant down. Concerning him the Scripture says: *Let not your mouth lead you into sin ...* (Qoh. 5.5)
> Rabbi Akiva ascended in peace and came down in peace. Concerning him Scripture says: *Draw me after you, let us run. The king has brought me into his chambers* (Songs 1:4).   (t Hag. 2.3 4, etc.)

Parables demand interpretation, and this one is no exception. For a modern reader the questions about the aims of this story are almost too numerous to mention. But the most important are probably the following: What makes entry into the Garden so risky? What is the Garden, in fact? The practiced reader of ancient texts knows that finding an answer to such questions is well-nigh impossible and that it is more productive to wonder what successive generations of Jewish mystics made of the story. What did they understand by "entering the Garden"? Some will perhaps want to go further and ask: Is this Garden still accessible now?

The phenomena of religious experience that we generally refer to by the term mysticism are so varied and numerous that the question of what is characteristic and essential in mystical experience cannot be suppressed. In other words: how do we define the phenomenon of mysticism and how do we distinguish it from other sorts of religious experience? It goes without saying that such a challenge must be accepted, but the attempts that have been undertaken with this goal show that the task is not an easy one. We may wonder whether the effort to bring all these phenomena into a single compact description in fact brings us any nearer our goal.

Matters become so much the trickier when we realize that "mysticism" in an abstract sense cannot exist. Anyone who wants to express something in words is dependent on a terminological apparatus and a language that is understood by his or her audience. What is more, complex experiences such as those which mystics speak of in their testimonies cannot even be passed on unless they are packaged in images and terms familiar to those concerned. In essence no individual emotion can be transferred to others—not even toothache, let alone religious feelings and experiences. But still we all feel a compulsion to do so. And when we want to express our feelings we are dependent on a language and a world of experience which the speaker and the hearer have in common. Musicians who want to convey emotions by means of their music will have to make use of the musical language of their culture in order to find a hearing, even if here and there they cross the boundaries of conventions and reinvent the musical language.

These general truths are essential for a good understanding of Jewish mysticism. Jewish mysticism is mysticism which speaks in the terms of Jewish religion and culture. Even if a Jewish mystic might have had the feeling that the customary images and terms were inadequate, still he would have had nothing other than the tradition available to help him express himself. Anyone who wants to understand his message needs to be familiar with this language—even, in fact all the more so, if the message wants to break through boundaries, creating new images. Even mysticism which desires to rise above the reality of existing religious traditions can only express itself with the aid of language from those same traditions.

It is the achievement of this book that it holds unswervingly to this elementary truth and so limits itself to what is possible within the terms of an Introduction. It provides the religious and cultural context in which Jewish mystical movements functioned and in which the mystics wanted to bring their message. It gives an insight into a long period of developments, some of which reached dead-ends, some of which were taken up again and adjusted to new ideas, and all of which were in some way or other committed to writing and given shape by Jewish tradition. Together they have also become a striking part of the the tradition as a whole. Anyone who realizes how many problems and uncertainties accompany even just the correct grasp of the historical facts will not be able to have anything but respect for the

"modesty" of this effort. The terminological apparatus of classic orthodox Judaism is extensive and complex, and the dimensions which
mysticism has added to them have vastly enriched the whole. It is,
then, no simple task to get through to the world of Jewish mysticism.

One thing, however, needs to be emphasized. The common description of Jewish mysticism as a "secret doctrine" is problematic.
Admittedly, it is part and parcel of mysticism to speak of secrets. The
term "mystery" (*sod*) is constantly on the lips of Jewish mystics too. It
is not uncommon for them to use obscure images and to dress them in
very symbolic language, full of allusions accessible only to the initiated.
A great deal of knowledge and erudition are necessary to gain entry
into this material. But despite all this the Jewish mystical texts strive to
impart information. They are intended to be understood, otherwise
they would not have been written. If we do not understand them, this
is sometimes due to the fact that knowledge of esoteric oral traditions
is assumed; more frequently still the distance from us in time stands in
the way of a good understanding. But anyone who surveys the extensive mystical and kabbalistic literature will have a hard time maintaining the view that so many words can be devoted merely to the
preservation of a secret. Of course, the whole of life is one great mystery, and consequently we try to get to the bottom of that mystery,
knowing that ultimately it will not give up its secret. The paradox of
all mysticism, namely that it wants to express the inexpressible, is characteristic of Jewish mysticism as well. The great challenge is precisely
that it was emphatically *not* kept quiet.

For this reason a systematic and historically ordered account of what
the Jewish mystical texts have to say is not only possible but also a
prime necessity. That is precisely what we have in this book; readers
will find their knowledge and insights greatly enriched.

Is it still possible, all this apart, to get through to the real mystery? It
is imaginable that some individual will not be content to digest all the
information offered but will want to make their own attempt at "entering the Garden". Although no one is going to block their path,
there is still reason for the reticence that is so emphatically recommended to us in the parable of the four. There is still reason to fear
that instead of arriving in the king's palaces, one will not be able to
come down again in peace. But that is not because the parable denies
us access to a mystery. Nothing is forbidden here. In any case, who or
what in our day could forbid us from studying admittedly often difficult but still readable texts and from learning what we want from
them? No, it is a matter of caution and respect. It is respect that must

keep us from trespassing on someone else's garden. To force one's way in is quite a different thing than being "brought by the king into his palaces". Respect is the only thing that can be asked, and at the same time it is the least that can be asked. With this in mind the reader is invited to enter into the encounter with Jewish mysticism.

Prof. Dr. Albert van der Heide
Leiden University, The Netherlands

Translator's Note

A debt of gratitude is owed to Martin Baasten, who devoted many hours to a close reading of the draft translation. He provided specialist advice, offered many suggestions for improvement and saved the translator from a number of potentially embarrassing slips.

David E. Orton

Preface

This book aims to provide the interested layperson with a picture of the main currents of mysticism in the past two thousand years of Judaism.

Existing literature on Jewish mysticism falls into two groups, both of which have shortcomings: scholarly studies and popular works. On the one hand the serious, scholarly literature seems inaccessible to many people. Considerable previous knowledge of Judaism, its history, literature and language, is necessary for a good understanding of the often complex problems of the different mystical currents. On the other hand, the more popularized literature on Jewish mysticism is indeed accessible, but obscures as much as it clarifies. This literature is characterized largely by an extremely subjective approach to the material and a great lack of detailed knowledge. Moreover, such publications often deal with matters which have virtually nothing to do with Judaism, let alone with Jewish mysticism. At the end of this book, when the reader has been able to gain an idea of the content and historical development of Jewish mysticism, we shall offer a critical discussion of a number of such books.

Between these two sorts of literature there yawns an unfortunate gap. This book is a modest attempt to go some way towards bridging this gap. On the one hand it aims to be a serious description, based on scholarly research, of the history of the main currents in Jewish mysticism. On the other hand, it aims to be accessible to a broader readership of interested non-specialists, without presupposing a great deal of prior knowledge.

Hence an attempt is made in this book to sketch in bold strokes the various mystical currents and the literature that has emerged from them. In the course of this, numerous smaller—though interesting—details are left untreated. Certain aspects of the background, which would be presupposed as already known in scholarly literature, are spelled out and explained.

The content of this book is based on existing scholarly research and does not rest on a personal interpretation. However, given that there

Jewish Mysticism

are a variety of views and interpretations on every aspect of Jewish
mysticism, there is no way that a book like this can avoid offering a
personal choice between divergent opinions. Where possible, in the
discussion of many topics, alternative opinions will be given in summary form.

To begin with we shall pay attention to scholarly research into Jewish mysticism. Then follows an overview of the historical backgrounds
of the Jewish people and the traditional literature of Judaism. Then we
shall ask ourselves what mysticism in general is, and what Jewish mysticism means in particular. After these introductory chapters a description follows of the content of the main mystical currents: ancient Jewish mysticism, the classical period of Kabbalah, Lurianic Kabbalah, the
Kabbalah of Shabbetai Zevi and the hasidic movement. This is followed by a concluding chapter devoted to one specific topic: language
mysticism.

To enhance readability, footnotes are not used. Readers who wish
to delve deeper into Jewish mysticism can find further literature in the
bibliography given by chapter at the end of the book. This chapter
also contains references to translations or commentaries on various
mystical texts in modern languages.

The transcription of Hebrew and Aramaic words is deliberately kept
as simple as possible.

I am especially grateful to two people with regard to the coming into
being of this book: first, Prof. Dr. A. van der Heide, who introduced
me to the field of Jewish mysticism during my studies in Leiden and
who gave me the idea of writing this book. He read the entire work
and provided it with useful detailed comments. Second, Drs. M.F.J.
Baasten, who acted as a willing and inspiring sounding-board throughout the whole writing process; in conversations with him many of my
ideas gained definitive shape. In addition, he meticulously read
through the entire English translation of this book. I am, further, in-
debted to Prof. Dr. J. Hoftijzer for his comments on the section on the
history of Ancient Israel and to Prof. Dr. L. Van Rompay for his conversations with me on gnosticism. Naturally, the final responsibility for
the content of this book rests entirely with the present writer.

J.H. Laenen
The Hague

1

Introduction

1. Scholarly research into Jewish mysticism

Scholarly research into Jewish mysticism and indeed Judaism in general is not so old. Up to the end of the eighteenth century, Judaism was seen primarily in terms of religion: the story of the chosen people, the Torah that was given by God to Israel on Sinai, the exile, the awaited redemption with the coming of the Messiah and such like. There was no consideration for Judaism in its historical development, a Judaism that had been constantly subject to change throughout the ages.

It was only under the influence of the eighteenth-century Enlightenment, an important current in the history of European culture, that we find modern attempts to reconstruct the Jewish past and to describe it in scientific historical terms.

The Enlightenment was marked by an absolute belief in the rational powers of human beings. By subjecting all areas of existence to investigation through human reason, it was thought that an end could be put to superstition, prejudice, submission to traditional thinking and all institutions and authorities that maintained these things. Developments in the empirical sciences, too, had shown that rational inquiry could render traditional values untenable. There arose an optimistic belief in human possibilities. People became convinced that the influence of reason on human actions would grow and grow and that all aspects of human life would be permeated by it and reshaped and improved by it.

In the religious arena these enlightened views came to expression in the desire to do away with dogmas and authority based on tradition. In the area of relations between nations and people, the Enlightenment stood resolutely against intolerance and absolutism, while such ideas as individual freedom and the equality of human beings were strongly emphasized.

This new cultural movement did not fail to impinge upon a large section of the Jewish community and it led to the emergence of the

Jewish Enlightenment, the Haskalah, in which the foundations were laid for a thorough change in Jewish consciousness and which brought about a sharp break in the continuity of traditional Jewish life. The universal, timeless validity of the Torah was restricted; the Hebrew Bible was brought back to being a book with a certain social function for a particular period in the history of the Jewish people.

One of the ideals of the eighteenth-century Enlightenment, the emancipation of oppressed and disadvantaged groups, appealed greatly to many Jews. After centuries of persecution and prejudice against Jews, under the influence of these enlightened ideas many felt the need to be accepted as Jews within Western European Christian culture. They wanted to play a part in the secular society of the various European countries, while still remaining loyal to their own culture and traditions. In order to be accepted as a full citizen in Christian European society, however, Judaism had to earn a certain respect. This required a decent knowledge of the cultural background of Judaism. It had to be shown that Judaism had a culture that was not fundamentally primitive or strange by comparison with Western culture and that the Jews were deserving of full emancipation. Partly as a result of the interest in the past that was growing in Romanticism, this desire led to the *Wissenschaft des Judentums*, Jewish scholarship which in the nineteenth century began studying the history of Judaism with in fact a single goal: to give the outside world a picture of Judaism which would command respect in European scholarly circles. Emphasis was laid on Judaism's individual and unique contribution to world culture.

It is not surprising that under the influence of the enlightened views of the time heavy emphasis was placed on the elements in Judaism that would arouse respect in the Christian environment. It was particularly the rational aspects of Judaism that were brought to the fore. In the eyes of this new *Wissenschaft des Judentums*, Judaism was the rational, abstract and monotheistic religion *par excellence*. Judaism was identified with these rational aspects: the rationalistic philosophy of Maimonides, for example, was regarded as the highpoint of Jewish monotheism, in which the spirit of Judaism attained its greatest purity. The heart of Judaism could be reduced to one "essence" of non-contradictory ideas.

On the other hand there was little understanding for those elements in the history of Judaism that precisely did not gel with the ideas of the *Wissenschaft*; everything that was not rational or not abstract in character was viewed as in fact non-Jewish. Thus Jewish mysticism as a whole did not fit the picture that *Wissenschaft* had of Judaism. It was not denied that such a thing as a Jewish mysticism had existed, but this was seen as a backwater on the periphery of real Judaism (that is to say, rational, abstract and monotheistic Judaism).

The thoroughly negative attitude of most great scholars of the *Wissenschaft des Judentums*, including Abraham Geiger, Leopold Zunz, Heinrich Graetz and Simon Dubnow, came to expression in the exclusion of mysticism. No independent place was credited to Jewish mysticism in Jewish history. Mysticism was seen as a polytheistic, reactionary and destructive element in Jewish culture, which represented everything that Judaism should not be; it was regarded as rebellion against enlightened progress. The use of manifold emanations in Kabbalah in order to describe God, for example, seemed contrary to reason as well as monotheism. The denial of a history of mysticism was given expression, among other things, in a metaphor of the core and the shell. The core stood for the "genuine" essence of Judaism and the various shells were the historical manifestations of it. But mysticism was a shell on top of a shell, a parasitic growth without organic connection to the actual seed. Mysticism could only serve the negative didactic goal of warning Jews against such dangers, which were undermining Judaism.

The messianic hope in the complete redemption of the whole Jewish people, which enjoys an important place in Jewish apocalypticism and mysticism, was similarly rejected by Jewish thought in the nineteenth century. Belief in a Messiah who would some day give the ancestral homeland of Palestine back to Israel had to give way to an acceptance of the European nations as the only real home. The desire that the Jewish people would enjoy a national return to the Promised Land was relinquished. Through belief in the permanent, unbroken progress of human existence, apocalyptic breaks in the historical continuity were denied. People no longer believed in a sudden reversal, the dawning of a messianic era. The "redemption" would be the result of the continuing further development of human progress and not an intervention by God.

Despite these overarching rational tendencies in the nineteenth century there were also scholars who adopted a more positive attitude towards mysticism. Thus Adolphe Franck made a serious attempt to describe the Zoharic tradition. Solomon Munk pointed to the influence of gnosticism on Jewish mysticism. Adolf Jellinek collected and published many texts of a mystical character. And it has to be said that in their attempt to depict Jewish mysticism as non-Jewish, perverse nonsense, some managed to make a contribution to our knowledge of the subject. Moritz Steinschneider, who came across many kabbalistic manuscripts in European libraries, laid the bibliographic foundations for future research. Heinrich Graetz too, notwithstanding his aversion to mysticism, had knowledge of mystical sources. Steinschneider and Graetz can be viewed in some regards as the founders of the academic study of Jewish mysticism, even though they did not apply their knowledge to giving an unprejudiced account of the subject. In general, incidentally, it was the case that the texts that were read were often barely understood, if at all; very little was known about Jewish mysticism. As yet, no one had a historical overview of mystical currents, ideas and writers.

At the end of the nineteenth century, under the influence of a changed political climate and a new wave of anti-semitism, belief in the emancipation of the Jews and the hope of a peaceful co-existence with another culture began to wane; partly as a result of this, the basis was laid for a national regeneration of the Jewish people. This was expressed also in Zionism, which advocated the return of the Jews to the Holy Land.

In consequence of this, the scholarly approach to Jewish history underwent a change. The tendency of the *Wissenschaft des Judentums* to separate the messianic hope in a return to the Land of Israel from Judaism, was no longer accepted by many. Jewish historiography now became more nationalistic in character; Jewish apocalypticism and messianism, in which the return to the Land of Israel was a central theme, were once again considered important. Often the aim was to show that Zionism was the climax and fulfillment of Jewish history, instead of the end of it, as the *Wissenschaft* had been proclaiming.

In the early twentieth century this changed attitude manifested itself among other things in a wider interest in the not strictly rational aspects of Judaism. The realization grew that the non-rational could also be studied scientifically. This resulted in a new interest in Jewish mysticism as an essential expression of Jewish existence. An attempt was made, away from one-sided rational assumptions or polemical points of departure, to undertake research into the origin, development, historical role and the social and intellectual influence of Jewish mysticism. In short: a study of the place of mysticism in the context of the internal and external forces which determined Jewish history. The pioneers of this new approach were S.A. Horodezky and E. Müller, but above all G. Scholem.

It was Gershom Scholem (1897-1982) who first undertook research into the history of Jewish mysticism on the basis of an objective methodological approach. Scholem's scholarly work proved an impressive beginning and has led to a reevaluation of and new attention to Jewish mysticism.

Scholem devoted great attention to careful study of the many previously uninvestigated mystical and kabbalistic texts. Although at some points he built upon the study of nineteenth-century scholars, most of the mystical literature was unknown to his predecessors and lay unread. On the basis of meticulous philological research of innumerable manuscripts which he collected, Scholem inquired what mystical currents there had been in the course of time in Judaism, what mystical ideas were developed in these currents, who the writers of the texts were and when they lived. Through attention to the biographical details of the authors of the various mystical works, many forgotten mystics were brought out of obscurity. For many texts which had been wrongly ascribed to certain authors, he was able to establish who had really written them. Gradually the tentative contours of these movements and their mutual relationships and influences came to light, which for the first time gave rise to a chronological picture of the emergence and history of Jewish mysticism.

After many separately published partial studies, the results of this research were published in 1941 in his book, *Major Trends in Jewish Mysticism*. In this work for the first time in history a coherent picture was sketched of the most prominent mystical currents and their literature within Jewish religion and culture. It contains the first analysis of the mystical movement known as ancient Jewish mysticism or Merkavah mysticism, which was described as a form of Jewish gnosticism. In addition, in *Major Trends* we find also for the first time a comprehensible treatment of the Ashkenazi Hasidim, a mystical-ethical movement in Germany in the second half of the twelfth and the thirteenth century. In addition, the book contains a study of Abraham Abulafia, a Spanish mystic who wrote his mystical works in the second half of the thirteenth century, as well as the result of a study conducted over many years of the authorship of the Zohar, the classic work of Kabbalah. The inclusion in Scholem's book of a chapter on Shabbetai Zevi was regarded as fairly revolutionary. The appearance of *Major Trends* signified a milestone and a turning-point in scholarly research into the history of Jewish mysticism. Indeed, some regard this book as the real beginning of scholarly research in this area.

Gershom Scholem can justly be called the pioneer of the study of Jewish mysticism. His work brought about a reevaluation of Jewish mystical literature. This is reflected, among other things, in the fact that Jewish mysticism has now gained its due place in general reference works on mysticism. Scholem was one of the founders of the Institute of Jewish Studies and of the Hebrew University of Jerusalem. Under his leadership, research into Jewish mysticism and its influence on Jewish culture developed into a mature and fully fledged discipline.

Despite the fact that Scholem devoted more than sixty years of his life to the study of Jewish mystical literature, there is still plenty of scope for further study. Various parts have been only sketched in broad strokes and many complex issues await further research. Thus the study of ancient Jewish mysticism, for example, did not really get underway until after 1975 and in the meantime it has made great strides. At other points Scholem's conclusions were disputed and subjected to new research. This is true, for example, of research on the mystical movement of Shabbetai Zevi.

In the meantime three generations of scholarly researchers, both within and outside Israel, have developed Scholem's work further and advanced the discussion at many points. Among them are an array of specialists in the field of the various mystical movements, such as Joseph Dan, Scholem's successor at the University of Jerusalem, Isaiah Tishby, Isadore Twersky, George Vajda, Ithamar Gruenwald, Moshe Idel, Peter Schäfer, David Halperin, Mark Verman and many others who cannot be mentioned here.

However important the results yielded by this groundbreaking scholarly research may be, discussion of the place of Jewish mysticism within Judaism is far from over. In essence it is a question of what, precisely, Judaism is. The *Wissenschaft des Judentums* saw Judaism as a rationalistic, abstract monotheistic religion, in which mysticism formed an alien and non-Jewish element, which could be put down to factors that had penetrated Judaism from the outside. Scholem, however, turned resolutely against such one-sided ideas. He emphasized the unique character of each mystical movement independently and the place which it occupied within Jewish religion and culture. He was convinced not only that Jewish mysticism had developed from within Judaism itself, as an authentic Jewish product, but more than this, that Jewish mysticism was an important dynamic force which, as a continuous undercurrent, in fact formed the source from which Judaism renewed itself time and time again; mysticism, according to Scholem, was the beating heart of Judaism. It is especially since Gershom Scholem's death that this discussion of the place of mysticism in Judaism has flared up again fiercely. The idea that Judaism is above all a rational religion is still shared by many. Later in this book, in the description of the various mystical currents, frequent reference will be made to this discussion.

2. The historical background of the Jewish people and its traditional literature

All too often, it seems that people who are interested in Judaism are put off by its great complexity and by the many aspects involved, which are difficult for outsiders to understand. This makes access difficult to much serious literature on the subject, certainly on Jewish mysticism. In such books considerable previous knowledge of biblical history, history of Judaism, Greek philosophy, the hellenistic world and Rabbinic literature is presupposed. This knowledge cannot be taken for granted for everyone.

Therefore, in order the better to understand the experience which underlies the various mystical movements within Judaism, a brief survey will now be given of some historical data that were of essential importance for the emergence of Judaism: biblical history, the Second Temple period, and the emergence of Rabbinic Judaism. Attention will also be paid to the most important works of rabbinic literature: Mishnah, Tosefta, Midrash and Talmud.

2.1 *Biblical history*

A central place in Judaism is taken by the Hebrew Bible (the "Old Testament"), which among other things tells the story of the first patriarch Abraham, with whom God enters into a covenant. This Abraham is indeed seen in Judaism as the forefather and the real historical beginning of the later Jewish people. The story relates how Abraham is chosen by God to be the father of a new and great people that will issue from him. God promises to give Abraham and his descendants the land of Canaan.

Abraham and his people are called Hebrews. At that point there is as yet no mention of "Israelites" or "Jews". God's promises to Abraham are inherited by his son Isaac, the second patriarch, and to *his* son Jacob, the third patriarch. After a nocturnal wrestle with "a man", Jacob is given a new name: Israel. Jacob (now called "Israel") has twelve sons who are the forefathers of "the twelve tribes of Israel" or "the Israelites".

As a result of a famine Jacob treks with his sons to Egypt, where Joseph—Jacob's favorite son—has become viceroy. The situation of the

Israelites in Egypt eventually deteriorates and they are forced into slave labor. It is Moses who then leads the Israelites out of Egypt (the so-called "Exodus"), after which the long journey through the wilderness to the Promised Land begins.

The central theme of this journey through the wilderness is the revelation of God to Israel on Mount Sinai, where Moses receives the Law from God, which he writes down in the Torah (the first five books of the Bible: Genesis, Exodus, Leviticus, Numbers and Deuteronomy, also called the "Pentateuch"). If the Israelites keep to God's Law they are God's chosen people.

At the end of the journey through the wilderness the people of Israel trek across the river Jordan and into the Promised Land, gradually taking it into their possession. Forced by social and political problems with other peoples, the need was felt for an earthly king. By means of the prophet Samuel God indicates the first king of Israel: Saul. With the coming of this first king God stops being king of Israel in the immediate sense. The period of true theocracy thereby comes to an end. Under king David, Saul's successor, and his son, king Solomon, Israel became a powerful kingdom. Solomon built a magnificent temple in Jerusalem. This temple became the center of the cult and symbolized the presence of God among the Israelites. The kings of the house of David were seen as theocratic kings, representatives of God, the true king of Israel.

Soon after king Solomon's death already the kingdom split into two pieces: the southern part consisted of the tribe of Judah, in which lay the city of Jerusalem, along with the area of the tribe of Benjamin. This area in the south is called the kingdom of Judah. The northern area, the land of the other ten tribes, with Samaria as its capital, was called the kingdom of Israel. Israel chooses kings who are not from David's royal line, while Judah remains under the rule of the Davidic dynasty.

In 722 BCE, Israel, the northern kingdom of the ten tribes, is deported and the kingdom of Israel comes to an end. Ten of the twelve tribes disappear into Assyria. In the middle ages numerous stories turn up in Europe telling where these tribes are supposed to have gotten to; according to many of these stories, the ten tribes spread out from Assyria into other parts of the world, constantly changing names. After the fall of the northern kingdom the kingdom of Judah remains intact.

In 586 BCE Judah too is conquered by the Babylonian king Nebuchadnezzar II. He sacks the temple of Jerusalem, has the last Davidic king's eyes put out, his sons killed and a significant section of the Judean population deported into exile to Babylon. This brings an end to the empire of Judah as an independent kingdom and to the rule of the royal household of David. With this the so-called Babylonian exile begins.

2.2 *The Second Temple period*

After the Babylonian Empire had been conquered by the Persians, in 538 BCE the Persian king Cyrus permitted the Judean exiles to return to Judah. They were also given permission to rebuild the ruined temple of Solomon in Jerusalem. Only some of the people took advantage of this opportunity to return; others indicated their preference to stay on in "Babylon".

The exiles who returned from the Babylonian exile made a start on the reconstruction of the temple, which was completed in 515 BCE. After the return from Babylon, which took place in various phases, Ezra set the Torah—the Law of Moses—again right at the center of social life. The Second Temple too again took a central place in religious life. This marked the beginning of a time known as the Second Temple period, which was to last until 70 CE.

From the time of Ezra onwards we may use the term "Jews" as a designation of the returned descendants of the earlier kingdom of Judah. We have already seen the term "Hebrews" used of Abraham and his people. From the time of Jacob, who was called Israel, we speak of the people of the twelve tribes as "Israelites". The term "Jews" is thus used only for the returnees from the Babylonian exile. In view of the fact that nothing remains of the ten tribes from the northern kingdom, so that the Jews, the descendants of the southern kingdom of Judah, are the only tangible remains of the people of Israel as a whole from the time before the division of the kingdom of Solomon, it has become common practice to equate the Jews with the people of Israel, or conversely to call the patriarchs Moses, David and Solomon "Jews". Strictly speaking, then, this is not correct.

An important change in relation to the period before the Babylonian exile was that the inhabitants of Judah no longer had a state of their own, but formed part of a larger kingdom. In the beginning they stood, as has been said, under Persian rule. The Persians were defeated by Alexander the Great, who conquered the whole of the ancient Near East around 330 BCE. With the coming of Alexander the Great the period of hellenism ensues, in which the Greek language and civilization exercised their influence on the areas he conquered.

Hellenism had a far-reaching influence on some circles in Judaism, while other groups were more suspicious towards Greek culture. An important source of conflict was religion. Judaism was after all based on a strict monotheism which was irreconcilable with the Greek multiplicity of gods. The tension between on the one hand assimilation to hellenistic culture and on the other the preservation of the purity of the Jewish religion was to have long-term effects.

Even after Judea—as the former Judah was now called—had become part of the Roman Empire in the first century before the common era, this tension persisted. In 66-70 CE it even led to a Jewish uprising against Roman domination, which was put down violently. In 70 CE the Romans sacked Jerusalem and the Second Temple.

2.3 *The emergence of rabbinic Judaism*

After the return from Babylonian exile the Law of God again came to have a central place in Jewish life, and of course it had to be applied to all kinds of everyday situations. In an ever-changing society, however, new, practical situations were always cropping up to which the regulations in the Torah offered no direct answer. This meant that, if it was to be applied at all, the Law had to be interpreted. We read in the Torah, for example, the prohibition of doing work on Saturdays (the *shabbat*). Anyone wanting to apply such a law in daily life has to know precisely what activities come under the category of "work" (and are thus forbidden activities) and which cannot be viewed as "work" (and are thus permitted activities). The text of the Torah gave no judgment on this. Using all kinds of methods, scribes (*soferim*) therefore had to find a way of deducing from the Torah the answer to concrete questions. As time went on traditions presumably came into being regarding the question of how the commandments and prohibitions of the Torah had to be applied under the changed circumstances.

The sacking of Jerusalem and the Temple by the Romans in 70 CE signified an end to the religious and national center of Judaism and the suspension of the sacrificial cult that had taken place in this Temple. Judaism now had to come to terms with an existence without a state of its own, but also without a Temple as the central element in religious life.

After the destruction of the Second Temple a group of scribes emerged in Judaism who were known by the name "Rabbis". They laid the foundation for rabbinic Judaism, the form of Judaism that is still familiar to us today. The Rabbis transformed Judaism, which

threatened to disappear, to such a degree that it was able to continue
to exist without motherland and Temple.

Now that the Temple, with its sacrificial cult, had disappeared,
study of the Torah came to stand alone in central place. The Rabbis
therefore attached great significance to the above-mentioned traditions
about the interpretation and the application of the Torah in daily life.
These traditions, which were said to have been transmitted orally from
generation to generation by the scribes during the period of the Second Temple, were now named by the Rabbis the Oral Law (or Oral
Teaching). In this regard, the Rabbis taught that apart from the written Torah God had also given Moses an oral Torah. This oral Torah
was an interpretation of the written Torah. Thus from the time of
Sinai a knowledge had already been transmitted which equipped
scribes to apply laws in the right way under constantly changing circumstances.

The Rabbis saw the Torah as the divine constitution of the Jewish
people. This Law, dictated by God to Moses, was in their view as
immutable as God himself. The divine character of both the written
and the oral Torah meant that the Law was perfect and covered the
whole of existence. No human norm or standard, however erudite,
ethical or eminent, could be accepted above or alongside this divine
word.

The close relationship between the oral and the written Torah was
one of the pillars of this new rabbinic Judaism. The one teaching
complemented the other and the two were inextricably linked. The
written Torah formed the fixed, unchanging element of God's Word,
while the oral Torah was the living, constantly changing aspect of it.

The custom was for the orally transmitted traditions not to be written down and fixed. However, the changed circumstances after the
destruction of the Second Temple quickly created the necessity for
them to be set down in writing after all, although in theory the prohibition remained operative. A start was thus made with the writing
down of the oral Torah, which formed the basis for rabbinic literature.

2.4 *Rabbinic literature*

By rabbinic literature we mean all the books produced by the Rabbis
("the Sages"). A wide variety of topics are addressed in this literature.
A very important element of course is the application and interpreta-
tion of the Law. The legislation which gives direction in the life of the
Jews into the greatest details of daily life, is called in Hebrew *halakhah*.
A great deal of literature in rabbinic literature is halakhic in character,

that is to say that it has a bearing on the *Halakhah*, the set of legal rules for practical daily living.

Besides Halakhah, rabbinic literature also contains material on other subjects. Thus we find all kinds of folkloric material, alongside theological viewpoints, parables, legends, apparently mythical stories, ethical anecdotes, etc., which are not directly concerned with the application of legal judgments in daily life. All this non-halakhic material is referred to by the term *Haggadah* (or *Aggadah*). The haggadic element too is an important aspect of rabbinic literature, for example in non-halakhic biblical interpretation.

The amount of orally transmitted traditions became very extensive, so that the need evidently arose for a systematic overview of all the halakhic decisions. It was probably shortly after 220 CE that such a systematic overview was compiled: the *Mishnah*. Innumerable rulings were brought together in it; both commandments and prohibitions already found in the written Torah as well as their interpretation and commentary on them from the oral Torah. The form in which this overview of the Halakhah is given in the Mishnah text consists mainly of pronouncements by various (schools of) Rabbis who discuss the laws. The generations of Rabbis whose interpretation is included in the Mishnah are called Tanna'im, and they lived roughly between 0 and 220 CE.

Alongside the Mishnah we have another work which largely mirrors the Mishnah and derives from roughly the same period. This work is known as *Tosefta* ("addition"). It is divided up in the same manner as the Mishnah and also contains rabbinic discussions of legal rulings. The great difference from the Mishnah, however, is that the Tosefta has picked up many traditions which are not to be found in the Mishnah. The editor of the Mishnah, Rabbi Judah ha-Nasi, made a selection for the Mishnah from all the available material, omitting many traditions, in particular those dealing with esoteric matters. Many such traditions we find included in the Tosefta. A tradition that is not adopted in the authoritative Mishnah is called a *baraita* (plural: *baraitoth*), which literally means "standing outside". In content they often differ from the Mishnah in their understanding of the Law.

The fact that the rulings in the Mishnah were viewed as normative religious laws did not mean that discussion of the Law ceased. There was a constant need for further deduction of new legal rules to suit ever new situations and problems in the daily life of the Jews. The rulings and discussions from the Mishnah began, therefore, to be provided with further commentary. This new commentary, the *Gemara* ("teaching" or "completion"), came into being roughly in the period between 220 and 600 CE, at the hand of generations of Rabbis called the Amora'im. The Gemara consisted of even more elaborate meticulous discussions of the rulings in the Mishnah: the how and why of the rulings, the theory behind them, further conclusions, deductions and special circumstances were discussed by the Amora'im in the smallest details. Various views were set over against each other dialectically in the form of dialogue. Mishnah and Gemara together form the *Talmud*.

There are two Talmuds: the Palestinian (or: Jerusalem) Talmud, which contains the views of the Rabbis from Palestine, and the Babylonian Talmud, which is the result of discussions by the Rabbis from the area of former Babylon. Of the two Talmuds the Babylonian has by far the greater authority. As a result of unfavorable economic and political circumstances from the end of the third century of our era, the importance of the Jewish community in Palestine dwindled considerably. The Jewish community in "Babylon" continued to flourish much longer and even became a very important center for Jewish scholarship.

Another, very well-known form of literature in rabbinic literature is *Midrash*, a method whereby a particular idea about or a viewpoint on all kinds of subjects is linked with the authoritative biblical text. In creative ways the Rabbis were able to link many new ideas to the old, familiar Scriptures. These new ideas thus also became part of the oral Torah. These *midrashim* vary considerably in character. They generally deal with haggadic subjects about which something is said in the light of the biblical texts, but also halakhic questions could be the subject of a midrash. In Palestine the extensive midrashic material was brought together in separate collections, while Babylonian Judaism included innumerable midrashim in the Talmud.

Rabbinic Judaism had an abiding and far-reaching influence on the character of later Judaism. Rabbinic tradition was—and for centuries remained—the religious framework of orthodox Jews; the Mishnah, the Talmud and the Midrash continued to be the objects of intensive study. The Jewish mystics too were completely oriented towards and permeated by this rabbinic tradition. It was only with the Jewish Enlightenment (*Haskalah*) in the eighteenth century that a section of the Jews began to withdraw completely or partially from rabbinic tradition.

3. What is (Jewish) mysticism?

In section 1 of this chapter, "Scholarly research into Jewish mysticism", a number of things were said about the problem of the place of Jewish mysticism within Judaism. Thus far we have not, however, posed the question, What, precisely, constitutes Jewish mysticism?

It is not so easy to answer this question. In fact the question falls into two parts. First of all we have to know what, precisely, mysticism is, and then we have to ask what it is that determines the character of specifically Jewish mysticism. It has, however, proved extraordinarily difficult to give a good definition of mysticism. A definition is a description which clarifies the content of a phenomenon and at the same time determines what exactly belongs to this phenomenon and what does not.

Imagine that we were to start with a broad, general definition of mysticism, for example along the lines of: "Mysticism is an awareness of a higher realm". In that case a great deal falls under the heading of "mysticism"; actually any expression of religious feeling has something to do with "a consciousness of the higher realm". According to this broad definition all forms of religion could be called mysticism. So a definition as broad as this does not get us very far.

If, however, we use a much narrower definition of mysticism we come up against other problems. A frequently used definition in literature on mysticism is: "Mysticism is the spiritual experience of a unification with God, the so-called *unio mystica*". This narrower definition fits certain forms of Christian mysticism extremely well, where the concern is indeed with the experience of absorption into or unification with God. One might think for example of the well-known Spanish mystic Santa Teresa de Jesús (St. Theresa of Avila, 1515-1582), who in her most important work, *Moradas del castillo interior* (Chambers of the Inner Castle) describes her path to unification with God. Jewish mysticism, however, is not familiar at all with such a form of unification with God. In all descriptions of the Jewish mystical experiences there is always talk of a difference between God and his creation; there always remains a distance between the mystic who is trying to approach God and God himself, and the two never become one. Thus if we were to stick to the narrow definition we would have to come to the conclusion that there is no such thing as Jewish mysticism!

There seems not to be any definition of mysticism which covers all of the world's mystical movements. The differences in the various approaches and points of departure are so great that it is impossible to capture them all under one common denominator and thus to speak of

"mysticism" as if it were a single entity. But even if we restrict ourselves to mystical currents in Judaism it proves to be impossible to give
a single comprehensive definition of "Jewish mysticism". The various
Jewish mystical currents seem to display so many differences that it is
difficult to designate them by a single definition.

So far, then, it has proved impossible to give a good and useful definition of the phenomenon of (Jewish) mysticism. Since there is little
point in giving an overview of the many, often contradictory opinions
of mysticism in general and Jewish mysticism in particular, for our
description of Jewish mysticism we shall have to make a choice. In the
context of this introduction to Jewish mysticism, the view of Gershom
Scholem is perhaps the most sensible. Without making any claim to a
comprehensive definition, he approaches the problem from quite a
different angle. According to Scholem it is better not to think first of
the theory of what Jewish mysticism is precisely in an abstract sense, in
order subsequently to see how this abstract idea is concretely realized,
but we have to tackle the matter the other way round: first investigate,
from the concrete, historical facts, the currents we find in the course of
Jewish history and which meet the broad criteria (to be given shortly),
and then to see what ideas we meet in each separate movement. By
this means we can arrive at a picture of the historical development of
Jewish mysticism. The question of whether particular movements still
belong to mysticism will be answered as we go along.

In his research Scholem assumes that for mystics there is a gulf between the human being and the divine world. Before there was any
question of this gulf, humans experienced the unity of everything that
had been created and unity between the created and the divine. The
mystic now endeavors to bridge the chasm between God and human
and to find the way back to God. By allowing spiritual activity to
flourish the mystic gives expression to his or her desire to throw a
bridge to God or to supernal reality.

The mystic gives expression to the desire for the divine world or
the lost paradise within his or her own religious framework and by
means of his or her own religious images, whether Jewish, Christian or
Islamic. Because mysticism is closely related to traditional religion,
Christian mysticism, for instance, is very different from Jewish or Islamic mysticism. The mystical interpretation of the suffering of Christ,
who performs a mediating function as a person between human and
God, is a theme that is of course entirely foreign to Jewish mysticism.

Jewish mysticism lies anchored in Judaism, in which a living God
manifests himself in the whole creation, in his revelation to the people

of Israel on Sinai, and in the Torah. Hebrew too, God's sacred language in which the Torah is written, forms one of the pillars of Judaism and thus of Jewish mysticism. This language formed the key to the deepest secrets of the Creator and creation. In the description of the mystical experiences of Jewish mystics from all mystical movements, these elements occupy an important place.

For the time being it is perhaps best to say that all the mystical movements in the history of Judaism together form Jewish mysticism as a single entity. Jewish mystics of all times have attempted by means of their spiritual activities to restore contact with an eternal divine reality, which lies beyond our finite human world. Each current, however, did this in its own entirely individual way, often differing in approach from an earlier or later mystical movement.

One of the factors underlying the sometimes considerable differences between the various mystical movements is the fact that they came into being in different periods. Each movement to some extent bears the marks of its time. To give just one example: the expulsion of the Jews from Spain in 1492—where Jewish culture had enjoyed a golden age—was experienced as an insurmountable catastrophe which, according to some scholars, subsequently led to a strong revival of messianism. This desire for the Messiah and for redemption manifested itself in Lurianic Kabbalah, which is entirely permeated by messianism.

There are of course points of agreement between the various Jewish mystical movements; they all speak of the development of spiritual activity in order to come to a direct experience of the divine world. Nonetheless we must not make the mistake—as is the case in much non-critical literature—of lumping the whole of Jewish mysticism together, but on the contrary we must look out attentively for essential internal differences.

The same may be said with reference to the differences between Jewish mysticism and that of other religious systems. Thus the kinship between the three monotheistic religions, Judaism, Christianity and Islam—with their common roots in the Old Testament—will be much closer than for instance in relation to an oriental religion. At least as important, however, are the differences in approaching the divine, which lie rooted in the religions concerned. If we lay too much emphasis on the agreements, the danger may arise that fundamental differences between the various mystical systems and experiences will not come sufficiently to light.

In the following chapters we shall attempt to sketch the characteristic features of the various Jewish mystical movements and to situate them against their historical background.

2

Ancient Jewish Mysticism

1. Merkavah mysticism and Hekhaloth literature

From what point may we speak of the very first appearances of Jewish mysticism? Some have tried to show that mysticism already existed in the Hebrew Bible. Religious experience as evidenced by certain psalms or visions of prophets like Isaiah and Ezekiel could indicate underlying mystical ideas. It seems better, however, not to view such religious phenomena as expressions of mysticism. Although it is not impossible that mystical currents existed in biblical times, there is no evidence of this at all and in view of the lack of data we are unable to make any such claims.

The first tangible historical evidence of the existence of Jewish mysticism is not found until the second century of the common era. The precise dating of this beginning is a matter of debate; estimates range from the second to the sixth century. These first mystical pronouncements are called "chariot mysticism" or "mysticism of the divine throne". This form of mysticism functioned in closed rabbinic circles which anxiously took care that the contents of their knowledge and their mystical experience did not become known by the public as a whole. In this form of mysticism the mystic made a visionary journey through the palaces of the seven heavens. The final goal of this journey was the privilege of beholding God, who was seated on his glorious throne in the seventh palace of the seventh heaven.

This image of God as a king seated upon his throne is borrowed from the first chapter of the biblical book of Ezekiel. There we may read how the heavens opened for the prophet Ezekiel in a vision. He saw four beings, each with a wheel next to it on the ground, which turned with every movement of these four. Above their heads and the turning wheels there was something like a canopy, with above it a throne on which sat a figure who looked like a human being. In the description of this vision the prophet Ezekiel nowhere speaks of a chariot—in Hebrew *merkavah*—but the way in which the vision is described calls to mind a picture of a throne standing on four wheels: a throne-chariot. Mysticism which centers on the vision of God on his throne is therefore generally referred to as Merkavah mysticism. Mystical texts speak of God's *merkavah*.

The central ideas and motifs as they appear in Merkavah mysticism in the mystic's journey through heavenly realms to God's throne, have their roots in extensive esoteric traditions which were preserved and taught in closed circles of Jewish scholars at the end of the Second Temple period (0–70 CE), earlier according to some. (Later in this chapter we shall go into the basic differences between esoteric traditions and those of Merkavah mysticism.)

The cradle of both these esoteric currents and the mystical currents must be sought in Palestine. From around the sixth century of our era, under the influence of the poor political and economic situation in Palestine, mystical activity shifted to the Jewish communities in Babylonia. Here the material from the preceding centuries was reworked, in the course of which, new interpretations were added to the earlier material. This process lasted until around the tenth century.

The literature about the early esoteric traditions as well as on mystical reports of the journey through the heavenly realms with the descriptions of the throne of glory are known by the collective name of Hekhaloth literature (*hekhaloth* is the plural of *hekhal*, which among other things means "palace"). The writings of this Hekhaloth literature derive from a long period of around a thousand years. It should be mentioned here that there are also other divisions of this literature; thus for example according to some, the esoteric traditions from the early phase should not be counted as Hekhaloth literature.

First of all we shall take a look at what has come down to us of Hekhaloth literature in manuscript form.

2. The problem of the extant material

Although the period of ancient Jewish mysticism lasted a long time and there must have been many groups and schools, scarcely anything has come down to us of the original work of these mystics. Over time the texts have constantly been rewritten. What is left of their literature consists largely of manuscripts dating from the fourteenth to the sixteenth century. These manuscripts contain tractates and fragments of what must once have been complete works by the Merkavah mystics and form the end result of a centuries-long process of reworking.

This process occurred in four phases. The earliest phase of Hekhaloth literature is formed by esoteric traditions as they were preserved,
taught and developed in closed circles in the first two centuries of our
era (or earlier, according to some scholars). In the second phase these
traditions were adopted by the first Merkavah mystics—between the
second and the sixth century—who summarized all this earlier material, revised it and put a new spin on it. Old motifs were given a new
meaning and quite different aspects than before were emphasized. In
this way the foundation was laid for a totally new literature. In the
third phase, from the sixth to the tenth century, later generations of
Merkavah mystics in turn revised this new literature once again and
supplemented it with new elements. Then, in the fourth phase, by far
the greater part of this material came into the hands of the Ashkenazi
Hasidim, a mystical movement in Germany from the twelfth and thirteenth centuries (see Chapter 3, § 2.5.3). This movement not only
preserved the material but also revised it to a considerable degree and
mixed it with a new and distinctive terminology and interpretation.

The end result of this process is then found in numerous manuscripts dating for the most part from the fourteenth to the sixteenth
century. This means that between the time of their original composi-
tion and the form in which we now have them, the texts of the
Hekhaloth literature that remain to us have undergone extensive
changes and will no longer contain much authentic material. It will be
evident that a reconstruction of ancient Jewish mysticism on the basis
of these corrupt—that is to say, unreliable—manuscripts will encounter considerable problems.

Besides the problem that we no longer have access to the original
works of ancient Jewish mysticism, so that it is difficult to form a picture of the development of the ideas, research into this period is made
even more difficult by the fact that almost all the works are pseudepigraphic, and we do not know who the real authors were. None of
them wrote his esoteric traditions or his mystical experiences under his
own name. They ascribed their works to biblical figures like Enoch,
Abraham or Ezekiel. Many tractates were also ascribed to famous
Tanna'im (the founders of the Mishnah), like Rabbi Johanan ben Zak-
kai, Rabbi Akiva and Rabbi Ishmael. The reader is given the
impression that these biblical figures and rabbinic teachers were the
real authors of such works and that they were in fact custodians of the
secret esoteric wisdom and mystical traditions. As a result we have no
details of the people who are the factual authors of the Hekhaloth

literature. It cannot be ruled out, by the way, that certain traditions found in these works do indeed go back to these Tanna'im.

Revision and pseudepigraphy have made it impossible to determine with any certainty from what period the texts date. Thus the Hekhaloth literature that derives from third- to fifth-century Palestine can no longer be clearly distinguished from the Babylonian Hekhaloth literature of the sixth century and later.

Notwithstanding all these problems it is still believed that roughly 25 distinct works from the original Hekhaloth literature can be discerned among the corrupt medieval manuscripts. Traditionally, various works from this literature are known by the names *Re'uyoth Yehezq'el* (Visions of Ezekiel) *Sefer Yetsirah* (Book of the Creation), *Sefer ha-Razim* (Book of Mysteries), *Harba de-Mosheh* (Sword of Moses), *Havdalah de-Rabbi Akiva* (Havdalah of Rabbi Akiva), *Shi'ur Qomah* (Measurement of the Divine Figure), *Hekhaloth Rabbathi* (Great Hekhaloth), *Hekhaloth Zutarti* (Minor Hekhaloth), *Sefer Hekhaloth* (Hebrew Book of Enoch, or *3 Enoch*), *Ma'aseh Merkavah* (Work of the Chariot), *Merkavah Rabbah* (Great Chariot), and *Massekheth Hekhaloth* (Tractate of Hekhaloth). Some of the most important of these works will be dealt with below.

In scholarly discussion of the question to what extent the surviving material still contains authentic tractates, or parts of them, opinions differ widely. Many of the manuscripts we have contain material from various tractates. In addition there are many different versions of each individual tractate. There are scholars who still assume the existence of separate tractates with a title of their own, others who think that we cannot speak of tractates like the Great Hekhaloth or the Minor Hekhaloth, in view of doubts that in the period of ancient Jewish mysticism there ever were separate tractates under these titles with a more or less fixed content. Much research remains to be done before a clear and reliable picture of Merkavah mysticism and its mystics can be obtained. A great deal of ancient Jewish mysticism is still unknown to us.

3. Esoteric traditions

As we have seen, the earliest phase in the Hekhaloth literature consists of esoteric traditions. This means esoteric speculations (i.e. ideas intended for the initiated), philosophical and reflective contemplations of subjects which go beyond what can be established empirically or logically. Although speculation relates to metaphysical subjects, it does not yet involve real mystical activity, in which a bridge is thrown to a supernatural reality, with the aim of directly experiencing the divine world.

It was long assumed that one can speak of Jewish mysticism already in the Second Temple period, from the second century BCE. Although some may still be inclined to this view, many are now of the opinion that at this early stage it is not a matter of real mystical activity in the sense of the ascent through the palaces to the divine throne. In the following we shall discuss various esoteric traditions in turn.

3.1 *Ma'aseh Merkavah*

One of the forms of esoteric speculation related to the vision of Ezekiel, as is described in the first chapter of the biblical book of Ezekiel. The various elements of the vision, such as God's chariot-throne (*merkavah*), the angels, animals, wheels, clouds and the firmament, become the objects of speculation and interpretation. This form of exegesis (interpretation) has been given the name *Ma'aseh Merkavah*, which means literally: "the work of the (throne) chariot". In the course of time various closed groups developed which preserved all kinds of esoteric traditions relating to God's throne chariot.

The tractate *Re'uyoth Yehezq'el* (Visions of Ezekiel), which is written in the form of a midrash, may serve as an example of such *Ma'aseh Merkavah* exegesis. The first chapter of the book of Ezekiel tells us that the prophet stood by the river Kvar and received a vision. This midrash now supplements the Bible story and relates—something which the Bible itself says nothing about—how Ezekiel looked into the sky reflected in the water. When the "holiness" opened the sky for him, he saw in it seven heavens, one about the other. There then follows an extended description of God sitting on his throne, along with the heavenly powers situated around the throne. The names of the heavens are interpreted and esoteric information is given concerning the structure of the heavenly realms viewed. Thus we learn that the distance from the earth to the heavens, and the distance from heaven to heaven, as well as the thickness of each individual heaven, each consist of a five-hundred years' walk. What is notable about this specific text is that the prophet views a throne chariot separately in each heaven, all of which are described independently. Later in the text there is also mention of an eighth heaven, in which God resides when he is not sitting on his throne.

3.2 *Ma'aseh Bereshith*

The story of creation in Genesis chapter 1 was also the subject of speculation. The biblical account does tell us about the origins of the world, but it still leaves many questions unanswered. In Genesis 1.1-2, for example, we read the following description: "In the beginning God created the heaven and the earth. And the earth was without form and void. Darkness covered the deep and the spirit of God hovered over the water." One may wonder, however, where that water suddenly comes from, whether it, too, was first created. The Bible text speaks, after all, only of the creation of heaven and earth and says nothing about the creation of the water. Nor does the creation story say anything about God's motives in creating the world. Questions of this sort then gave rise to further speculation.

As in the case of *Ma'aseh Merkavah* esoteric traditions developed about the origins of creation (cosmogony) and about the structure and arrangement of creation as a dynamic and ordered whole (cosmology). These exegetical traditions concerning creation are known by the name *Ma'aseh Bereshith* (literally, "the work of creation") and thus form speculations concerning things the Bible says nothing about.

As an example of such a *Ma'aseh Bereshith* tradition we may mention a tractate called *Sefer Yetsirah* (Book of Creation). This tractate contains a concise treatment of cosmology and cosmogony and hints at hidden knowledge of the creation of heaven and earth. The opening paragraph explains that God created the world with 32 wondrous paths of wisdom which form the basic structure of the whole creation. These are the 10 *sefiroth*—a newly coined word which means something like "primordial numbers"—which together with the 22 letters of the Hebrew alphabet form the 32 paths of wisdom and thereby the elements or building blocks of the whole creation. They form as it were the instruments which God used in the creation process and by means of which the creation could take place.

In this tractate the 10 sefiroth stand for the primordial elements and the points of the compass. The 22 letters of the alphabet are divided into three groups: three "mother letters", seven "double letters" and twelve "single letters". The cosmos too is divided into three areas: the universe, time, and the human body. It seems that the letters of the Hebrew alphabet have an influence on all three of these areas of the cosmos, setting their stamp, as it were, on everything in the whole world.

The three mother letters, *aleph, mem* and *shin,* correspond with the three basic elements, light, water and fire, through which everything comes into being. In the area of time, the mother letters are represented in the three seasons of the year: the warm season, the moderate season and the cold season. Besides this we have an analogy in the human body, which is divided into head, chest, and belly. The seven double letters, *beth, gimmel, kaph, peh, resh* and *taw*, also have an analogy to the three areas of the cosmos. Among other things, on the universal plane they correspond with the seven planets, in the realm of time with the seven days of the week, and in the body with the seven bodily orifices. Similarly the twelve remaining single letters have an analogy, among other things, with the twelve signs of the zodiac (universe), the twelve months (time) and the twelve most important organs (body).

The Book of Creation had an enormous influence on the later medieval Jewish mystics of the Kabbalah and on Jewish philosophers of that time. Contrary to what is often maintained, this book was not the first kabbalistic mystical work. Underlying the Kabbalah, which came into being only in the second half of the twelfth century, lie quite different ideas than those we find in the Book of Creation. The misunderstanding is due to the term sefiroth, which occupies such a prominent position in later Kabbalah as well. In the Kabbalah, however, this term has quite a different meaning than that which the Book of Creation attaches to it (see Chapter 3, § 2.2).

3.3 *Magic: theory and practice*

Alongside the topics of *Ma'aseh Merkavah* and *Ma'aseh Bereshith* in Hekhaloth literature we also find all kinds of traditions which had magic as the object of esoteric speculation. These traditions cannot be counted as mysticism either, because there is no talk of mystical activity here. Very probably this esoteric, theoretical knowledge of magic was developed already in classical antiquity. The neo-Platonic philosophers in particular developed vast theories on demonology. Jewish speculations on magic reflect the influence of magical traditions from the late hellenistic world. This knowledge was the property of an intellectual scholarly elite.

Apart from the theoretical knowledge of magic there also developed traditions in which this knowledge was applied for practical purposes. A good example of this is the tractate *Sefer ha-Razim* (Book of Mysteries), which contains detailed instructions for all kinds of practical purposes, such as the healing of people, the overcoming of one's enemies or love potions. In addition we find instructions on dealing with supernatural powers, divination, influencing the course of events and such like. In line with the Merkavah tradition the book is divided into seven chapters giving a description of the seven heavens. The lower, first heaven is full of magic. The higher one gets, the lesser the role played by magic; in the seventh and highest heaven there is no longer any question of magic and we have to do with pure Merkavah material: a description of God sitting on his throne of glory. Other tractates dealing almost exclusively with magical subjects are *Harba de-Mosheh* (Sword of Moses) and the tractate Havdalah of Rabbi Akiva.

In their mystical activities, the later Merkavah mystics also applied the knowledge they possessed of theoretical magic for practical purposes. As a result, both theoretical and practically applied magic belongs to the integral components of later Merkavah mysticism.

3.4 *Physiognomy*

Besides the elements already mentioned, esoteric speculations in reference to the determination of the character of a person on the basis of physical features (physiognomy) are an integral part of Hekhaloth literature. According to the authors of these texts information could be read from a person's body about his or her character, spiritual and moral qualities, health, future and such like. These perceptions were supported by astrological knowledge.

The art of discerning someone's character was an extremely elaborate system, which was divided into various parts. Much attention was paid to the form and lines of the hand (chiromancy) and to facial features, in particular the lines of the forehead (metoposcopy). But also other parts of the body, including the genitals, could be taken into account for interpretation. An important part is played by the letters of the Hebrew alphabet, which according to these traditions were engraved in particular parts of the human body.

The origins of these traditions should perhaps be sought in the ancient Near East, although we know nothing of the means by which they found their way into Hekhaloth literature. The basis for these traditions was the biblical expression *hakkarath panim* in Isaiah 3.9, which can be translated as "the perception (or: knowledge) of the face". Although in the biblical context this expression is not yet connected with secret knowledge relating to the link between the character of a person and his or her bodily features, this passage was taken in esoteric circles for the first time around the beginning of our era as being a reference to physiognomy. In rabbinic literature we find no clear indications of the application of physiognomic methods. Among the Dead Sea scrolls, however, we do have some texts that are physiognomic in character.

The texts relating to physiognomy are usually written in an unclear, technical idiom, which does not always give us a good picture of what precisely is meant. In general these texts are found spread throughout various works of Hekhaloth literature, and often it is the introductions to these works that contain physiognomic material.

The various esoteric traditions in Hekhaloth literature are in reality not so strictly distinguished as described above. The work *Re'uyoth Ye-hezq'el* (Visions of Ezekiel), in which *Ma'aseh Merkavah*, the exegesis of the throne, is paramount, also contains cosmological traditions which belong with *Ma'aseh Bereshith*. *Sefer ha-Razim* (Book of Mysteries), with its strong emphasis on magical speculations, was written against the background of *Ma'aseh Merkavah* traditions. Alongside the esoteric speculations on the origins of the creation, in *Sefer Yetsirah* (Book of Creation) we also find *Ma'aseh Merkavah* elements, and one can even find forms of language mysticism in them.

These speculations are taken up, sometimes in adapted form, in practically all the later mystical texts.

4. From esoteric speculation to mystical activity

We have seen above that Hekhaloth literature contains traditions on various subjects which on closer inspection cannot be regarded as forms of mysticism, since they do not speak of a spiritual activity that is oriented towards a direct experience of the divine world and its inhabitants. At a certain stage, however, it seems that a transition took place to a new phase which can indeed be called mysticism in the true sense. The question of how this transition took place, from closed groups with their esoteric traditions to the mystical activities of ascent through the heavenly palaces to God's throne, cannot be easily answered, since we have no knowledge of many of the relevant historical details. Despite these objections it has been possible to arrive at a feasible reconstruction of this change on the basis of other facts.

The early traditional literature from the time of the Tanna'im, the rabbinic teachers of the Mishnah, seems at one point to contain two new elements. First, an entirely new approach is added to the traditional allegorical exegesis of the Song of Songs, suggesting that God had given a description of himself in the Song. Second, esoteric speculation on the vision of the prophet Ezekiel, which contains a description of seven heavens, was inclined to develop into an active "ascent" through the heavenly realms to the throne of glory. These changes seem to occur in and around the school of Rabbi Akiva, in the second century CE.

It was traditionally assumed that the wise king Solomon was the author of the Song of Songs. This book of the Bible offers an unselfconscious description of sensual love between a bridegroom and a bride. The physical charms of each are sung about in turn, as well as their passionate desire to unite with each other.

From the discussions that were conducted concerning whether the Song of Songs should be adopted in the canon of the Hebrew Bible, it is clear that the sacred character of this book was not firmly established. Precisely this book was now called by Rabbi Akiva the holiest book of all the scriptures, given by God on Sinai just like the Torah. That means that the author of the Song of Songs is not Solomon but God himself. That the book comes directly from God is also expressed in another tradition by means of a wordplay: the author of the Song of Songs is not king Solomon (*ha-melekh shelomo*), but "the king who possesses peace" (*ha-melekh she-ha-shalom shelo*), which means God himself.

The bridegroom in the Song of Songs, who is also compared with a king who resides in his palace, is now God himself. When the bride sings of the physical features of her beloved, the king, and exclaims that his cheeks are like balsam beds, his arms like golden scrolls, his legs like white marble columns and his body like a piece of ivorywork, God is in fact thereby giving descriptions of himself.

Alongside these new ideas of the Song of Songs there is still another new element that could indicate a change, in which as well as ordinary exegesis there is also a question of spiritual activity in the form of ascent through the divine world and of viewing the secrets in these heavenly rooms. The Tosefta tractate *Hagigah* 2.3-4 contains a parable in which four learned Rabbis enter into the *pardes* (garden). These were Ben Azzai, Ben Zoma, Aher and the already mentioned Rabbi Akiva, who—as we have seen—is connected with the new interpretations of the Song of Songs.

This parable relates how the four scholars enter the *pardes* or garden. When they emerge from the garden Ben Azzai dies. The second scholar, Ben Zoma, loses his rational faculties, while the third, Aher, loses his faith. Only the fourth scholar, Rabbi Akiva, proves capable of emerging physically and spiritually unscathed from his experiences in the garden. A striking feature of this story is not only that Rabbi Akiva is said to have *ascended* in peace and to have *come down*—the oldest versions still have "went in" and "left"—but also that his ascending and descending is linked with a biblical text from the very same Song of Songs (1.4), where we read: *Draw me after you—let us make haste! The king has brought me into his chambers.*

The two new elements in the esoteric exegesis described above seem to form the beginning of the emergence of mystical activity. The view of the Song of Songs as a self-portrait by God was to develop into the picture of God on his throne of glory in the seventh palace of the seventh heaven, which formed the final destination of the heavenly traveler. The *pardes* or garden from the Tosefta story becomes more clearly the paradise or the heaven(s) to which the ascent is made. The chambers of the king then stand for the palaces of the celestial realms.

Not all modern scholars are agreed that the *pardes* story forms one of the first indications of a development of esoteric traditions towards mystical activity. Some see it as a simple parable concerning Torah study, which does not contain any mystical elements. Nonetheless the development described above is generally regarded as very probable. For the first time in the history of Judaism we have to do with mysticism, a whole new phenomenon with an individual and unique character.

A text which builds further upon the new mystical elements is the tractate *Shi'ur Qomah* (Measurement of the Divine Figure). It contains a very detailed description of the figure of God as creator of the world, which is based on the description of the male lover in the fifth chapter of the Song of Songs. According to this tractate the figure of God contains all the secrets of the creation. The mystery of God is expressed in the various members of the divine body, in their mystical names, and in the measurements of these divine parts.

The various measurements of the body parts are expressed in gigantic numbers, in units of thousands or tens of thousands of parasangs (an old Persian measure). The divine figure is thus given astronomical, unimaginably large measurements. All the members and the separate parts of them have esoteric names. These names consist of strange and sometimes unpronounceable combinations of letters, often without any clear meaning, which exceed our comprehension.

In the first instance a description of God's figure in terms of the human body—this text speaks of God's head, his hair, neck, beard, arms and so on—is a shock for orthodox Judaism. So it is no surprise that in some Jewish circles this tractate was viewed with horror. But the question is whether the Measurement of the Divine Figure is really concerned with the representation of God as a human being (anthropomorphism). The measurements of the divine members given are so far outside what can be rationally conceived of, that it seems more likely that the author of this tractate is trying to say precisely the opposite: God's form is beyond human conception.

The later medieval mystics, the Kabbalists, saw this tractate as an important source for working out the Kabbalistic mystical symbols with which the various powers of the divine world were described.

5. The heavenly journey and the vision of the divine throne

5.1 *Prerequisites and preparations*

The closed groups of Merkavah mystics carefully screened their esoteric and mystical traditions from the outside world. In order to be admitted to such a group or school, one had to fulfill certain conditions. To begin with, a novice had to meet a number of moral requirements. Above all, he had to follow strictly all the commands of the Halakhah, the rules for daily Jewish life. Then he was subjected to a chiromantic (palm-reading) and metoposcopic (face-reading) examination; anyone who wanted to ascend through the heavenly realms thus necessarily had to have the right character to be able to successfully complete such a journey.

After a novice had been admitted to the mystical group and had been initiated into the esoteric and mystical traditions he could prepare for a journey through the palaces of the seven heavens. Each heavenly traveler, whether this was the first journey he had undertaken, or one of many, had to prepare very carefully for the journey. After extensive preparations, which were ascetic in character—among other things it was necessary to fast for several days—the mystic had to take account of what others had already experienced on another heavenly journey. Then he assumed a sitting position with his head between his knees. In this position he recited prayers and ecstatic hymns in a whisper, which gave rise to a sort of self-hypnosis. Absorbed in a state of deep self-obliteration the mystic saw in his mind's eye the heavenly palaces loom up through which he had to travel, and the journey could begin.

5.2 *Ascent through the heavenly palaces*

The reports of mystical experiences in the various Hekhaloth texts are not all precisely the same in content. Not only did each mystic experience the heavenly journey in an entirely individual way, but the various periods in which certain groups of mystics were active also produced variations in content, shifts of emphasis and changes of terminology.

The descriptions by the Merkavah mystics give a picture of the ascent through heavens situated one above the other. Around 500 CE the strange fact emerges that the mystics were also called "descenders to the throne-chariot" (*yordei merkavah*). From that moment on practically all the mystical reports present the process with two opposing images: on the one hand they speak of "ascent" through the heavenly realms, while on the other hand there is talk of "descending" to the Merkavah. Why this terminology changed, remains obscure.

The mystic's visionary journey led him through seven heavens, each of which in turn contained seven palaces. The mystic had just one aim in his journey: to view the Divine Figure on his heavenly throne of glory. The trip was not without its dangers, and as the journey through the heavenly rooms progressed, the difficulties grew. Without thorough preparation such a journey was doomed to fail.

To get from one palace to another the mystic had to move through heavily guarded gates. The gatekeepers were angelic beings, who were looking to hinder the traveler or do him harm. At each room to which the traveler wished to be admitted, he had to show the gatekeepers the right seals (*hotamoth*). These seals consisted of divine names, secret formulas or arbitrary combinations of letters of the Hebrew alphabet, which gave the mystic the power to overcome the dangers and to ascend through the divine worlds. The important thing was that the mystic knew the names of the angels on the way. By knowing the name of the angel in question the traveler had a certain power over him. In addition, the heavenly traveler could protect himself against great dangers by singing hymns in which God was praised or by using magically charged images.

As the degree of difficulty of such things increased, the risk also grew that at some point one would make a mistake, so that the watchers or enemy angels could simply refuse entry to a higher area. The higher one ascended, the more difficult it became to get the heavenly powers to give information and secure their help. The traveler had to struggle with misleading visions and had to come to terms with destroying angels, who tried to confuse him.

The most difficult test of the whole process was the transition from the sixth to the seventh and last room. Here the mystic had to show that he could distinguish marble from water. This distinction was evidently very difficult. If at any time he took marble to be water, he would not pass the test. In that case enormous masses of water would swamp the traveler and there could be no question of his completing the heavenly journey.

The element fire also played an important part during the procession through the heavenly realms. Some reports relate that the body of the mystic was suddenly consumed by fire as soon as he made a wrong judgment or did not know the right formula. Other reports speak of fire as an ecstatic experience on entering the first palace.

The literary form of the reports of the ascent is sometimes one of dialogue. In a conversation between two or more Rabbis, for instance, there is talk of the right way of attaining visions of the heavenly kingdom. A Rabbi who had already made the trip on a previous occasion tells the others of his experiences, the dangers he had met and the prayers, hymns or names consisting of particular combinations of letters which he had used to achieve his progress through the palaces. The others respond to this by asking questions or by relating their own experiences. Frequently the dialogue is more or less instructive in nature. Not only is the traveler given the content of what the heavenly beings will say or sing, but there is teaching about what precisely must be said or answered, and what formulas are necessary in connection with the summoning of the various angels in the different phases of the ascent.

5.3 *The vision of the celestial throne*

After the person who descended to the Merkavah had passed all the tests after a long and difficult journey through the heavenly realms, he finally reached the goal of his journey: the vision of the Holy One on his throne of glory. Here in the seventh palace of the seventh heaven God, the holy king, who had come down from an area unknown to humankind, had taken his place on his throne of glory. The traveler is completely overwhelmed by the sight of the mysteries of the divine throne.

The Holy One was clothed in dazzling heavenly raiment, radiant with white light, and wore a crown which shimmered with rays of light. From the throne itself, made of sparkling crystals and sky-blue lapis lazuli, flowed rivers of fire, crossed again by bridges. God, seated on his throne, surrounded by angels who incessantly sang hymns in praise of him and his kingdom, revealed his hidden glory to the mystic's soul.

When the traveler ascended, there were sometimes companions sitting next to him on his left or right, who quickly wrote down what the mystic was experiencing in ecstasy. These reports by the Merkavah mystics reflect in their ecstatic descriptions an enormous respect for the holiness of the throne world. There are reports which speak of a curtain or drape (*pargod*) behind which the divine figure on the throne was screened and which separated him from all other beings and things belonging to the throne chariot. On this curtain, which was held up by angels, the archetypes—ideas or thoughts of God—were embroidered, the pre-existent original patterns of everything that appears from the beginning to the end of life on earth. Anyone who viewed these patterns knew the secrets of creation and the redemption of the world.

5.4 *Basic ideas*

Merkavah mysticism is not a polished mystical system. Not all the motifs we find in it can be made to fit into a coherent system. We shall therefore deal below with some of the main topics in the literature of the Merkavah mystics.

Language mysticism. We have seen that the use of language—in the form of divine names, knowing the names of the angels and the right formulas and combinations of letters—plays an important role. One of the pillars of Merkavah mysticism, then, is language mysticism. An important principle of language mysticism is that the Hebrew language and the letters of the Hebrew alphabet have inherent powers. (At the end of this book a separate chapter will be devoted to the interpretation of the Hebrew language in Jewish mysticism.) In Hekhaloth literature this idea was given practical application in the form of language magic. By making use of knowledge of the powers in the letters and the spoken word, the Merkavah mystics were able to ascend through the heavens.

In all the extant texts language magic occupies an important place. We often encounter long summaries of angelic names. The "angels" in Hekhaloth literature are divine powers, each of which has its own name. This name indicates the specific divine qualities of the angel concerned. Everything in this literature seems to revolve around knowledge of the names of the angels. By magical use of the name of a particular angel one could gain power over that angel. Without knowledge of the secret names of the divine powers it was impossible to ascend to the highest heavenly room, the seventh palace of the seventh heaven, to view the king on his heavenly throne.

The many angelic names found in the mystical texts are constructed from various combinations of the 22 letters of the Hebrew alphabet. Some of these are long and unpronounceable and have no discernible meaning; others consist of particular systematic combinations of letters. In order to enhance the (magical) powers of the letters, the Merkavah mystics used a specially designed script. Both the sounds of words and names and the form of the written letters played a large part in this. This can be clearly seen, for instance, in one of the later Hekhaloth tractates, *Otiyoth de-Rabbi Akiva* (Alphabet of Rabbi Akiva), which incorporates many of the Merkavah traditions associated with language.

In the section on esoteric traditions we already looked at the esoteric character of magical traditions, which probably go back to an intellectual elite (see § 3.3). There is a great deal we still do not know about the exact content of these traditions. Nor do we know what attitude this elite adopted towards the application of esoteric knowledge in practical magic. The precise relationship between esoteric, theoretical knowledge of magic and its practical application is also an issue in Merkavah mysticism.

On the one hand in mystical works we are confronted with a large quantity of magical formulas, incantations, spells and above all the magical use of (divine) names. In addition, in many texts the acquisition of wisdom is a central topic. Wisdom in the form of a thorough knowledge of the Torah and the Oral Law could only be acquired after years of study. By means of magic and spells the heavenly traveler tried to gain possession of this wisdom without the need to make efforts of his own. In particular the secret divine wisdom which Moses was supposed to have received from God on Sinai was earnestly desired by many mystics. At first sight these facts might give the impression that Merkavah mysticism is concerned only with magic. This view is indeed defended by some modern scholars, who assume that the magical element is the most important feature of Merkavah mysticism, whereas the ascent through the heavenly realms was only a minor issue.

On the other hand there are many scholars who think that Merkavah mysticism should not be reduced to mere magic. Magic only makes sense if it can be applied practically; or in other words, when it is clear what the precise use is for a particular name or spell. But this does not always seem to be the case in Hekhaloth literature—not by a

long way. Very often we find long lists with divine or angelic names
which are theoretical and abstract in character. No explanation is given
of the application or the practical use of such names. It must therefore
be considered improbable that a mystic was able to use such names for
practical magic. The ample attention given in the Merkavah literature
for the innumerable divine and angelic names has to do with a cosmological interest: the mystic's so ardently desired insight into the
divine realms which are densely populated by powerful beings.
Knowledge of the angelic names was a means for establishing the
structure of the divine world. In this view it is the mystical knowledge
of the divine names that takes central place in Hekhaloth literature. In
the second place this knowledge has on a lower plane a practical application in magic. The mystic thus did have knowledge of magic, which
he was also able to use for the purpose of ascending and viewing the
throne world, but the magic was a means and not the real objective of
Merkavah mysticism.

Hymns and prayers. An important place in Hekhaloth literature is
occupied by numerous hymns and prayers, the main element of which
is the praise of God. Constantly the holiness and the majesty of the
Divine Figure on the throne and the glory of his kingdom are sung
about by the angels around the throne chariot. Hymns are sung both
by the celestial beings in the palaces and by the heavenly travelers
themselves. They could also take the form of a dialogue between God
and traveler or between two or more Rabbis describing the heavenly
realms, during which the ascending mystic was given instruction.

The rhythmic recitation of hymns served to arouse ecstasy. By
means of mechanically executed movements, the long monotonous
repetition of similar-sounding words, the regular return to key words,
emphasized in a cyclical rhythm, and by means of magical incantations
expressed in a crescendo, the mystic attained a state of ecstasy. Language magic again played an important role in this.

The traditional Hebrew vocabulary of course often proved inadequate for describing the ecstatic experiences of the heavenly travelers
in the divine rooms. The language in which the hymns are composed
is to us rather bombastic and bizarre, riddled with obscure word combinations and neologisms. Despite the abhorrence and resistance from
non-mystical rabbinic circles towards what in their view was an exag-
gerated and excessive praising of God, the hymns and prayers of
Merkavah mysticism left traces in the later traditional liturgy of Judaism.

Metatron. With regard to the world around the throne an important part is played by the Metatron traditions. Metatron may be viewed as the most powerful being in the divine world, in second place next to God. Metatron is seated on a throne subordinate to the divine throne of glory and is initiated by God into all the divine secrets, including those of creation. In mystical reports this highest of the angels tells of his metamorphosis from a human being to an angel and of the hierarchy of the throne and the angels. Further, he reveals the mysteries of the Merkavah to the mystic. Originally Metatron was a human being who had made his way up to the position of the first angel, the highest of all created beings. Another name for Metatron is the Prince of the Countenance (*Sar ha-Panim*). The Metatron traditions have their roots in Jewish apocalypticism, a spiritual movement from the Second Temple period, which we shall look into more closely below (§ 6.1). Within apocalypticism many esoteric speculations developed around the figure of Enoch, of whom the Bible says that *he walked with God, and he was not, for God took him* (Gen. 5.24). Here Enoch is led to heaven, where divine mysteries, the end of the world and the coming redemption are revealed to him. These esoteric speculations developed over time into the angel Metatron in Merkavah mysticism.

The Prince of the Torah. Beside the mysticism of the ascent and the description of the divine world and its inhabitants, in Hekhaloth literature we find quite a different tradition which again is to be found spread about in the various manuscripts. The main figure in this tradition is the Prince of the Torah (*Sar Torah*), who like Metatron reveals divine secrets to the mystic. The motifs surrounding the Prince of the Torah, however, differ in one important regard from the rest of Merkavah mysticism. Whereas the texts usually speak of the mystic's ascent to the heavenly realms in order to receive revelations, here it is not the mystic himself who ascends; the Prince of the Torah descends to the earth—or is forced to do so—in order to provide the mystic with the desired knowledge. To date there is still no systematic research available on these traditions.

5.5 *The literature of ascent*

In practically all the mystical writings concerning the ascent through the heavenly realms and the vision of the throne of glory we find the mystical components which have been pointed out in the previous sections.

In line with what has been said in relation to the problems concerning the extant material (see § 2 of this chapter), we can state that the many traditions and motifs from Hekhaloth literature are found spread throughout various manuscripts in ever new combinations. The Hekhaloth texts thus resemble one another, even though each of the various texts presents the same tradition in its own way. Why this happens is usually not known; the origin of some mystical components or traditions remains obscure.

For specialists in this field, who are interested in the historical development of Merkavah mysticism, the sometimes small differences or similarities are highly significant. The sudden appearance of a specific angelic name for example, or another detail that is not found elsewhere, can throw new light on the history of ancient Jewish mysticism. Within the framework of this book, however, it would not seem so useful to give a summary of all the minor differences from and correspondences with other texts for each individual Merkavah tractate. The most prominent agreements between the various tractates have been presented in the previous section. We shall therefore content ourselves with a concise description of a number of specific elements in each of the best-known mystical works.

The tractate *Hekhaloth Rabbathi* (Great Hekhaloth) is generally regarded as the classic and best-known work in Merkavah mysticism. The chief figure in it is Rabbi Ishmael, one of the famous heroes of Merkavah mysticism. It is notable here that God does not always sit on his throne in the divine palace. The throne itself bows before God and asks him to sit down. It seems then that there is another, eighth heaven above the throne world, where God generally stays hidden. The seventh palace functions, as it were, as a public court in which God takes his seat a few times each day, in accordance with the times at which the people of Israel say their prayers.

In the tractate *Hekhaloth Zutarti* (Minor Hekhaloth), it is precisely Rabbi Akiva who is the most important figure. It is interesting that this text also speaks of revelations to the heavenly traveler during the ascent and not exclusively at the end of the journey. A large part of the text relates to magical incantational names and is very technical in character. The work is very important for the study of magic in ancient Jewish mysticism. Among other things, secret methods of magical incantation are given for the study and memorization of the Torah. The book starts from the premise that apart from the "ordinary" Torah, Moses received revelation of an extensive, secret, magical-mystical knowledge. The acquisition of this knowledge constitutes a significant element in ancient Jewish mysticism. The impression is given that the Minor Hekhaloth itself is the book that was revealed to Moses and that it thus contains all the secrets of the world and the Torah.

In *Sefer Hekhaloth* (Book of Hekhaloth), also called the Third Book of Enoch, we again find Rabbi Ishmael as the chief character. Mainly this work is more a summary of Jewish apocalypticism and mystical traditions. From the artificial way in which the traditions are combined in this tractate, we can deduce that the Book of Hekhaloth is not an original work but is an arbitrary selection from various older sources, which often do not fit well together. The greater part of the work consists of revelations by the angel Metatron to Rabbi Ishmael of secret knowledge about the divine world. In the previous section we saw that the Metatron traditions emerged from apocalyptic traditions surrounding the biblical figure of Enoch. It is remarkable that only here, in the Book of Hekhaloth, is the figure of Enoch explicitly equated with that of Metatron. Certain themes familiar from the other Hekhaloth literature are missing from this tractate. Thus for example here we read nothing of the adjuration of the heavenly inhabitants or the showing of magical seals to gatekeepers. Nor does this work contain instructions in relation to the techniques of ascent.

The tractate *Ma'aseh Merkavah* (Work of the Chariot) consists of a dialogue of Rabbi Ishmael with Rabbi Nehunia and Rabbi Akiva. In section 5.4 we discussed language mysticism and the magic of language. This text shows such a view of and use of language; it is the ritual power of language which enables the ascent. The ascent is brought about by the pronouncing of prayers, hymns, divine names, magical formulas and word-combinations. The text is constructed in such a way that there is an analogy between the structure of the various heavens and the structure of the different hymns which describe the heavens. The dialogues in the text contain exclusively instructions on the ways of using language: what and how a traveler should speak and what he himself hears spoken from the heavenly realms.

6. The relationship between ancient Jewish mysticism and other religious currents

In the previous sections we have looked at various topics which are under discussion in scholarly research into Jewish mysticism. We have seen that opinion is still divided on such questions as the reliability of the transmitted material, the canon of Hekhaloth literature, the way in which the transition to true mystical activity took place, the extent of the influence of magic and the problem of the chronological development of ancient Jewish mysticism.

Besides this, research finds itself confronted by what is possibly the most difficult question, namely that of the relationship between ancient Jewish mysticism and the earlier and contemporary religious currents, both within and outside Judaism. We shall therefore take a look at how ancient Jewish mysticism relates respectively to apocalypticism, gnosticism and rabbinic Judaism.

6.1 *Merkavah mysticism and apocalypticism*

Hekhaloth literature shares some conceptual elements with Jewish apocalypticism, a religious current which existed from the second century BCE and had its heyday in the first century BCE. Apocalypticism was a spiritual current for a very select group, which occupied itself with the end of time and the terrible horrors with which the end of our world would be associated. This end was connected with the coming of the Messiah, the redeemer and preparer of the way for a completely new world. The apocalypticists speculated on the way in which God led the world and how this divine economy might be discerned from the course of history. At the same time the doctrine of the apocalypticists assumed a divine world inhabited by angels and demonic powers, a world in which such subjects as the throne of glory and the assumption to heaven of biblical figures played a role. The apocalypticists, who desired to share in the world to come, endeavored to bring their lives into line with these heavenly realms. They therefore speculated on the structure of the divine world, on the fate of souls in the world, on the secrets of creation and on the revelations which they received from angels and the deity.

Apocalyptic literature contains many elements to be found in the later traditions of *Ma'aseh Merkavah*, *Ma'aseh Bereshith* and Merkavah mysticism. Initially it was thought that the mystical activity of the ascent through the heavenly realms and the descent to the throne of glory had to have its roots in the last two centuries before the destruction of the Second Temple, perhaps even earlier. As we have seen, however, most scholars are now convinced that there is no question of mystical activity earlier than around the third century CE. In the periods before that it is a matter of esoteric speculations, in which the ascent played no part.

Besides Hekhaloth literature, apocalypticism has left traces also in the so-called Dead Sea scrolls. These scrolls are probably the literary remains of a religious community in Qumran which existed from the second century BCE to the first century CE. This community lived in separation from the rest of the Judaism of the time and could not come to terms with the way in which the temple cult was directed in Jerusalem. They tried in their own way to live according to what they took to be the true interpretation of the divine Word. Alongside documents that were specific to the community, their library also contained many texts that give us an insight into the literary culture of Palestine at the time. Not only do aspects of the content of this literature raise huge problems, but also the question of the relation between the writings of this separatist group and those of apocalypticism, ancient Jewish mysticism, rabbinic Judaism and religious currents outside Judaism, presents scholarly research with no mean task.

6.2 *Merkavah mysticism and gnosticism*

The relationship between Jewish Hekhaloth literature and gnosticism—a spiritual current which has its roots in Hellenism—presents us with a huge problem. The conquest of the East by Alexander the Great between 334 and 323 BCE resulted in Greek language and culture being introduced into the area extending from Egypt as far as the borders of India. Alongside the diversity of language and culture in this area that remained there arose also various mixed forms of Greek and indigenous culture, which we refer to by the collective term of "hellenism". This hellenized world, which displayed a certain degree of cultural unity by virtue of its Greek element, was not to come to an end until the rise of Islam in the seventh century CE.

On the one hand, a consequence of the hellenization of the East was that with the aid of systematic Greek thinking all kinds of Eastern religious elements now gained expression in coherent ideas. On the other hand, there were also eastern ideas that were unacceptable to the hellenistic world of the time. These disappeared into esoteric subcurrents, about which we know little, except that from the first century BCE they emerged in a whole range of manifestations. The core of all these underground currents has been called by Hans Jonas—a well-known scholar in the field of gnosticism—"the gnostic principle". The gnostic principle was expressed in various ways: in the reemergence of Babylonian astrology, in the spread of mystery cults, in new philosophical currents such as neo-Pythagoreanism and neo-

Platonism. In its purest form, however, this gnostic principle was expressed in divergent directions, which we call gnostic currents.

Gnosticism is the sum of varying dualistic systems, in which a sharp distinction is drawn between, on the one hand, the highest divinity and his world of light, and on the other hand, our world, the cosmos, which is called the realm of darkness. Our world was not created by the divinity himself, but by inferior powers, the *Archons*, which were led by the *Demiurge*. The earth is surrounded by seven cosmic spheres, each of which is ruled by one of the Archons.

Within the human being too a sharp distinction is drawn between body and spirit. Each person has a divine spark (*pneuma*), which comes from the divine world of light and has fallen into this world. The Archons try with all their might to keep these sparks imprisoned on earth and in humans, so as to prevent them from ascending to the divinity, of which they were originally a part.

The divine spark or inner person is asleep, but must awaken and be liberated by means of knowledge (*gnosis*) both concerning God and humanity and its world. This knowledge is gained when an envoy from the world of light manages to get past the Archons to wake up the inner person and give him or her gnosis, by means of which he can ascend and force the Archons to let him through.

Ancient Jewish mysticism displays clear points of contact with gnosticism. The descriptions from Hekhaloth literature of the ascent through the seven heavens with their palaces have, among other things, parallels with the seven cosmic spheres of gnosticism. The motif of the gatekeepers in Merkavah mysticism corresponds with that of the gnostic Archons. Some of the Hekhaloth tractates seem to suggest a connection between the figure of the angel Metatron and that of the demiurge. In both currents, there is frequent use of magical and incantational techniques. Further, many gnostic symbols and myths are very similar to those we find in the ecstatic descriptions of the throne world. In addition, the strongly dualistic features of Jewish apocalypticism and the literature of the Qumran community, mentioned above, have points of contact with gnosticism, though these have not yet been fully elucidated.

One of the hottest potatoes is now the question of the exact relationship between ancient Jewish mysticism and gnosticism, partly because this is tied up with the question of the emergence of Christianity. A precise picture of the relationship would have to provide an answer to the question: Is Jewish mysticism a product of external—i.e.

non-Jewish—influences, or is it a matter of a dynamic spiritual development within Judaism itself?

Some saw gnosticism as a product of "heretical" Christian groups. In this view, the agreements between Jewish mysticism and gnosticism can be explained as the result of influences of Christian heresies on Judaism. Others have put forward the possibility that gnosticism emerged not only completely independently of, but also earlier than nascent Christianity. Many have even expressed the opinion that the origins of this pre-Christian gnosticism should be sought within Judaism, while this "Jewish gnosticism" is considered to be of enormous importance for the emergence of Christianity. Alongside these views another theory has gained ground, namely that both Merkavah mysticism and Christian gnosticism, as well as other gnostic currents, are products of one and the same religious impulse, which we have referred to above as the "gnostic principle". This principle, which came to expression in a large number of spiritual movements, was simultaneously expressed in a specifically Jewish form in ancient Jewish mysticism. The fact that any form of dualism—so characteristic of many gnostic currents—is missing in the Jewish gnostic variant, Merkavah mysticism, does not detract from this view. The gnostic principle was expressed in many gnostic currents in mythical images of a divine realm of light, a realm of darkness, and fallen divine sparks, which wanted to be redeemed and longed to return to their original divine home. In ancient Jewish mysticism we find this gnostic principle in the system of the seven heavens with their palaces and the world of the throne, but without dualistic elements. The latter could not be reconciled with the Jewish principle of monotheism, since belief in one God absolutely ruled out the existence of two separate powers.

From the latter point of view, ancient Jewish mysticism then proceeded in the first instance from an internal and dynamic spiritual development within Judaism itself. It is obvious that there would in addition have been external non-Jewish influence on this development within Judaism; Palestinian Judaism was very much a part of the hellenistic world of the time. In its dynamic development Jewish mysticism drew its inspiration not only from spiritual currents within Judaism, such as Jewish apocalypticism, but also from non-Jewish spiritual currents. In its turn, ancient Jewish mysticism also had an influence on other currents, such as Christian gnosticism.

The extent to which Jewish mysticism can be called precisely gnostic, is difficult to determine: no clear definition has yet been given for the phenomenon of gnosticism; it is extremely difficult to determine what belongs to gnosticism and what does not.

6.3 *Merkavah mysticism and rabbinic Judaism*

At the beginning of this chapter we pointed out with reference to the question of the relationship between Hekhaloth literature and official rabbinic Judaism that Merkavah mystics must be sought in rabbinic circles.

An indication in this direction is the fact that in traditional rabbinic literature we encounter passages which are at first sight incomprehensible. On closer inspection it turns out that a clearer picture emerges if these passages are read in connection with the mystical Merkavah writings. An example of this is a saying of Rabbi Akiva in the Talmud (*b. Hag* 14b): "When you come to the pure marble stones do not say, 'Water, water!', for it is written: *No deceiver shall dwell in my house; the speaker of lies shall not stand in my eyes* (Ps. 101.7)."

The meaning of this saying ascribed to Rabbi Akiva is not at all clear within the context of the Talmudic passage. However, if we read this passage in relation with what we know from the Merkavah texts, it seems quite clear what its background is. We saw of course that the mystical descriptions of ascent report the extremely difficult transition from the sixth to the seventh palace. Here the heavenly traveler is tested on his ability to distinguish marble from water. Anyone who took marble for water was not worthy of admittance to the throne world. Akiva's saying relates to this. The cited verse from the psalm is then applied to the unworthy mystic: he was not allowed into God's house. The Talmudic passage thus only has meaning against the background of Merkavah mysticism.

On the basis of this example, and on the basis of other texts in rabbinic literature also, many scholars have concluded that Merkavah mysticism developed in the heart of rational, legalistic and normative rabbinic Judaism and formed part of that same culture. This conclusion dispenses with the view of the nineteenth-century scholars of the *Wissenschaft des Judentums* that this mysticism arose on the periphery of Judaism and only long after the closing of the Talmud, as a degenerate form of religiosity resulting from non-Jewish influences. As we saw in the previous section, the question of the extent to which Jewish mysticism is authentically Jewish played a role as far as the relationship to gnosticism is concerned. There too, the conclusion was that though there is indeed evidence of influence of gnosticism on Jewish mysticism, this does not mean that Jewish mysticism was simply a product of non-Jewish influence.

There are also, by the way, scholars who—in some cases in the trend of the *Wissenschaft des Judentums*—deny any connection between such passages in rabbinic literature and Merkavah mysticism. What makes it so difficult to gain a full picture of this question is that in rabbinic literature we also find indications of rabbinic circles who were opposed to mysticism and resisted the influence of gnostic ideas. A picture of rabbinic Judaism thus emerges which is less homogeneous than is often assumed.

7. Mysticism moves to Western Europe

The end of the period of ancient Jewish mysticism from Palestine and Babylon lies somewhere in the late ninth or the beginning of the tenth century. From the second half of the twelfth century we find two Jewish mystical currents in medieval Europe: in Germany, especially along the Rhine, there arises the movement of the Ashkenazi Hasidim, while in Provence and on the Iberian Peninsula we find the beginnings of Kabbalah.

What developments occurred in the intervening period in the way of mystical activity is not known. The new medieval mystical currents in Western Europe had a character all their own. We can, however, confirm that they adopted and elaborated a great deal of material of an earlier date. Many elements of Hekhaloth literature recur in these twelfth and thirteenth-century currents, sometimes in unaltered form, sometimes also by means of radical reinterpretation. Alongside traditions from ancient Jewish mysticism we also find clearly gnostic myths and symbolism which do not crop up within earlier Jewish sources and whose origins cannot always be determined.

Because we have no mystical literature from the centuries between ancient Jewish mysticism and the later mystical movements we cannot determine for sure how the transition of ancient mystical tradition to Western Europe occurred. That something from Palestine and Babylon was indeed handed down, is, however, evident from sparse indications in the Jewish writings preserved from this period. Late collections of midrash, for example, sometimes took up traditions containing mystical elements. In the many commentaries from this period on *Sefer Yetsirah*, too, we read views which we meet again in later mysticism.

On the question of the way in which, and the channels by which
earlier ancient Jewish mysticism and gnosticism now reached Western
European Jewish mystical movements, many theories have been developed. Some of them have assumed the existence of "underground"
Jewish schools, which would have provided a framework in which
many traditions could have been handed down.

The new medieval Jewish mystical currents in Western Europe differ in content from Merkavah mysticism in one important respect. For
the Merkavah mystics the human being as an individual had no part to
play. The central topic was the vision of the divine throne world.
Consequently Merkavah mysticism does not contain any moral teaching of significance that is directed to the perfection of the human as a
person. A person's relationship to God did not hold the attention of
these mystics. In medieval mysticism, on the other hand, precisely
these matters assume an important role.

In the following chapter we shall go into the content and historical
origins of the new mystical currents that have been mentioned. In the
course of our discussion we shall illustrate the problem of the transfer
of Jewish mysticism to Western Europe with some concrete examples.

3

Classical Kabbalah

1. Basic concepts in classical Kabbalah

1.1 *Introduction*

At the end of the twelfth century and the beginning of the thirteenth, to the north and south of the eastern Pyrenees, with apparent suddenness there appeared a Jewish mystical movement that was to become known as Kabbalah. Shortly after its appearance in Provence Kabbalah moved to Gerona in the county of Catalonia. Both Provence and Gerona belonged at that time to the area of the Catalan-Aragonese monarchy; the present-day state boundaries between France and Spain did not yet exist.

It was in the Jewish centers of Provence and Gerona that the formation of the earliest Kabbalah took place. From Gerona Kabbalah spread out over the Christian kingdoms of the Iberian Peninsula, where it reached the height of its classical development at the end of the thirteenth century with the appearance of the *Zohar*, the main book of Kabbalah, which was to enjoy great authority not only among later kabbalists, but also in broader circles within Judaism.

In Chapter 2 we saw how the mystics of ancient Jewish mysticism pictured the divine world in a system of seven heavenly realms with the throne world. The Kabbalists now attempted to describe the divinity in quite a different way, namely by means of the doctrine of the sefiroth. It will not be possible to arrive at an undersatnding of kabbalistic thought without insight into the basic principles that underlie the system of the sefiroth.

Since Kabbalah consists of a multiplicity of mystical currents and betrays no evidence of a unity of thought, it is not possible to speak of Kabbalah as a single entity. This fact does not make it easy to sketch a clear picture of classical Kabbalah. It was only after four generations of kabbalists that the sefirotic system and kabbalistic symbolism crystallized into a more or less fixed form; before that time we have to do with very many different systems, each with its own details and angles of approach. For the sake of clarity we shall therefore proceed initially on the basis of this fully-fledged form. The danger of course is that we might otherwise quickly lose sight of the overall picture.

In this overview, alongside a description of the sefiroth system we shall also pay attention to a number of other general aspects, such as the mythic character of Kabbalah, the role of symbolism and the points of contact between Kabbalah and the theories of the Swiss psychologist C.G. Jung. We shall then give extensive attention to the relationship between Kabbalah and Jewish philosophy.

After taking account of the overall picture, we shall devote attention to the various mystical currents and persons of classical Kabbalah in their chronological order. In the course of this the various phases of development will be discussed which preceded the crystallized form of classical Kabbalah. We shall also offer a description of the most important mystical literature which these currents produced.

1.2 *The doctrine of the sefiroth*

The kabbalists assumed that underlying the visible reality surrounding us was another reality, a divine world. In the eyes of the kabbalists everything that belongs to our created world—including humans and everything they have produced—was rooted in this presumed divine world. In order to imagine the divine world the kabbalists used the system of ten *sefiroth* (plural of *sefirah*). The doctrine of sefiroth which they developed is in the literal sense of the word a theosophy; it is a wisdom which relates to the character of the divine. (The term "theosophy" in this sense has nothing to do with the Theosophical Society which was set up by Mme. Blavatsky in New York in 1875.)

Figure 1 offers a schematic representation of this world of the sefiroth with the associated terms. Although the sefirotic system was not originally fixed as regards their precise order and their individual names, some time after the emergence of the earliest Kabbalah a more or less uniform system developed.

The first sefirah is called Kether (crown), the second Hokhmah (wisdom), the third Binah (intelligence), the fourth Hesed (love, or mercy), the fifth Din (stern judgment), the sixth Tif'ereth (beauty), the seventh Netsah (lasting endurance), the eighth Hod (majesty), the ninth Yesod (foundation), and the tenth and last sefirah is called Malkhuth (kingdom). Some of these names are borrowed from the Bible

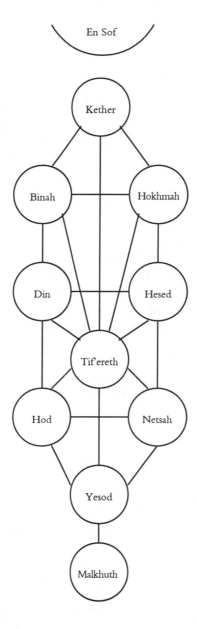

Figure 1
Schematic representation of the sefirotic world

(1 Chron 29.11), while others derive from traditional Jewish literature.

These ten sefiroth flow or proceed from En Sof, the highest principle. The technical term for this process is emanation. The sefirah Kether (crown) first emanated from En Sof. Then from this first sefirah Kether, Hokhmah (wisdom) emanated as the second sefirah. From this in turn emanated the third, and the process continued up to the emanation of the last sefirah Malkhuth (kingdom). Together with En Sof the ten sefiroth thus formed the realm of the godhead. This divine realm is closely related to our created reality.

We shall follow the whole emanation process step by step, from "above" to "below". En Sof means literally "there is no end", or "without end". This term refers to that aspect of God that cannot be comprehended by us humans and which lies beyond anything we can imagine. This aspect of God has no attributes, that is to say that nothing can be said about it. No name can be given to this aspect of God; the divinity in his highest aspect, in En Sof, simply cannot be named. When En Sof is indicated by such terms as "God in himself", "the Eternal" or the "Infinite"—as often happens in kabbalistic literature— this is simply the consequence of the human inability to say anything about En Sof. When we speak of the infinity of En Sof, we point to a world or state where eternity reigns and where concepts of ours like beginning and end do not have the meaning that we would attach to them, neither in time nor in space. In short: for humans, En Sof is something, a world or state, which cannot be described and cannot be imagined.

From this unknowable En Sof, this impersonal, absolute and infinite deity, the ten above-mentioned sefiroth emanate. With the coming of the ten sefiroth the hidden and for us unknowable God displays ten different aspects, qualities or attributes of himself. From the hiddenness of En Sof God reveals ten aspects of his hidden life. Kether, the first sefirah, is regarded as the highest and most elevated of all the sefiroth. It is the first manifestation of the hidden deity, in which its will to reveal itself is expressed. Kether is also sometimes called Ayin (nothingness) and is very close to En Sof.

The next step in the emanation process is the second sefirah, Hokhmah. In Hokhmah, the divine will to create, present in Kether, becomes a spiritual blueprint of our world. Hokhmah contains the divine ideas, the "archetypes" (see § 1.5) of all things that must come into being. Our whole visible reality lies inside Hokhmah as a model. Since the divine will in Kether is unfolded in Hokhmah, through Hokhmah the human being can get to know the divine will.

The third sefirah is Binah. In this sefirah the still undifferentiated model of creation, contained in Hokhmah, is distinguished in all its components. Here all things gain a more or less distinctive identity. The kabbalists saw Hokhmah as an active, masculine power, by contrast with which Binah stood as a passive feminine power within the deity. Thus they created two powers which were opposed to each other, a principle which comes to the fore also in the sefiroth which still remain to emanate. In much kabbalistic literature Hokhmah and Binah are characterized by the symbols *abba* (father) and *imma* (mother), from whose union the seven sefiroth which now follow will be "born".

With the emanation of the fourth and fifth sefiroth, Hesed and Din, there emerge two powers which, like the two previous powers, Hokhmah and Binah, are in opposition to each other. Hesed (or Gedullah, "greatness"), is the representative of God's grace and love—divine qualities which cannot be measured by human standards. To ensure that this divine grace and love will not overreach its goal by swamping everything unchecked, Hesed has the sefirah Din as its opposite, which keeps the divine love within certain boundaries and sets limits on it so that there remains room for creation. Din (or: Gevurah, "power") is generally viewed as the principle of strictness, of the just but immutable law, a power which sets limits and determines the boundaries. Unconditional love (Hesed) stands opposite unrelenting justice (Din). These two sefiroth are viewed by the kabbalists as the origin of innumerable apparently irreconcilable opposites in human life, such as for example good and evil, love and hate, the sacred and the profane as well as reward and punishment.

In the sixth sefirah, Tif'ereth, the two opposing powers of Hesed and Din are united in a harmonious whole and merge into a synthesis. Tif'ereth thus harmonizes the expanding principle of Hesed with the limiting and restraining principle of Din. By analogy with this reconciliation in the spiritual world due to Tif'ereth, in our visible reality too harmonization takes place between apparently irreconcilable differences.

The seventh and eight sefiroth, Netsah and Hod, are again two opposing powers, which are united in a harmonious synthesis in the ninth sefirah, Yesod. These last three sefiroth constitute a further elaboration of the sefiroth Hesed, Din and Tif'ereth. They are as it were a lower or coarser manifestation of these. By means of the sefiroth Netsah, Hod and Yesod, in the spiritual world the deity lays the basis for a creation in which life in general and human life in particular

are possible. The fact that the planets follow exact paths in the firmament, that the seasons follow one another, that there is an alternation
between day and night, that there are animals and plants, that the human body works—all such things have their origins in these three
sefiroth.

Unlike the preceding nine sefiroth, the tenth and last sefirah, Malkhuth, has no qualities of its own. As in a bowl, Malkhuth collects the
end result of the dynamic processes that have been played out within
these nine sefiroth. Since Malkhuth unites all the sefiroth in itself
without adding anything, this sefirah forms the whole of the sefiroth.
The sefirah Malkhuth is the last in a hierarchical system of ten sefiroth,
in which we can see a process of increasing differentiation and density.
The last sefirah marks the completion of the self-revelation of the deity
and the unfolding of its total personality, to the extent that it can be
known by humans. From En Sof there flows an unbroken stream of
divine life towards the sefiroth and ultimately on into Malkhuth. This
tenth and last sefirah is closest to our own reality; it forms the border
between God and the world.

Malkhuth always held a special fascination for the mystics. After all,
the totality of the sefiroth that is reflected in Malkhuth forms in fact
that part of God that is turned towards us. In the sefiroth—and thus in
condensed form in Malkhuth—the deity revealed itself as a person
whom according to the kabbalists one could get to know and learn
about. For the mystic, Malkhuth formed the point of contact, the first
step on the path to the recovery of God. Through the convergence of
all the sefiroth in Malkhuth the receptive principle that characterizes
this sefirah was associated by the mystics with the feminine side of the
deity, which is called Shekhinah. Later in this book we shall go into
the concept of the Shekhinah in more detail (§ 2.2 of this chapter).

In the course of time the various kabbalistic schools and individual
kabbalists developed systems to elucidate the phases of emanation. A
common system is a division of the sefiroth into three triads—according to the neo-Platonic model (see § 1.7)—complemented by the
tenth sefirah, Malkhuth. The emanation of the first three sefiroth,
Kether, Hokhmah and Binah, is referred to by the term "the intellect"
(*ha-muskal*), since in these first three sefiroth the divine idea unfolds
concerning the origins of creation. The second triad in this system—
Hesed, Din and Tif'ereth—is often referred to as "the psychic" (*ha-
murgash*), while the last triad of Netsah, Hod and Yesod, from which
the conditions for life emerge, is called "the natural" (*ha-mutba'*).

In kabbalistic literature, alongside the system of three triads we also frequently come across a division into three and seven sefiroth. Here the first three sefiroth are so close to the hidden divinity of En Sof that they are more or less hidden from us. On the other hand the seven lower sefiroth that follow in this view belong to the divine realm that is indeed accessible to humans. Another system frequently found in kabbalistic writings is the one that presents the phases of emanation as concentric circles, by analogy with the medieval picture of the ten spheres of the cosmos.

In the teaching of Kabbalah we thus have to do with one God, who on the one hand has an impersonal aspect, beyond all human description, which resides in itself and is unknowable (En Sof), but who on the other hand has a personal aspect, in which he reveals his hidden being (the sefiroth).

The ten sefiroth, the revealed aspects or lights of the hidden deity, are often regarded as the faces of God directed towards the world. They do not say anything about the deepest nature of the hidden life of the deity, but form the side of God that is turned towards the world and which is knowable and can be experienced by humans. The deity reveals itself by unfolding in the sefiroth.

In much of kabbalistic literature the relation between En Sof and the sefiroth is clarified by means of two similes. One is that of the coal and the flame. The coal (En Sof) can exist without the flame (sefiroth), but the latent and hidden forces of the coal come to expression only by the light of the flame; the two form a unity, even though they are not identical. The other simile is that of soul (En Sof) and body (sefiroth). People show themselves to others by means of their behavior, thoughts and emotions, which can often be contradictory in character. All these qualities are manifestations of their non-perceptible soul. In the same way God cannot be known in his deepest essence, although by means of the ten sefiroth a fair amount comes to expression as to who and what God is.

The sefirotic world can be described in two ways. In the first place we can describe the ten sefiroth as a fundamental unity, within which together they constitute the universe of God's hidden life. In their totality they form as it were a mystical organism in which the dynamic processes of this hidden life are played out. In kabbalistic literature the pattern of the ten revealed aspects in which God rises out of his deep and hidden life is described in a great variety of ways and with a great many different symbols.

Secondly, each sefirah can be described separately. Each sefirah has a completely individual and unique function, within which again dynamic processes are at work. Not only does the work of one sefirah complement that of another, but each sefirah is reflected in the totality of the other. Each sefirah in separation is really a world of its own of an unlimited richness and depth with a very great range of effects. The possibilities of the relations between the sefiroth are infinite. Just as countless numbers can be made up of ten numerals, so too there are many possible combinations—or configurations—of the ten sefiroth. These infinite possibilities of the sefiroth form the dynamic processes in the divine world.

How, then, does our visible reality relate to this divine world of the sefiroth and En Sof? The kabbalistic writings are not at all univocal concerning the relation between the divine world and our own. There is a variety of opinions on the question of how the lowest sefirah, Malkhuth, is connected to our world. It is in any case clear that the two worlds are connected and that the spiritual worlds constitute a higher—that is to say, more authentic and closer to En Sof—stage of our physical reality. Each physical thing and each living creature in our world stands in a relationship to and is a reflection of the sefiroth and their configurations. With the various configurations of sefiroth the innumerable patterns are woven which finally reach concrete form in our creation. The whole material creation is thus an external manifestation of a single process, which is at work both above and below. The dynamic processes in the world of the sefiroth and everything that happens in creation are therefore comparable with communicating vessels; the two worlds after all are in a constant state of interaction.

In this process of interaction, an important role is played by the divine energy or light from En Sof, which streams through the channels of the sefiroth to our creation. For this is the life-source of all worlds, including our own. The interplay consists in the fact that the energy coming from En Sof not only streams into our world from above to below, but that conversely also the human has an influence on the higher worlds and thus on the descending streams of energy. Not only concrete human action, but also the thoughts, imagination, intentions or inner contemplations of humans exercise an influence on the dynamic processes of the world of the sefiroth and thus also on the quantity, nature and quality of the divine light which descends to the earth.

The influence of human action on the divine realms is one of the most important topics in the teachings of Kabbalah. Why is human

activity so fundamental in kabbalistic doctrine? The importance of
human action in our reality has a close connection with the fall of
Adam in the biblical creation story. Adam, the primordial man of
paradise, transgressed the divine prohibition on eating from the tree of
the knowledge of good and evil (Gen 2.17–3.7). According to the
mystics of Kabbalah this transgression had far-reaching consequences.
Originally our reality was a pure reflection of the divine world. Our
world—not yet in today's material form of course—formed a perfect
image of the higher realms. This situation, called the Garden of Eden
or paradise, was spoiled by the "transgression" of Adam, which destroyed the original harmonious unity of both the higher worlds and
our own world. A tear ran, as it were, through all the worlds from top
to bottom, so that a disturbance arose also in the downward flow of
the divine energy.

The *Zohar*, the main work of Kabbalah, presents this disturbance in
mythic images. The book relates how as a result of Adam's transgression the originally androgynous divine world split into two separate
parts: a male half and a female half. The two halves originally constituted a unity. Adam too, who according to a well-known midrash
(*Genesis Rabbah* 8.1) was originally an androgynous human being, lost
his androgynous character; he too was split into a male and a female
half, in complete accordance with what happened in the world of the
sefiroth.

The question of how the fissure that ran across all the worlds could
be repaired and the original "wholeness" of things regained, was one
of the most important matters that occupied the kabbalists. Throughout the whole history of Kabbalah great emphasis is placed on the
restoration of this original condition. The various kabbalistic currents
and individual kabbalists did think very differently about the extent to
which and the way in which human action could contribute to this
restoration. The point of departure for all the mystics, however, was
that appropriate action could heal the break, while wrong actions
could exacerbate the split which ran through all the worlds. A very
important aspect of appropriate human action was of course the observance of the commandments in daily Jewish life.

Apart from concrete action it was also possible for humans to contribute to the restoration through a correct insight into the divine
world. The kabbalists were convinced that an insight into the inner
dynamic life of the deity, such as the latter revealed in the realms of
the sefiroth, contributed to the restoration of the primordial harmony.
In order to bring about this restoration they endeavored to get to

know the various stages of emanation and to delve ever deeper into
the order and the hierarchy of the sefiroth, into the mutual relations
between the divine worlds and the essential analogy between our
world and the divine world.

With the system of the ten sefiroth the kabbalists tried to conceptu-
alize one single all-embracing reality, in which there was a place for
both the divine and the human, and also for the world around humanity. Various aspects of the teaching of the sefiroth which have
been mentioned here in broad terms will be supplemented and elaborated upon later in this book.

1.3 *Kabbalah and myth*

The question of what myths really are is in fact just as difficult to answer as the question of what mysticism is. For practical reasons we
shall proceed from the definition of a specialist on the history of religion, Mircea Eliade. He defines a myth as a sacred story about gods or
divine powers that expresses "something" that cannot be grasped by
human reason.

One of the most striking features of the various kabbalistic currents
is their strongly mythic character. In Kabbalah, myths—that is to say,
stories in which God is described in all his aspects—represent a reality
which goes beyond all logic. This reality cannot be reduced to something that can be fully grasped logically and must therefore be
approached via myth. In order to conceive of the processes and laws of
the hidden life of the deity, the kabbalists constantly created new
myths. The study of Kabbalah is an encounter with mythical worlds
full of archetypal images and symbols. An example of such images in
many kabbalistic writings is the description of the divine world
through the mythic image of a primordial tree planted by God, the
roots of which symbolize En Sof and ten branches symbolize the ten
sefiroth. In Kabbalah we also find myths which speak of masculine and
feminine powers within the deity or of a gigantic struggle between
good and evil which is acted out in the world of the sefiroth. Further
on in this chapter we shall meet many other examples of mythical
elements in Kabbalah.

The fact that Jewish scholars who were positively disposed towards
mysticism in the late twelfth and early thirteenth century in Provence
and Gerona apparently suddenly felt the need to dream up new myths
to describe the emanations of the deity in a symbolic way has given
rise to many questions. It is not only with reference to Kabbalah, by

the way, that the role of myths is a much-disputed topic, but also for Judaism in general. Of the divergent scholarly opinions on this point, we shall present the three most important.

As we pointed out in Chapter 1 concerning scholarly research into Jewish mysticism, under the influence of the Haskalah, the Jewish Enlightenment, there arose a picture of Judaism as a strictly rational, abstract and monotheistic religion. In this view Judaism was exalted far above all myths. In fact, the Jewish principle of monotheism was fundamentally opposed to the pagan, polytheistic myths. Kabbalah with its strongly mythical element was viewed as a strange, non-Jewish by-product. The explanation for the mythic character of Kabbalah, according to this view, should be sought in influences from outside Judaism. This view is still maintained by many scholars.

Over against this evaluation stands the opinion of other scholars who claim that myths were certainly an important and influential factor in the history of Jewish spirituality. Some of them think that the religion of ancient Israel already had a mythic character. From the time of the prophets, however, two trends emerged. On the one hand, a demythologizing tendency appeared, in which relics of ancient eastern myths were divested of their original symbolic power by the prophets and transformed into metaphors in order to arrive at a "pure" picture of God. This demythologizing tendency was ultimately to reach its climax in the medieval Jewish philosophy of Maimonides. On the other hand, however, this tendency was apparently restricted to a small spiritual elite, while the ordinary folk were kept completely outside. Among the common people many still held on to myths, which in their graphic descriptions did more for the imagination than a "purely" abstract notion of God. According to the scholars who represent this view, throughout the whole of Jewish history there was a tension between the two tendencies: a religious experience which is wary of myth, and a popular sub-current with a perception in which myth was paramount. In this struggle sometimes one side was in the ascendancy, sometimes the other. While the demythologizing tendency was strongly emphasized and reinforced by the rational thought of medieval Judaism, the popular, mythically charged sub-current would have been fertile soil for later Jewish mysticism. In this second view, then, the explosion of myths in Kabbalah is the result of the reemergence of a popular sub-current, which had always been present in Judaism.

Others, on the other hand, have expressed a more radical understanding and are of the opinion that a demythologization process took place neither in the religion of ancient Israel nor in later Judaism

These scholars claim that even the Torah is ultimately based on a myth—though not a polytheistic one—and that it remained active throughout all the centuries. In the emergence of Kabbalah they therefore see the strong emphasis on mythical elements not as a new eruption of a popular undercurrent but merely as a reformulation of one and the same myth, which had underlain the whole of Judaism from the very beginnings.

From the above it will be clear that discussion is still continuing as to whether Judaism is a strictly rational religion in which mystical currents with corresponding myths are at best a byproduct of external factors, or whether a constant field of tension existed between the abstract notion of God and a sub-current which held firm to living, graphic myths, or again whether Judaism as a whole lies under the sway of a single great monotheistic myth. In section 1.6.5, where the opposition between myth and philosophy will be described, we shall go more deeply into the function of myth in Kabbalah.

1.4 *Kabbalah and symbolism*

In the preceding sections we saw that the world of the sefiroth lies far beyond any human understanding and expression and how this world could, among other ways, be depicted in mythical stories. The kabbalists nonetheless felt the need to convey their inner experiences to others or to commit them to writing. Since human language is inadequate for conveying experiences and truths from another reality than our own, they expressed themselves in symbols.

So what, precisely, is a symbol? Originally "symbol" (Greek: *symbolon*) meant the converging of two halves of something cut or broken in two, or also "sign". A symbol presupposes the presence of two worlds. It is a sign of another reality that is present in our reality. The symbol shows us not only that another world or reality exists, but also that a connection is possible, a convergence of one reality with the other.

In the eyes of the kabbalists, the dynamic processes in the divine world of the sefiroth were reflected in our natural world, in the human being and in human life in general. Everything around us that we can perceive with our senses—such as the mineral world, the world of plants and animals, with their multiplicity of forms, the human being in its totality, the universe, but also the history of human beings and their world, in which wars and disasters occur—is a reflection, or rather, a symbol, of divine processes in another reality which underlies our own. For the mystics of Kabbalah the symbol formed a bridge to the divine world. And they sought the intangible reality hidden behind the symbol. By means of the symbol another reality revealed itself, a reality of unfathomable depth, an ineffable, mysterious truth. Since the divine, the infinite, shone through its representation by the symbol, the symbol became, as it were, transparent.

It was this experience of the divine world that the mystic tried to convey. By means of symbolic images he communicated with his surroundings as it were via symbols about truths which cannot be measured, known, or evaluated by our human standards. When the mystic speaks for example of an emanation process of sefiroth, one should not fall into the trap of taking this process literally as if one sefirah did indeed proceed from the other, streaming out or overflowing. With this symbolic notion the mystic aims to describe a process that he has seen as it were in a vision and has experienced in his heart. With the term "emanation" (*atsiluth*), which is to be taken symbolically, he refers to a relationship between the various sefiroth, which cannot be grasped by our human intellect and which occurs in a world which lies far beyond human language, understanding and expression. The sefiroth themselves too are symbols, which we should not in any way try to conceive of concretely.

Thus, for example, in the description of the sefiroth we have seen that the tenth sefirah Malkhuth in kabbalistic literature is often conceived of as the feminine aspect within the deity. In view of the fact that we are talking about an aspect of the deity, a side of another reality, this feminine side of the divine can never be fully known by us. Here on earth it never appears in its pure form but always as a pale reflection of it. This feminine power within the divine is expressed by the kabbalists in such terms as "the bride", "the woman", "the mother" or "the sister". These earthly manifestations of the female should be taken as indications of the female aspect of the unknown divine reality; they are merely symbols of it. The kabbalists used hundreds of symbols to depict the female power within the deity. These symbols show innumerable aspects of this side of God. Nonetheless real knowledge of this power was an impossibility, since its full content is by definition unfathomable. No one can ever be in a position to grasp and experience the full divine potential of the feminine as a whole.

Two very important topics in which the kabbalists' symbolic approach is in evidence are the Torah and the Hebrew language. The Bible and rabbinic tradition after all taught that the Torah had been given to

Moses on Sinai as the revelation of God. When God gives something, this means that the gift has a divine origin. A rabbinic midrash tells of the preexistence of the Torah: the Torah was already in existence before God created the world. The Torah thus forms as it were the blueprint for the whole of creation. If the Torah is preexistent, Hebrew—the language in which the Torah is written—automatically originates from before the creation and is thus of divine origin. The fact that the Torah and the Hebrew language were of divine origin automatically implied for the kabbalists that they must be symbols: crystallizations in this world of something that derives from another, divine, reality.

The dynamic processes in the world of the sefiroth find their reflection in each of the letters of the Hebrew alphabet, while conversely each Hebrew letter forms a symbol referring to processes in the divine world. Not only individual letters but also whole words—which of course are composed of letters—form complex symbols. Thus the Torah itself, consisting of many Hebrew letters, words and sentences, is for the kabbalists in fact one huge symbol of God. The concrete letters and the words which we can read in the Hebrew Bible are "signs", that is, symbols of another reality than our own. In the eyes of the kabbalists it was no coincidence that the Hebrew word for "letter" (*oth*) is also the word for "sign".

To read the Torah is to read texts which have a symbolic meaning. The kabbalists were thus convinced that their kabbalistic teaching was reflected in the Torah texts. According to them the stories in the Torah contained symbolic references to the sefiroth. Thus for example the stories of the three patriarchs were related to the dynamic processes of the sefiroth Hesed (Abraham), Din (Isaac) and Tif'ereth (Jacob). The chapters in the Torah about the patriarchs could thus be read on the one hand as a story concerning the lives of three people, but on the other hand also as a symbolic reference to a cosmic drama in the world of the sefiroth. Similarly, the creation story, in the first chapter of Genesis, is not only concerned with the history of the creation of our world, but at the same time forms a symbolic description of the emanation process of the sefiroth.

In the worldview of Kabbalah the whole visible reality that we see around us formed one great *corpus symbolicum*. Absolutely everything that we know in our world was seen as a symbol of the hidden divine aspects and processes in another reality. Such things as the sun, moon and stars, the four seasons of the year, the elements—fire, earth, air and water—the dawn of the day, the dusk of the evening, the fact that things have certain colors in nature, birth and death, marriage and family life, good and evil, love and hatred, etc., everything had its own *sign*-ificance for the kabbalists. Thus the kabbalists refused to acknowledge our visible world to be the only existing reality. They viewed the whole pathway from En Sof to our creation as a divine ladder—"ladder" of course should be taken as a symbol too—which led down from the most exalted point, from an original unity within the divine world to our visible reality with its astonishing variety, which to our human powers of conception often seems not to display any coherence. The mystical activities of the kabbalists were oriented towards investigating the divine world and the various stages in the descent or compression process of creation, which are hidden behind our earthly symbolic appearances. In this way the mystics tried to experience the divine unity and harmony that underlie the pluriformity of our creation, a unity in which our visible reality coincides with the invisible reality.

1.5 *A psychological approach*

In some studies of Kabbalah we meet the terms "archetype" and "archetypal" in relation to the mythic and symbolic character of the sefiroth. The use of the term archetype refers to the psychological theory developed by the Swiss Carl Gustav Jung (1875-1961). At the annual Eranos conferences in Ascona, which were devoted to such broad issues as Jungian psychology, religion and history, Gershom Scholem gave many lectures on a whole variety of subjects in Jewish mysticism. Neither in Scholem's work nor in the work of other authors is the term "archetype" clarified or the connection between Jung's theories and Jewish mysticism explicitly elaborated. Since Jung's theory of archetypes can be illuminating in some respects for our understanding of Kabbalah, we shall go into the matter in a little more detail.

According to Jung, the human psyche consists of a conscious part, which we know, and an unconscious part, which is unknown to us. The unconscious is then divided into on the one hand a personal unconscious, the area of all the personal things that we have repressed and forgotten, and a collective unconscious (referred to in what follows as "unconscious"). It was primarily in the latter part of the psyche that Jung was interested.

The unconscious in a person forms an infinite area which is hidden and inaccessible to us, since it is not linked with the conscious layer in

the human individual. The realm of the unconscious can be investigated only by indirect means, namely by observing the conscious and
knowable part of the human psyche and drawing conclusions from it
with regard to the underlying unconscious. Jung discovered that in the
unconscious there were certain fixed structures that belong to the psyche of every person. These unconscious inner structures Jung called
"archetypes", following the Greek *archetypos*, "primordial form". Here
he was reaching back to a Platonic understanding of "ideas" as the
basic principles of reality, which existed already in Antiquity. Archetypes are spiritual primordial forms, immaterial primordial ideas; they
reside in an area that we cannot directly observe and that cannot be
measured and analyzed with scientific yardsticks. They can, however,
be observed by indirect means, namely by the way in which they
manifest themselves in our conscious reality, both in the concrete external world and in the human soul. Before all material things appear
here, there already exists in spiritual form a primordial principle, the
archetype. The original spiritual form thus already exists and is observ-
able by us when it expresses itself concretely, in an infinite number of
variations. Archetypes are thus dynamic spiritual force fields working
in the background, on which all phenomena and expressions of life in
our visible reality rely.

A frequently cited comparison designed to clarify the archetype is
that of a crystal. When a process of crystallization takes place in a
chemical solution, we see forms created according to a particular pattern of geometrical shapes. This pattern, the idea of this geometrical
shape, is already present in the solution before the crystallization, but
cannot itself be observed. It is only when the pattern manifests itself in
a particular crystal that we see the realization of it. Although separate
crystals can be infinitely varied and different in shape, they all give
expression to one and the same underlying pattern: the archetype. Just
as the principle of the crystal can in practice be expressed in innumerable ways, so too a single archetype manifests itself in countless
different archetypal images, notions or motifs. In other words, various
archetypal images are structured by a single archetype.

An example of an archetype is that of "the mother". The mother
archetype can manifest itself in an infinite number of concrete images
and motifs—one's own mother, of course, but also the grandmother,
the stepmother or mother-in-law, or children's nanny, etc. All these
instances can have both a positive and a negative meaning, such as the
loving and the loveless mother. At the same time everything that gives
us a feeling of security and safety—a quality that is generally associated

with motherhood—can be taken as a symbol that refers to the mother archetype. In this case we think, for example, of hollowed-out shapes, such as a cave, a womb or a nest, which enclose us protectively.

The manifestation of archetypes in our conscious reality occurs autonomously. They lie beyond the influence of a person's conscious "I". According to Jung, archetypes also occur as unconscious ordering principle in the formation of human ideas and theories. An archetype can thus manifest itself in a dream. The dream images are at the same time symbols; they refer to (an aspect of) an archetype. In Jung's view myths come into being in the same way as dreams; both myths and dreams are a creation of the unconscious. Hence there is a close connection between symbolic images in dreams and those in myths. The universal images, notions and motifs are in evidence not only in myths, but also in sacred writings of religions and moral lore as well as in fairy-tales.

If we take the above into account, Jungian psychology seems in some respects to bear interesting points of contact with the mysticism of Kabbalah. Just like the unconscious, the divine world of En Sof and the sefiroth is unlimited, inaccessible and not measurable by human standards.

When in literature on Kabbalah the sefiroth are designated as archetypes, this is an implicit reference to agreements in their content. Like archetypes, sefiroth are primordial spiritual forms, ideal models which contain a non-material foreshadowing of the concrete forms—as in the example of the crystal—which are found in our material reality. In all instances the kabbalists saw symbols that refer to spiritual powers, which they called sefiroth. Like the content of archetypes, that of the sefiroth cannot be fully known; just like the archetypes, the sefiroth are inexhaustible in their concrete forms of expression and thus they are never fully knowable to us. Whereas Jungian psychology speaks of the regulating action of archetypes in all forms of our visible existence and in the human psyche, Kabbalah sees the divine realm of En Sof and the sefiroth as the basic, original pattern of our visible creation, which determines its various manifestations.

In section 1.3 we saw something of the strongly mythic character of Kabbalah. According to Jung myths should be taken as stories in which the symbolic images have an archetypal content. This archetypal content can affect a person in a most profound way, since the images exude a numinous effective power. That is to say that the images are "accompanied" by something of the irrational, the mysterious or the divine. It is not so much the image itself that speaks to us but rather the numinous or divine aspect that speaks from it. Later on in this chapter (§ 1.6.5) we shall see how the devout Jew can, by means of mythic stories, experience the divine as a living reality, a transcendental or spiritual reality, which forms a single entity alongside the external reality of life.

Study of the Jungian view of the archetype can enrich our insight into parts of the kabbalistic doctrine of the sefiroth, kabbalistic symbolism and the mythic character of Kabbalah. Despite various striking points of agreement in content, however, mysticism should not be equated with modern terms from Jungian psychology. In this regard, Moshe Idel, a leading scholar in the field of Jewish mysticism, has pointed out the danger of applying Jungian categories rather too superficially to Kabbalah. He acknowledges that psychological theories can in certain regards contribute to our understanding of Kabbalah, but on the other hand he is rather skeptical about the way in which Jung claimed to have understood Kabbalah. Although the literature of Jungian psychology regularly speaks of a "kabbalistic parallel", the fact that both phenomena cannot automatically be equated may explain why in literature on Kabbalah, by contrast, there is usually no explicit reference to such a parallel.

1.6 *Kabbalah and Jewish philosophy: a controversy*

When Kabbalah emerged as a mystical current, in the late twelfth and early thirteenth century, this was at a time and in an environment in which Jewish philosophy was dominant. For it was philosophy that formed the intellectual framework of the time and determined the religious climate. An important feature of early Kabbalah was its need to determine its attitude towards this Jewish philosophy. To come to a better understanding of early Kabbalah and its relation to philosophy we shall need first to pay some attention to Jewish philosophy.

In section 2.1 of Chapter 1, on biblical history, we saw that the Hebrew Bible (the Old Testament) has central place in Judaism and that Torah is viewed as the revelation of God to the people of Israel. When the Jews came into contact with Greek thought, however, they met a world that differed greatly from that of the Hebrew Bible. In Greek philosophy *reason* is paramount; reality is approached through the rational capacity of the human being. Greek philosophers sought rational explanations of the phenomena that we experience, as well as causal connections between them. In this exercise they proceeded quite systematically: the various ideas and concepts were defined precisely and put into a coherent framework. The world of the Hebrew Bible on the other hand reflects a religious spirit in which God's *will* provides the explanation for all phenomena, so that there is no need to seek a rational cause by a process of reason. The ideas put forward in the Hebrew Bible are not formulated in a logical or systematic way. In the discussions between early rabbis, too, there is no evidence of the strict systematization and abstract conceptualization of Greek philosophy. The conversations between rabbis were carried out in an associative way; one subject led automatically to another. If we wanted to know what the rabbis thought for example about life after death, we should have to read through the whole of rabbinic literature, and we would encounter some rather divergent opinions in the process; we cannot simply look up the chapter on "Life after Death" in some systematic theological work by the classical rabbis, since no such work exists.

Between these two approaches, the religious spirit and the human capacity for thought, there is a constant tension, which is evident also in the history of Judaism. Right from the beginning of hellenism there are scattered signs which indicate an encounter between the world of the Hebrew Bible and that of Greek thought. But a first attempt to link revealed Jewish writings and Greek philosophy in a systematic way was undertaken by the Jewish scholar Philo of Alexandria (35 BCE–50 CE). Philo was convinced that besides the Law, the Torah also contained a philosophical doctrine. However, since the Torah was written in the form of stories and not as a book on philosophy, the philosophical ideas have to be deduced from the text by taking the stories as allegories which refer to these ideas (see § 1.6.1 on allegory and symbol). When Philo suggests that the Torah should be understood as a revelation of the Logos (reason), this means that the divine revelation on Sinai must be amenable to reason. Philo is primarily concerned with showing that the Torah is not in contradiction with, but precisely in agreement with the principles of Greek philosophy. Nonetheless, Philo of Alexandria cannot be seen as the real beginning of Jewish philosophy. Although the most important topics of later Jewish philosophy are evident in his work, no one in Jewish circles really built directly upon Philo's thought. His influence on Judaism thus remained quite limited. We have to wait until around 900 CE before we can really speak of the emergence of Jewish philosophy.

In the ninth and tenth centuries the most important Jewish centers lay within the cultural domain of Islam, in present-day Iraq. Since it was mainly Syrian Christians who had translated the works of Plato and Aristotle and the late antique commentaries on them from

Greek—sometimes through Syriac—into Arabic, the Islamic world had come into contact with Greek philosophy. A religious philosophy had thus developed within Islam which took it upon itself to define the truths of the traditional revealed scriptures of Islam with the help of this Greek-hellenistic logic and metaphysics. Since the Jews played a full part in Islamic culture, they came into contact with Islamic religious philosophy. This provided a stimulus to develop a Jewish philosophy as well. The religious climate of the time was very conducive to the emergence of a Jewish-religious philosophy in view of the fact that adherents of Islam, Judaism and Christianity, as well as adherents of many other eastern religions, were constantly embroiled in heated faith disputes, in which each claimed to possess the absolute truth. The defenders of the religion could not simply appeal to the authority of their own revelation but had to fight their opponents with the same weapons: the persuasiveness of rational argument.

Judaism had to face up to various challenges. First of all there was the Greek scientific and philosophical worldview, which proceeded from reason as the ordering principle and not from a personal god who had created the world. Then Islam and Christianity each claimed that their revelation was superior to that of the other monotheistic religions, while all kinds of eastern religions queried the feasibility of the monotheistic principle as such. But the Jewish religion was also attacked from within—in particular by the sect of the Karaites, which with its refusal to accept the authority of the Oral Law threatened to undermine the legitimacy of the Talmud and the religious authority of the rabbis. The rabbis were, as it were, forced to defend Judaism's right to exist and the authority of the Torah and tradition—in their eyes the only true divine revelation—and to show that these were in accord with human reason. Judaism had to learn to reformulate its own fundamental concepts and to place them in a coherent theological system, so that they formed an understandable and rationally justifiable whole.

In the main, the theological topics that arose were concerned with the apparent contrasts between the unity of God and the multiplicity of his attributes, between the free will of the human being and his/her predetermination, between God's supernal nature and the anthropomorphic (human-like) way in which he is often presented in the Bible and Midrash, as well as between the divine revelation in the Torah and the rational knowledge that the human mind can grasp. The philosophical system demanded that within the religion faith had to be logically consistent. That meant that "solutions" had to be found for all these apparent contradictions, theories by means of which it could be shown that the topics concerned were indeed only *apparent* contradictions.

The first real Jewish philosopher was Rabbi Sa'adyah Gaon (882–942), head of the famous Babylonian academy of Sura. After him Jewish philosophy developed much further; Judaism's approach on the basis of Aristotelian philosophy permeated broad circles of Jews who, alongside an appeal to the receipt of revelation, sought for other, intellectual means of experiencing their religion. Jewish philosophy reached its climax in the teaching of the most famous Jewish philosopher, scholar, doctor and theologian, Moses Maimonides (1135/8–1204), of Córdoba.

When the mystical movement of Kabbalah arose on both sides of the Pyrenees in the late twelfth century, this ushered in a period which saw the end of the dominant role of Jewish philosophical thought. The kabbalists turned against the rationalization of the Jewish religion, which in their view was fundamentally undermined if one tried to make it subordinate to the limitations of human reason. After Maimonides' death the differences of opinion between philosophers and mystics came to a head. This dispute, which was conducted in waves during the late thirteenth and early fourteenth century, is known in the history of Judaism as the "Maimonidean controversy".

In the sections that now follow, on the basis of some examples we shall see how much philosophers and kabbalists stood opposed to each other in their differing views on the interpretation of their traditional religious heritage. It should be borne in mind that philosophy can be roughly divided into two strands: the Aristotelian tradition, which was mainly based on the works of Aristotle and was strictly rational, and the neo-Platonic tradition, which was oriented towards the works of Plato and the late antique interpretations of his thought by the neo-Platonists. The controversy between mystics and philosophers applied especially to Aristotelian philosophy, which had become the dominant current by the time Kabbalah emerged. Neo-Platonism, as we shall see (§ 1.7), was easier to reconcile with a mystical view of reality.

1.6.1 *Allegory versus symbol*

The philosophers set themselves the objective of showing that the world of the Bible and rabbinic tradition in fact taught exactly the same as Greek philosophy, which was held in such high esteem. The

value of the Bible and rabbinic tradition, according to the philosophers, lay precisely in the fact that these writings really expressed the
ideas of Aristotle. The interpretive method which the philosophers
used for this was that of *allegory*.

In an allegorical interpretation an image used in the text is replaced
by another image. That is to say: though the text mentions a particular
thing, the text has to be interpreted as if it says something else. Thus,
the Bible verse, *Wisdom has built her house, she has set up her seven pillars*
(Prov 9.1), was understood allegorically by the philosopher Joseph
Kimhi. He posited that the image of the "seven pillars" was actually a
reference to the seven ways in which humans acquire knowledge: the
five senses, the information obtained from others, and the science of
deductive reasoning. And he claimed thus to be able to discern a medieval theory of knowledge, based on Greek philosophy, within the
biblical text. In the same vein Maimonides saw the creation story in
Genesis 1 as a representation of the Greek sciences, and the vision
from the first chapter of Ezekiel as a description of Greek metaphysics.
Now the allegorical understanding of a biblical text was not a new
phenomenon introduced by the medieval Jewish philosophers as a
exegetical technique. The Song of Songs, for example, had traditionally always been taken allegorically: the love between bride and
bridegroom in fact stands for the love between God and Israel; wher-
ever in the Song of Songs it says "bride", one should read "Israel", and
"beloved" simply means "God". It was only with the medieval philosophers, however, that allegory was applied as a systematic means of
exegesis to all possible biblical texts.

In section 1.4 we discussed the great significance of symbols in Kabbalah. In the kabbalists' view the whole Torah should be taken
symbolically, as a reference to another, higher reality, which underlies
our own: the world of the sefiroth. An example of such a symbolical
interpretation can be seen in the kabbalistic exposition of Gen 1.1 in
Hebrew: *be-reshith bara' elohim et ha-shamayim we-et ha-arets*, which
means literally: in-beginning created God the-heaven and the-earth.
The mystical interpretation of the words of this verse ran as follows:
"By means of (*be-*) the sefirah Hokhmah (*reshith*; which in the traditional literature was always linked with wisdom, but was understood
by the kabbalists specifically as the sefirah Hokhmah) He emanated
(*bara'*; the actual subject, En Sof, remaining unmentioned), the sefirah
Binah (which in kabbalistic literature is also frequently called *elohim*),
together with (*et*) the sefirah Tif'ereth (also frequently called *shamayim*,
"heaven") and the sefirah Malkhuth (which has the nickname *arets*,

"earth")." Hidden behind the words of this first verse of the Bible there lay, therefore, for the kabbalists a succinct description of the whole emanation process: *By means of the sefirah Hokhmah En Sof emanated the sefirah Binah, together with Tif'ereth and Malkhuth.*

Both the kabbalists and the philosophers were thus convinced that the revealed scriptures of the Jewish religion contained a hidden, esoteric meaning. The above examples clearly illustrate how each one saw his own truths reflected in the traditional religious literature. The philosophers read in the Torah the philosophical teaching of Aristotle, while the mystics recognized in it their doctrine of the sefiroth. The way in which that hidden meaning was exposed, however, varied considerably; the philosophers made use of the allegorical method, while the kabbalists practiced a symbolic type of exegesis.

The kabbalists were sometimes fiercely opposed to the allegorizing biblical exposition of the philosophers. So what, precisely, were their objections? First of all the mystics reproached the philosophers for in fact elevating Greek philosophy as the highest standard. The philosophers tested the religious ideas of Judaism as to the degree to which it agreed with reason, with rational human faculties. And by so doing they tried, in the view of the kabbalists, to make eternal divine truths subordinate to contemporary human standards, which, furthermore, came from outside Judaism.

A second objection by the kabbalists ensues from the first. Since everything in the Bible and in Jewish tradition had to be brought into agreement with human reason, the philosophical interpretation of the tradition always applied to things that were knowable, perceptible and understandable by humans. Since philosophical interpretation is concerned with expressible truths, an allegorical picture corresponds precisely with the content; what was meant can be expressed exactly by means of the allegorical image.

The third objection related to the fact that philosophical allegory bore an inherent danger. Since in allegory the original image stands for something else, the literal meaning of the biblical text can be lost. If the creation story is nothing but a presentation of the Greek sciences, the details of the seven days, of sun and moon and so on, no longer need to be taken so seriously; the deeper meaning, after all, is not at all concerned with the creation of the world as the Bible story suggests on a literal level. (Philo of Alexandria had already warned of this danger.) Furthermore, if the deepest meaning of the Torah really lay in the fact that it taught the ideas of Greek philosophy, it was only a short step to the conclusion that it would be better to study the works of Aristotle

directly instead of via the roundabout route of an allegorical interpretation of the Torah.

Although the kabbalists sometimes themselves applied the allegorical
method, they were primarily concerned with symbols. For them, symbols went much further than allegory. As we saw in the section on
symbolism, a symbol constitutes a reference to quite another world, an
ineffable world which lies far beyond human comprehension. In that
respect a symbol is superior to an allegory. By taking something as a
symbol one recognizes that the thing it refers to is in essence ineffable.
The symbol is thus merely an aid by which the ineffable can become
transparent. While an allegorical image is thus limited to our knowable
world, a symbol represents something that lies beyond our imagination. An allegorical image can be understood and interpreted by
reason; the content of a symbol can only be felt intuitively. The Castilian kabbalist Moses of Burgos expressed this by claiming that the
kabbalists began at the point where the philosophers ended.

An important difference between allegory and symbol is thus that
with a symbol the literal meaning always remains operative. Since the
symbol constitutes a link between two realities—our concrete reality
and that of the divine—the literal meaning of the symbol remains an
essential part of the whole. With the symbol there is an intrinsic connection between the literal image and what it expresses in the divine
world; with allegory the relationship is wholly arbitrary. For the kabbalists the deeper meaning they give to the Bible is thus an addition to
the literal meaning, and not its replacement. In the section on the
commandments (§ 1.6.4) we shall see that this difference between
allegory and symbol is paramount.

1.6.2 *The unity of God versus the multiplicity of creation*

One of the daily prayers of the Jewish people, the so-called Shema,
begins with the exclamation: *Hear, O Israel, the Lord our God, the Lord
is One* (Deut 6.4). Under the influence of Jewish philosophy the
meaning of this declaration of the unity of God was elaborated further.
The philosophers understood this verse as an indication that God was
in essence indivisible, that his being could not be divided up into all
sorts of separate qualities. God had no physicality. His being was eternal, that is to say not susceptible to change. Since any statement on the
character of God, any ascription of qualities, implies a limitation of
God's all-embracing unity, in the view of the philosophers God does

not actually have any features. The essence of God was transcendent, lying beyond all human imagination.

One problem for the philosophers was that although they concluded that no features could be ascribed to God, the Bible and Jewish liturgy did indeed ascribe properties (or attributes, called *middoth*) to God: God is merciful, gracious, jealous, vengeful etc. All these properties seemed to point rather to a multiplicity and changeability of God than to his unity and immutability. So the question arose of what can in fact be said about God. The problem of the doctrine of attributes was an important topic in medieval philosophy. Maimonides went into this problem in the most extensive way. He established that many of the properties or attributes ascribed to God in the Bible are not really attributes of God. So-called "attributes of action" of God do exist: properties which establish nothing of the essence of God but only say something of his actions in relation to this world. Seen from the world, God can have an effect on the world in various ways, while his essence is still one and indivisible. (See the following section 1.6.3, "anthropomorphisms").

The kabbalists too subscribed to the notion of the unity of God. Nothing can be said about the innermost essence of God; it is unknowable and cannot be defined in any way at all. This unknowable, "highest" part of the deity, which also played a part for the philosophers, the kabbalists called En Sof. However, where the philosophers spoke of the middoth, the divine attributes, the kabbalists thought in terms of sefiroth, which formed the wholly individual, independent states (hypostases) within the deity. These properties of God however were not understood by the kabbalists as mere metaphors, as expressions that had to be taken as only "a manner of speaking", but as revealed aspects of the hidden and unknowable En Sof. The sefiroth contained much more than the philosophers' middoth; they were emanations, effusions from the hidden deity. The sefiroth were the varying aspects or the mystical countenances of God. For the kabbalist it was indeed possible, by means of the sefiroth, to get to know something about God.

For the kabbalists, the way in which the unknowable God revealed himself in the world of the sefiroth agreed with the concept of the God of the Bible: a personal God who is concerned for his creation and his creatures and maintains a personal relationship with them. Everything that the Bible relates about God and his relation to creation, refers to the world of the sefiroth and not to En Sof. Even when a person approaches his personal God, as in prayer, for example, this action is directed to the sefiroth and not to En Sof. Through the system of the sefiroth the Jewish mystics saw the chance of building a bridge between on the one hand the absolute unity of God, the impersonal, abstract and unknowable God, and on the other hand the personal God of the Bible.

The kabbalists emphasized that the various aspects of God as expressed in the sefiroth did not imply a multiplicity or mutability of the deity; the whole emanation process had to be seen as something that took place within the one and indivisible God. There was thus no question of a God who was divided into various components. The kabbalists saw no inherent contradiction in the sefirotic system between the unknowable God of En Sof and the self-revealing personal God of the Bible, who was identical with the sefiroth.

But there is something paradoxical in this understanding. In the kabbalistic literature a process is described in which the God of En Sof gives up his resting in himself and allows something to flow out. And thereby indeed a difference emerges between the situation within En Sof and that outside it, a form of duality or multiplicity instead of an unbroken unity. The kabbalists did not see it this way. For the limited human mind it may seem that one could speak of an inside and an outside, but since all this concerned processes that lie beyond human imagination, this is not really the case. The fact that humans can put into words these processes in our reality only in a paradoxical way does not mean that they must necessarily be taken as an abandonment of the unbroken divine unity. Nonetheless in the whole of kabbalistic literature it is not made clear how, precisely, the transition of En Sof to the world of the sefiroth should be viewed. There are varieties of opinion as to the extent to which the sefiroth can be counted as God's deepest essence and the extent to which they in fact lie outside it.

1.6.3   *Anthropomorphisms*

Closely connected with the topic of the unity and properties of God is the problem of anthropomorphisms. The Bible often describes God in human form (anthropomorphically): God speaks, breathes, stretches out his hand or is a war-hero, and so on. In countless passages we also find descriptions of God as if he has human-like feelings (the so-called anthropopathisms): God gets angry, rejoices or becomes vengeful.

Although in rabbinic literature we also find anthropomorphic descriptions of God, alongside this there was a certain caution with respect to references to God in terms of the human body. For Jewish philosophy, however, striving for an image of God that was as pure and abstract as possible, all anthropomorphic descriptions were abhorrent and completely at odds with the idea of the absolute unity and indivisibility of the God of Israel. In the eyes of the philosophers, all references in which God was depicted in a human way had to be taken allegorically. They should certainly not be taken literally, since after all the nature of God was unknowable, could not be grasped and lay beyond all human yardsticks. When for example the Bible speaks of "the arm of God", then this could not possibly be meant literally; God does not have an arm and the expression is only a manner of speaking. The concept merely uses the human arm as an example.

The mystics of Kabbalah however proceeded from quite another principle. When the Bible or rabbinic literature speaks of "the arm of God", the kabbalists do indeed take it literally: the divine really does contain an aspect that coincides with the term "arm". Furthermore, the only real arm is God's arm; the human arm here in our reality is merely a weak reflection of this higher reality. In other words: when the Bible says, "the arm of God", it is not a matter of an anthropomorphic description of God at all, but the reverse. When a person speaks of his or her own body with such terms as "arms", "legs" etc., this is in fact a theomorphic (i.e. "God-shaped") description of that person. After all, the human being was created in the image of God (Gen 1.26) and not the other way round. The fact that people have body parts can only exist on the basis of this divine or higher reality. The human arm is merely a symbol that refers to God's arm, which is something real and existent in the divine realm. The kabbalists were concerned with the experiencing of the divine reality hidden behind the symbolically understood human arm. The mystics thus had no problem in describing one of the parts of the divine body. They could simply leave the literal meaning of the Bible intact while at the same time a new layer of meaning was tapped in the Bible.

The difference between the philosophical and the kabbalistic vision is thus a question of the point of departure. The philosopher takes the "arm" as a human concept; "arm" is something human, something that really exists in our human world. When we then use this human term for God, this is only a metaphor in the divine world, since God does not have human arms in real life. For the kabbalist all this is precisely the other way round. He takes the "arm" as a divine concept, an aspect within the divine, which really exists there. If we use this divine term for humans, this is merely a metaphor (or better: symbol) in the human world itself, since with all their physical limitations humans do not really have this divine arm.

The fact that the human being was created in the image of God led the kabbalists to the idea of depicting the sefiroth as a representation of the "human" body (see Figure 2). According to one particular arrangement the sefiroth Kether, Hokhmah and Binah coincided with the human head, the sefiroth Hesed and Hod with the legs, the sefirah Yesod with the genitals, while the last sefirah, Malkhuth, reflected the body as a whole. Alongside this there existed other systems for arranging the sefiroth by analogy with the human body. Thus the world of the sefiroth forms a great divine body (macrocosm) of which the human body (microcosm) is a pale reflection.

1.6.4   *The commandments*

Another important topic with which both philosophers and kabbalists occupied themselves was the Halakhah, the set of regulations which gives detailed directions for daily Jewish life. The Halakhah is perhaps the subject that gave the most cause for conflict between philosophy and Kabbalah.

According to tradition, the Torah has 613 commandments. These 613 regulations are divided into 248 positive commandments, i.e. regulations that must be performed, and 365 negative commandments, which include everything that one should not do. Commandments and prohibitions are called in Hebrew *mitswoth* (singular: *mitswah*).

Aside from a few exceptions, the Bible never mentions a reason for a particular commandment. God charges his people Israel to obey these mitswoth without explaining why. Rabbinic literature then repeatedly indicates that the reasons for the commandments (*ta'amei ha-mitswoth*) are hidden and that a danger lurks within any attempt to inquire into a justification for a particular commandment.

As we saw in the previous section, the philosophers attached great value to human reason. They therefore were keen to show that there was a rational explanation for the biblical commandments, however illogical they might sometimes appear. It was now the job of the human being to discern the rational explanation of all the commandments and also to explain why Jews had to do so many of these material, physical actions with their bodies. Of all the philosophers Maimonides contributed most to an exposition of the commandments that is acceptable to human reason. He opposed the mechanical observance of a commandment, since this did not achieve the goal of understanding the why and wherefore of that commandment.

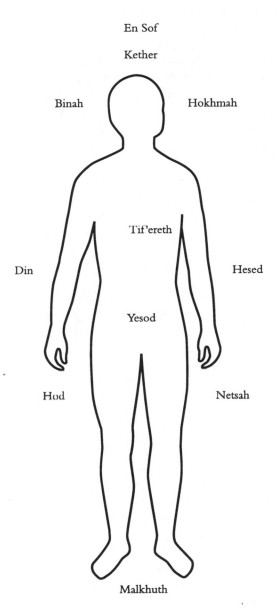

Figure 2
The analogy between the sefiroth and the human body

According to Maimonides many mitswoth served a particular practical purpose. All forms of unclean food were forbidden since such food was bad for one's health; pork was forbidden because the pig was a dirty animal. The incense used in the Temple had no other function, according to Maimonides, than to disperse the stench of the sacrificial animals. The prohibition of revenge was intended to make antisocial behavior impossible. Many commandments were in his view exercises to teach people proper behavior and the right mentality. Further, Maimonides explained many commandments as measures against idolatry. Sometimes he also saw particular commandments as time-bound, in that they had had their use, especially earlier, in the time of the Bible, but were less relevant in Maimonides' own day. He was convinced that any individual commandment could be rationally explained. In cases where the logical reason was not clear to someone, it was that person's fault and not that of the commandment. As far as he was concerned, there were only very few commandments for which he could not see the reason.

Quite unlike the philosophers, the kabbalists brought the meaning of the commandments into connection with the world of the sefiroth. In the section on the sefiroth we discussed the interplay between our world of space and time and that of the divine world, in which human actions can have an influence on the restoration of the chasm that runs through all the worlds as a result of the fall of Adam. In the previous section we also saw how the sefiroth world was viewed as the body of the deity, of which the human body forms a reflection, as a microcosm (§ 1.6.3).

Taken as a whole, the commandments that Jews are to observe, which govern daily life, are related to the body of the deity. Because of the mutual dependency of the divine world and our creation, the kabbalists were convinced that the practical observance of the commandments had a direct effect on the world of the sefiroth. The commandments were not only to be understood as symbolic actions that reflected analogous processes in the divine world, but also as actions which influenced these processes. Since Jews observe the commandments with their bodies, they participate actively in the processes of the divine body.

So it is not without reason that so much importance is attached throughout kabbalistic literature to human actions—in particular the daily observance of the commandments. After all, the performance of these mitswoth makes an important contribution to the restoration of the chasm that runs through all the worlds, bringing about a return of the original harmony and unity. Thus for instance the observance of the regulations with reference to married life had a reinforcing effect on the relations between the sefiroth Tif'ereth (as the male principle) and Malkhuth (as the female principle). Each human action in which love or mercy played a role, had an influence on the sefirah Hesed. Great value was attached to ritual hand-washing, since the ten human fingers symbolized the ten sefiroth.

Sometimes the idea that the daily practice of the commandments contributed to the restoration of the original unity of all things led to extremes. Thus there is a kabbalistic writing in which we read that the eating of *matsah* (unleavened bread) at Pesach has a reinforcing effect on the first joint of the right thumb of the divine being!

Mystical writings and commentaries by well-known kabbalists almost unanimously present the conviction that though the meaning of the commandments can never be fully grasped, by practicing the commandments people were imitating the divine. Each mitswah is after all the symbolic representation of particular divine principles and processes. Through the observance of the commandments not only was the human will brought into agreement with the divine will, but at the same time a concrete contribution was made to the restoration of the original situation of paradise. In abiding by the commandments people attained contact with the divine; simply by doing them the hidden God became known.

In the writings of the great kabbalists like Nahmanides, Jacob ben Shesheth, Moses de Leon and Joseph Gikatilla, a strong resistance is evident against Maimonides' attempt to rationalize the commandments. According to them the rationalization of the commandments cast doubt on their divine origin, which could lead to neglect of the Law. They were also opposed to Maimonides' statements that the details of certain commandments were not relevant or that some commandments were even out of date. Each regulation, each work and each letter of any of the commandments contained, for the kabbalists, divine mysteries. The wrath of these mystics was directed especially against those Jews who had become assimilated to the non-Jewish society of their day to such an extent that they thought it unnecessary to continue to live by the commandments. Many of them had a philosophical attitude and, having "understood" the mitsvoth allegorically, considered themselves no longer bound to their daily observance.

Those who were inclined to neglect the commandments frequently made an appeal to Maimonides himself. This was not justified, since

Maimonides always clearly stated that the understanding of the mitswoth should never be at the expense of their literal meaning and
observance. His opinion was that the commandments should be literally lived by, since they helped people in body and soul to become
fulfilled beings. The more perfect in body and soul, the greater the
practical and moral virtues which for Maimonides were the precondi-
tions for a correct understanding of the faith. Besides this the mitswoth
in his view brought about a just society, in which the individual human being was enabled to become a fully rational being.

Gershom Scholem and others are of the opinion that the philosophers, unlike the Kabbalah mystics, did not succeed very well in
renewing the commandments and inspiring devout Jews to keep to the
practical rules of daily Jewish life. When philosophers interpret some
commandments as originally gentile or as representing an outdated
morality, this cannot exactly be seen as a reinforcement of the will to
live by them. The kabbalists, by contrast, are considered by these
scholars to have indeed succeeded in reinforcing and inspiring the
foundations of the religious life of the devout Jew, by elaborating the
meaning of the commandments in detail. The kabbalists after all had
transformed Halakhah into a complex of sacramental actions and mystical rites, behind which lay profound divine secrets and mysteries.

Finally it should be noted that alongside those who adhered to a
philosophical or kabbalistic view of the daily commandments, there
were also non-philosophical and non-mystical traditional adherents of
the Jewish religion. For them, the fact that God had laid these commandments upon them was more than sufficient; there was no other
reason for the mitswoth than the will of God. They preferred to subject themselves to the commandments without further ado and not to
ask questions, instead of deciding for themselves what was the right
way to act. Any attempt to bring these divine regulations into connection with rational explanations or mystical dimensions was rejected by
this group.

1.6.5   *Philosophy and myth*

In sections 1.3 and 1.5 the topic of myths already came up for discussion. We saw there how the kabbalists tried to approach the divine by
creating new myths in which God is described in all his aspects. Now
we shall first of all look more closely into the difference between the
conceptual thinking of the philosophers and the symbolic-mythical
thinking of the kabbalists and proceed to present an example of how

the kabbalists transformed biblical motifs and traditional haggadic stories into a myth.

For the philosophers the purity of the monotheistic idea of God had pride of place. As they sought abstract formulations to indicate the unity of God, there arose an extremely abstract and pure but also distant picture of a transcendent God. Such an abstract idea of God does not of course sit well with descriptions of the deity which make use of mythic and anthropomorphic images and symbols.

For the kabbalists, however, mythic stories with their engaging images and symbols were a living reality. In their view, God came alive for people by means of myths, and the deity became a living and personal God, a God one could visualize and experience, a close God who above all else was involved in human life. Mystically inclined Jews saw their deepest religious feelings reflected in the symbols and in the archetypal character of the myths they created. God was experienced as a living reality in all his aspects. However sublime the purely abstract theological-philosophical formulations of God might be, for the kabbalists they were inadequate; the living reality of God in his infiniteness could not be reduced to logical, rational terms.

This is not to say, of course, that the philosophers' picture of God was limited and accessible, while that of the kabbalists was infinitely elevated. It is true both for the philosophers and the kabbalists that the secret of the divine remained intact. Just as for kabbalists there was never an end to knowing the unfathomably deep processes of God and his divine world, the philosophers too realized that they would never be able rationally to think the deity right through to the end.

In the preceding section we were able to read how the kabbalists expanded Halakhah, the commandments regarding daily Jewish life, into cosmic dimensions. With the transformation of the commandments into holy sacraments and mystical rites, they created a form of myth, since every commandment had an effect on the hidden life and body of God and the dynamic processes in it.

Just as in the area of the commandments the kabbalists tapped into deeper layers in the haggadic elements from rabbinic literature: folklore material, parables, legends, fairytale-like stories, ethical anecdotes etc. (see Chapter 1, § 2.4). Here too the kabbalists extended the traditional material into cosmic dimensions, in which the mythic element played an important part. As an example we shall take the biblical story of the expulsion from paradise (Gen 3). If we approach this Bible story about Adam's fall from a human perspective we come across various aspects which seem illogical to us: the expulsion from paradise takes place as a result of one simple fact—Adam transgresses the divine prohibition against eating of the fruit of the tree of knowledge. For this one fact he is banished for good from the Garden of Eden, a punishment which extends to the present day for all his descendants. Humanly speaking we can ask questions of this story. Isn't a punishment for such a transgression rather drastic? Would it not have been better if God had prepared Adam better, informing him or explaining to him what consequences the transgression would have? Doesn't this story give the appearance that a vengeful God has two duffers running around in the nude fall into a cleverly set trap, not even allowing them to complain about their banishment to a totally different world? If God is almighty and has any regard for humans, couldn't he have arranged things so that Adam would not have been so stupid as to eat of the fruit? Then at least his descendants would not have had to suffer so pitifully. Furthermore, how do things stand with the commandment, *Honor your father and mother* (Exod 20.12)? Does this commandment apply to the very first father too, then?

We see clearly that it is not possible to say that this and many other Bible stories are particularly logical. The kabbalists, however, did not assume that the Bible had to be *logically* explicable. The Torah with its stories was after all a creation with a divine origin (see § 1.4), which like the sefiroth had come down from the hidden essence of the deity through all the worlds, to take shape finally in our world. The Torah thus comprised all worlds, including our own. The story of the expulsion from paradise, as we find it in the Torah, was according to the views of the kabbalists merely an external wrapping of—or a symbolic reference to—divine mysteries that underlie our creation and are encompassed in the doctrine of the emanation of the sefiroth. The images, words and letters of this story, which are to be taken symbolically, all refer to these mysteries. Conversely, one can also say that these mysteries in turn are given shape in the graphic story of the fall of Adam. The story of Adam's fall thus teaches anyone with good understanding something quite specific about God himself. So the Torah is not to be taken as a book that tells beautiful, logically defensible stories according to human norms. If it were a matter of the beauty of the stories in the Torah, says the Zohar, we should be able to think of much better and more attractive stories that those we find in the Torah.

The same notion, that the Bible stories make something clear about the "structure" of God, is also found in the mystical exegesis of a haggadic midrash in rabbinic tradition (*Genesis Rabbah* 8.1), which relates how God had created Adam as an androgynous being with two faces, after which He sawed him through and provided each of the two parts with its own back. This midrash, which was originally intended as a clarification to accompany the Bible passage on the formation of the woman from Adam's side (Gen 2.21-23), was now linked by the kabbalists with their view of the emanation process. The story of the splitting of Adam was already a symbolic representation of a specific occurrence in the sefirotic world. According to the kabbalists precisely this occurrence was now illuminated further in the rabbinic midrash: Adam lost his originally androgynous character by splitting into a male and a female half, an occurrence which ran parallel to a split in the world of the sefiroth; the sefiroth world too was originally androgynous in character and also split into a male and a female part. The kabbalists thus considerably broadened the meaning of this Bible passage and the midrash that belongs to it. Both the biblical story and the midrash were transformed by the mystics into a complete myth on the split within the divine world, and thus into an occurrence of gigantic cosmic proportions. It is self-evident that more rationally-minded philosophers were rather dismayed by a mythological exegesis like this. Philosophical exegetes generally read in the splitting of Adam a depiction of the Aristotelian dual division into matter and form.

1.7 Neo-Platonism

As we pointed out in section 1.6, Kabbalah arose at a time and in an environment in which the Aristotelian version of Jewish philosophy was dominant. We also saw a number of important points of contention in the controversy between Kabbalah and Aristotelian philosophy. As we already said there, however, there existed another school within philosophy besides the Aristotelian tradition, namely neo-Platonism.

The founding father of neo-Platonism was Plotinus, who lived in Italy in the third century CE and who reinterpreted the philosophical system of the Greek philosopher Plato (429-347 BCE). The philosophy which Plotinus developed on the basis of Plato's work contained in its basis a mystical doctrine, which was completely foreign to the Greek philosophy that preceded it.

Plotinus's teaching speaks of "the One" as the highest principle, which stands above all opposition, precedes all that exists and cannot be grasped in conceptual terms. Since the fullness of the One as it were overflowed (emanated), our material reality finally emerged by means of a gradual process of progressive condensation. One might compare this with a bucket filled to the rim with water which in accordance with a fixed law of nature overflows at some point. According to Plotinus the emanation process took place by stages through three different spheres of being. The first emanation he called *nous* (Intellect), which coincides with what Plato understood by Ideas. According to Plato our total visible reality derived from a world of ideas, separately existing realities in a world outside our own, a transcendental world which underlies our visible creation (see also § 1.5). The second emanation in Plotinus's scheme is that of the Soul or the Psyche. The third is that of Matter, which is associated with our reality and is where evil resides.

What distinguishes Plotinus's scheme so fundamentally from Greek philosophy is the theme of return. Just as everything that exists emanated from the One, so shall everything return again to the original cause; that which streamed out of the One will stream back into it. Individual human souls here on earth also have a divine origin, since they all flowed out of the One. As the souls entered more deeply into matter they forgot their origin in the One. The further they entered into it the more their knowledge of their origin and of themselves waned. The more independent the souls thought themselves from their original home port, and the more they became identified with this material world, the more they neglected their origins. According to Plotinus the highest objective of humans is to come to realize they have strayed, to retrace their steps and to ascend to their origin. There is no higher conceivable happiness for the human soul than its reunion with the divine from which it proceeded.

Like Aristotelian philosophy, neo-Platonic philosophy had an influence on various Jewish thinkers. Three important Jewish thinkers whose work displays neo-Platonic influence in varying degrees are Solomon ibn Gabirol (ca. 1020–1050/8), Judah Halevi (ca. 1075–1141) and Abraham ibn Ezra (1092 1167). It is clear that neo-Platonic philosophy can be more easily related to a revelatory religion than the Aristotelian system. For the Aristotelians the emphasis lay on the proof that the content of the Torah met the requirements of logic, on getting to know God by way of reason, as well as on the denial of his attributes. By contrast, such a figure as Judah Halevi posited that at many points there was indeed a fundamental opposition between reason and revealed religion. He ascribed only a limited validity to philosophy; there are simply areas about which human reason can say nothing of importance. Judah Halevi allowed more room for a non-rational experience of God. For him the aim of the devout Jew was rather to approach ("cleave to") God, through which a person experiences a living contact with God. He was more concerned with the emotional experience of God's presence than with rational knowing.

The development of nascent Kabbalah cannot be seen separately from the encounter with neo-Platonism. In particular with regard to its view of the structure of the celestial world, Kabbalah adopted elements of neo-Platonism and reinterpreted them. We do need to bear in mind, however, that between Plotinus's scheme and that of Kabbalah, which functioned within a monotheistic religious framework, there were areas of tension.

An important difference between them is that Plotinus saw the emanation process as a completely automatic, involuntary occurrence in accordance with the laws of nature, without there being any question of a conscious will on the part of the One to move on to the creation of the world. The kabbalists on the other hand understood the emanation process as an entirely conscious act of will by the hidden deity. Further, there is the difference that by contrast with the impersonal One of Plotinus Kabbalah focuses on the God of the Bible: a personal God who reveals himself to humans in the Torah. This aspect of self-revelation by the deity is completely absent in Plotinus. While the biblical God is concerned with his creation, the One of Plotinus takes no part in this created world. An another difference lies in the fact that Plotinus saw the emanation process as a gradual materialization of the highest principle as far as the visible world. The kabbalists understood the emanation process as something that was played out completely *within* God, while the divine world was reflected as a single entity in our creation.

In the descriptions of the emergence of the earliest kabbalistic movements we shall see how Plotinus's image of the impersonal One and the Bible's image of the personal God permeated each other in kabbalistic thought. From the neo-Platonic concept of the One the kabbalistic view of En Sof developed—that part of God that remains entirely hidden, is unknowable and has no properties. This hidden part of God is not mentioned at all in the Bible, according to the kabbalists. Moreover, the hidden side of God cannot even be mentioned in the Bible; for the Scriptures are concerned with the part of God that he reveals of himself to humans. This revealed side of God, which forms his personal aspect, finds expression in the sefiroth. We see how in this way the kabbalists succeeded in constructing a bridge between the neo-Platonic idea of the impersonal One and the biblical, personal God.

In the second part of this chapter we shall acquaint ourselves with some further neo-Platonic elements which in one way or another found their way into Kabbalah (§§ 2.3, 2.4 and 2.6.4).

1.8 Concluding remarks: Kabbalah and philosophy

Philosophers and kabbalists in the twelfth and thirteenth centuries found themselves confronted with an enormous difference between the contemporary view of the world and the worldview that is evident in the Bible and the traditional literature. Both for the philosophers and the kabbalists, the relationship with traditional rabbinic Judaism had become something of a problem. Since a break with the Torah and everything that had been handed down on the basis of tradition was inconceivable both for philosophers and kabbalists, they endeavored to build a bridge between the worldview of their own day and that of the Bible and rabbinic literature. Both blew new life into the tradition by reinterpreting it. So philosophy and Kabbalah are two opposing, alternative approaches to the traditional Jewish religious heritage.

Here the question must not be asked whose interpretation of the tradition was right. We cannot say, of course, that the mystical approach was by definition better that the philosophical, or vice versa. It is true that around 1500 CE philosophy had lost a good deal of its attraction—we shall return to this question in Chapter 4, § 2—while Kabbalah was enjoying considerable popularity among large groups of Jews. This does not mean that Kabbalah was a superior system. In the seventeenth century we see, as Scholem aptly describes it, the originally so triumphant Kabbalah in turn become hopelessly tangled up and go under in its self-constructed mythical labyrinth.

In the previous sections, for the sake of clarity the controversy between philosophers and kabbalists has been no more than sketched in broad brushstrokes. However, in the case of almost every part of this controversy there are numerous nuances to be brought out and interesting details to be added. The true relation between philosophy and Kabbalah is of course much more complex than has been presented here. It is clear, for example, that despite their great differences, the two movements influenced each other and also became intertwined: philosophy adopted elements from mysticism and mysticism contained philosophical aspects. The philosopher Judah Halevi, for instance, was viewed by the kabbalists as in some regards one of their precursors. Others, such as Isaac ibn Latif or Bahyah ben Asher, were both kabbalists and philosophers. In addition, kabbalists like Abraham Abulafia were inspired to a significant extent precisely by the philosophy of Maimonides.

The complex relations between philosophy and Kabbalah find expression, among other places, in the sphere of the terminology used. In the formulation of the doctrine of the sefiroth and mystical symbolism the kabbalists made use of philosophical terms. On the one hand it looks as if kabbalists and philosophers were thinking and writing about the same things, while on the other hand we have to realize that initially the mystics had no other terms available to them to describe their entirely individual ideas on the divine world of the sefiroth. For the expression of what lay beyond what could be expressed, the kabbalists thus used words that had quite another content for the philosophers. This fact can of course lead to misunderstandings in the interpretation of the kabbalistic writings.

There are also scholars who prefer not to draw such a sharp contrast between philosophy and Kabbalah. Precisely because of the complexity sketched above they have more regard for the agreements between the two movements than for the differences. These scholars claim, for instance, that the terms allegory and symbol do not reflect two totally different approaches but are rather both references to the search for the deeper meaning of the Bible and Tradition. They point to the creative philosophical interpretations of some of the commandments, which do not differ essentially from those of the kabbalists.

In the first part of Chapter 3 we became acquainted with the themes of the most important aspects of classical Kabbalah. We shall now pay attention to the historical development of Kabbalah up to the expulsion of the Jews from Spain in 1492. In this process a range of movements, writings and mystics will be met in chronological order, along with the various views on them that are current in today's scholarly research into Jewish mysticism. The basic knowledge we have gained in the preceding sections must serve as the background for the treatment of the separate movements. On the basis of this background we have a better understanding of what the Jewish mystics were really about and what their main points of contention were. In what follows we shall regularly refer back to this knowledge.

2. Historical overview of the movements

2.1 The problem of the emergence of Kabbalah

As we have seen, the emergence of Kabbalah as a mystical movement
has to be sought in Provence, to be precise in the western part, the
Languedoc, between 1150 and 1220. The Languedoc was home to
some important Jewish communities, where the study of Torah and
tradition had come to flourish in such towns as Montpellier, Arles,
Lunel, Carcassonne and especially Narbonne, which for centuries had
been a leading center of Jewish culture—according to some even an
independent Jewish principality from 768 to 900. These centers to the
north of the Pyrenees maintained relations with other Jewish communities, such as in northern France, the Rhineland, the Iberian
Peninsula and the Middle East.

From a cultural and religious point of view the twelfth century was
a dynamic period for Provence. The Languedoc was the center of a
highly developed courtly and feudal secular culture in which, among
other things, the poetry of the troubadours flourished. In the religious
realm the presence of the heretical movement of the Catharists led to
great tensions in this area. With religious zeal the Catharists turned
radically against what to them was the corrupt Catholic Church, the
clergy and society in general.

In the teaching of the Catharist movement the dualism of gnosticism plays a large part. This teaching is connected historically with that
of the Bogomils of Bulgaria. There are points of agreement between
the Catharist form of gnosticism and that of the Manicheans, a gnostic
movement founded by Mani in Persia at the beginning of the third
century CE. Yet there is no convincing evidence of a historical relation
between the Catharists and the Manicheans. The dualistic character of
the Catharist teaching seems in part to be due to the fact that alongside
God there is talk of a Satan who created our world. The Catharists had
a negative view of visible reality, which they saw as merely a sort of
provisional order from which the human soul had to find a way to free
itself.

In the fight against this heresy the Church used all the means available to it to regain its power over the Catharists and over that part of
the nobility that supported this movement. Nonetheless it lost a great
deal of influence and authority. This deep-seated conflict was not limited to Provence but affected the whole of the country. It was only
after the intervention of the French kings that the Catharists could be

brought to their knees and the Catholic Church was able to regain its power.

It is against this very social background of religious, cultural and social tensions in Provence at the end of the twelfth century that we see the mystical movement of Kabbalah emerging. The Jews in Provence are bound to have known about these goings-on. After all, great Jewish centers like Narbonne and Toulouse provided the backdrop for continual clashes and intrigues between the Church on the one hand and the Catharists and the secular culture of knights and troubadours on the other. Scholarly research into the very complicated question of the emergence of Kabbalah as a completely new mystical movement has of course also wondered to what extent all the factors and conditions just mentioned could have influenced Kabbalah and whether they can shed more light on the history of the emergence of this form of Jewish mysticism.

It turns out, however, to be very difficult to determine the exact nature of relations between Catharists and Jews, or to what extent the secular social milieu was influential. The oldest kabbalistic documents from Provence that have come down to us unfortunately contain scarcely any clear information on the historical developments which led to the emergence of Kabbalah. They do, however, give quite a good picture of the mystical world of ideas as it came to expression after the appearance of Kabbalah. By subjecting the various elements in this literature to a close investigation, scholars have tried to reconstruct something of the prehistory of Kabbalah.

From the earliest kabbalistic documents it seems that Provençal Judaism must have taken over traditions from various sources. What these were, precisely, where they came from and how they arrived in Provence, is in many respects still an unsolved issue. We must leave open the possibility that the traditions in question derived ultimately from the Middle East.

In view of the importance and the influence of the kabbalistic movement within Judaism, the question of the roots of Kabbalah—this has been called one of the most difficult questions in the history of Judaism after the fall of the Temple—is indisputably of great significance. Despite all the research that has been carried out, a great deal is still unknown regarding the emergence of Kabbalah. Various problems that play a role in this will be encountered in the following sections on the Book Bahir and the first kabbalists.

2.2 The Book Bahir

As far as we know, *Sefer ha-Bahir* (Book Bahir)—which means something akin to "radiant light", after Job 37.21—is the first mystical work in which we meet the symbolic structure of the sefiroth, which is so characteristic of later Kabbalah. The book has the form of a traditional midrash written in Hebrew and Aramaic: sundry comments on Bible verses and passages in rabbinic literature which are attributed to existing and non-existing rabbis from the time of the Mishnah and later. The text is carelessly edited and follows no particular train of thought; it jumps from one subject to another: cosmology, cosmogony, the Hebrew language, the Divine Name, rituals, commandments, prayer etc. The form of the Book Bahir as we have it now originates from Provence, probably dating to the middle of the twelfth century. The text is clearly the result of repeated editing. Some layers cannot be older than the twelfth century, while other passages seem, in view of their ideas and use of language, to go back to much older sources.

In Chapter 2, on Hekhaloth literature, reference was made to the great influence which *Sefer Yetsirah* (Book of Creation) had on medieval Jewish mystics (§ 3.2). It was studied by practically all the mystics of the time and was a source of inspiration in the development of kabbalistic ideas concerning the divine world. The term *sefiroth* in the Bahir is borrowed from the Book of Creation. In the latter work, however, this term stands for the ten primordial numbers and nowhere is there any mention of these sefiroth emanating from God and being in a dynamic relationship with each other. It is only after the Book Bahir that the term sefiroth gains the meaning of aspects or properties of God, or individual emanations in the divine world. Here the sefiroth are also the ten *ma'amaroth* or *logoi*, the "utterances", with which God created the world, according to the Mishnah (*Avoth* 5.1). In the Bahir these ten divine utterances become independent properties of God in their own right—the sefiroth.

The structure of the sefiroth in the Bahir does not yet have the fully-fledged form as described above in section 1.2. Thus the sefirah Yesod, which occupies ninth place in the structure of the canonical system, is in seventh place in the ranking of the Bahir. The written Torah, which is brought into connection with the third sefirah in the Bahir, was eventually to fall under the sixth sefirah. Another important difference with the system of later Kabbalah is that at this point there is still no mention of En Sof, the realm of the hidden and unknowable deity. According to the Bahir the first sefirah is Thought (*Mahshavah*). This Mahshavah is the primordial Idea, the divine Knowledge that stands at the beginning of the creation process, in which a well-considered and ordered plan for creation lies enclosed. In the Bahir we learn nothing of a possible higher, unknowable principle standing above this Thought. It is only later, when the first kabbalists start to get on with neo-Platonism, that the idea of En Sof from which the sefiroth emanate develops. This process finally came to completion with the kabbalists of Gerona.

The way in which the sefiroth are described in the Book Bahir has much in common with ancient gnosticism. The latter was occupied with the idea of "fullness" (Greek: *pleroma*), the realm of the divine. This divine world of perfection and absolute harmony was filled by *aeons* or divine powers. The lower worlds emerged from this heavenly world. In the Book Bahir this gnostic idea now appears in an altered, Jewish-monotheistic form. The Gnostic-mythic character of the imagery is also evident in the Bahir's presentation of the sefiroth as a cosmic tree, planted by God, the roots of which are above and the ten branches of which grow downwards through a fixed structure.

Not only in relation to the sefiroth, but also at other points the Bahir contains gnostic elements. These are expressed above all in the way in which the Bahir deals with three important subjects: the question of the origins of evil, the presence of a separate female power within the divine world, and the issue of reincarnation.

The origin of evil. There is much speculation in Kabbalah about the origins of evil. The Bible does not give an explicit answer to this question, although the idea does emerge that God wove evil deliberately into his creation; God is the creator of light *and* darkness, of good *and* evil (e.g. Isa 45.7; Prov 16.4). For Jewish philosophers, however, the thought that evil could come from God, in any way at all, was absolutely unacceptable. In effect they tried to explain away evil by supposing that it did not really exist as something of itself, but was merely the absence of good, just as darkness can only exist in the absence of light. The kabbalists resisted this philosophical reasoning. They took the biblical view of evil as their point of departure and built upon it. According to the kabbalists, evil, contrary to the philosophical point of view, was a genuine reality which could by no means be underestimated or avoided.

In the kabbalistic speculations about the nature and origin of evil, in general two views stand out. In the first view, evil has a place within the divine world. Evil thus also belongs to the structure of the created world and is not dependent on human behavior; it is God himself who determines in his creative acts that evil must come into being. According to the other view evil is not woven into the structure of creation but only really comes to expression as the result of the fall of Adam; evil thus is primarily associated with human behavior.

The classical kabbalists assumed above all that the origins of evil should be sought in the divine world. The idea that evil is connected with human behavior was not very influential in early Kabbalah. This last view, initially developed by the kabbalists of the Castilian school (§ 2.6.3), was not to be given detailed elaboration until the sixteenth century in Lurianic Kabbalah. In the Bahir, evil is an entirely independent manifestation within the world of the deity. In the Bahir, evil emanates from the divine tree and has a role in the realization of the divine plan of creation. It is connected with the sefirah Din, or alternatively sometimes presented as the fingers of God's left hand.

The female aspect of God. Another, entirely new phenomenon in the Book Bahir is the presence of a female power within the world of the deity. This feminine aspect, called Shekhinah, is associated with the last of the sefiroth, Malkhuth. The term Shekhinah is found already in traditional rabbinic literature. The word derives from *shakhan*, "indwell"; the Shekhinah is seen in this literature as one of the names of God, which refers to God's presence ("indwelling") here on earth and his nearness to humans. Often the Shekhinah is imagined as watching over the people of Israel; when Israel goes into exile, the Shekhinah goes with them, and when Israel misbehaves, the Shekhinah withdraws. In rabbinic literature the Shekhinah is generally described in feminine terms.

Whereas before the appearance of Kabbalah there was never any talk of the Shekhinah as something that could be distinguished from God himself, in Kabbalah, this traditional notion of the Shekhinah is transformed into a separate, independent female power within the celestial world of the sefiroth. This power is referred to in Kabbalah with a large number of female symbols, especially as the bride or the wife of the deity. After the hidden God had revealed himself in the first nine sefiroth, these sefiroth finally emanated into the last sefirah, Malkhuth. This brought about something at the end of the emanation process that stood as female over against the deity, seen as male, at the beginning of the process.

In the Bahir and the writings of the early kabbalists the Shekhinah stands on the boundary between the divine and the non-divine world. The Shekhinah—often also symbolized as the heavenly mother or the caring and protecting aspect of the deity—remains among her people, the Community of Israel (*Kneseth Yisra'el*), without relinquishing its stay in the world of the sefiroth. God can get into contact with the world through his bride, the Shekhinah, since the latter lives in both worlds. Later Kabbalah was to see in the Shekhinah also the means of access for the mystics to enter into contact with the divine world of the sefiroth. God and his divine world could only be approached via his Shekhinah. Knowledge of the Shekhinah was the precondition for insight into the dynamic processes between the sefiroth.

In the Bahir, then, the idea first emerges of a male and female dualism within the divine realm. While the Bahir refers to the processes between male and female powers in the divine world in an indirect and cautious way, in less than a hundred years' time the Zohar was to describe these mutual processes in unveiled and robust sexual symbolic imagery.

Reincarnation. In traditional literature, Talmud and Midrash, we find nothing in relation to the transmigration of the soul. Jewish Aristotelian philosophy totally rejected the possibility that the human soul could take a physical body several times. It is striking, therefore, that in the Bahir we first encounter the issue of reincarnation in a positive sense. Moreover, reincarnation is presented here as if it is the most ordinary thing in the world, as if it is a matter of a familiar, traditionally accepted truth which needs no justification of any kind.

The Book Bahir presents the transmigration of souls in the form of parables, in which souls return to earth over and over again. They "wander" around in this world and yearn to return to their origin, the fatherly home in heaven. All souls are repeatedly given the possibility of correcting their faults and becoming righteous, which is a precondition for their return to God. These ideas are connected with such Bible verses as Eccl 1.4, 12.7, Ps 105.8 and Isa 43.5. The parables and symbols which the Bahir uses for all this are often obscure to us. The book does not use a fixed term for the concept of reincarnation; it was not until several generations later that finally the term *gilgul* became current.

The gnostic character that speaks from the parables in relation to reincarnation has raised the question of whether its source should be sought in the similarly gnostic teaching of the contemporary Catharists. There is, however, no conclusive evidence for the theory that Kabbalah took over the idea of reincarnation from the Catharists; in the following we shall see that its origins must be much older than the Catharist movement. In the Lurianic Kabbalah of the sixteenth century, in particular, the issue of reincarnation had considerable influence and almost attained canonical status.

In the Book Bahir we meet completely "new" ideas and motifs not found in earlier Jewish literature. Although Hekhaloth literature contains numerous gnostic motifs, these cannot account for the world of thought that is evident in the Book Bahir. In the traditional rabbinic literature of Talmud and Midrash, too, we look in vain for clear parallels to many passages in the Bahir. This fact presents us with a difficult but important question: What are the sources of the Book Bahir? From where does it derive its inspiration? We have already seen that with the Book Bahir we are at the beginning of the current that we refer to by the term Kabbalah. In research into the history of the emergence of Kabbalah, then, the question of the origin of the ideas of this writing is also an important issue.

Discussion of the origin of the Book Bahir—and thus of Kabbalah—generally centers around two different opinions. The first is that of Gershom Scholem, which is still widely accepted. This view posits that some ideas and new elements in the Bahir and in nascent Kabbalah go back to non-Jewish, ancient gnostic motifs and traditions. These traditions, which we do not find in Merkavah mysticism and rabbinic literature, would thus have been transmitted in certain Jewish esoteric-mystical circles and have ultimately found their way into the Book Bahir. This process of transmission, however, is hidden from us; from the centuries before the appearance of the Bahir we unfortunately have no writing or any kind of indication of orally transmitted traditions concerning these ideas. We do not know for sure where these traditions on the *pleroma* and the aeons, which probably came from Palestine and Babylonia, first made their appearance and where they were further elaborated with reference to the new sefirotic doctrine. In one way or another this material must have entered Provence from old sources around the middle of the twelfth century. It is suspected that an "original", older version of the Bahir arrived in Provence and that it was subsequently reworked until it ultimately reached the form we have today. Probably the Book Bahir was disseminated among scholars and kabbalists soon after the emergence of the "definitive" version, and further developed by them in a creative way. Underlying the emergence of Kabbalah, then, according to this first view, are gnostic, non-Jewish ideas which were elaborated in a particular, Jewish way before finally finding their way into the Bahir.

The second opinion is defended by the scholar Moshe Idel and others who do not agree with what they label the "gnostification" of Jewish mysticism. According to them recent research into gnosticism in antiquity is bringing more and more clearly to light that the nascent gnostic literature of that time is influenced precisely by Judaism, and not the other way round (for discussion of this see Chapter 2, § 6.2). There would never have been any question of the adoption of gnostic motifs by ancient Jewish mysticism, which were then reshaped in a specifically Jewish form. On the contrary, it was esoteric Jewish motifs that found their way into early gnosticism. These esoteric traditions simply remained, however, within Judaism and resurfaced in Kabbalah by way of a long chain of links. According to these scholars there can therefore be no question at all of a demythologizing tendency in classical Judaism (as described in § 1.3). Mythic elements have always been an integral part of Judaism. The myths that were reinterpreted during the emergence of Kabbalah were thus originally Jewish myths. We have already pointed to the fact that we have no evidence of the links through which this material would have been transmitted; in this connection Idel speaks of a "quiet growth of ancient Jewish esotericism". The conclusion of the second opinion with regard to the emergence of Kabbalah is thus that it was not gnostic, non-Jewish roots that underlie the Bahir, but originally Jewish traditions which were operative in closed circles within Judaism from the earliest days.

Scholars like Moshe Idel see the emergence of Kabbalah as a reinterpretation of essentially Jewish esoteric motifs; it was not a matter of a sudden and almost inexplicable explosion of gnostic myths and esoteric traditions in the center of Judaism, but of a new impulse of something that was already present in Judaism in an older form. This would also explain why Kabbalah was accepted pretty well without protest or dismay by so many authoritative, conservative-minded orthodox rabbis, many of whom where themselves kabbalists. This opinion also chimes better with the image that the kabbalists had of themselves, namely of bearers of an old tradition which contained an esoteric interpretation of Judaism.

It is true of both views, by the way, that in the form in which it emerged in Provence and Catalonia, Kabbalah is a new phenomenon. Although it clearly reinterprets older traditions, it cannot be said that in its thirteenth-century form Kabbalah derives as a whole from an older period.

Not only for the first kabbalists in Provence, but also for the kabbalists of the Iberian Peninsula in the thirteenth century, the Book Bahir was an authoritative book. It was viewed as an old and authentic source, of the same value as haggadic midrashim and the writings of Merkavah mysticism. After the publication of the Zohar in 1286 the Bahir was replaced by the extensive Zoharic literature, since the system developed there was preferred over the obscure and fragmentary character of the Book Bahir.

2.3 The first kabbalists in Provence

The Book Bahir is the first work to show us anything of the characteristic doctrine of the sefiroth. The work is, however, anonymous; the people behind this writing remain unknown to us. Recognizable historical persons who were occupied with this new mystical doctrine are not found in leading circles of rabbis in Provence until the twelfth and the early thirteenth century. From the period before 1200, however, no authentic documents have come down to us; what we know of the first historical phase of the kabbalists derives from reports by the third generation of kabbalists from the Iberian Peninsula. Since these kabbalists also had at their disposal all sorts of fragments ascribed to the mystics in Provence, which they quoted in their own writings, we are able today to form some kind of picture of the ideas and backgrounds of these first mystics.

According to reports by later kabbalists the first kabbalists formed strictly closed circles of mystics who were supposed to have received revelations from the prophet Elijah, who in rabbinic Judaism was held to be the guardian of sacred traditions. Elijah gives new information in dreams or visions to supplement the traditions of the rabbis. The revelations concerned were direct, visionary revelations of heavenly mysteries, which the mystics received in the course of their contemplation of the world of the sefiroth. These contributed to the emergence of completely new kabbalistic ideas. Opponents of Kabbalah saw in this new teaching the rising of strange and heretical influences. For the kabbalists themselves the matter was quite clear: the fact that the revelations, however new, had come from the prophet Elijah as a recognized source of supernal knowledge was a guarantee for their reliability.

The new kabbalists were totally convinced that what had been revealed to them in the way of mysteries was part of Jewish tradition. Precisely for this reason they referred to their teaching by the term *qabbalah*, derived from the verb *qibbel*, "receive"; *qabbalah* is what is received and transmitted—tradition. The mystics consequently called themselves *mequbbalim*, i.e. "those who have had a tradition handed to them". It is certainly clear that from that moment on they used the term *qabbalah*, which originally meant "tradition" in a general sense, with the more specific meaning of "mystical or esoteric tradition". They saw themselves as heirs of a secret teaching which, despite its visionary character, had also been orally transmitted for generations.

The later kabbalists viewed the mystics of Provence as the masters of Kabbalah. One of the best-known Provençal mystics, Isaac the Blind, was the teacher of most of the kabbalists of the somewhat later school of Gerona in Catalonia (see § 2.4). Since the school of Gerona followed closely after Provençal mystics and the latter moreover were their teachers, we see that two important topics broached in Provence came into their own in Gerona.

The first of these topics which played a role in both currents was the meeting of nascent Kabbalah with neo-Platonism. Through this encounter the mystics were challenged to bring Plotinus's image of the impersonal God into agreement with the image of the personal God in the Bible (see above § 1.7). This process, which was to lead on to an image of God that consists of an unknowable, hidden component alongside a personal, knowable aspect, can be clearly followed in the kabbalistic writings in the development of the Hebrew terminology. New terms are deliberately sought for the highest hidden principle in God which emphasize the impersonal and general character, such as "the Root of Roots", "the Hidden", "the undivided Unity" and "the self-hiding Light". Slowly we see another term arising, however, for the impersonal aspect of God: *En Sof.* In the period before Kabbalah the term *en sof* occurs only in an adverbial sense in combination with a preposition, such as *ad le-en sof*, "infinitely, to the infinite". In Provence too the term is still used in this way, although it is already clear that it means more: an area that stands out because of its infiniteness. It is only with the kabbalists of Gerona, however, that we see the term appear unambiguously as a noun: *En Sof*, "the Infinite", or "Infinity".

The second problem that had to be solved in the early Kabbalah of Provence and Gerona was the relationship between Thought and Will within God. Greek philosophy in both its Aristotelian and its neo-Platonic garb explained the world primarily from the point of view of thought, logic and the existence of natural laws. For Judaism, on the other hand, reason did not lie at the basis of creation, but the Will of God; things happen because God desires that they should so happen (see also § 1.7). As a result of the meeting between Jewish mysticism and Greek philosophy the kabbalists came face to face with the question of what principle actually underlay creation: was creation the result of the Thought of God or did creation emerge primarily from an act of the divine Will? Or in other words: is the personal God who emerges from En Sof and reveals himself in the world of the sefiroth, a thinking or a willing God? Although this question is of direct significance for the division of the sefiroth, the kabbalists initially had no clear answer to it. The kabbalists in Provence initially still had a preference for describing the character of the first sefirah as the Thought of God. They therefore called this sefirah the *Mahshavah*, "the Thought", in which the whole plan for the world was contained. But little by little we do see a growing inclination to associate the first sefirah with the divine Will as the cause of all things. In Gerona there is then finally talk of Kether as the first sefirah, who forms the divine Will to self-revelation and to the creation of the world. In the Gerona system the Thought of God only gains a place in the second sefirah, Hokhmah (see above, § 1.2).

The precise relationship between the early kabbalists of Provence and Catalonia and the Book Bahir is not completely transparent. Certain points of agreement between the Bahir and the early kabbalists seem clear, but on the other hand we also encounter noticeable differences. One of these differences is that later sources derive the traditions in Provence from revelations given by Elijah, while this is never claimed for the content of the Bahir. It is, furthermore, evident that in the elaboration of particular ideas early Kabbalah uses quite different sources and symbolism than the Bahir.

A clear example of this relates to the idea of reincarnation. The kabbalists of Provence and Gerona derived the transmigration of souls from other biblical texts—Exod 34.7, Deut 3.26, 2 Sam 14.14, and the book of Job—than the Bahir did. They also made use of the biblical conception of levirate marriage (Deut 25.5-10). This provides for the fact that if a married man dies without leaving a male heir, one of his surviving brothers has the duty of marrying the widow of the deceased so as to guarantee descendants for the deceased after all. According to the kabbalists this conception was a symbolic reference to the transmigration of souls; the son who issued from the levirate marriage was supposed to be a reincarnation of the deceased. For the first time in Kabbalah we also come up against the idea that a soul, which has its roots in the world of the sefiroth, can only be reincarnated among kindred souls. In Lurianic Kabbalah the subject of the kinship of souls was to become a central component of the doctrine of transmigration. Unlike in the Bahir, where reincarnation is presented completely openly and unapologetically, in Provence and Gerona the subject was viewed as a profound mystery that should not be openly talked about.

So in early Kabbalah we only find vague allusions to this topic and nowhere do we find clear, systematic explanations.

The fact that the early kabbalists used motifs and forms of symbolism which are not met in the Bahir gave rise to the question of their derivation. Outside the traditions that have made their way into the Bahir there must therefore have been others which contributed to the rise of early Kabbalah. Although we know that the kabbalists were aware of the existence and of the religious views of the contemporary Catharists, and although both movements display a number of common elements, we cannot demonstrate that the kabbalistic ideas that were developed were influenced by the gnostic doctrine of the Catharists. As was pointed out in the previous section, the sources must lie in antiquity (on this see also §§ 2.5.1 and 2.5.2).

The kabbalistic sources mentioned above tell of revelations to a number of leading persons in Provence. Around these persons an important kabbalistic group assembled, about whom we unfortunately know very little. Nor can we tell to what extent they already had recourse to a developed system of kabbalistic symbolism. It seems clear that many different traditions came together and established themselves in this circle. The first person known to us from this circle by name is Abraham ben Isaac of Narbonne (1116-1179), president of the rabbinic court. In order to prevent the spread of mystical ideas among the uninitiated he did not write any kabbalistic work; according to later witnesses the only thing that Abraham ben Isaac set down in writing about kabbalistic matters was a list of key terms, which could only be understood by the initiated.

The second person to whom revelations from Elijah were ascribed is Abraham ben David of Posquières (Rabad; 1125-1198), the son-in-law of Abraham ben Isaac. Just like the latter, Rabad too did not write a single kabbalistic work. Rabad is known for his many commentaries on Talmudic tractates as well as for his critique of Maimonides' halakhic work, *Mishneh Torah*. In his work he merely alluded indirectly to kabbalistic topics when he considered this necessary. The passages in his work which have a mystical angle to them are deliberately vague and kept indirect. Sometimes Rabad also tries to veil the mystical content of his exposition in deceptively ordinary language, so that in his case too only an initiate would be able to grasp his real intentions. He does appear, remarkably enough, to base himself on direct revelations—also in relation to halakhic matters.

The third person we know is Jacob ben Saul of Lunel, nicknamed Jacob the Nazirite, a colleague of Rabad, who belonged to an ascetically minded group of scholars who devoted themselves entirely to the study of the Torah. According to later witnesses Jacob received traditions in Jerusalem concerning mysticism and angelology (the doctrine of angels). Jacob the Nazirite made an important contribution to the development of new mystical views of the liturgical prayers. We shall look into the mysticism of prayer in more detail later in this book (§ 2.4).

The fourth person, finally, is Isaac the Blind, mentioned earlier (ca. 1165-1235), the son of Rabad. He is the first kabbalist whose historical personality and ideas emerge with any clarity. Isaac was the first to devote the whole of his work to mysticism. Besides his best-known book, a commentary on *Sefer Yetsirah* (Book of Creation), we also have a large number of extant fragments that are ascribed to him as well as a few letters. Isaac the Blind enjoyed considerable respect among the other mystics and exercised great influence on them. If we are to believe what his students say of him, Isaac possessed the ability to read the human aura and so to determine whether people had new or old souls.

Building on oral traditions he had received from his father and grandfather, Isaac developed a contemplative mysticism which proceeded largely from meditation on the sefiroth. His commentary on the Book of Creation is the first kabbalistic work that contains a systematic treatment of the sefiroth and the symbolism that goes with it, which is elaborated much further than in the Bahir. While in the Book Bahir it was still the Mahshavah that stood at the beginning of the creation process, Isaac the Blind alludes to "something" that seems to lie above that, the "cause" of the Mahshavah, although he did not yet use the term En Sof for this. For Isaac, the first sefirah is still the Mahshavah, unlike later in Gerona, where Kether stands at the top as the divine Will.

Of the many aspects of Isaac's mystical system—his view of good and evil, of the commandments or of prayer etc.—we shall deal with one topic in more detail: kabbalistic language mysticism. Isaac's commentary on the Book of Creation is the first kabbalistic work to contain, alongside the systematic treatment of the sefiroth, a complete mystical theory of language.

Isaac the Blind's view of language. We have already seen a number of times how the mystics symbolically express the process of the self-unfolding deity by means of the sefiroth. With Isaac the Blind we see that the process in which God reveals himself can also be described in a quite different way, namely by making use of symbols borrowed from the world of language. Sefiroth and language are in fact two different ways of expressing the same process in a symbolic manner; it is just a matter of a choice between equal symbols. A kabbalist can therefore choose whether he makes contact with the celestial world by means of contemplation of the sefiroth or by thinking through the nature of language.

In his view of language Isaac the Blind built upon rabbinic traditions of the divine origin of Hebrew, on old midrashim on language as well as on traditions on language from Merkavah mysticism. He connected all this, however, with direct mystical experiences, which resulted in a completely new mystical view of language. The rabbinic view of language, according to which God created the world by pronouncing words, was adopted by Isaac the Blind and reinterpreted. He was also familiar with traditions that assumed that the world had come into being when God pronounced his Name. Isaac the Blind posited that the whole world emerged from the one Divine Name, which subsequently developed in stages into the language which we know as humans. Where the Bahir still uses the image of the sefiroth which form the divine tree, Isaac extends this symbolic image into a tree whose roots represent the one Name. Just as trunk, branches and twigs develop from the root, so do the letters and words develop from the one Name. Thus by means of a gradual differentiation process all language develops from the one Name of God.

Central to Isaac the Blind's description of the emanation process is the word *davar* (plural *devarim*), which can mean both "word" and "thing". When Isaac speaks of *davar* he means simultaneously "word" and "thing"; the coincidence of these two meanings is of great significance for Isaac's thought. The "spiritual things" (*devarim*) which represent the world of the sefiroth are at the same time the "spiritual words" (*devarim*) in which the deity manifests himself. In practice, both symbolic systems, that of the sefiroth and that of language, are frequently used together. Instead of the claim that language has its origins in the one Name which in turn forms the blueprint for language, we also find statements that language has its origins in the sefirah Hokhmah.

From the highest principle, the developed principle of En Sof, the idea of language flows into the first sefirah, Mahshavah: it is only in the second sefirah, Hokhmah, that the beginnings of language and speech really lie. As we have seen, Hokhmah is the spiritual blueprint

for our world, since this sefirah contains the divine ideas, the archetypes of everything that will appear. Our whole visible reality after all
lies contained as a model in Hokhmah. So in this second sefirah,
which can be viewed as the one Name from which everything pro-
ceeds, the origin of language also lies. Just like the chain of the
sefiroth, the things (*devarim*) that flow out of Hokhmah, at the same
time, by an analogous process, the letters and words (*devarim*) come
into being.

The connection between the sefiroth and language is also apparent
in Isaac's view of the twenty-two letters of the Hebrew alphabet. Each
separate letter agrees with a certain configuration—or combination—
of the ten sefiroth and forms a world of its own. There are thus
twenty-two configurations of the ten sefiroth. The still spiritual letters
can in turn combine into a configuration as words. Our concrete
language, the totality of words that we use, is the result of a gradual
coarsening of these spiritual language elements, a reflection on a lower
level, a condensation or crystallization. This process of coarsening of
language runs parallel to that of the condensation of the rest of
creation; *davar* was after all both "word" *and* "thing".

The written letter, according to Isaac the Blind, is made up of sacred lines, which form the reflection of a power from another world.
The form of each letter contains secret references to all stages of the
divine world which it passed through in this crystallization process. In
the area where language is still the pure thought of God, there is as yet
no question of sound, but the letters form unpronounced principles. It
is only at a later stage of emanation that sounds become audible. The
written letters are thus symbols referring to the hidden worlds where
they come from. By occupying oneself with the symbolism expressed
in the letters, one can get through to the spiritual area, the divine
realm. In this process the letters become, as it were, transparent, and
one perceives another reality which forms the roots of our visible reality. According to Isaac, the originally spiritual language finds its
reflection in the Torah. (We have already discussed in some detail the
symbolic approach to the Hebrew letters and their function in the
Torah, see above § 1.4.)

With Isaac the Blind's commentary on the *Sefer Yetsirah* (Book of
Creation) the real history of kabbalistic literature by identifiable medieval authors begins.

2.4 The kabbalistic school in Gerona

Between the Jewish communities of Provence and Catalonia there were close ties. We have already seen that the kabbalists of Gerona were direct or indirect students of the kabbalists of Provence, in particular of Isaac the Blind. Already during the latter's lifetime the center of gravity of Kabbalah shifted from Provence to Gerona, which developed between 1210 and 1260 into an extremely dynamic kabbalistic center, which had considerable authority. From the material handed down to us we know about twelve kabbalists by name. These mystics were strong and notable personalities, all of whom were closely involved in the controversy concerning the writings of Maimonides, which, particularly between 1232 and 1235, gave rise to great commotion in the Jewish world of the day. They had a great influence on the later development of Kabbalah on the Iberian Peninsula. An important part of the terminology and basic ideas from Gerona, can, despite all the changes in kabbalistic thinking, still be found in Kabbalah in succeeding centuries. In Gerona we see that the ten sefiroth and the symbols which the separate sefiroth represent became a more or less fully-fledged fixed system, although the canonical form we described in section 1.2 was not yet achieved. Besides agreements that characterize the group as a whole, the writings of the Gerona circle also display differences, however; each kabbalist came up with a completely individual and creative approach to Kabbalah.

With the emergence of Gerona as a kabbalistic center, Kabbalah changed fundamentally in character. The mystics to the north of the Pyrenees had done all they could to keep their kabbalistic doctrine secret and to hide it from non-initiates. While they did their daily work as eminent rabbis within the Jewish community, nothing of the content of the secret kabbalistic circles around them ever came out. The Provençal kabbalists were thus extremely reluctant to set down their mystical experiences in writing. The kabbalists of Gerona, on the other hand, in part broke with the closed character of Kabbalah in Provence. Many wanted to develop the material from Provence more openly, to write it down and disseminate it. There is an extant letter of Isaac the Blind in which he expresses his displeasure with the kabbalists in Gerona who in his view were bringing the secret doctrine into the open, so that it was becoming the subject of conversation "in the street and at the market". According to him familiarity with such secrets among the general public could only lead to incomprehension and misunderstanding. The protests of Isaac the Blind could not prevent great literary activity. The writings of the Gerona group are

reasonably well preserved; on the basis of this material, which is unfortunately often difficult to understand, we have been able to form a
picture of their ideas and mystical activities. Nonetheless there were in
Gerona also kabbalists who, in the Provençal tradition, wanted to limit
Kabbalah to a closed circle.

The best-known kabbalists of the Gerona group were Azriel of
Gerona, Ezra ben Solomon, Jacob ben Shesheth, Nahmanides, Asher
ben David, Abraham ben Isaac Hazzan, Judah ben Yaqar, Meshullam
ben Solomon da Piera and a certain Ben Belimah. In what follows we
shall take a brief look at the first four of the mystics mentioned and
their work.

Azriel of Gerona is seen along with his colleague Ezra ben Solomon as
the founder of the Gerona circle. They broke with the strictly secret
character of Kabbalah and made a start with the opening up and dissemination of kabbalistic teaching. Azriel developed the ideas of Isaac
the Blind further by reformulating them and adding new facets to
kabbalistic doctrine, especially with regard to the sefiroth and prayer.

The works that have come down to us under the name of Azriel are
all kabbalistic in character. They contain lucid and largely systematic
discussions concerning kabbalistic doctrine. In Azriel's work we encounter the term *En Sof* for the first time as a wholly separate divine
area that lies beyond all human imagination. We see in Azriel's work
that Kether represents the first sefirah as the divine Will, differently
from Isaac the Blind, for whom the Mahshavah, the divine Thought,
was still viewed as the first sefirah. Azriel wrote various works: one
intended for beginners and non-initiates concerning the ten sefiroth
(*Sha'ar ha-Sho'el*) which is presented in question and answer form,
various commentaries on the Book of Creation, a commentary on the
haggadic parts of the Talmud (*Perush ha-Aggadoth*) and several works
on the prayers. Azriel was furthermore the first kabbalist to devote a
complete work to the mysticism of prayer.

We have not yet said anything about the role of prayer in Jewish
mysticism, so we shall go into this topic at this point. The first kabbalists were of course familiar with the traditional prayers and the
halakhic regulations concerning liturgy. Jews directed their prayers to
the God of the Bible, a God who was personally concerned for people
and for their struggles in this world, a God who listened to their prayers. When under the influence of Aristotelian philosophy the idea
came to the fore that the essence of God was indivisible, beyond all
human imagination, and that no properties could be ascribed to it, in

short that the essence of God was transcendent and immutable (see
§ 1.6.2 of this chapter), this had far-reaching consequences for the way
in which prayer was understood. After all, if the essence of the deity is
eternal and unchanging, this deity cannot possibly listen to prayers or
allow himself to be influenced by them. The unchanging God cannot
receive new information; for if the information was really new to
God, this would mean that God did not know about it beforehand.
The conclusion would be that human prayer cannot be directed to the
unchanging God.

We have seen too that the kabbalists subscribed to the idea of God's
immutability and that the kabbalists called this unknowable and "highest" part of the deity *En Sof*. For the kabbalists, the sefiroth through
which the unknowable God revealed himself coincided with the notion of the personal God of the Bible. If a mystic wanted to approach
God in prayer he directed his prayer to the sefiroth and not to En Sof.

In the Book Bahir we already find some passages from which it appears that prayer is brought into connection with the sefiroth, without
further details becoming clear. The first kabbalists in Provence, in particular Jacob the Nazirite, laid the basis for a technique in which
specific words and sentences in the traditional prayers were directed to
specific sefiroth by means of a special concentration or intention of the
praying mystic. This technique of intention is called *kawwanah* (pl.
kawwanoth; "directing"). The mastery of these mystical *kawwanoth* demanded not only a great exoteric and esoteric knowledge, but also
considerable spiritual training. Jacob the Nazirite already gave complete instructions on the way in which prayer could be connected with
the sefirotic world. These indications describe how the separate words
or blessings, spoken aloud in traditional prayers, are related to particular sefiroth. During prayer, the mystic had in his mind to direct his
various words or blessings to the specific sefiroth as appropriate.

As we have said, Azriel of Gerona was the first to devote a complete
work to the mysticism of prayer. For almost every separate word of
the main prayers he indicated which sefirah it related to. In Azriel we
see how prayer actually forms a symbolic reiteration of the dynamic
processes in the divine world. This becomes clear on the basis of a
comparison that he draws in his commentary on liturgy (*Perush ha-
Tefilloth*). The original eighteen blessings in the Prayer of Eighteen
Benedictions correspond with the eighteen human vertebrae (following the anatomy of the Babylonian Talmud, tractate *Berakhoth* 28b). As
in the human body the spinal fluid spreads out from the brain as its
origin, so too all the blessings in the Eighteen are comprised in the first

blessing, which therefore demands a very special *kawwanah*. We see that according to Azriel both the human body and the Eighteen are a symbolic representation of the sefirotic world; the sefiroth too are all comprised within En Sof, where they originate.

By means of *kawwanoth* the human being contributes to the unification of the sefiroth. Absorbed in meditation on the prayer, the praying mystic internally observes the celestial world in which he ascends through the sefiroth phase by phase. During this process, in which he comes into direct contact with God and the celestial world, the mystic learns hidden secrets. The extent to which in the mystical *kawwanoth* as described by Azriel we have to do with magical elements, is a question that is not easy to answer. It is impossible to determine precisely where the mystical intention, the total heart-and-soul orientation to the celestial world in order to come into personal and intimate contact with the deity and his world, merges into the hope that the sefiroth can be more or less coerced by the praying person into letting something of their divine powers descend on them. (Further on in this chapter, in section 2.5.3 on the Ashkenazi Hasidim, we shall go into other aspects of mystical prayer.)

Ezra ben Solomon is the second important kabbalist of the Gerona school. This colleague of Azriel's, as we said above, was one of the founders of the Gerona group and also one of the kabbalists who broke with the originally secret character of kabbalistic doctrine. Kabbalists from Burgos, where another kabbalistic circle formed, were instructed by Ezra ben Solomon. Among other things he wrote a mystical commentary on the Song of Songs, in which he also paid attention to the mystical background of the ten commandments. This work contains symbolic systems which are difficult for us to penetrate. An example of this is his interpretation of *We will make you ornaments of gold, studded with silver* (Songs 1.11). Ezra points out that "silver" refers to the Written Torah, in line with the sixth sefirah, Tif'ereth, and "gold" to the Oral Torah, in line with the tenth sefirah, Malkhuth. Since one might have expected that the Written Torah would be equated with gold and the Oral with silver, Ezra explains that from the human perspective gold comes before silver, but from God's perspective silver comes before gold. Ezra finds support for this in the biblical verse Haggai 2.8, where God speaks the words *The silver is mine, and the gold is mine*, where silver is mentioned first.

Besides this important commentary on the Song of Songs, Ezra also wrote a commentary on the haggadic elements in the cosmologically oriented Talmudic tractate *Hagigah*. In addition he must have written a commentary on the Book of Creation; this work was still in existence at the end of the thirteenth century, but was unfortunately lost after that. A striking feature of Ezra's work is the self-assured way in which he opposes the kabbalistic teaching to the views of the Aristotelian philosophers.

The third important figure in Gerona, Jacob ben Sheshet, was an original and creative kabbalist who brought forward completely new mysteries and mystical explanations of the commandments as no one before him ever had. He scarcely referred back to the work of his teachers Isaac the Blind and Nahmanides, and did not develop their ideas further. While the latter two exercised the utmost caution in writing down kabbalistic secrets and discussing them deliberately in a vague and indirect way, Jacob did not place any such restrictions on himself in this regard. He was extremely contentious in his polemics against the followers of Maimonides. It is striking that he did not direct his criticism to Maimonides himself but to his followers, who in Jacob's view distorted the teaching of Maimonides and mixed it with heretical ideas. His anger was directed in particular against Samuel ibn Tibbon, who had translated Maimonides' work from Arabic into Hebrew; not only had Samuel failed to understand anything of Maimonides, but he had also deliberately set out to mislead people with his translation.

The last kabbalist to whom we shall turn our attention is Rabbi Moses ben Nahman (1194–1270), usually called simply Nahmanides or Ramban, an eminent rabbi in the Jewish community in Catalonia. Since he enjoyed great authority as exegete, halakhist, poet and physician, he contributed to the acceptance of Kabbalah in conservative rabbinic circles on the Iberian Peninsula. The fact that Nahmanides stood behind Kabbalah was for many of his contemporaries the guarantee that the novel and sometimes daring kabbalistic ideas did not constitute a divergence from rabbinic tradition.

When the Maimonidean controversy broke out in 1232, Nahmanides played an important role in it. He tried not to polemicize too much and sought a compromise between the disputing parties. Nahmanides was, however, very critical towards those who were charmed by Greek philosophy. So for instance he was fiercely opposed to the allegorization of the commandments.

Unlike Azriel and Ezra, Nahmanides was very much against any great dissemination of Kabbalah. He wanted to pass on his kabbalistic ideas only to his trusted disciples, who in turn avoided the dissemination of kabbalistic secrets, in particular by not setting them down in writing and by passing them on exclusively by oral means to their disciples. It was only in the late thirteenth and the early fourteenth century that this strictly hidden and secret character of Kabbalah came to an end, though a certain section of the mystics still adhered to this principle.

In consequence of this we have very little written material by Nahmanides dealing with Kabbalah, especially compared with his extensive "traditional" work. In addition, in this small amount of material Nahmanides discusses kabbalistic teaching only indirectly and deliberately in veiled terms; usually he simply alludes to what he really means, so that his kabbalistic views are only intelligible to someone who is already very much at home in the material. Kabbalistic allusions are found, among other places, in his commentary on the Book of Creation, in his sermons and liturgical poems and in his commentary on the book of Job, which alludes largely to the mystery of the transmigration of souls. In Nahmanides' best-known work too, his commentary on the Torah, we find allusions to kabbalistic ideas. In the introduction of this work he warns that the uninitiated must not try to reconstruct kabbalistic ideas from the written text, since this can only lead to misunderstandings.

We can state that Nahmanides largely succeeded in his attempt to keep his kabbalistic teachings secret; it is still very difficult for us to gain a picture of them. To date there is no comprehensive study dealing specifically with Nahmanides as a kabbalist.

2.5 Intermezzo

Much of the literature on the historical development of Jewish mysticism implicitly assumes, following Gershom Scholem, a linear development of early Kabbalah, supposing that one mystical movement leads directly into another. Thus the mysticism and symbolism of the Book Bahir were adopted by the first kabbalists of Provence, after which the material they developed was subsequently passed on to the kabbalists of the Gerona group. The mystical doctrine of the Gerona group was then continued in several mystical currents spread over various kingdoms on the Iberian Peninsula, all of which finally made their way into the Zohar. A number of critical footnotes have to be set alongside this view, however.

2.5.1 Jewish mysticism: a linear development?

It has become clear from recent research that early Kabbalah did not develop in a straight line. To begin with, it cannot be said that the first kabbalists from Provence are a direct continuation of the Book Bahir. They did of course borrow material from that book, but the greater part of their symbols seems not to derive from the Bahir. That would mean that these mystics also adopted material from other sources, which evidently existed alongside and independently of the Bahir. From this we can conclude that the Book Bahir is not the exclusive manifestation of Jewish mysticism in the twelfth century.

In the meantime many more historical facts have surfaced with regard to the existence and the content of other mystical movements at the time of the Book Bahir and the kabbalists of Provence and Gerona. It seems that these movements had, independently of each other, developed alternative mystical systems and teachings, in which there was no place for the doctrine of the sefiroth. In this earliest period of Jewish mysticism in Provence and Gerona, the mystical current that developed the system of the sefiroth was only one of several mystical systems by which the deity could be described. For this reason it is not correct to speak of a linear development of Jewish mysticism, in view of the fact that there was no question of one particular mystical current leading into the next.

The situation is that in the late twelfth and the early thirteenth century the doctrine of the sefiroth—after a process of fermentation, the details of which are still difficult for us to determine—gradually gained the upper hand over the other mystical systems which were in circulation. It was this sefirotic doctrine that ultimately formed the basis of what we now know as Kabbalah per se, as it emerges more and more clearly in the school of Isaac the Blind, the Gerona group and finally in the Zohar. In retrospect we can thus see a scarlet thread running from the Zohar via Gerona back to the Bahir. But in the late twelfth and the early thirteenth century there was nothing to indicate that the doctrine of the sefiroth in particular would form the mainstream of later Jewish mysticism.

Below we shall give attention to two mystical currents which are not based on the doctrine of the sefiroth. One of these currents is known by the name of the Iyyun circle and has its origins in Provence or in Castile. The other current is known as that of the German Hasidim, the origins of which have to be sought in the Rhineland. The two currents roughly coincide with the earliest period of the doctrine of the sefiroth.

2.5.2 The writings of the Iyyun circle

From the work of the kabbalists of the kingdom of Castile, including that of Rabbi Isaac ha-Cohen of Soria (see § 2.6.3) we know of the existence of a specific group of mystics who gave descriptions of the spiritual world which are not based on the sefirotic doctrine. Gershom Scholem was the first to do research into the history and basic ideas of these descriptions. He believed that in all 32 tractates by this group have survived. Because all these texts are anonymous or pseudepigraphic in nature, we know nothing of their authors. For want of a better name, Scholem called them "the writings of the Iyyun circle", after the main work of this circle, *Sefer ha-Iyyun* (Book of Contemplation). If we are to believe the above-mentioned Rabbi Isaac ha-Cohen, the mystics of this circle drew material from a source called the Book of Rab Hammai. However, we know of no historical person with this name. If the book did exist, then it was lost in the vicissitudes of time.

The members of the Iyyun circle too used the term *qabbalah* for the theosophy and the description of the celestial world that they developed. The basic ideas we meet in the most important writings of the Iyyun circle cover such topics as the primordial ether, light and color symbolism as well as language and number mysticism. When studying their texts one is struck by the fact that numerous concepts and symbolic images are not explained. The authors apparently assumed that these were familiar to their readers. So for us it is often not an easy task to understand what the texts mean precisely. The main lines of the theories of this circle of kabbalists, however, can generally be ascertained.

The main idea behind light mysticism is that the essence of the deity can be expressed by means of the symbol of light. The various manifestations of the deity or the ways in which it reveals itself, are then expressed by means of various colors. Just as the colors are present in the still unbroken light, so too these divine manifestations are still contained in the unity of the divine being. Here one might think of the parallel of sunlight, which can be split up by means of a prism into the colors of the spectrum.

In the teaching of the kabbalists of the Iyyun circle, the primordial ether (*awir qadmon*) occupied an important place. From this primordial ether, the original root of everything that will come into being, issues a sort of explosion of lights which consequently are separated into thirteen pairs of opposing lights which in turn split up into an unending play of colors. After the still unbroken light has unfolded completely into this thousandfold splendor of colors, all the revealed lights return to the primordial foundation from whence they emerged. The principle of the cyclical movement in all the processes by means of which the hidden life of the deity is described, is also frequently encountered in the writings of the Iyyun circle.

The way in which the primordial ether is described varies from text to text. Sometimes the primordial ether is imagined as "the source of incessant light" or "the original light", which is white in color and from which the lights spread out like a shower of sparks. Often the light of the primordial ether is called "darkness" or "the light that is too dark to shine". The mystics did not mean by this that all light was absent from it; this image of darkness serves as a symbolic reference to a reality which cannot contain or bear any creation and which is beyond all knowledge. By seeing light and colors as symbols, the mystics endeavored to discover the processes and laws of the deity and to bring them into connection with our visible reality. Just as the kabbalists worked with their own sefirotic symbolism, the mystics of the Iyyun circle discovered how the hidden nature of God revealed itself by means of the symbols of light and colors. They saw how the hidden life of the deity with its laws, harmonies, lights and colors was reflected in the colorful splendor of our visible creation.

In developing their color symbolism the mystics of the Iyyun circle often drew upon biblical and rabbinic motifs. Although the Bible itself does not know the idea that colors are symbols of the revealed deity, the mystics found inspiration in, among other things, the rainbow in the flood story (Gen 9), in the colors of the priestly garments (Exod 28) or in the colorful descriptions such as we find in the visions of the prophet Ezekiel (Ezek 1). The theory of the primordial ether as the source of the original light that is white in color, can for example be brought into connection with a midrash (*Pesiqta de-Rav Kahana* 21.5) in which we read that God clothed himself in a coat of white light when preparing to begin the work of creation.

In section 2.3 on Isaac the Blind's commentary on the Book of Creation we looked into the expression of the emanation process by means of language symbolism. The same idea is found in the writings of the Iyyun circle. From the primordial ether—viewed as the original root—the language movement takes its beginnings. From the original root the *aleph* emanates, the first letter of the Hebrew alphabet. From the *aleph* the Tetragrammaton emerges, the Divine Name which is formed by the letters *yod–heh–waw–heh*. The Tetragrammaton symbolizes a sort of primordial condition in which the powers which underlie all further processes exist alongside one another in a balanced unity. According to some fragments the four letters of the Tetragrammaton coincide with four separate aspects of the deity, two of which are male and two of which are female in character. From the Tetragrammaton the separate letters split off, which are then formed into names or words, after which a further differentiation follows in which separate letters or words are combined with each other in an infinity of permutations. As in light and color mysticism, here too all the language elements that have unfolded finally return to their place of origin.

There are also texts which do not proceed from the letter *aleph* but from the *yod*, the tenth letter of the alphabet, as the deepest principle from which the language movement is born. It is difficult to determine whether with the *aleph* and the *yod* it is a question of two separate notions of language movement or whether the symbolism of the *yod* forms a part of that of the letter *aleph*.

As in the emanation of lights, the differentiation of the language occurs from the original root in thirteen pairs of opposites. How the latter precisely operates is not clear from the texts. The principle of pairs of opposing names comes to expression also in the language mysticism of the divine names. In the Iyyun circle the foundation was laid for a system of divine names in which they were placed in pairs opposite one another so that they could then be merged into a single name. As an example one can mention the Tetragrammaton *yod–heh–waw–heh* and the divine name *Adonai*, which is written in Hebrew with the letters *aleph–daleth–nun–yod*. The two names each count four letters, and when they are merged together we get the eight-letter name, *yod–aleph–heh–daleth–waw–nun–heh–yod*. A formation of this kind is called a *yihud*, a "unification", or "union". The 72-letter divine name—which is also frequently found in the magical traditions—also plays an important role, placed opposite the 42-letter divine name. Later Kabbalah adjusted the *yihud* principle to the system of the sefiroth, which in the meantime had become canonical, and elaborated it further. There too the opposing names are interpreted as male or female elements which merge into a unity. Sometimes within a single name a difference is also made between male and female elements.

The texts of the Iyyun circle contain a wide variety of ideas. At many points, for instance, we find the influence of neo-Platonism (see § 1.7), while influence of the Catharist movement—in particular with reference to light symbolism—is very likely. Many ideas and motifs in various texts indicate a relationship with those of the Irish philosopher Johannes Scotus Eriugena (810-877) as well as philosophical writings by Pseudo-Dionysius the Areopagite from around the year 500. Besides this, in many texts there is evidence of a borrowing of elements from Merkavah mysticism. Components of the throne world from Merkavah literature are transformed by the mystics of the Iyyun circle in an entirely new way into independent powers of the deity. Within this circle *Sefer Yetsirah* (Book of Creation) too was a rich source of inspiration, especially the 32 paths of wisdom which appear in it.

The traditions surrounding the thirteen pairs which play such a fundamental role in the light and language mysticism of the Iyyun circle ultimately derive from the classical rabbinic interpretation of Exod 34.6, where thirteen properties or attributes (*middoth*) of God are mentioned. The traditions which in the Iyyun circle led to the transformation of these thirteen properties into separate stages within the deity are entirely separate from the doctrine of the sefiroth. As the sefirotic system gained influence, however, the kabbalists of the Iyyun circle made attempts to bring the system they had developed into agreement with that of the sefiroth. In the earliest texts of the circle there is no reference to be found to the sefiroth. In the texts of the period after that, the sefiroth are mentioned occasionally, while in the texts of the last period of the circle the sefiroth have clearly come to take a dominant place. Conversely, the kabbalists who brought the sefirotic system gradually to development adopted much of the light, color and language mysticism and adapted it to their own system. Thus the opening sentence of the Zohar contains a clear reference to light and color mysticism as developed within the Iyyun circle. The mutual adaptation had a more or less artificial character for both parties. The traditions from which the system of the ten sefiroth developed were completely different from those of the thirteen pairs in the Iyyun circle. The two systems are actually very difficult to reconcile with each other.

Gershom Scholem conducted his research into the Iyyun ciricle between 1928 and 1948. The work lay idle for some decades after that, until some scholars, especially Mark Verman, critically investigated several of Gershom Scholem's theories and supplemented them with new insights. Scholem had not formulated any criteria to determine which texts belonged to the Iyyun circle and which did not. Nor had he paid attention to the question of the correct chronological sequence of these texts—i.e. the order in which they were written over time— and their relationship to each other.

Mark Verman points out that in the writings of the Iyyun circle not only is *Sefer ha-Iyyun* (Book of Contemplation) of central importance, but also the tractate *Ma'ayan ha-Hokhmah* (Fountain of Wisdom), which was written in the same period. Texts which display no sort of relation with these two tractates do not, according to Verman, belong with the works of the Iyyun circle. On the basis of this criterion it is possible to identify about forty texts by anonymous authors which derive from this circle. Besides this Verman supplemented Scholem's work by paying attention to the relations between the texts and their chronological sequence.

Another point of interest is the precise dating of the Iyyun circle. According to Gershom Scholem the most important works appeared between 1200 and 1225, simultaneously with the writings of Isaac the Blind. Later, between 1225 and 1240, a number of shorter works by this circle were published. After the earliest work of the Iyyun circle had come into being in Provence, some of these writings would have made their way to the kingdom of Castile, where in Burgos and Toledo among other places they encountered kindred spirits. Mark Verman on the other hand is of the opinion that there are sufficient arguments to be adduced for the assumption that the most important works appeared much later, between 1230 and 1270, and moreover not in Provence but in Castile. It was only afterwards that they became known among the kabbalists of Provence. According to Verman, here we have to do with the largest group of kabbalists of the period, at least thirty different authors, who were literarily active from 1230 to the early fourteenth century. This contrasts with all the other groupings which numbered far fewer members and whose literary activity extended over a much shorter time-span.

The above is a clear example of how uncertain some things still are in the description of the historical development of early Kabbalah. Even as far as the main lines are concerned, it is perfectly possible to arrive at other and new insights. With regard to the place of the Book Bahir, for instance, Verman considers the possibility that this work came into being in Provence not in the middle of the twelfth century, as Scholem assumed, but only some 70 years later.

2.5.3 The Ashkenazi Hasidim

Another current that is difficult to fit into the linear historical development within Jewish mysticism sketched above is that of the Ashkenazi Hasidim, also known as the German Pietists. This esoteric-mystical movement, which cannot be classified as Kabbalah, flourished between 1170 and 1240 in the Rhineland, primarily in the cities of Mainz, Speyer and Worms. The movement formed around a number of members of the eminent family Kalonymus, in particular Rabbi Samuel ben Kalonymus the Pious, his son Rabbi Judah the Pious and Rabbi Eleazar ben Judah of Worms, disciple and cousin of Judah the Pious.

A striking feature of the writings of the German Hasidim is the fact that they indicate where they got their own traditions from—by contrast with early Kabbalah. If we are to believe their reports, their earliest source goes back to a certain mystic and magician, Rabbi Aaron ben Samuel of Baghdad. This Aaron, son of the head of the Jewish academy in Babylonia, had fallen from grace and was banished for having misused his knowledge of magic. He made his way to southern Italy, where he passed on his esoteric-mystical and magical knowledge to the sages of the Kalonymus family. When this family moved from southern Italy to Mainz in the Rhineland in the ninth century, they took the traditions and secrets they had received from Aaron of Baghdad with them. These related in particular to the Book of Creation, Merkavah mysticism and the true meaning of prayer.

In the various schools and currents within Hasidism commentaries were written on the writings of the Hekhaloth literature and the Book of Creation. Through the often extensive anthologies they made of this literature, a good deal of material from the period of ancient Jewish mysticism has come down to us (see Chapter 2, § 2). In addition, all these traditions handed down from Palestine and Babylonia were reformulated and transformed into something completely new.

By far the best-known work of this movement is *Sefer Hasidim* (Book of the Pious), written by Judah the Pious (died 1217). This work contains the description of a community of pious Jews and of an ethical doctrine, a system of moral behavior towards which the pious Jew was supposed to strive. The lives of the individual members of this community were marked by a total dedication to the service of God and an absolute obedience to his will. The leadership of this religious brotherhood was in the hands of sages (*hakhamim*) who were described as charismatic figures who had access to great knowledge of the will of God and the way in which one could obey it. These leaders passed on their knowledge to the pious, gave advice and meted out punishments to whose who in their view had strayed away in sin. Within the community a distinction was made between a pious elite, which was supposed to submit to a very strict code of moral behavior, and a group of ordinary pious people, for whom less strict requirements were made. This way of life, which also contained various mystical exercises, was viewed as preparation for mystical experience.

In order to display their unfailing devotion to God, the Hasidim were keen to do more than what the "ordinary" commandments committed them to. So they examined the Scriptures in order to discover hidden duties which had not been explicitly revealed in the Written and Oral Torah. They saw their lives in this world as a preparation for the coming world; God subjected the pious constantly to trials and temptations in order to test them. In the Book of the Pious we read that the pious were to withdraw completely from worldly affairs; they were to stay well away from innocent enjoyment, such as playing with children or superficial talk about daily matters. Everything had to be directed towards overcoming one's humanness; human nature was in conflict with what God demanded of a person. The pious brought themselves into situations where they were exposed to temptations in order to test themselves. They also created situations where they could demonstrate their ability to resist evil, hatred or insults. When a pious person failed in a particular regard, there was an elaborate system of repentance to restore oneself from a sin one had committed, which was viewed as an insult to the deity. People subjected themselves to various forms of self-chastisement, such as for instance fasting for long periods, being dipped in icy water during the winter, exposing their bodies to bees in the summer, or lying naked on an anthill.

Besides the Book of the Pious, other Hasidic writings have come down to us. While the Book of the Pious gives a description of a community of pious Jews, the writings of Eleazar of Worms (died ca. 1230) lay emphasis on the pious person as an individual. In view of the fact that beyond the Book of the Pious none other of the Hasidic works mentions the existence of such a community, there are various views of its historicity. Some see in the description of the community of the pious no more than an ideal model that was never realized. Others do not doubt that the community existed, while others again think that this community may have existed only for a very short time.

Prayer occupied a very important place among the German Pietists. Until the late twelfth century the traditional prayers in Judaism were discussed only with regard to halakhic matters. From that moment a whole new view of liturgy emerges, according to which the text of the prayers was treated with the same veneration as the text of the Torah. The two earliest works in which the prayers are commented upon as if they were Torah text are by Judah the Pious and Eleazar of Worms. Of Judah's book, however, we only know fragments in the form of quotations in the work of other authors.

As has already been stated a number of times, according to tradition the Torah is of divine origin and forms a blueprint for the whole of creation. The Ashkenazi Hasidim then saw the same divine structures reflected in the text of the prayers as those contained in the Torah. This did not mean that the prayers were also of divine origin; but the rabbis who fixed the text had done this out of a profound insight into the divine structure of the Torah, which they had also laid in the texts of the prayers. So the German Pietists studied the prayers in the same way as the Torah, since they wanted to bring the hidden divine structures and their harmony to light.

If the comparison between Torah and prayers is a view we have not previously encountered in the historical development of Jewish esotericism and mysticism, no less new was the way in which in their search for the divine structure the Ashkenazi Hasidim made use of numerical patterns—which in their view were embedded not only in the Torah but also in the prayers. In the prayers they discovered numerical connections as they paid attention to the number of letters in a sentence or a certain word and the number of times that a word, (final) letter or name occurred in a prayer. Thus we read in a quotation from Judah's lost commentary that the word *ashrei*, "happy the one who", occurred precisely nineteen times in a certain part of the morning prayer, the same number of times as the word *elohim*, "God", is mentioned in the first pericope of the book of Exodus. These and other words that occurred nineteen times were, according to Judah, related to each other in some profound mystical sense. At the same time they also used *gematria*, a technique based upon the numerical value of the Hebrew letters. This technique, which was applied to a limited degree as an exegetical method already in rabbinic literature, was elaborated by the German Hasidim into a very extensive system. For the first time in the history of Jewish mysticism numerical connections and gematria form part of the mystical tradition. (An overview of the Hebrew letters and their corresponding numerical value can be found at the end of this book in the chapter on language mysticism. At that point we shall also deal with the use of gematria.) It is not surprising that a view in which prayer is seen as a reflection of the divine world, in which numerical connections between letters, letter combinations and words had a decisive place, regarded any change or supplement to the text as completely inadmissible. Anyone who for any reason at all makes changes to the prayer text will not only disturb the divine structure of the prayer, but also its effective power.

Like the kabbalists, the Ashkenazi Hasidim asked themselves the question to which aspect of the deity their prayers should be directed. They were familiar with the efforts of Jewish philosophy to attain as pure and abstract an image of God as possible and its abhorrence for anthropomorphic descriptions of the deity, which in the view of the philosophers was totally at odds with the idea of the absolute unity and indivisibility of the God of Israel. In this view God could not possibly listen to prayers, since the nature of the deity is eternal, immutable and transcendent. And as we have seen, this philosophical view does not accord well with the traditional practice of prayer, in which Jews directed themselves to the (anthropomorphic) God of the Bible, a God who was personally concerned with individuals in their struggle in this world (see also §§ 1.6.3 and 2.4). One of the first Jewish philosophers, Rabbi Sa'adyah Gaon (882-942), solved this problem by presenting the theory of the Kavod ("glory" of God). On the basis of the use of the word *kavod* in the Bible and Talmud, among other things, Sa'adyah concluded that the Kavod was the highest of the angels, created by God with the aim of revealing himself by means of this power. When God wanted to reveal himself, he took form and shape through the Kavod. With this theory Sa'adyah was able not only to preserve the character of the eternal, immutable transcendent deity, but also the anthropomorphic description of the God of the Bible. The theory of the Kavod became the cornerstone of the various emerging mystical movements in the late twelfth and early thirteenth centuries, especially of the Iyyun circle, though everyone had their own variations on Sa'adyah Gaon's original theory. The Ashkenazi Hasidim, too, adopted the idea of the Kavod, albeit in a radically altered form. In the teaching of this current, the Kavod was a power emanating from God that was partly hidden and partly revealed. So they directed their prayers to the lower, revealed part of the Kavod.

Another difficult point with regard to this movement is the role of magic. On the one hand the pious person in the texts stands out as someone who disposes of magical powers with which he can manipulate everything and everyone. The Hasidim had various techniques for bringing about paranormal states of consciousness. In order to reach an ecstatic state of consciousness and to experience the divine world—often described as an erotic passion between God and the mystic—use was made, among other things, of letter magic, i.e. lengthy recitation of and meditation on letters and divine names, the uttering of letter combinations and the creative combining of letters. These techniques also played a part in prayer as a means of making contact with the celestial world. In the work of Eleazar of Worms we find for the first time instructions on how to create a *golem*, a person made of clay, with the aid of letter magic. On the other hand it is clear that not everyone was happy with these magical practices. Judah the Pious, himself convinced of the effectiveness of magic and the reality of witches and demons, turned against the practice of magic. According to him a devout person should above all be humble, not demanding anything at all for himself, and not a proud magician. It remains somewhat unclear where the precise boundary lay between what was permissible and what was not, or under what conditions magic could or could not be practiced.

The ethical teaching of the Book of the Pious with its emphasis on repentance and humility had a great influence on the development of the ethical ideas of later Judaism, through to the present day. The influence of the Ashkenazi Hasidim on emergent Kabbalah, however, is not so great; the developing system of the sefiroth, for example, seems not to have been influenced by the Ashkenazi pietists. The kabbalists did, however, take up some of their ideas in an adjusted form. They took inspiration, for instance, from the theories on the Kavod and prayer. In the second half of the thirteenth century the Hasidic theories on the numerical values, gematria and esoteric-mystical and magical techniques had great influence on the ecstatic or prophetic Kabbalah of Abraham Abulafia (see § 2.6.2) and on the Cohen brothers (see § 2.6.3). Eighteenth-century Hasidism (see Chapter 6), despite a number of points of contact, cannot be seen as a direct continuation of the Ashkenazi Hasidim of the twelfth and thirteenth centuries.

2.6 The spread of Kabbalah over the Iberian Peninsula

The development of the classical period of Kabbalah on the Iberian Peninsula extends over a period of almost three centuries: from the late twelfth century to 1492. From political, economical and religious points of view the thirteenth century was a relatively favorable period by comparison with the fate of Jews in other European countries. This situation certainly helps to account for the fact that Kabbalah was able to develop and flourish. In 1137 a new dynasty was created by a marriage between the House of Catalonia and the heir to the throne of Aragon. The two states were then linked in a personal union with common sovereigns. This dynasty brought the whole of Catalonia, Aragon and large areas to the north of the Pyrenees under its authority and developed into one of the great powers of the southern European world. Both under the Catalan-Aragonese dynasty and under the kings of Castile, the leading power on the Iberian Peninsula, Jews had eminent positions at the court or occupied important government offices. Although each kingdom had its own legislation with respect to the Jews, under Alfonso X in particular, king of Castile and Leon (1252-1284), the social climate was relatively tolerant and favorably disposed towards the Jews. Alfonso X, nicknamed "the Wise" (*el Sabio*), was king of a country in which people of three religions lived together: Islam, Christianity and Judaism. This king was also the driving force behind the famous Toledo school of translators, where Jewish, Islamic and Christian scholars devoted themselves to the translation of Arabic literature, philosophy and science into Castilian and Latin.

When in the fourteenth century the situation of the Jews deteriorated in all the realms of the Iberian Peninsula, the hey-day of Kabbalah was also over. An increasing oppression of the Jewish section of the population by the Christians took place, which came to a climax in the fifteenth century. By the marriage in 1469 of Isabel of Castile and Fernando II of Aragon, of which Catalonia was a part, a process of national unification of the realms on the Iberian Peninsula got underway. From 1489 we can speak of the nation of Spain. Under the government of this royal couple, known as the Catholic Kings (*los Reyes Católicos*), in 1476 the Inquisition was introduced. The oppression and persecution of the Jews came to a climax during the rule of Fernando and Isabel, and in 1492—the year in which Granada, the last Moorish stronghold, was conquered and Columbus "discovered" America—all the Jews were expelled from Spain. With the expulsion of the Jews Kabbalah also disappeared from the Iberian Peninsula.

At the beginning of the thirteenth century Kabbalah spread from the kabbalistic center in Gerona over the Iberian Peninsula. It is not possible within the compass of this book to deal with all the movements associated with Kabbalah and all the individual kabbalists. We shall restrict ourselves to the most important: *Sefer ha-Temunah* (Book of the Figure), ecstatic Kabbalah, the kabbalists of the Castilian school and the Zohar. We shall then offer a brief summary of developments from the appearance of the Zohar to the expulsion of the Jews in 1492.

2.6.1 The Book of the Figure

A special place in the history of Kabbalah is reserved for a remarkable book entitled *Sefer ha-Temunah* (Book of the Figure). The ideas presented in this work play an important part not only in the kabbalistic literature of the thirteenth century but for centuries after that they were interpreted and adjusted in a range of variations. The Book of the Figure gives an elaborate kabbalistic view of the idea that the history of the world develops in a sequence of cosmic cycles (*shemittoth*, sg.: *shemittah*). The idea of successive world cycles is not only found in Jewish mysticism; even before the advent of Kabbalah this motif was known to the Jews from Indian and Arabic sources, as is evident from Jewish astrological writings, among others.

The Book of the Figure, as it has come down to us, is the work of an unknown author and was published around 1300. The doctrine of the cosmic cycles, however, seems to have been known to kabbalists through the whole of the thirteenth century, in particular those of Gerona. By some means or other this teaching made its way to Provence, presumably from the East, and later became connected with the sefirotic doctrine. Between 1200 and 1300 simpler versions of the Book of the Figure must already have been in circulation.

According to the anonymous author the seven lower sefiroth can also be seen as the original seven days of creation or as world cycles. (The three highest sefiroth are left out of consideration because of their elevated character; they have no perceptible effect on the visible creation.) Each separate sefirah rules a cosmic unit (*shemittah*), which determines the character of world history for a 7000-year period. Just as the sefiroth reveal a particular aspect of the deity in the sequence of their emanation, so too they make their mark on world events in the successive cycles. Each cycle of 7000 years thus hides a quite separate aspect of the divine. When all the phases have unfolded after seven world cycles, 49,000 years in total, the divine powers will have come to their full manifestation in creation. In the fiftieth millennium the seven lower sefiroth return into the bosom of the third sefirah, Binah, from which all seven emerged (see § 1.2 of this chapter), since the purpose of creation would then have been fulfilled. Underlying the doctrine of the world cycles, clearly, are the biblical regulations with reference to the sabbath and jubilee year (Deut 15, 31 and Lev 25).

The Book of the Figure links the seven lower sefiroth as cosmic eras with the mystical understanding of the Torah. According to the kabbalists the Torah has its roots in a primordial Torah (*Torah qedumah*). The latter is associated with the sefirah Hokhmah, one of the three highest sefiroth, in which our whole reality lies embedded as a spiritual model. This primordial Torah, written with the primordial letters, is spiritual in character and has such a high position in the celestial world that it cannot be reached or grasped by humans. In each separate world cycle this primordial Torah takes on a completely different shape, in agreement with the individual character of the sefirah which determines that particular phase in world history. This brings about an agreement between a world cycle which unfolds a specific aspect of God's intention in history, and the form of the Torah, which comprises a special aspect of the divine revelation. The seven world cycles, then, each have their own separate, corresponding Torah. Although the primordial Torah is manifested seven times in a different form—in each period of world history the Torah has a different content—its essence does not undergo any change at all. The unchanging nature of the primordial Torah merely takes on another external form—just as when a person changes clothes, despite the external change that person remains essentially the same. The external changes relate to the structuring of the Torah into various books, the form of the letters, which have a different appearance in each shemittah, as well as the sequence of the letters and their combination into words. The title of *Sefer ha-Temunah*, the Book of the Figure, refers to these constantly changing forms.

The era in which we live at present, corresponds, according to the anonymous author, with the sefirah Din, the second of the seven lower sefiroth. The cosmic period that preceded our own belonged to the sefirah Hesed, the seventh in line in the seven. The Book of the Figure describes this first world cycle of Hesed as a period in which the human resembled the heavenly person such as the prophet Ezekiel saw sitting on the throne in his vision (Ezek 1.26). The whole of creation was bathed in a divine light and evil was completely absent. The letters in the Torah of the Hesed cycle were simpler in form than the letters we know.

The period of Din, however, our reality, is dominated by the principle of limitation, strict law and justice. Our world knows evil, exile and sin. In order to make restitution for committed sins, souls in this world are forced to transmigrate. In order to conquer evil in our era, God placed on humans the yoke of negative and positive commandments for daily life. And this is the reason why the Torah that belongs to the cycle of Din consists of regulations for what is and what is not allowed. Through the limiting power of Din, the divine light cannot reveal itself fully in our cycle. The Torah in its present form reflects the limiting aspect of Din; the impure, evil character of this world cycle imbued the Hebrew letters with such a degree of abhorrence that initially they refused to enter into the combinations that were to provide the meaning of the present Torah.

That the Torah that we know is imperfect is made clear in two different ways. First of all it is posited that the Hebrew alphabet in which the Torah is written, is incomplete. In the Book of the Figure this is evident from the idea that the form of the letter *shin* is imperfect. In the alphabet known to us this letter has three downstrokes (ש), while originally it would have had four. Other kabbalists in this tradition go further and even speak of the existence of a twenty-third letter, which is invisible in our Torah. The fact that in the present Torah strict laws and regulations are to be read is, in this view, simply the result of the omission of the one letter or the imperfect form of the *shin*. Secondly, the imperfection of the present Torah is evident from the fact that it consists of five books, whereas the original Torah comprised seven books, corresponding to the seven lower sefiroth.

The period that follows our world cycle dominated by Din is described in the Book of the Figure in utopian terms. This third cycle again has a paradisiac nature and involves a return to the pure character of the first. Evil has gone, the bad side of humanity has disappeared, so that the human is no longer capable of sin. The transmigration of souls has become superfluous. The Torah that corresponds to this new age again has a holy and pure character and will once again consist of seven books. The invisible letter will re-appear, and the character of the Torah will be completely changed; the yoke of the commandments and prohibitions belongs to the past and the combinations and forms of the letters will manifest an entirely different revelation of God. The kabbalists speculated a great deal about these first three world cycles, and especially the coming third cycle fascinated them greatly. In the following chapters we shall repeatedly return to the utopian aspect of the coming age. On the four cycles that were to follow the first three, the kabbalists were extremely vague.

At first sight the theory of the "different" Torahs is extremely daring and unorthodox. Tradition states after all that God's revelation is immutable and given for all time. Nonetheless it seems that authoritative, orthodox rabbis such as Nahmanides from the Gerona school had little problem with this bold concept. The principle of the eternal and unchanging Torah was guaranteed in their eyes by the idea of the primordial Torah; while the essence of the primordial Torah, the true revelation, remained unchanged, its content assumed a different form in each of the various cosmic periods.

2.6.2 Ecstatic Kabbalah and Abraham Abulafia

From a conceptual point of view, in the historical development of Kabbalah, two main streams can be distinguished: theosophical Kabbalah and ecstatic Kabbalah.

All kabbalistic movements that we have discussed so far belong to the theosophical current. Theosophical Kabbalah is theocentric: it presents God himself, above all, as central and develops an elaborate theory of the structure of the divine world, the doctrine of the sefiroth. The kabbalist as an individual only played a role to the extent that he was capable—especially by observing the commandments—of exercising an influence on the divine world and thereby on the repair of the chasm that ran through all the worlds. The "manipulation" of the deity by means of human activity is called theurgy. This is how theosophical Kabbalah comes to be referred to also by the term theosophical-theurgic Kabbalah (see also § 1.6.4).

Ecstatic Kabbalah, on the other hand, is anthropocentric: it is the human being that is in central position instead of God. In this current the focus is on the attainment of an ecstatic awareness of the individual mystic, without the latter being concerned about the restoration of the internal harmony of the divine world. In order to bring about ecstasy, the experience of a direct relationship with the deity, the mystic made use of various mystical techniques. These are often non-legal in character, that is to say that they are not rooted in the regulations of Torah and Talmud. Sometimes such techniques are difficult to distinguish from magic. The mythic element, symbolism and the teaching of the sefiroth which we met in theosophical Kabbalah have little part to play in this form of Kabbalah.

Unlike theosophical Kabbalah, ecstatic Kabbalah is not specifically a product of the Iberian Peninsula. The tradition of ecstasy goes back much further than the thirteenth century. As we saw in Chapter 2, the Merkavah mystics already directed their attention to the ecstatic experience of the contemplation of the divine throne after the ascent through the heavenly palaces. Ecstatic Kabbalah did not really flourish on the Iberian Peninsula. As a result of the hostile attitude of the theosophical kabbalists towards this form of Kabbalah, with Abraham Abulafia ecstatic Kabbalah disappeared from the Iberian Peninsula (see below). From 1280 theosophical Kabbalah completely dominated fur-

ther developments. Ecstatic Kabbalah moved from the Iberian Peninsula via Italy to the Middle East. In Lurianic Kabbalah, which arose in
the sixteenth century in the town of Safed in the north of Palestine,
theosophical and ecstatic Kabbalah were to come together.

Oddly enough, in research into Kabbalah by far the most attention
has been directed to theosophical Kabbalah. Since Gershom Scholem's
devotion of a whole chapter to ecstatic Kabbalah in his 1941 work,
Major Trends, it has more or less been forgotten. Almost unnoticed,
this gave rise to the idea that Kabbalah is only theosophical-theurgic in
character. From 1976, however, the scholar Moshe Idel attempted to
deal with this one-sided view of Kabbalah in a series of books and
articles. He posits that throughout the whole history of Kabbalah, the
theosophical and ecstatic currents existed alongside each other as two
equal main types.

Through his extensive attention to the aspect of mystical experience, Idel came to a remarkable conclusion in relation to the *unio
mystica*, the union or merging of the mystic with God. Following
Scholem, almost everyone—as we also did in Chapter 1, § 3—assumes
that in Jewish mystical experience there is no question of a real unification with God, since there always remains a distinction between
God and his creation. This important distinction is supposed to be
expressed in the Hebrew term for mystical experience, *devequth*, which
means "cleaving (to God)", which is not the same thing as "union".
On the basis of an extensive investigation of numerous, in many cases
still unpublished, manuscripts, Moshe Idel opposes this view. According to him, this material appropriately describes the experiences of
many ecstatic kabbalists as a *unio mystica* and the term *devequth* can thus
very well stand for a real merging between God and the mystic.

Abraham Abulafia (1240–ca. 1291). The exponent of ecstatic (or
prophetic) Kabbalah on the Iberian Peninsula is Abraham ben Samuel
Abulafia. He was born in Zaragoza in the kingdom of Aragon. His
youth was spent in Tudela in the neighboring kingdom of Navarre.
Shortly after the death of his father, at the age of twenty he left for
Palestine, among other things to seek the river Sambation, beyond
which, according to tradition, the ten tribes of Israel were supposed to
live (see Chapter 1, § 2.1). By force of war he moved through Greece
to Italy, where he was to remain for ten years. Here he studied philosophy, especially Maimonides' *Moreh Nevukhim* (Guide of the
Perplexed). In 1270 Abulafia returned to the Iberian Peninsula, where
in Barcelona he devoted himself to the study of Kabbalah, in particular

the Book of Creation. The divine revelations he received in 1271 brought him to travel around the Iberian Peninsula to teach select groups about his mystical ideas on the attainment of ecstasy. In so doing in the kingdom of Castile he came into contact with the leading kabbalists Moses of Burgos and Joseph Gikatilla. He soon encountered great opposition from the theosophical kabbalists, who were opposed to his meditation techniques. They were wary of Abulafia's view that the ecstatic experience could be attained by self-taught methods, since they feared that by this means his view of Kabbalah would become known by the general public, which according to them was not ready for such knowledge. The theosophical kabbalists thought that mysticism had to be taught by educated rabbis and was reserved for a small, privileged group.

In 1274 Abulafia again left the Iberian Peninsula and traveled through Italy and Greece. In 1280 in a vision he was given the task of going to Rome to bring the difficult situation of the Jews to the attention of Pope Nicholas III and to persuade him to do something to make the life of the Jews more bearable. On Abulafia's arrival in Rome, however, the Pope had him arrested and condemned him to burn at the stake. Because the Pope suddenly died shortly afterwards, the sentence was not carried out and Abulafia was released.

Most of Abulafia's numerous works were written in Italy between 1279 and 1290. Besides a commentary on the Torah and on the Book of Creation, he wrote a number of handbooks which contain a systematic theoretical and practical guide to the attainment of ecstasy. In various writings he also set down his mystical and messianic views. Of the latter works, however, not much is left.

Central to Abulafia's mysticism is language, in particular the Hebrew language. In this regard he referred among other things to ancient ecstatic traditions from Merkavah mysticism, to the Book of Creation and especially to the mystical-magical techniques of the Ashkenazi Hasidim, all of whom made extensive use of language. This material he transformed into something quite new. Thus he developed a complete system, *hokhmath ha-tseruf*, "the knowledge of combination", involving infinite combinations of the letters of the Hebrew alphabet which were meditated upon. Besides this, Abulafia also adapted the technique of permutation, whereby letters were given different positions in the word or were replaced by other letters. He also made much use of the system of numerical values of the letters (*gematria*).

Abulafia was convinced that the true nature of language can only be exposed if one makes use of the system of letter combinations. The proof of this he saw, among other things, in the fact that the numerical value of the letters of the "combination" is equal to that of the word "language". For the convenience of the reader we give these Hebrew words in transliteration, their spelling with the names of the letters and after that the numerical value of each letter. The word "combination" is *tseruf* in Hebrew and is spelt *tsade(90)–yod(10)–resh(200)–waw(6)– peh(80)*, which is 386 in total. The word for language is *lashon*, which is spelt as follows: *lamed(30)–shin(300)–waw(6)–nun(50)*. The total of this is also 386. The fact that the two words represented the same numerical value meant for Abulafia that there was a connection between them.

In combining the letters Abulafia also made use of words and sentences in the Bible. The letters of which the words or sentences consisted were taken out of their context and regrouped into other combinations that meant something else, or which sometimes had no concrete meaning at all. That most of these combinations had no plain meaning was irrelevant for Abulafia; he assumed that the letters had meaning in themselves, and that it was these "original meanings" that were combined. For Abulafia, each separate letter was already a divine name, a world of its own (see also § 1.4 of this chapter). Thus for example he re-arranged the letters of the term "Tree of Life" to form another expression: "The Life of the Essence". In Hebrew "Tree of Life" (*ets ha-hayyim*), is spelt *ayin–tsade heh–heth–yod–yod–mem*. "The Life of the Essence" (*hayyei ha-etsem*) is spelt *heth–yod–yod heh–ayin– tsade–mem*, precisely the same letters as those comprised in the first expression, but in a different order.

In the combination or permutation of the Hebrew letters, the letters of the divine names take a special place. In Abulafia's writings whole tables are to be found of repetitions of two letters of the divine names combined together, each time with different vowel characters, which in fact form an attempt to explore the infinite possibilities lying hidden in the divine name. An important element in Abulafia's system is that all these combinations had to be recited extensively, in which process music played an important role.

In order to describe the character of the "wisdom of combination", Abulafia drew a comparison with music. Just as the tones lead in infinite combinations to ever new melodies, so too can the letters of the Hebrew alphabet bring divine harmonies to expression in ever new combinations. The enjoyment that people experience in listening to

various melodies constructed of a limited number of tones is comparable with the mystic's enjoyment in the contemplation of the various
letter combinations that are constructed from a limited number of
letters.

For Abulafia the aim of these techniques was an ecstatic experience,
the ultimate awareness of the divine. By means of meditation on the
letters, their combinations and permutations, a process was set in motion by which the soul of the mystic released itself from everyday
reality. In order to attain this ecstatic experience Abulafia also made
use of a number of other techniques, such as music, recitation and
breathing techniques, as well as physical positions which are reminiscent of those practiced by Indian mystics (yoga).

After the soul had released itself from the senses, a path opened up
through the celestial world. The mystic climbed up by means of a
mystical ladder and on arrival at the highest rung, the hidden source of
divine life revealed itself. In a state of supreme ecstasy the mystic received a prophetic vision in which he was made aware of the deepest
mysteries with reference to the deity and his creation.

Abulafia was very much aware that the practical side of the search
for ecstasy could carry with it great and dangerous risks for the insuffi-
ciently prepared mystic. A mystic who did not proceed systematically,
did not reorder, exchange or replace vowels and letters in the right
way, misread them or made a mistake, could fall victim to both mental
and physical injury.

A striking element in the work of Abulafia is that he allowed himself to be deeply influenced by philosophy. Abulafia had great
admiration for Maimonides' work, the Guide of the Perplexed, and
saw no contradiction at all between philosophy and mysticism. Rather,
he viewed his own mystical doctrine as the continuation and the definitive perfection of Maimonides' philosophy.

2.6.3 The kabbalists of the Castilian school

In the second half of the thirteenth century we find in Castile a group
of mystics who together composed the kabbalistic school of Castile.
The circle formed around Rabbi Jacob ha-Cohen of Soria, and especially around his sons Jacob ben Jacob ha-Cohen and Isaac ben Jacob
ha-Cohen. Among their students were such outstanding kabbalists as
Rabbi Moses of Burgos and Rabbi Todros ben Joseph Abulafia of
Burgos and Toledo; the latter was one of the leaders of Castilian Judaism.

In the work of the sons Jacob and Isaac there is noticeable influence from the Book Bahir, of the kabbalists of Provence and Gerona, but especially also of the Ashkenazi Hasidim (on this cf. § 2.5.3). Despite this influence the work of the two brothers stands entirely alone and can be regarded as extremely original. In their mystical considerations they claimed to draw upon personal visions and revelations, as well as discoveries of their own in relation to gematria and other numerical relationships. Besides this, however, they claimed to be in possession of ancient, secret mystical traditions.

One of the best-known works of Jacob ben Jacob ha-Cohen is his *Perush ha-Otiyoth* (Commentary on the Hebrew Letters). In this work Jacob displays great interest in each separate aspect of the Hebrew language. Not only does he deal with the letters in this commentary, but also with their form, the sound of the consonants and vowels in pronunciation, the signs with which the vowels are indicated as well as those which denote the melody of the biblical text. In illustration of his mystical language theory we shall show how Jacob regards the first letter of the Hebrew alphabet, *aleph*, as the letter from which all the other letters derive, with their forms.

If we look at the shape of the letter *aleph* א more closely, we see an oblique line with two symmetrical points on each side of the oblique, thinning out in a downward direction. In the oblique line Jacob sees the letter *waw* ו (numerical value: 6) and the two points running off as the letter *yod* י (10). The letter *aleph* is thus made up of a *yod* (10), a *waw* (6) and another *yod* (10). The total numerical value of the parts of the letter *aleph* thus amounts to 26. Jacob then connects this first letter and its numerical value with the four-letter divine name of the God of Israel. As we have seen, the Tetragrammaton consists of the letters *yod* (10), *heh* (5), *waw* (6) and *heh* (5). Now if we count up the numerical value of the Tetragrammaton, we obtain, just as with the letter *aleph*, a total of 26. This agreement between the Tetragrammaton and *aleph* (which represents the numerical value of 1) Jacob uses to emphasize the unity, indivisibility and immutability of God, as is also evident in *Hear O Israel, the Lord our God, the Lord, is One* (Deut 6.4). Just as God is one, the *aleph* is the first letter; just as the whole creation issues from God without God ceasing to be God, so do all the letters issue from the first letter of the alphabet with the *aleph* ceasing to be *aleph*; just as God is one and hidden from all creatures, so is the pronunciation of the *aleph* as first letter "in a hidden place at the back of the tongue" (the pronunciation of the *aleph* after all is marked by soundlessness, the glottal stop). In order to clarify the analogy between the unity of God and the *aleph*, Jacob adds that not only is the numerical value of the

letter *aleph* 1, but that also the Hebrew cardinal number one (*ehad*)
begins with an *aleph*, just as the first word of the ten commandments,
"I (*anokhi*) am the Lord your God" (Exod 20.2) begins with an *aleph*.

Jacob's brother Isaac is especially well known for his view of the
origins of evil in this world. In a tractate on the so-called sefiroth of
the "left emanation" (*ha-atsiluth ha-semalith*) Isaac presents a completely
new starting-point in relation to evil. Before going into this we shall
first pay attention to the kabbalistic views of the origins of evil which
preceded Isaac's publication.

In section 2.2 on the Book Bahir we saw that the early kabbalists
viewed evil as an entirely independent power within the world of the
deity. In the Book Bahir evil is spoken of only in general terms: evil
emanated from the divine sefirotic tree and fulfilled a role in the divine
plan of creation. After the Book Bahir we see the development of two
more views of the origins of evil. According to one of these, there was
a connection between the emergence of evil and the two trees which
stood in paradise, while the other saw the roots of evil in a disturbed
relationship between the sefiroth Hesed and Din.

It was particularly the symbolism of the two trees of paradise, the
Tree of Life and the Tree of the Knowledge of Good and Evil that
seems to have been of lasting influence in the history of Kabbalah. The
kabbalistic view of the paradise story sees Adam, the (primordial) human, as a spiritual being, acting in a spiritual world. In this spiritual
Adam the unity and harmony of all the powers in the divine realm
were reflected as in a microcosm. The Tree of Life is associated with
the right-hand side, the good inclinations, peace and harmony, while
the Tree of the Knowledge of Good and Evil has to do with the left-
hand side, the evil inclinations and disharmony. In the world of the
deity, in the realm of the sefiroth, therefore, the possibilities of good
and evil are contained, and they are reflected in the human being.

The two trees stand in two different places in paradise, but under
the ground they are linked together by their roots. As long as the two
trees are linked together in unity, the effect of the Tree of Life has
supremacy over the Tree of Knowledge. As a result it is not possible
for the latter tree to do any evil. However, if the two trees were to be
separated from each other, the Tree of Knowledge could become independent, so that it would indeed be possible for the evil impulses to
be realized. Instead of Adam maintaining and strengthening his contact
with the spiritual reality, bringing his will into line with the divine will
and thus fulfilling the aim of creation, he allows himself to eat of the
fruit of the forbidden tree.

This deed had far-reaching consequences. The original harmonious unity of both the higher worlds (sefiroth) and our world was broken. Not only did a chasm run through all the worlds from top to bottom as a result of Adam's fall, but also the roots which linked the two trees of paradise were severed. Since the Tree of Knowledge was now separated from the Tree of Life, evil could manifest itself. Adam absorbed these evil powers and united with them, so that he lost his spiritual nature and became a mortal being. In symbolic terms this is often depicted by saying that Adam's soul became separated from the Supreme Soul.

The symbolism of the two trees of paradise refers to a unity of opposites. Just as the two trees were originally one—since they grew from one common root—so too all opposites were united in a holy harmony. Originally, then, such opposites as male and female, left and right, soul and body, were linked in a harmonious unity. By Adam's fall the unity was broken and everything became as it were displaced, both in the world of the sefiroth and in our world. As a result of Adam's fall it is no longer possible for humans to see the harmonious connections between things, since everything has lost its proper place. The moral nature of the human individual and the view that a person has of reality are affected by Adam's fall; humans no longer see male and female, body and soul or any opposition as two things that are one and linked in harmony. Evil arises because the human being—in particular the first human, Adam—disturbs the existing harmony by means of his actions.

The other version of the emergence of evil which is frequently found in kabbalistic literature is concerned with the relationship between the sefiroth Hesed and Din. Although the symbolism used is different, this view has a lot in common with the symbolism of the trees of paradise; it seems to be an attempt to say the same thing in a different form. There is a correspondence between the Tree of Life and the sefirah Hesed on the one hand and between the Tree of Knowledge and the sefirah Din on the other. In the description of the symbolism of these two sefiroth at the beginning of this chapter we described Hesed as the manifestation of God's mercy and love, which has its counterpart in Din as a power of strictness and limitation, which must keep the constant stream of divine love within boundaries. (The opposition between Hesed and Din as attributes of God was an idea accepted already in classical rabbinic Judaism.) Just as the Tree of Life initially held sway over the Tree of the Knowledge of Good and Evil, so too Hesed held sway over Din. As soon as the latter sefirah released itself, however, and separated from Hesed, evil gained the possibility of dominating everything. Early Kabbalah speculated greatly about the sefirah Din and its relationship to evil. The two views with their varying symbolism can be reduced to the same principle: evil can only come into being when two connected things are separated or if something is removed and isolated from its proper place within the divine order.

Isaac ben Jacob ha-Cohen has a much more radical approach to the emergence of evil than the kabbalists before him. He created a complete myth of evil in which there was even talk of two emanations, each of which had ten separate sefiroth; on the right-hand side stand the ten holy or good sefiroth, on their left as counterparts the ten evil sefiroth. We now no longer have to do with two things that are connected in unity with each other and may not be parted—although this idea remains present in the background—but with two separate, opposing sefirotic structures. In these two structures everything develops in parallel pairs, in which good and evil find themselves opposite each other in a constant mythical struggle in the celestial world. Each good power in the sefiroth of the right emanation has an evil opposite number in the sefiroth of the left emanation. Thus for instance the female power within the right emanation, symbolized in Eve, has its counterpart in Lilith, the female demonic power in the left world. The male power symbolized in Adam has Samael as its counterpart, the male satanic power.

With reference to the emergence of the left emanation, Isaac posits that God tried a number of times to bring creation into existence. These attempts were frustrated by strong powers that had permeated the already emanated worlds with their evil. God thus found it necessary to destroy these failed emanated worlds. These worlds, according to Isaac, emerged from the sefirah Binah. Binah, as we have seen, is a female sefirah, in which everything that is to appear is already embedded in a differentiated form. After the destruction of the failed worlds, everything returned to the maternal lap of Binah. It was only after this that God managed to bring into being what he considered to be a perfect creation. A residue of these destroyed worlds remained, however, which continued to exist after the emergence of the definitive worlds, like material that has become separated from the divine being. From the remains of the lost worlds the emanations of the left-hand side ensued. The idea that God created worlds and then destroyed them is already found in traditional rabbinic literature (*Genesis Rabbah*

9.2). This theme is further elaborated by Isaac and connected with the world of the sefiroth and the left-hand emanation.

Isaac's tractate on the left emanation also contains the idea that the struggle between good and evil powers will only be decided by the Messiah, at the end of time. The Messiah himself will exact retribution for all the suffering caused by evil and subdue the evil powers. Isaac is the first in kabbalistic literature to speak of a mythical, messianic struggle against evil in apocalyptic terms. Messianism does also occur in the work of the kabbalists of the classical period, but their interest was more in the secrets of creation hidden in the past than in the messianic time in the future. In the following chapter we shall deal with this topic in more detail, in our discussion of Lurianic Kabbalah, in which messianism occupies a central position.

Following Gershom Scholem the kabbalists of the Castilian school are often called "the Gnostics of Castile" or "the Gnostic Brothers" on account of the dualistic character that was said to mark their work. In our discussion of the Book Bahir we looked in detail at the question whether Kabbalah goes back to ancient gnostic motifs and traditions or not. Only when scholarly research has succeeded in answering this question will it be clear whether the name "Gnostics" is appropriate or inappropriate for this group of mystics.

With the doctrine of the left emanation Isaac added a new element to kabbalistic ideas which was to be a continuing source of inspiration to Kabbalah for centuries.

2.6.4 The Zohar

General features. The appearance of the Zohar (*Sefer ha-Zohar*, Book of Splendor) at the end of the thirteenth century forms the culmination of the development of classical Kabbalah. The work provides a comprehensive system in which all aspects of Judaism are interpreted mystically by means of complex symbolism. The Zohar is a literary monument, engagingly written and exuberant in tone, in which numerous ideas and symbols from earlier kabbalistic currents are brought together and further elaborated in a creative way. All the currents and ideas that we have described in our preceding discussion belong to a period in which Kabbalah was still as it were seeking its definitive form. With the appearance of the Zohar this period comes to an end and Kabbalah gains its classic shape.

From a bibliographic point of view the Zohar forms an extremely complex whole, which in five different parts—around 2400 pages in

total—contains some 23 separate books, which moreover are not
clearly separated in the various manuscripts but are intermingled. The
book is written in the form of a Midrash, following the classical rabbinic method in which particular views of all sorts of subjects are
connected to the authoritative biblical text (see Chapter 1, § 2.4). The
most important part of the Zohar is formed by a mystical commentary
on the Torah. Other books sometimes contain narrative passages of all
kinds or also midrashim on other books of the Bible such as the Song
of Songs, Ruth and Lamentations.

The mystical commentaries are often homiletic in character, that is
to say that they have the form of a sermon. The sayings in the Zohar
are placed on the lips of various rabbis from the Talmud, in particular
Rabbi Simeon ben Yohai, a student of Rabbi Akiva's, who lived in
Palestine in the second century CE. At various points we read how he
assembled students around him in order to reveal to them the hidden
mysteries of the Torah. In most of the Zohar this Simeon ben Yohai
and his circle take pride of place. On the basis of what they experience
together, for instance on walks or in encounters with others, the
reader gains an impression of the life of such a mystical circle and the
mysteries with which they occupied themselves. Simeon ben Yohai is
credited with an unimaginable and almost supernatural insight into the
secrets of the Torah. In greatness, power and insight he would not be
inferior to Moses himself.

Age and authorship. From the appearance of the Zohar at the end of the
thirteenth century the antiquity of this work has been the subject of
discussion. The question was whether the Zohar was really a very old
Midrash which preserved mystical traditions from the time of Simeon
ben Yohai or whether the book was written by Moses de Leon, an
eminent kabbalist who lived in Castile in the second half of the thirteenth century. An interesting testimony on this question has come
down to us which dates to shortly after the appearance of the Zohar.
This is a fragment from the diary of a certain Rabbi Isaac of Acre, who
was forced by the violence of war in 1291 to leave Acre in Palestine.
He probably heard tell of a Castilian kabbalist, Moses de Leon, who
was supposed to be in possession of a very old book, the Zohar, which
apparently contained the mystical teachings of Rabbi Simeon ben Yohai. This Moses de Leon copied parts of this ancient book, which he
disseminated among other kabbalists. Isaac of Acre tells us how he
traveled on further to the Iberian Peninsula, where he met Moses de
Leon in the town of Valladolid in Castile. On that occasion Moses de

Leon promised to show him the book in his home town Avila. But Moses de Leon died in Arévalo on the way to Avila shortly afterwards, and the appointment was not met. Isaac of Acre then heard from a third person that a certain Joseph of Avila was prepared to marry his son to the daughter of the late Moses de Leon on the condition that he would receive in exchange for this the original book of Simeon ben Yohai. The widow however was said to have declared that no such book had existed, but her deceased husband had written the book himself. Isaac of Acre conducted an investigation in order to find out precisely what the situation was in relation to the Zohar and spoke with various kabbalists. Interestingly enough he found opinions fiercely divided already as early as this; some were convinced of the genuineness and antiquity of the Zohar, while others maintained that their contemporary Moses de Leon must have been the author.

The discussion on the antiquity of the Zohar that had run since the thirteenth century did not come to an end until the first half of the twentieth century. After a comprehensive fifteen-year investigation, in which the problem was studied from every conceivable angle (philological, historical, linguistic, and conceptual), Gershom Scholem could come only to one incontrovertible conclusion: the Zohar was written by Moses de Leon at the end of the thirteenth century. Despite this scholarly conclusion, some orthodox circles still hold fast to the authorship of Simeon ben Yohai.

A meticulous study of the linguistic aspects of the Zohar, which with the exception of a few parts is written in Aramaic, showed that as regards style and content, the same personal characteristics are in evidence everywhere in the work. This indicates that the work must largely be the work of a single author. Furthermore, the Aramaic used by the author has an artificial feel about it; it is not the living language of Palestine from the time of Rabbi Simeon ben Yohai, but a mixture of Aramaic dialects which Moses de Leon knew from later Jewish literature, especially the Aramaic of the Babylonian Talmud. In addition, behind the Aramaic the structure of thirteenth-century Hebrew is clearly visible; this is Hebrew in Aramaic dress.

A critical investigation of the literary form of the book makes it clear that the whole thing is played out in a non-existent Palestine and that the author himself has evidently never been to Palestine. The romantic description of the hills of Galilee is more like a description of the Castilian mountains, and the author makes frequent mistakes with regard to the topography of Palestine. A clear example of this is that Moses de Leon misunderstands a passage in the Palestinian Talmud about the Jews of Cappadocia (in Asia Minor) and assumes that this is a place in Galilee; thus, he has Rabbi Simeon ben Yohai and his followers go on frequent visits to the village of "Kapotkia". Moses de Leon also makes mistakes in the chronology of the older rabbis; among the disciples of Simeon ben Yohai he mentions rabbis who lived generations later.

As has been said, the Zohar is written in the form of a midrash. It is, however, clear that the content and form of the midrashim in the Zohar do not closely resemble ancient midrashic collections from the time of the Mishnah which the author is attempting to follow, but rather are more like medieval midrashim. At countless points Moses de Leon betrays the fact that he is au fait with kabbalistic literature of the thirteenth century, in particular with the writings of the Gerona group, the Cohen brothers and the Ashkenazi Hasidim. In addition, the Zohar contains here and there references to contemporary events such as the Crusades or polemical allusions to Islam and Christianity.

From the above it appears that the Zohar dates from the end of the thirteenth century. An extensive comparison with the works Moses de Leon wrote under his own name shows that the author of the Zohar can be none other than Moses de Leon himself. Arguments from both content and style point in this direction. Two books in the Zoharic corpus however form an exception to this: *Ra'ya Mehemnah* (Faithful Shepherd) and *Tiqqunei ha-Zohar* (Supplements to the Zohar). Both books are by anonymous authors and were written probably quite shortly after the death of Moses de Leon in 1305, in imitation of the original Zohar, of which they were subsequently to form part. By means of a reconstruction of the innumerable facts that had emerged from his research, Scholem came to the conclusion that Moses de Leon must have completed the work in 1286.

It is no great surprise that Moses de Leon placed the teachings of the Zohar on the lips of Rabbi Simeon ben Yohai; a great deal of mystical and kabbalistic literature is pseudepigraphic. The kabbalists assumed that all true knowledge of the secrets of the Torah had already been given to Moses on Sinai and that it had since been preserved and transmitted as oral tradition. If a kabbalist had a "new" idea, and had the feeling that it was true, he thought that this idea must therefore also be old and known already to Moses, Solomon or an ancient rabbi. Genuinely new ideas which Moses had never had simply could not be true. By placing the mystical sayings in the Zohar on the lips of Rabbi Simeon ben Yohai and his circle, Moses de Leon gave expression to his conviction that the mystical knowledge contained in the Zohar was already ancient and thus authoritative.

Following Gershom Scholem other scholars have also occupied themselves with the study of the Zohar. At some points they come to somewhat different conclusions. Isaiah Tishby, for instance, is of the opinion that Moses de Leon did not complete the Zohar in 1286 but must have continued to work on the book until his death in 1305. Yehudah Liebes came to the conclusion that the Zohar must be the literary product of a group of mystic friends in Castile, who would have started working on the book as early as 1250. Though Moses de Leon played an important part in this group, he should not be viewed as the sole author of the Zohar.

One thing at any rate has been incontrovertibly demonstrated: the Zohar is not an ancient work from the time of Rabbi Simeon ben Yohai. Nor is it a work consisting of various layers which came into being through the course of the centuries as the product of various authors. The Zohar saw the light of day in Castile in the late thirteenth century.

Basic ideas. The Zohar contains a range of kabbalistic themes. Some of the most important of these we have already discussed in connection with the doctrines of classical Kabbalah in the first section of this chapter. The general, fully-fledged form of Kabbalah which we presented there is in fact Kabbalah as we find it in the Zohar. The concern here is with the description of the world of the sefiroth, their position and their names, the influence of humans on the divine realm, the significance of the fall of Adam and the bringing about of the restoration of the divine harmony (see § 1.2). The same applies to the attitude to anthropomorphisms (§ 1.6.3) and partly to the commandments (§ 1.6.4) as well as the symbolism of the Torah and the Hebrew alphabet (§ 1.4). Below we shall deal with another important theme from the Zohar: the central role occupied by the human being in the creation. Other motifs are connected with this, such as the tripartite division of the soul, sleep, dream and death, as well as married life.

The central role of the human. The Zohar is strongly anthropocentric. That is to say that the whole of creation centers around humanity; the human being forms the culmination point of creation. Everything that God brought forward in creation he made for the sake of man. The whole creation is then reflected in the human as a microcosm. At the moment that humans came on the scene, the goal of creation was reached and everything was in place.

As we have learned, through Adam's fall the spiritual character of humankind was lost, which allowed evil to come into the world. With a few variations, Moses de Leon takes over the doctrine of the left emanations from Isaac ben Jacob ha-Cohen. The left emanations are designated in the Zohar by the "Other Side" (*Sitra Ahra*). More so than the kabbalists of the Castilian school, however, Moses de Leon connects this doctrine explicitly with the place of the human being in the creation process. Also he does not trace the origins of the left emanations back to the sefirah Binah, as Isaac did, but to the sefirah Din. Since our reality and the human being form a reflection of the higher worlds—both realities are of course connected like communicating vessels—good and evil are present intertwined in the human. In our reality, in which the world of Din holds sway, the human stands in between the principles of good and evil. It is the human that forms the decisive factor in the conquest of evil and the restoration of the original harmony. All the doings of humans are seen in the Zohar as closely connected with the ten holy sefiroth on the one hand and the ten evil sefiroth on the other.

The tripartite division of the human soul. According to the Zohar the human consists in the first place of a soul, which has its origins in the divine, in the world of the sefiroth. Since the human soul corresponds to the structure of the sefiroth, it possesses something of the substance of God. The soul is formed by the union of the masculine sefirah Tif'ereth and the feminine sefirah Malkhuth. The soul as a spark of divine essence thus comes from the interchange between a male and a female principle. The human body—equally in the image of the sefiroth, but constructed from the elements of our earthly material—forms an outer garment enveloping the soul.

According to the author of the Zohar the human soul consists of three separate parts: *nefesh*, *ruah* and *neshamah*. The basis of this tripartite division was a mixture of medieval neo-Platonic and Aristotelian philosophical understandings. Although the passages on the threefold division of the human soul are generally obscure, complicated and contradictory, the broad lines can still be extracted. The neshamah is the highest part of the soul; it is what constitutes the divine within the human. It is due to the neshamah that the human being is formed in the image of God. It is therefore also symbolized as a divine spark. The nefesh as the lowest part of the soul, often referred to as the natural soul, is closely connected with the body. The nefesh contains the forces that are necessary to keep the body functioning and in good condition. Between the highest and lowest parts of the soul stands the ruah, which forms the connection between neshamah and nefesh. When the three parts of the soul are interacting well, the ruah has the task of giving the divine light of the neshamah through to the nefesh and of ensuring that the nefesh can maintain itself in the body.

All human souls have their origin in the sefirah Hokhmah, in the spiritual blueprint of everything that will come into being. Corresponding to this process in which the deity unfolds its whole personality in the world of the sefiroth, the soul begins from Hokhmah with a process of descent or individualization. In this process the specific individual character of the soul is gradually revealed, until it reaches its definitive individual form in the sefirah Malkhuth. In this last sefirah, often depicted as Paradise, all the souls that will ever appear on earth are present. From Malkhuth as the storehouse of the souls the transition begins to our physical appearance, the body in our reality. By analogy with Adam's fall, after which Adam changed from a spiritual being to a mortal one, the descent of the soul into the body is also understood as a fall or a form of impurity.

All three parts of the soul are not necessarily always present in the body. The presence or absence of all three is dependent on the level of the person. Just as the ruah forms a bridge within the human soul, so the neshamah, as the divine part of the soul, forms a bridge between God and man. Whenever a person makes mistakes or commits evil, the neshamah separates from the two other parts of the soul and leaves the body. An impure neshamah from the Other Side then takes its place. Whenever a person does good, on the other hand, he strengthens the connection with his neshamah.

The nefesh, which is closely connected with the body, is associated in the Zohar with the Other Side, the opposite of everything that is holy. In order to understand why Moses de Leon posits this correspondence, we must refer to what we said about the two trees of paradise and the sefiroth Hesed and Din. In the literature the two trees and the sefiroth are compared with the symbol of the unity of body and soul. The soul, viewed as essence or kernel, is surrounded by the body; the two form a unity. In the symbolism of the kabbalists the principle of the kernel or the essence is depicted as "right" and "masculine", while everything pertaining to shape and appearance is associated with "left" and "feminine".

In the Zohar this symbolism is elaborated by Moses de Leon in a special way. Just as the two trees and the sefiroth Hesed and Din become separated and their unity is broken, so too the nefesh breaks the one-ness with the neshamah, after which the latter is subsequently able to leave the body. Once free from this unity the nefesh and the body incline towards evil and can become embroiled in the satanic realm of Sitra Ahra.

In principle every person has the possibility of possessing all three parts of the soul. After Adam's fall, however, the possession of a neshamah is reserved for only very few. The restoration or maintenance of the connection between the nefesh and the neshamah is dependent on the behavior of the individual. Reckoned among the good deeds of a person in the Zohar are, among other things, the study of the Torah, penetration into its secrets and the strict observance of the daily commandments. A person who has contact with his neshamah comes closer to God—after all the neshamah was the bridge between God and human—and thus manifests the divine in his or her own nature. Among the evil actions of a person, inspired by the Other Side, are in fact all human actions that are not oriented towards the restoration of the original unity but rather reinforce the chaos and disharmony. These may include identification with the external side of life, the satisfaction of all bodily needs, failure to observe the commandments, as well as the practice of black magic, in which a person exploits satanic powers that can be helpful in the realization of his or her own personal aims.

It is the Zohar that makes a connection between the actions of a person and the divine energy or source of light (*shefa'*)—examined above in our discussion of the sefiroth—which flows to our creation by way of the channels of the sefiroth. This stream is the source of all life, without which no life can exist. The uppermost three sefiroth are always provided plentifully with this divine stream of light by virtue of their special elevated character, but in the seven lower sefiroth the through-flow is not always smooth. Important in this regard is again the relationship between Hesed and Din. Initially the divine light sources which flow from Hesed were kept within certain boundaries by Din. After the breaking of their unity the limiting element of Din gained the upper hand and the stream of light from Hesed became overly weakened. The result of this was that the powers of Din flowed too strongly towards our creation and formed the source of increasing evil. It now depends on a person's deeds how much he contributes to redressing the shortfall of Hesed light and decreasing the dominance of Din, so as to restore the balance.

Sleep, dream and death. The threefold division of the human soul also plays a part in the interpretation of sleep and dreams. When someone falls asleep, the soul separates from the body. It leaves the body and

rises through the divine world. Only a very small part of the soul remains in the body to keep it alive and to maintain the connection
between body and soul. The Zohar describes this ascent as a process in
which the soul is judged on its actions, including the words a person
has spoken in the course of the preceding day. Judgment is made according to the extent to which a person has succeeded in making a
contribution to the restoration of the original harmony. Here we
should not think in human categories of good and evil, since this is a
matter of things in a reality beyond our own.

Before reaching the divine realm, the soul must first pass through
regions where the Other Side holds sway. Demonic and seductive
powers try to arrest the ascending soul in their region. In sleep, most
souls quickly become entangled in the satanic world of the Other Side
and get stuck there the whole night long. The height to which a soul
can rise is, however, dependent on the person; souls of the righteous
are immune to the influence of the Other Side, so that the quickly
pass through this area and ascend further into the divine world. The
souls that ascend during sleep to their origins in the upper realm, receive instruction there in the secrets of the Torah and gain new
insights. All this comes to expression in their doings the following day.
The awakening in the morning is seen as a form of resurrection. The
dreams a person has during sleep are depictions of the experiences of
the soul in the higher worlds. Souls which get stuck in the satanic
areas of the Other Side have misleading dreams in which false information and demonic powers manifest themselves. Souls which by
virtue of their character can surmount the areas of evil, can have
dreams which have the nature of revelations or which show future
events in our human world.

Repeatedly sleep is compared with death. The processes which take
place each night during sleep—a form of temporary "death"—are
repeated in death itself but then have a permanent character. After the
physical death the three parts of the soul return to their original area:
the neshamah to Hokhmah, the ruah to Tif'ereth and the nefesh to
Malkhuth. After death a comprehensive judgment follows on a person's doings during the whole of his or her earthly life. Which people
will die each year is determined at the beginning of the Jewish New
Year; impending death is then announced already in all the spiritual
worlds. The dying person views in visions the celestial world through
which the soul returns and sees at the same time everyone who has
died before him. As in sleep, however, the soul of the deceased can get

stuck in the dark realms of evil instead of ascending to its original home.

Marital life. The central role of humans in creation is also expressed in the interest the Zohar attaches to marriage between a man and a woman. As has been said, the Zohar knows of no higher goal than the restoration of the break that was the result of the fall of Adam. The re-merging of the separated parts into a unity is portrayed in the Zohar by means of the symbolism of human sexual union. The dynamic processes of the sefiroth among themselves are then also viewed as permanent interchanges between male and female powers. Everything that forms a pair in some way or other is depicted in sexual terms. Thus heaven and earth correspond to the masculine and feminine principle, while the Written and Oral Torah are related together as male and female. The description of the divine world in the Zohar is in essence the depiction of one great sexual event, in which male and female powers earnestly desire to overcome their separation and to meld together into a unity.

Moses de Leon sees marriage between man and woman as a reflection of the relationship between male and female powers in the cosmos. The author ascribes a sacred character to married life, especially to sexual relations within marriage. The sexual act embodies in our world the divine relations in the higher world. According to Moses de Leon, sexual union in marriage even has a stimulating effect on relations that occur between male and female powers in the upper world, in view of the fact that both worlds are related like communicating vessels. God's commission, *Be fruitful and multiply* (Gen 1.28), is taken as a reference to the unification of male and female powers within the deity: it is from this union that souls emerge. Accordingly, a marriage should produce offspring, not only as early as possible, but also to as great an age as possible.

Within marriage, according to Moses de Leon, the woman, as the reflection of the Shekhinah (the female power within the deity), played an important, if indirect, role. The commandment to reproduce is the responsibility of the man; the woman then puts him in a position to fulfill this assignment and thus to bring about the heavenly union. The indirect character of the role of the woman is also evident in the observation that the woman does not have the right to do anything without the permission of her husband. Blessings which come from God go to the man first, and reach the woman only through him. The most important quality of the Jewish woman, according to the Zohar, is modesty: women who remain at home and do not go outside are modest and suitable for bearing worthy children.

It is clear that the Zohar attaches enormous importance to the sacral role of both the man and the woman within marriage. In the cosmos it is all about the continuing connection between male and female powers; in the connection between these two poles, in their unification, a divine element lies hidden. Marriage thus forms a mirror image of this divine connection between male and female. In this regard it is all the more striking that the book also contains passages which appear to contradict this—something that we often encounter in the Zohar, by the way. At various points one of the two holy poles, the woman, is suddenly depicted as very unholy. For us at the threshold of the twenty-first century, such passages seem even to be woman-hostile—according to Gershom Scholem Kabbalah as a whole deserves this label—and discriminatory. Thus the Zohar states, for instance, that women are connected with the Other Side, the realm of impurity and evil. This is evident from the "fact" that women are naturally disposed towards magic and sorcery, especially during menstruation, and are also experts in this area. Women have a persistent inclination towards murder and killing; if Heaven did not hold them back, women would murder everyone in the word. Incidentally, it is not only women that are connected with the Other Side in the Zohar. All non-Jewish peoples and religions fall under the sway of evil. Moreover, non-Jews who are unable to fulfill the Torah and the commandments have no neshamah at all, the divine part of the human soul. Such contradictory and to us discriminatory passages must of course be seen in the context of thirteenth-century Judaism. Pronouncements in this vein by the author of the Zohar clearly fit within quite other frames of reference than our own.

The Zohar and chariot mysticism. In conclusion another important motif from the Zohar needs to be mentioned: throne-chariot (*merkavah*) symbolism. Though in the early kabbalistic literature from the Book Bahir to the Zohar we find references to Merkavah mysticism, it still cannot be said that the writings of the ancient Jewish Merkavah mystics played an important role in this period of Kabbalah. The early kabbalists were more interested in the emanation doctrine than in the vision of the throne. Instead of the spiritual activity of the Merkavah mystics, which was directed towards the ascent through the heavenly palaces to God's throne and to the attainment of ecstasy, there emerged a symbolic reinterpretation of the mystical descriptions from the ancient period of Jewish mysticism. The reports of the heavenly journey now served as an object of kabbalistic meditation. In the Zohar, however, for the first time in a long period extensive attention was paid to the throne chariot. We find elaborate descriptions in which each component of the chariot turns out to be a symbol within the world of the sefiroth. In this view the model of the throne chariot from the book of Ezekiel corresponded with the divine system of the world of the sefiroth. Here the Zohar speaks even of two chariots, the higher chariot corresponding with the symbolism of En Sof and the first three sefiroth, and the lower one—inspired by Gen 41.43—corresponding with the symbolism of the seven lower sefiroth.

The reception of the Zohar. Initially the Zohar was only known to kabbalists. After the expulsion of the Jews from Spain in 1492, however, the situation was to change. In the sixteenth century there was great interest in the content of the Zohar (cf. Chapter 4) not only among mystics but also in large sections of the Jewish population, as well as in its artistic character. Gradually the Zohar acquired an aura of holiness and as a printed book the work even gained the status of a canonical text, ranking equally with the Talmud in traditional literature. After 1492, especially from around the middle of the sixteenth century, Talmud and Zohar were seen as two different aspects of the divine revelation in the Torah: the Talmud was the body, or the exoteric aspect, of the Torah, while the Zohar constituted its soul, or its esoteric aspect. For the mystics of the time, the Zohar was the point of departure and the source of inspiration in the development of all new mystical ideas. The kabbalistic literature from before the Zohar was not forgotten of course, but for the mystics it was primarily the Zohar that came to occupy central position.

In the nineteenth century, for adherents of the Jewish Enlightenment, the *Haskalah*, there came an end to this exalted status of the Zohar. As we have mentioned a number of times in this book, during the Jewish Enlightenment the rational aspects of Judaism were strongly emphasized. Judaism was identified with the rational philosophy of Maimonides, who was viewed as the leading exponent of Jewish monotheism. Everything that was at odds with rational, abstract and monotheistic Judaism—such as mysticism, among other things—was seen as non-Jewish. During the Jewish Enlightenment, the fact that Greek philosophy could not exactly be regarded as a purely Jewish product was evidently less of a problem. Twentieth-century scholarship has restored not only the Zohar but also the history of Jewish mysticism as a coherent whole to its place in the history of Judaism (for details see Chapter 1, § 1).

2.6.5 Kabbalah from the Zohar to 1492

After the appearance of the Zohar at the end of the thirteenth century, various works were written in the course of the fourteenth century which imitated the Zohar and tried to develop its symbolism. Various compilations and interpretations were put together on the basis of the Zohar and other currents. In this period, however, there is little that points to a separate, independent creativity in the further elaboration of the material that had already been developed. In addition we see that all kabbalistic currents predating the appearance of the Zohar continue into the fourteenth century, especially those of the kabbalists of Gerona. Thus the school of Rabbi Solomon ibn Adret occupied itself in particular with the unveiling of the "secrets" of Nahmanides, one of the most important of the Gerona kabbalists. As we saw in section 2.4, Nahmanides had written kabbalistic doctrine in an indirect and deliberately obscure way, so that the mystical element in his work could only be grasped by someone with good understanding. The school of Adret endeavored to study and expound these vague allusions to Kabbalah in his work. The work *Kether Shem Tov* by Rabbi Shem Tov ibn Gaon is devoted entirely to this subject.

In this period Kabbalah found its way also to other parts of Europe, especially Italy. Even in Constantinople and Persia systematic kabbalistic discussions appeared. An important representative of the teaching of the Zohar in Italy was Menahem Recanati. His two main works, a commentary on the Torah and an interpretation of the reasons for the commandments, are based on the symbolism of the Zohar (see also § 1.6.4 on the commandments). Another important work is the anonymous *Sefer Ma'arekheth ha-Elohuth* (Book of the Divine Hierarchy), which served many as a manual for Kabbalah.

In the fifteenth century the political and religious climate for Jews on the Iberian Peninsula deteriorated to such an extent that there was scarcely any question of real kabbalistic literary activity. Many kabbalists had already sought safety in other countries before the expulsion of the Jews in 1492. In Italy, however, Kabbalah was still able to flourish. The rise of neo-Platonism there went well with the kabbalistic teaching. By means of translations of kabbalistic works into Latin, Kabbalah became a popular subject among Christian scholars too, who started to engage actively in Jewish mysticism. Christian kabbalists such as

Giovanni Pico della Mirandola and Johannes Reuchlin were of the opinion that Kabbalah confirmed the truth of Christian teaching.

Two of the most important books from this period are *Sefer ha-Qanah* (Book of [Rabbi Nehunyah ben] ha-Qanah) and *Sefer ha-Peli'ah* (Book of the Miracle). The former is a commentary on the reasons for the commandments in the form of miraculous anecdotes concerning Rabbi Nehunyah. The latter is a collection of older mystical traditions with an emphasis on mythical symbolism, in which the topic of messianic redemption also comes to the fore. In the classical period of Kabbalah, the messianic redemption played only a modest role. In the following chapter, however, we shall see that in Lurianic Kabbalah the mystical interpretation of the messianic element constitutes precisely a central component of kabbalistic doctrine.

4

Lurianic Kabbalah

The expulsion of the Jews from Spain in 1492 came as a horrendous and shocking catastrophe which left deep scars in the spiritual development of Judaism. A feeling of total bewilderment and despair confronted the Jews with pressing questions: What is the meaning of this disaster? What is the significance of the dispersion of the Jews? Is there still hope for the future?

These were the questions occupying all those who were affected by the event. The disaster of 1492 also had far-reaching consequences for Jewish mysticism. From that moment we see in Kabbalah a strong revival of messianic ideas—a complex of beliefs and ideas associated with the expectation of the coming of a Messiah. This messianism came to expression in Palestine in particular, in the Galilean town of Safed, where a kabbalistic movement developed that was to become known as Lurianic Kabbalah. Lurianic Kabbalah of course could draw upon messianic ideas that had been developed earlier, which in turn were based partly on motifs in the Hebrew Bible.

Before giving a survey of the prime features of Lurianic Kabbalah, we shall first look in more detail at Jewish messianism in order to gain some idea of the way in which the kabbalists adopted messianic ideas into their kabbalistic system.

1. Intermezzo: Messianism

1.1 Future expectation in the Hebrew Bible

The messianic idea in Judaism, as it developed from around 200 BCE to about 70 CE—in the so-called intertestamental period—derives partly from various ideas in the Old Testament, which were further developed and reinterpreted. In what follows we shall draw attention to some of the most important elements of these.

The term *mashiah* occurs in the Hebrew Bible with the meaning of "anointed one". Mashiah derives from the Hebrew verb *mashah*, "anoint". The Old Testament is familiar with the custom of anointing things or persons with oil for secular or sacred purposes. The term "anointed one" is used among other things for the reigning king of Israel or Judah or for a king in general whose kingship begins after he has undergone a rite of anointment. By means of the anointing an intimate relationship comes into being between God and the king; the king becomes sacrosanct and is endowed with the Spirit of the Lord. Besides the Israelite kings the Persian king Cyrus is also called a *mashiah* (Isa 45.1), because as God's instrument he allowed the Judean captives to return to Judah from Babylonian exile and gave permission for the ruined Temple of Solomon in Jerusalem to be rebuilt. The term *mashiah* is also sometimes used in connection with the high priest and on rare occasions in relation to the patriarchs. In the Old Testament the term "anointed" can clearly not be understood in the sense of the later idea of *the* Messiah, the eschatological figure who will appear at the end of days to bring in the Kingdom of God.

Another element we encounter in the Hebrew Bible is the theme of the future expectation of the people of Israel. In Chapter 2, section 2.1, on the history of ancient Israel, we have already seen how an end came to the united monarchy of Israel under kings David and Solomon after the latter's death. The kingdom split into two parts: the kingdom of Judah in the south and the kingdom of Israel in the north. We saw further how in 722 BCE northern Israel was deported to Assyria and how in 586 BCE a significant part of the Judean population was taken into exile in Babylon, and the Temple built by Solomon was destroyed. In the prophecies of the biblical prophets the future expectation of the people of Israel, stripped of its former glory, occupies an important position. The prophetic descriptions of what will befall the people of Israel in the future are very diverse; in this regard the Old Testament does not give a clear, firmly contoured, coherent and complete picture.

The loss of the former glory is due to the disruption of the relationship between God and his people, since Israel does not keep to his law. God metes out punishments to Israel and Judah, such as famine, plague, natural disasters, war, subjection to enemies and deportation, so that Israel will come to repentance and the disturbed relationship can be restored. At a future moment which God will choose, on the Day of the Lord, God will pass judgment on everything that is ungodly, on foreign nations, foreign gods, and the transgressions of his own people. Parts of the world and its population will be destroyed and swept away. Over against this prophecy of disaster in reference to the judgment on the Day of the Lord stands a prophecy of salvation which promises rescue. God promises rescue to those who have remained loyal to him. Sometimes there is also talk of a remnant in the prophecy, a remnant that will come to repentance at the last minute and will be spared. The people of Israel—or a remnant of it—will be saved by God. The same applies to other nations or at least to part of them.

A motif that also plays a role in the salvation is the political and national restoration of the people of Israel. The exiles of the kingdoms of Israel and Judah are collected, the northern ten-tribe Israel is reunited with the southern kingdom of Judah and the reunited people of Israel returns to the Promised Land. Israel's former time of glory and flourishing under kings David and Solomon is restored, while Jerusalem and the Temple on Mount Zion will be rebuilt. All the nations, or remnants of them which remain after the judgment, will recognize the God of Israel; besides the national character of prophecy a universal aspect is evident in the proclamation of salvation. God's reign over the world comes definitively into its own; Mount Zion with the Temple becomes the center of the restored kingdom and becomes meaningful for all nations of the world.

An important feature of these prophecies of salvation is formed by the appearance of a future king from the House of David. Not only does the people return to the Promised Land, but also the old monarchy is restored. Thus God's promise to king David that his House will exist forever is fulfilled. Although the salvation takes place on God's initiative alone, the leadership of this operation lies with the anointed king from the Davidic dynasty; he brings about the national and political restoration of Israel. With this restoration not only does a time of peace and justice break out, but also one of welfare and earthly happiness.

As with the term *mashiah*, so also in the case of the anointed king who will restore the monarchy in the future, this figure in the Old Testament cannot be equated with *the* Messiah who will appear at the end of time. Precisely the same applies, by the way, to other allusions we sometimes meet in the Hebrew Bible; such terms as "son of man" (Dan 7.13), the "servant of the Lord" (e.g. Isa 42.1-7) and "Shiloh" (the meaning of which is unclear; Gen 49.10-12) can certainly not be regarded as allusions to the eschatological figure of *the* Messiah.

As has been said, it is not possible to derive a fixed and coherent picture of messianism from the Hebrew Bible. Study of the prophecies of calamity and salvation by the various biblical prophets separately will produce a much more complex and nuanced picture than we have sketched here in summary form. Each prophet who takes up the theme of judgment and salvation in his prophecies does this in his own way, placing emphasis at different points. Sometimes, by the way, we simply have to recognize that the precise meaning of a particular prophecy escapes us.

Clearly present in the background in the prophets' descriptions are the political and social conditions of their own day. In line with their view of their own time the fixed pattern of catastrophe, salvation and restoration were projected onto contemporary events. Expectations of a utopian future arise—though not always—in times of suffering, injustice or oppression. The prophet Amos, who lived before the conquest of the kingdom of Israel by Assyria (722 BCE), projected the process of crisis, salvation and ideal time completely into the future. The prophet Jeremiah, however, who witnessed the destruction of the Temple in Jerusalem (586 BCE), was of the opinion that the crisis or catastrophe took place in his own time, while he placed the salvation and the ideal time still in the future. The prophecy of Deutero-Isaiah (Isa 40ff.) is played out against the background of the Persian king Cyrus, who in 538 BCE allowed the Judean exiles to return to Judah from Babylonian exile and to rebuild the ruined Temple of Solomon. According to Deutero-Isaiah, crisis and catastrophe (destruction of the Temple and Babylonian exile) had taken place in the past and the time of salvation (the return) had begun in his own time. Only the ideal time was still projected into the future. In later times too we shall see that there is a constant relationship between the sort of future expectation and the contemporary circumstances.

A feature of all biblical future expectations is the fact that the events described take place in one world—the world we know. All events will be realized visibly for everyone in this world. The time that precedes judgment and salvation runs directly into the time of national and political restoration of the people of Israel. The verdict on the Day of the Lord of which the prophets speak is thus not the very last thing that will take place in our world and so cannot be taken as the later developed idea of the Last Judgment at the end of time. Another feature of the biblical concept of salvation is that this always has a collective character: it is for the people—or several peoples—as a whole; salvation does not relate to the individual person. We clearly see, moreover, both a restorative and a utopian element coming to the fore in the biblical future expectation. The expectation that the time of the former glory of Israel will return can be characterized as restorative; people look back into the past and expect the restoration of everything that was lost. In contrast with this there stands the expectation that in the future something will be realized that has never previously taken place. This way of looking to the future can be characterized as utopian. An example of a utopian picture would be the prophecy that in the ideal future the wolf will lie down in peace with the lamb (Isa 11.6) or that all nations will go on a pilgrimage to Mount Zion (Isa 2.2-4). The restorative and utopian elements, however, are not strictly distinguishable; in the visions of the future one finds both the restoration of everything that has been lost and elements that have never previously been realized. Below, and in the following chapters, we shall see that in the historical development of Jewish messianism there has always been a tension between restorative and utopian visions of the future.

1.2 Jewish apocalypticism and eschatology

In the intertestamental period we see that future expectations undergo an enormous growth in relation to what we find in the Hebrew Bible. It is in this time that we meet a strong apocalyptic and eschatological current.

The term *apocalypse* means "revelation, unveiling" and relates to a form of literature which has to do with mysterious revelations that are transmitted or interpreted by supernal beings such as angels. In these revelations an eschatological picture is sketched, i.e. a picture of events at the end of time (the term comes from the Greek *eschaton*, "the last"). Jewish apocalypticism was a current which arose from the third or second century BCE and came to flourish in the first century BCE; it further extended and reinterpreted future expectations found in the Hebrew Bible. The experiences and ideas of the apocalyptists have come down to us in their pseudepigraphic writings; they placed the revelations on the lips of great biblical personalities such as Enoch, Moses, Abraham, Solomon and Baruch or some supernal being.

Within this apocalyptic current the figure of the Messiah occupies an important position. Here we encounter for the first time a figure who comes to save the world at the end of time. The biblical *Mashiah*, "anointed one", not only became *Messiah* under the influence of Greek (*Messias*), but at the same time it underwent an expansion of

meaning. Gradually the biblical concept of the anointed one was extended to a person to whom God had assigned a very special task. This
latter meaning then developed again into *the* Messiah, someone who at
the end of time would appear as the savior and redeemer of humankind and the world and introduce the Kingdom of God. All the Old
Testament texts concerning the future anointed king of the House of
David which play a part in the national restoration of the people of
Israel, and the texts about "the son of man", "the servant of the Lord"
and "Shiloh", are now related to this one specific eschatological Messiah figure.

A second important feature of apocalyptic literature is the view of
the end of time. The apocalypticists foresaw in the future an abrupt
and absolute end to our known world and its history, after which a
new world order would come into being, which would be radically
different in character. While the Hebrew Bible is familiar only with
one continuous world, in apocalypticism we find a sharp break in
time, two totally different and opposing periods or aeons: *this* world
and the *World to Come*. In their descriptions the apocalypticists placed
strong emphasis on the dramatic and catastrophic aspect of the end, an
end which moreover would include many supernatural and miraculous
elements. Redemption would go hand in hand with the most horrendous events, disasters and wars. The former world, which is associated
with a dominion of darkness, disappears in order to make room for a
new world of the reign of God.

For the apocalypticists God's judgment as in the Old Testament becomes the Last Judgment which will take place in this world. While
the biblical notion describes the judgment and the salvation in collective terms, the individual person is now also involved in the transition
from this world to the World to Come; in the course of the Last
Judgment his or her deeds are weighed in the balance. Closely connected with the Last Judgment is the resurrection of the dead, an idea
that can also be found, to some extent, in the Old Testament (e.g.
Ezek 37.1-14). In most apocalyptic works this resurrection is understood very concretely. As soon as the end of time has begun and the
Last Judgment has taken place, the souls of people who have already
died will emerge from their resting place and reunite with their bodies
which lie buried here on earth. This resurrection is necessary, since
otherwise those of the deceased who lived a good and just earthly life,
would not be able to be part of the imminent messianic kingdom,
while those of the deceased who had lived their earthly life in sin
would escape their punishment. During the Last Judgment, then, jus-

tice will be done to the dead and the living. With regard to the fate of righteous and sinful souls after physical death, and the nature of their resting-place in other realities, ideas in the apocalyptic literature differ considerably.

Another difference between the Bible and apocalyptic literature is that biblical prophecy of the national restoration of Israel and the Davidic dynasty is situated in a much larger, cosmic framework. It is not just a national affair, but a matter of events that have affected the whole of humankind and the whole of history from beginning to end. In the view of the apocalypticists all the biblical prophecies concerning the messianic future had to be interpreted and read in the light of the absolute end of this world, the Last Judgment and the dawn of a radically new age for the whole cosmos. We have to note, by the way, that no rounded and uniform picture emerges from the apocalyptic literature either. Various works give divergent views, while within a single book we also encounter contradictory ideas.

A feature of Jewish apocalypticism is the way in which it transformed biblical ideas of the future into a secret knowledge. The apocalyptists believed firmly that by means of revelations they had received knowledge previously hidden by God, with reference to events at the end of time. While in biblical prophecy nothing is to be found concerning a hidden knowledge—not even in the book of Daniel, the only apocalyptic work that is included in the Hebrew Bible—we see in apocalypticism the emergence of closed groups which occupied themselves with esoteric speculation on the way in which God directed the world and on the awful horrors which would accompany the end of our world. What precisely the background was to the transition from biblical prophecy to the view of a hidden knowledge known only to initiates, is still not fully clear.

In Chapter 2 we referred to the complex relationship between apocalypticism, Gnosticism, the origins of Christianity and the Dead Sea scrolls. Here we shall indicate just one fundamental difference between Christianity and Judaism in reference to messianism. Christianity recognized all the expectations regarding the Messiah ("anointed" is translated into Greek as *christos*) in the historical person of Jesus of Nazareth. For Christianity the eschatological figure had thus indeed come, while in Judaism expectations were still directed to the future. For the Jews the messianic age could not possibly have dawned in an unredeemed world which remained full of injustice, sin, oppression and war.

1.3 Messianism in the rabbinic period

Messianic ideas are found arbitrarily scattered throughout rabbinic literature. There is no chapter to be found in which a coherent picture is given of rabbinic ideas on the catastrophe at the end of time, the Messiah and the World to Come (on the problem of system in rabbinic literature see also Chapter 3, § 1.6). At this point we shall discuss a number of the important aspects.

Some of the rabbinic messianic traditions build upon themes of apocalyptic literature. Rabbinic Judaism too, which emerged after the destruction of the Second Temple, had an apocalyptic current. The rabbinic apocalyptists formed one section of the closed groups that cherished esoteric traditions handed down from the intertestamental period. These traditions on the horrors of the end time, the Messiah, this world and the World to Come, the Last Judgment and the expectation of the national restoration of Israel and the Davidic dynasty, are echoed in a whole variety of forms in the Talmud and the midrashic collections. Around the third century CE many elements from esoteric apocalyptic traditions were to form part of the mystical activity of the ascent through the heavenly realms and the descent to the throne of glory (for the transition from esoteric speculation to mystical activity see Chapter 2, §§ 4 and 6.1). During the ascent, those visions dealing with in particular what awaits the individual in the hereafter occupy an important position. In addition, in rabbinic literature we also find further elaborations of biblical ideas about the future.

An important point for the rabbis was how the transition from this world to the utopian kingdom of peace would occur. Broadly speaking, there are two views on this. According to the first, the coming of the Messiah would be preceded by disasters and horrors, called the "birthpangs of the Messiah" (*hevlei ha-mashiah*). The old world disappears in the catastrophe and the new age dawns, the time of the Messiah. The messianic age or the World to Come thus begins after the catastrophe. According to the second view the Messiah appears still in this world. His coming is the sign that catastrophe and Last Judgment are at hand and the redemption of this world of darkness is about to dawn. According to this view the days of the Messiah and the World to Come are not the same thing. The messianic age is played out in this world and forms a transition between this world and the World to Come; it will come to an end as a result of the catastrophe and the Last Judgment.

In the rabbinic period we see the question arise whether humans can accelerate the process of redemption through their deeds. Neither the Hebrew Bible nor apocalyptic literature knows the idea that a person can speed up the redemption. Both the Bible and apocalypticism assumed that the redemption was an unexpected and sudden breakthrough of the divine world into our world. History does not develop gradually towards salvation according to a fixed, predictable pattern; there comes an end to history at a moment, a day and an hour known only to God. A person cannot influence this intervention of God. In relation to the question whether the redemption presupposes a passive or an active human role, we see a certain ambivalence emerging in rabbinic literature. On the one hand there is the view that a person can do nothing other than wait passively until redemption dawns, and on the other hand we encounter the opinion that a person can actively bring the redemption closer through his or her actions. The rabbis wondered whether the coming of the messianic age was linked to particular conditions or not. Against the opinion that only God knows the day and hour, which humans cannot influence, there was the opinion that Israel must first be brought to repentance before God intervenes. Many tried by means of complicated calculations to establish in advance when the time of redemption would dawn. Later in this book we shall see that both the opinions described above concerning the character of the transition from one age to the other as well as the tension between a passive and an active approach to messianism, were to play a significant role in Jewish mysticism.

Although tradition contains many different statements about the Messiah, he still remains a rather vague figure. The traditional literature does not allow us to form a sharp picture of precisely who the Messiah is, as a person, what his name is and what qualities he possesses. There were also rabbis who had no truck with apocalyptic and messianic currents within Judaism and who actively resisted them. They did not give credence to bold notions of disasters, miraculous events and the coming of a new heaven and earth, but believed that the difference between this world and the messianic age was merely that Israel was no longer subjected to other peoples. We shall meet this polemic between apocalyptic and anti-apocalyptic below in our discussion of Maimonides and his followers (§ 1.4).

In the rabbinic tradition we regularly meet the idea of two messianic figures. One of these is the Messiah, son of Joseph, and the other the Messiah, son of David. The Messiah ben Joseph, who is associated with the northern, ten-tribe Israel, leads the armies in the fight against Israel's enemies. He dies a hero's death in this struggle, after which he is succeeded by the Messiah ben David, who is associated with the

kingdom of Judah and the Davidic dynasty. This Messiah ben David
will ultimately triumph. The origins of this tradition are not very clear,
though possibly some passages in Zechariah 3 and 4 contributed to the
idea of two eschatological figures.

Another idea is that of the wars of Gog and Magog. In Ezekiel 38
and 39 a vision is presented in which God wages war against Gog, the
king of Meshech and Tubal, from the land of Magog. Remarkably
enough, later traditions speak of two persons, Gog and Magog. The
war which God waged was connected with the wars at the end of
days, the birthpangs of the Messiah and the Last Judgment. All earlier
wars and horrors pale into insignificance in comparison with the
apocalyptic wars of Gog and Magog which will precede the messianic
age.

One of the important events which will take place in the end-time,
according to rabbinic tradition, is the reunification of the ten lost tribes
of the northern kingdom of Israel with Benjamin and Judah, the tribes
of the southern kingdom of Judah. It was believed that the descendants
of the northern, ten-tribe kingdom of Israel deported to Assyria in 722
BCE still exist somewhere in the world. According to the tradition the
ten lost tribes lived beyond a river by the name of Sambation. At the
end of time these tribes from beyond the river would reappear, to
reunite with the tribes of Benjamin and Judah, to reconstitute the
restored Israel.

One of the works with a strong apocalyptic-messianic bent is the
pseudepigraphic Book of Zerubbabel, which was written some time
after the completion of the Talmud. This work stands entirely within
the realms of future expectation and the end-times. The book contains
a vision placed on the lips of Zerubbabel, a Judean leader from shortly
after the Babylonian exile, although the story takes place against the
background of the wars between Byzantium and the Persians, before
the emergence of Islam. The vision describes in detail the events of the
end-times. It tells of the time before the coming of the Messiah, when
a certain Armilus is king of Rome. This satanic king brings the whole
world and all religions under his domination. With the exception of
the Jews, all nations put their faith in this Armilus, who is described in
this book as a monster and viewed by the anonymous author as an
incarnation of Jesus. The Messiah ben Joseph leads the armies against
Armilus and he is helped in this by a woman named Hephzibah, the
mother of the Messiah ben David. After Armilus has conquered and
killed the Messiah ben Joseph, Jerusalem is saved by Hephzibah. Then
the Messiah ben David arises. With his triumph over Armilus the

messianic kingdom commences. The ideas we find in the Book of Zerubbabel had a great influence on medieval Judaism. The book became the model for anyone who wanted to describe the coming of the Messiah and the disasters and wars at the end of days.

The biblical, apocalyptic and rabbinic ideas discussed above, as well as other themes, found their way into all layers of religious Judaism. Messianic ideas became a fixed component of the religious views of Judaism. We see this most clearly in the liturgy, which often gives expression to longings for the Messiah. In due course an extensive apocalyptic popular literature evolved, in which free reign was generally given to the imagination; it served as a support and comfort to people, especially in difficult times and circumstances.

In the following section we shall see what line was taken by classical Kabbalah and Jewish philosophy with regard to the traditional notions of apocalypticism and messianism.

1.4 Messianism in Jewish philosophy and classical Kabbalah

In the previous chapter we looked in detail at the various ways in which philosophy and Kabbalah tried to breathe new life into the tradition by interpreting it in a new way. In this section we shall add another theme to this: messianism.

With the exception of just a few philosophers, among them Sa'adya Gaon, Jewish philosophy had little affinity with apocalyptic feelings and utopian notions of the World to Come. Rational philosophy in the middle ages was predominantly restorative in nature; the utopian element was pushed into the background as much as possible. The reason for this is clear: the highest goal of philosophy was a universal knowledge of God. By means of Greek thought, the study of Torah and the observance of the commandments, a person should come to the true understanding of God. To attain this, however, the philosopher did not need to wait for the future; his efforts were not dependent on an apocalyptic picture of the end of time. Some philosophers, Maimonides among them, then had no truck with apocalyptic and catastrophic notions which shook the world to its foundations, like those circulating among the common people.

Moses Maimonides formulated his attitude to apocalypticism and messianism in his law codex *Mishneh Torah* (the tractate on the Laws of the Kings, chs. 11-12 and the tractate on repentance and penitence, chs. 8-9) and in his commentary on the Mishnah (introduction to *Sanhedrin* 10). He expresses the conviction that the Messiah will appear in the future, that the Davidic kingdom will be restored to its former glory, that the Messiah will gather all the exiles of Israel from the diaspora and will rebuild the Temple—in brief, above all a restorative view.

Like the Hebrew Bible Maimonides saw no absolute end of history nor a radical break in the historical process. He emphasized that the world we know will simply continue to exist and that everything will be played out in it. There is no talk of a Last Judgment or of a World to Come that would be a completely new creation ("a new heaven and a new earth"). On the contrary, the messianic age is not a world of miracles; in the days of the Messiah precisely the same natural laws apply as in the preceding time. Just as creation will not undergo any change, so too the revelation, which has been given for eternity, will not undergo any changes; the commandments will not be revoked, but will simply retain their binding validity. Maimonides emphasizes that the Messiah is not a figure who will perform great miracles, such as bringing people back from the dead. The true Messiah cannot be recognized by the miracles he will perform but by the extent to which he succeeds in his worldly mission. If this figure succeeds in rebuilding the Temple and gathering the exiles, this is the proof that he is the true Messiah.

The only utopian element in Maimonides' picture of the future lies in the fact that in the messianic age all humanity will recognize the God of Israel; Torah study and contemplative knowledge of God will become the primary occupations in life, while Israel will no longer sigh under the yoke of its enemies.

Maimonides liked to see his own views of these things accepted as authoritative. To support this he would quote an anti-apocalyptic passage of rabbinic literature that supported his opinion, leaving contrary viewpoints unmentioned. The diversity of opinions which are evident both in the Bible and in rabbinic literature, Maimonides explains as follows: the biblical statements about the future must sometimes be understood allegorically and in other regards they are not always clear; further, the rabbis possessed no tradition on the matter and did not agree among themselves. For anyone who still doubted after these arguments, Maimonides stated that the whole question of the messianic age did not in any case belong to the main features of religion and that it was much more important to strive towards the spiritual perfection of the individual in the World to Come.

One of Maimonides' objections to what in his view were erroneous expectations of a utopian future was the potentially antinomistic nature of apocalypticism; even just the idea that the commandments might no longer be valid in a new age was abhorrent to him. Although Maimonides did not succeed in silencing apocalyptic viewpoints, since his time the anti-apocalyptic tendency in Judaism has been constantly represented.

From its origins until the expulsion from Spain, classical Kabbalah added no new or revolutionary ideas to the body of messianic material as it had developed from the time of the Bible through to rabbinic Judaism. Messianism is, to be sure, present in the works of classical kabbalists, but it does not play any prominent role. Classical Kabbalah was not so interested in the end of this world; it directed its attention to the past, to the primordial beginnings of creation. For the kabbalists, redemption meant an individual, inner process of return to the perfect state of before the fall. They investigated the whole process from the emergence of creation, the precise sequence of all phases that led up to our creation, and the question of how the original state of perfection had become disturbed by the fall of Adam. The kabbalists thus tried to seek out the secrets of the primordial origins. By placing emphasis on a redemption that has to be sought in the restoration of the original situation, classical Kabbalah marks itself as predominantly restorative. The end of history, the catastrophes and the national and political restoration of Israel did not occupy the kabbalists so much, although they did not deny or ignore these ideas. The idea that the redemption could be accelerated by human actions is not found in classical Kabbalah.

Still, the utopian element is not completely absent from classical kabbalistic literature either. We find, for example, statements that at the moment of redemption, creation will take the form that God originally intended. After the redemption the original character of creation, which had remained hidden from humans as a result of the fall, would be revealed. The secrets of the Torah would also be revealed; the mystical meaning which the kabbalists unveiled in the Torah would become the literal meaning of the Scriptures in the World to Come. With a few exceptions, in this regard the Zohar more or less constitutes a reiteration of utopian elements from traditional midrash: the miracles that accompany the redemption are given detailed attention, as also the theme of the birthpangs of the Messiah.

Closely connected with messianism is the question of the nature of the Torah. The kabbalists were convinced of the preexistence of the Torah (see Chapter 3, § 1.4) and wondered what this original Torah looked like before the cosmos had been thrown off course by the fall.

Partly on the basis of an old tradition according to which the real sequence of the Torah was not known to humans, they came to the
conclusion that the Torah we know, which anyone can read, is not
the same as the perfect Torah from before creation. In classical kabbalistic literature a distinction is also made between the Torah of
Emanation (*Torah de-Atsiluth*) and the Torah of Creation (*Torah de-
Beri'ah*). The Torah of Emanation is a spiritual and perfect Torah
which forms a unity with God himself in the world of the sefiroth. In
our concrete world, the post-fall world, this spiritual Torah could only
become crystallized to a very limited degree in the Torah as we know
it in our reality and which the kabbalists refer to as the Torah of creation. By virtue of the imperfect character of our world the spiritual
Torah could only take the form of a collection of commandments and
prohibitions. Observance of the commandments which indicated precisely what was good or evil, pure or impure, and what was permitted
and what was not permitted, was seen as the way in which humans
could restore the original state from before the fall. Nonetheless, the
spiritual aspects of the Torah of Emanation are present in hidden form
in our Torah, and can be discerned by the mystic.

The kabbalists indulged in a great deal of speculation about the nature of the spiritual Torah, hidden from us. What, then, would this
have looked like, precisely? This problem was automatically connected
with the question of what the nature of the Torah would be if, at
some point in the future, the chasm running through all the worlds
were to be repaired and humans were to regain their original pre-fall
state. In the future messianic age—the kabbalists were agreed about
this—the spiritual aspects of the Torah of Emanation would be fully
revealed. One important question had to do with the Torah of Emanation and the Torah of Creation, which were contrasted with each
other for the first time in *Ra'ya Mehemna* (Faithful Shepherd) and
Tiqqunei ha-Zohar (Supplements to the Zohar), the two anonymous
works within the Zohar corpus. In rabbinic literature of the third
Christian century already, people had wondered whether with the
coming of the Messiah the commandments would be rescinded or that
the Torah we know would remain fully valid in the messianic age (*b
Sanhedrin* 99a). The classical kabbalists too debated whether the yoke
of the commandments would be revoked in the messianic age and
under the spiritual Torah. Some, like Maimonides, were convinced
that the present commandments would be eternally valid. Others, on
the other hand, believed that there was no room any more in the Torah of Emanation for commandments and prohibitions. The idea of

various manifestations of Torah—a Torah of spirituality, a Torah of this creation and a Torah of the messianic age—was given a worked-out application in *Sefer ha-Temunah* (Book of the Figure), in which each world cycle has its own Torah (see Chapter 3, § 2.6).

The topic of the nature of the spiritual Torah in the messianic age was to play a large part in Lurianic Kabbalah and in particular in the Kabbalah of Shabbetai Zevi. The expulsion of 1492 meant the beginnings of a complete transformation of kabbalistic doctrine. Whereas before 1492 Kabbalah was oriented towards the original perfection in the past, Jewish mysticism after that time had, above all, a utopian notion of a World to Come in the future. With regard to the messianic age, the classical kabbalists adopted a waiting, passive attitude, while from 1492 Kabbalah worked towards active participation in the process of redemption.

2. Messianism after 1492 and the rise of Safed

After the misery of the expulsion from Spain, the feeling grew among many Jews that redemption from this world must be close at hand. As often happened in the past in times of crisis, the familiar structures of catastrophe and redemption were projected into one's own time (see §§ 1.1 and 1.3 of this chapter), and many interpreted the expulsion from Spain as the dawning of the catastrophe of the end-time. The birthpangs of the Messiah had begun; the Messiah would now come quickly, after which the exile of the Jewish people would end and the ideal age could dawn.

Shortly before the expulsion of 1492, but especially in the period after it, we then also see a vigorous revival of apocalypticism among a section of the kabbalists. (This is not of course to say that messianism and apocalypticism necessarily or always emerge as a result of historical crises.) People prepared themselves for the wars associated with the end and the coming messianic kingdom. The appearance of Martin Luther, for instance, was seen as an indication that the power of the Church was about to collapse and as a sign that the end would soon come. The first decades after 1492 are marked by an energetic development of emotionally-charged, messianically-tinted apocalyptic visions.

With the Spanish kabbalist Joseph de la Reina (ca. 1470) we already find the beginnings of the swing from a passive to an active form of messianism; by means of practical Kabbalah—the application of magical techniques—he aimed to force a breakthrough of the end of time.

One of the last Jewish philosophers of the middle ages, Isaac Abrabanel (1437–1509), who personally experienced the expulsion from Spain, wrote a systematic overview of all the apocalyptic and messianic ideas in Judaism. Like many others of his day he too occupied himself with calculations of the time of the end. In this regard he had a very concrete and also political view of the course of events. On the basis of his interpretation of the book of Daniel, Abrabanel came to the conclusion that the redemption would dawn in 1503. It need occasion no surprise that each forecaster arrived at a different year, depending on his point of view.

A well-known proclaimer of the imminent redemption in this period was the kabbalist rabbi, Abraham ben Eliezer ha-Levi. On his travels through many countries he spread an apocalyptic interpretation of his own time. He called his hearers to repentance and caused great consternation with his pronouncements that the birthpangs of the Messiah had begun in 1492 and would end in 1531.

From the steadily growing stream of apocalyptic works two well-known anonymous works are worthy of mention which clearly reflect the spiritual climate of this period: *Kaf ha-Qetoreth* (Incense Vessel) and *Sefer ha-Meshiv* (Book of the Revelation). In both works—the Incense Vessel interprets the Psalms and the Book of the Revelation is a commentary on the Torah—the Bible is read in the light of the events of the end-times; everything pointed in a symbolic way to the exile of the Jewish people in the diaspora and the imminent redemption from this world by the Messiah. The Psalms are viewed as apocalyptic battle-songs which constitute a secret magic weapon in the wars of the end in order to defeat the powers opposed to God.

Roughly from the time of the expulsion we see an important new development in the history of Kabbalah taking place. Thus far, Kabbalah had been the preserve of a small elite of scholars; the mystical teaching was not easily accessible to the ordinary person. When, under the influence of the expulsion from Spain, the messianic body of ideas became a fixed component of Kabbalah, a change came about in this situation. Instead of the difficult kabbalistic theories about the world of the sefiroth, precisely the apocalyptic and messianic elements lent themselves extraordinarily well to popular interpretation. Gradually the Kabbalah began to permeate through to broader layers of the Jewish population. This expansion of Kabbalah resulted in a great demand for systematic kabbalistic manuals; in this period we see introductory commentaries appear, as well as standard works and compilations of all sorts of mystical traditions. The work *Avodath ha-Qodesh* (Service of

God) by Rabbi Meir ibn Gabbai, which attempts to give a comprehensive overview of Kabbalah, is an example of the great need to take cognizance of kabbalistic doctrine. Kabbalah study per se became a part of the intellectual development of the educated Jew; people studied the Zohar, for instance, as one of the great works of Jewish literature. From this point on, Kabbalah counted as a integral part of Jewish culture.

Approximately forty years after the expulsion from Spain, when all hope and expectation of a speedy redemption had still not been fulfilled, apocalyptic activism collapsed. Because of the emotions concerning the exile, which had become almost unbearable, the traumatic experience of the expulsion and the feelings of disappointment with regard to the non-appearance of the redemption, many Sephardic Jews (i.e. originating from Spain and Portugal) began to seek ways of finding an answer to the whys and wherefores of exile and suffering. People began to ponder over the origins and circumstances of the expulsion. Now that the concrete external redemption had not arrived, attention shifted to a spiritual, mystical understanding of redemption. As a result, between 1540 and 1580 a whole new mystical movement emerged in which apocalyptic-messianic and kabbalistic ideas were definitively connected with each other.

Both the kabbalists of the classical period and those of the first forty years following the expulsion had added little new material to traditional ideas concerning the Messiah and redemption. While people were still convinced, after the expulsion, that the beginnings of the end-times had set in, it was thought that the dramatic events could be explained on the basis of traditional views of the last days. In this period there is no noticeable inclination to arrive at a reinterpretation of Judaism against the background of the expulsion from Spain. Why should one develop new ideas if the end had already announced itself? As soon as the realization dawned, however, that the end had not yet begun after all, the situation changed considerably.

In the town of Safed in the north of Palestine a new form of Kabbalah arose, in which messianism formed a very important element. In Safed, which was already a flourishing community at the time of the expulsion, a section of the kabbalists had congregated who had left for North Africa, Turkey, Syria, Palestine or other countries. The kabbalists of Safed began to think about explanations for the expulsion from Spain. They wondered what, precisely, was the nature of this world, in which the Jewish people had to live in exile. Why had the expulsion hit the Jews, of all people? What was the meaning of all the trials and all the suffering?

An important reason given for the current misery was that the Jews had not kept the commandments sufficiently well. Strict observance of the commandments was given renewed attention and study of the Halakhah in general was again undertaken seriously. Many blamed the philosophers in particular for all this; after all, with their allegorizing philosophy they had contributed to the fact that many people in Spain had no longer taken observance of the daily commandments so seriously. It had to be said that philosophy in general did not seem capable of formulating satisfactory answers to the pressing questions of the meaning of suffering. Its abstract ideas about the purity of the monotheistic notion of God and its detached definition of evil as the absence of good did not strike a chord with people in times of great crisis (cf. also Chapter 3, § 1.6.5). This probably accounts for the fact that philosophy lost its popularity for a number of centuries.

Various groups and schools formed in Safed, individual students of which also began their own schools. Safed produced great halakhists and kabbalists. To the greats of the city belonged, among others, Rabbi Joseph Taitatsak, Rabbi Jacob Berav and Rabbi Solomon Alkabets, as well as Rabbi Moses Alsheikh, who was famous for his homilies (synagogue sermons) and his mystical ethics. We shall give attention below to two great personalities who made a significant contribution to the standing of Safed before the appearance of the Kabbalah of Luria: Joseph Caro and Moses Cordovero.

2.1 Joseph Caro

Rabbi Joseph ben Ephraim Caro (1488-1575) was born on the Iberian Peninsula and after the expulsion came via Turkey to Palestine. He was famous as a halakhist, among other things on account of his codification of the regulations for daily Jewish life, entitled *Shulhan Arukh* (Set Table), a work which still enjoys great respect today.

As well as being a halakhist, however, Joseph Caro was a convinced kabbalist. He was inspired by a *maggid*, a spiritual force which revealed itself and spoke to him. Caro had always felt a strong affinity for the Mishnah (see Chapter 1, § 2.1). This maggid presented itself to him as the spirit of the Mishnah: "I am the Mishnah that speaks through your mouth; I am the soul of the Mishnah; I, the Mishnah and you are united into one soul." The maggid generally appeared at night; while Caro lay motionless, the voice rang out through him. This voice was clearly audible to bystanders through Caro's mouth. Although they recognized Caro's voice in this voice, Caro experienced it as something that did not come from himself. After the maggid had manifested himself, Joseph Caro could always remember precisely what the maggid had told him.

He kept a sort of mystical diary of these sayings, in which he recorded all his spiritual experiences. This work is known by the title *Sefer ha-Maggid* (Book of the Maggid), also called *Maggid Mesharim* (Maggid of Uprightness). The term maggid is ambiguous in this context: it can mean both "preacher" and also a spiritual power which reveals itself to the mystic. The latter meaning was ascribed to the word *maggid* particularly in the Safed of the sixteenth century.

Not only did the maggid converse with Joseph Caro about the secrets of the Torah and kabbalistic questions of how the sefiroth had developed from En Sof or their function and relationship; it also spoke to him about Caro's own marital life and other personal matters. The maggid directed him to live an ascetic life, admonishing him if he had gone astray in any matter, if he had had more to drink than was strictly necessary, had sat too long at the dinner table or had gone to bed too late. It is striking that if Joseph Caro had a guilty conscience about something—for instance at having spent too much time on worldly pleasures instead of Torah study—the maggid immediately appeared and comforted or admonished him, chastised or stimulated him. In general the maggid confirmed the ambitions that Caro cherished; thus for example he promised Caro that he was worthy to lead the largest body of students in Israel. Occasionally the maggid passed on to Caro greetings from God himself and the members of the heavenly Talmudic academy.

Joseph Caro ardently desired to be allowed to die a martyr's death at the stake. The maggid confirmed repeatedly to him that his wish would be granted. He was very much inspired in this desire by the striking figure of Salomo Molcho (ca. 1501-1532). This rabbi, mystic and diplomat from Portugal made a great impression on everyone who came into contact with him, by virtue of his great erudition, coupled with a smart appearance and charming manner. Like Caro, Molcho also had a maggid. But through this maggid, as well as in his dreams and visions, all kinds of events were revealed to him in relation to the speedy coming of the Messiah. During his wanderings through Italy and Turkey—where he may have come into contact with Joseph Caro—he gave heavily politically-charged addresses on the coming messianic age, to both Jewish and Christian mystics. He was to be found in the higher echelons of society, at the court and even in church circles. Pope Clement VII and other church authorities were very much impressed by his personality and protected him. Despite the protection of the pope and the church authorities, through the machinations of his arch-enemy, the Jewish physician Jacob Mantino, Molcho ultimately fell into the hand of Emperor Charles V, who handed him over to the Inquisition. In Mantua in 1532, Molcho was executed at the stake as a heretic. After his martyrdom he was regarded as one of the "saints" of Kabbalah. There has always been a great deal of speculation as to the extent to which the promises, favors and predictions made to Joseph Caro by the maggid, had been fulfilled. One thing is sure, in any case: despite the "promise" of the maggid that Caro would find his so-desired death at the stake, he died a natural death in 1475 at the age of eighty-eight.

Among those who are inclined to see Judaism as a rational, abstract and monotheistic religion par excellence, opinions about Joseph Caro are very much divided. Some refuse to take Joseph Caro seriously because of what for them is the pathological and absurd nature of his personality. Others praise his halakhic standard works and ignore his kabbalistic activities or emphasize that the halakhic work should be seen quite separately from his kabbalistic work. Others again think, against the weight of evidence, that the Book of the Maggid was not written by Joseph Caro.

Even among those who study Jewish mysticism seriously one can often detect great reservations with respect to anything that smacks of magic in Kabbalah. The reality, however, is that the kabbalists of Safed—among whom were many leading figures—occupied themselves, alongside their theoretical interest in the divine world, with all sorts of practical magical techniques. Having a maggid was no exception for mystically inclined rabbis of this period. Further on in this chapter we shall look in more detail at the connection between theoretical and practical aspects in Kabbalah (see § 3.2.5).

2.2 Moses Cordovero

Rabbi Moses ben Jacob Cordovero (1522-1570) was one of the greatest kabbalistic thinkers and writers of this period. The most striking feature of his work is the systematic approach that speaks from it; where other kabbalists write things that are sometimes mutually contradictory or restrict themselves to a certain aspect of Kabbalah, Cordovero attempted to bring together the various currents and ideas from the rise of Kabbalah into a single, ordered and systematic whole. His attempt to meld the often contradictory ideas into a synthesis betrays a sharp and profound way of thinking.

The Zohar in particular held Cordovero's special attention. He wrote a very extensive commentary on each page of the Zohar, which we know by the title *Or Yaqar* (Precious Light). Apart from the fact that this work contains Cordovero's own views on the subject of Kabbalah, it also gives us an insight into numerous earlier kabbalistic ideas, which he mentions and discusses. In another important work by his hand, too, *Pardes Rimmonim* (Garden of the Pomegranates), the Zohar occupies an important position. *Pardes Rimmonim* is a thematically arranged handbook of Kabbalah: each chapter contains a systematic treatment of one particular kabbalistic topic. Through the systematic arrangement and the clear manner of exposition this book gives an excellent overview of the various aspects kabbalistic doctrine.

In several of his works, Cordovero displays special interest in the relationship between En Sof and the sefiroth. As we know, there was a great deal of speculation about this problem in Kabbalah (see also Chapter 3, § 1.6.2). An important aspect of the relationship between En Sof and the sefiroth was the question whether the sefiroth were of the same divine substance as the deity of En Sof, or whether they were merely instruments or vessels by means of which the deity performs its various activities in the world. We might summarize this question in our own words as follows: If we imagine that God is water, are the sefiroth then drops of water, or are they the cups in which the water is carried to the world? Most kabbalists up to the time of the Zohar were of the opinion that the sefiroth were of the same substance as En Sof. However, from the time of the writing of *Tiqqunei ha-Zohar* onwards, it was commonly supposed that the sefiroth were merely vessels or instruments. Since Cordovero still thought that *Tiqqunei ha-Zohar* was part of the Zohar (see Chapter 3, § 2.6.4), here he stumbled on what was apparently an internal contradiction in the Zohar. From his systematic perspective Cordovero attempted to reconcile the two views. For him the sefiroth were *both* divine in substance *and* vessels; though the sefiroth formed the vessels or instruments by means of which the divine substance is operative in the world, at the same time they were so saturated with divine substance that in practice there could be no noticeable difference between them. In comparison Cordovero pointed to the frequently mentioned relationship between soul and body in the human being, which though not identical, still form an inseparable unity.

Additionally, Cordovero wrote a large number of commentaries and treatments of all kinds of mystical subjects. One of the best known of these works is the short tractate *Tomer Devorah* (Palm Tree of Deborah). Here he draws a connection between kabbalistic views and ethical norms (see also Chapter 3, § 2.5.3 on ethics among the Ashkenazi Hasidim). In the course of ten chapters Cordovero discusses how in all regards the human being should strive to follow God; just as God is merciful, the human should be merciful, and so on. With this idea Cordovero continues a tradition already found in rabbinic literature. In *Tomer Devorah*, however, the moral behavior of a person is related to the processes in the world of the sefiroth; the ethical actions of a person had a direct influence, in Cordovero's view, on the sefirotic realm. This is in no way a new idea in the history of Kabbalah, since the kabbalists before him had already supposed that human behavior could influence the divine world for good or ill. The distinctive thing about Cordovero, however, is that he presents the material so systematically and coherently.

A person's every deed is brought into relation with a particular sefirah. Hokhmah, for instance, corresponds with love for all things and care for all creatures, Binah with sincere repentance, Tif'ereth with the study of Torah and Malkhuth with making sacrifices for the sake of Torah and meeting one's marital responsibilities. By occupying oneself with the study of Torah in the right way, one can gain the quality of Tif'ereth. Anyone who acts humbly in Torah study will ensure that the sefirah Tif'ereth will descend and let its divine energy or radiance flow out over that person. But anyone who acts arrogantly in the study of the Torah will cause the sefirah Tif'ereth to avoid him, which has the opposite effect of restricting the divine flow from Tif'ereth.

It is striking that we scarcely find anything in Cordovero's work of new tendencies in Kabbalah which were emerging in particular after the expulsion from Spain, such as messianism, for example. In that respect he is a classical kabbalist; Cordovero gives a clear and well considered account of the kabbalistic ideas that had preceded him. The emergence of Lurianic Kabbalah, at the end of Cordovero's life, rang in a period of a completely new kabbalistic current which differed greatly in content from earlier Kabbalah.

3. The Kabbalah of Isaac Luria

3.1 Luria's life

With the exception of the last two or three years of his life, which he
spent in Safed, very little is known for certain of the life of Rabbi Isaac
Luria (1534–1572). In Safed Luria was also known by the name of
Isaac Ashkenazi, in reference to his father, who emigrated from Germany or Poland to Palestine. Isaac was born there in 1534. After his
father's premature death, his mother moved to live with her brother, a
wealthy tax franchiser in Egypt. The description of Luria's life in
Egypt by his later biographers is so interwoven with hagiographic details that it is difficult to distinguish true facts from legend. In Egypt
Luria worked as a grain merchant, but he also occupied himself with
rabbinic literature, Halakhah and esoteric works. Alongside the Zohar
in particular he studied contemporary kabbalistic literature, such as the
work of Moses Cordovero. It is possible that it was also in Egypt that
he wrote one of his very few works, a commentary on *Sifra di-
Tseni'utha* (Book of Concealment), a section of the Zohar which contains a compact mystical exposition of the beginning of Genesis. This
is quite a different work, however, from the kabbalistic teaching that
Luria was later to develop.

In the year 1569 or 1570 he moved to Safed, where he was to be
found among the disciples of Moses Cordovero. It was not long, however, before he began to gather a circle of disciples around himself, and
to disseminate his own kabbalistic ideas. Luria instructed his disciples
orally, often in the course of long walks in the surroundings of Safed.
He was the charismatic leader of a hierarchically organized circle, presumably based on the spiritual level of his students. Luria taught on the
basis of his spiritual intuition and divine revelations, which he claimed
to have received from the prophet Elijah. He always resisted the dissemination of kabbalistic teaching as it developed within the group.
Nor was he inclined to take just anyone into his closed circle; even
such great personalities as Moses Alsheikh and Joseph Caro were refused entry. In Luria's view, for instance, Caro's soul was unsuited for
the receipt of higher wisdom than the kabbalistic system of Cordovero.

Isaac Luria's mystical activities in Safed were restricted to just two or
three years. He died in consequence of an epidemic on 15 July 1572
in Safed, where his grave is still visited by pilgrims. After his death he
was to gain enormous fame as a kabbalist. He was known primarily by

the name of *ha-Ari*, "the Lion", an acronym of the Hebrew *ha-elohi rabbi yitshaq*, "the divinely inspired Rabbi Isaac".

3.2 Lurianic doctrine

Luria often spoke to his disciples of his inability to set down in writing the revelations, visions and ideas he had received. He was, moreover, convinced that his teaching was scarcely suited to being written down in a coherent and systematic overview. The way in which he taught was similarly lacking in coherence and system. It was Luria's disciples who wrote down what he said and preserved it for posterity. Three of his most important followers were Hayyim Vital, Joseph ibn Tabul and Israel Sarug. Of the very little that has come down to us from Luria in person, we have already mentioned the commentary on the Book of Concealment, and there are a number of commentaries on various passages of the Zohar, a small number of other tractates and mystical poetry—Luria was also known as a poet—including three hymns for the sabbath meals.

Although Luria's ideas can be described as extremely original and revolutionary, and seem sometimes to form a radical break with the past, in some respects they draw upon older sources, in particular the Zohar, the writings of Moses Cordovero and traditional rabbinic literature. Luria viewed his own work in many respects as an interpretation of the Zohar on the basis of new revelations from the prophet Elijah, in whom he saw his direct teacher. These visionary revelations occupied a very central position in the Lurianic circle. An important aspect of Isaac Luria's leadership within the school was connected with the fact that he himself received more extensive and more far-reaching visions than all other members of the circle. (According to Luria the kabbalists had not received any divine revelations from Elijah since the days of Nahmanides, one of the most important mystics of the Gerona school.) Luria never referred to a maggid such as the one Joseph Caro had.

Lurianic teaching contains, among other things, an elaborate description of the process in which God reveals himself. This description is strongly anthropomorphic; the self-revealing God is depicted in human terms. This whole process is full of dramatic mythical events, which are reminiscent of gnosticism. (On Kabbalah and gnosticism see Chapter 3, § 2.2.) Since the descriptions of these mystical events are extremely graphic, one is liable sometimes to forget that the concern is with symbols which refer to a reality in worlds beyond our own, which cannot be adequately put into words.

As we have said, Lurianic Kabbalah does not lend itself very well to a coherent and systematic treatment. In the case of many ideas it is not clear how the kabbalists conceived of them, while numerous internal inconsistencies can be pointed to. Lurianic doctrine often is more a collection of loose, apparently unconnected elements, and sometimes only the main lines are clear. Any attempt to arrive at a logical and comprehensive overview of Lurianic teaching is doomed to failure. This has everything to do with the fact that the teaching is largely based on experiences gained in mystical contemplation. Mystics thereby glimpse another reality which lies beyond human language, understanding and expressibility, and thus cannot be grasped logically by the human intellect.

We shall now look into three important elements in Luria's myth, which at the same time represent various phases in the cosmos: the "withdrawal of God" (*tsimtsum*), the "breaking of the vessels" (*shevirath ha-kelim*) and the "cosmic restoration" (*tiqqun*).

3.2.1   God withdraws

From the emergence of Kabbalah to Moses Cordovero, all kabbalists saw the emanation of the sefiroth from En Sof as a direct linear process. When God reveals ten different attributes of himself, this occurs in a single direction, in a movement that takes place from the innermost part of En Sof in an outward direction—or from above to below. With regard to the creation process, however, Luria saw the following problem: if God is all-embracing, there can be nothing that exists outside him. But this means that it is not possible for something simply to flow "out" from God, since there is no "outside" God. Earlier kabbalists had not offered any solution to this question, or rather did not give it serious attention. Isaac Luria's attempt to give an answer to this problem leads him to a completely different understanding of the beginning of the creation process.

According to Luria, at the beginning of the emanation process God had no choice other than first to create a space *within* his own area of infinity. This occurred by means of a "withdrawal" (*tsimtsum*) of God out of a part of his infinity. There arose thus a primordial space which is called *tehiru* (Aramaic for "pure emptiness") in the Lurianic writings. One might think of En Sof as a house completely filled with the divine essence. When God decides that a creation should come into being, he withdraws from one particular room in this house in order to create space for creation. By contrast with classical Kabbalah, where the deity of En Sof reveals itself in a movement from the inside to the outside, Isaac Luria speaks precisely of an inward movement; the very first action of the deity is one of withdrawing within itself. Instead of a God who reveals himself, we see here a God who withdraws into himself.

Although the creation of primordial space was an important part of God's tsimtsum, the withdrawal of the deity into itself also has to do with another aspect: the origin of evil in creation. In this regard too the teaching of Isaac Luria constitutes a radical break with earlier ideas in Kabbalah concerning the origins of evil. For the classical kabbalists the deity of En Sof was an indivisible unity which could not be separated out into various loose attributes. Luria, in contrast, daringly posited that the God of En Sof did not form a perfect unity. Within En Sof, in his view, all the divine lights or powers existed in a harmony that cannot be grasped by us. The divine lights of Hesed and Din also were part of this still undifferentiated harmony. Despite the state of divine harmony within En Sof, God realized that the powers of Din were capable of acting disharmoniously within the deity (see Chapter 3, §§ 2.6.3 and 2.6.4 on the sefirah Din and the roots of evil). In the Lurianic view, there were thus already powers present within En Sof which could potentially develop into evil powers.

By comparison with earlier Kabbalah, this view of the deity of En Sof and the roots of evil constitutes a radical innovation. While for Isaac Cohen of the Castilian school and in the Zohar, evil was only a byproduct of processes within the relationship between the sefiroth Hesed and Din, in Lurianic teaching evil was seen as something eternal within God himself. It is no surprise that some later kabbalists had great difficulty with the "heretical" idea of a dualistic principle within En Sof and sought other explanations for the origins of evil.

The second aspect of tsimtsum is concerned with the fact that the deity wants to purify itself of the elements of Din. For this purpose God withdraws with all his divine lights from one particular place within his infinity, in which process the lights of Din remain in the primordial space thus constituted. A frequently used image in this connection is an empty pail of water in which some moisture always remains. The lights of Din, the roots of evil, are thus isolated. This remaining residue is called *reshimu*. The relationship between the divine lights of the powers of Din will constitute the scarlet thread that determines the meaning of creation in the whole further process of creation and in the world which we know.

Luria's symbolism of God's withdrawal contains another view which had not come up before: the exile of the deity. Since God withdrew from a particular space during tsimtsum, from a place where he had previously been present, he is now actually in a state of exile: there is an area where God used to be but is no longer. This is a much more fundamental view of God's exile than is to be found in rabbinic literature. The rabbis were familiar with the idea that an aspect of God, the Shekhinah, accompanies Israel into exile in this world. In Luria, however, this idea is taken much further: right from the very beginnings, before there was any question of a creation, the deity is in exile.

The withdrawal of the deity has been called one of the most revolutionary ideas in the history of Kabbalah. Although Luria's originality in this regard cannot be disputed, he was still inspired by ideas that had been developed earlier. Already in a tractate of the Iyyun circle from early Kabbalah, we read that in the creation of the world God withdraws into himself, like someone holding his breath, after which a darkness arises in which the emanation process takes place. Isaac Luria adopted the idea and elaborated it into the theory of tsimtsum as a fundamental principle of his teaching.

We shall now look at the theme of the breaking of the vessels, which constitutes the second phase of the creation process in Lurianic doctrine.

3.2.2 The breaking of the vessels

When the elements of Din were left in the primordial space following God's contraction, a beam of divine light proceeded from En Sof into the primordial space, which touched the lights of Din. The deity first withdrew, therefore, in order subsequently to send part of its lights into the vacated space. This movement of withdrawal and emission of light—which can also be described as the inhalation and exhalation of the deity—forms the basis of the whole creation process in the Lurianic system. After the emission of the beam of light a to-ing and froing movement begins between En Sof and the primordial space, which gives rise to the ten sefiroth. These emanated sefiroth take the shape of an enormous, cosmic human form, the Adam Qadmon, or "primordial human", who forms a sort of spiritual foreshadowing of the earthly human. The goal of the emission of the beam of light from En Sof and the formation of the shape of the primordial human was to reach a harmonious balance between the divine lights from En Sof and the light powers of Din. The two different sorts of light, the lights from

En Sof and the lights of Din, had to work together in order to bring
the sefiroth into existence in the form of the Adam Qadmon. The
Adam Qadmon is described as a shape through which the lights of the
sefiroth shine; the divine light streams out of the eyes, mouth, ears and
nose of the primordial human being. The sefiroth can be imagined as
vessels filled with light, while the casing (the vessel) forms an inseparable unity with the center (the light).

The process of the formation of Adam Qadmon, however, is not
completed, since a cosmic "accident" occurs. Before the shape of the
primordial human reached its definitive form, the forces of Din refused
to collaborate further. They thus withdrew from the harmonious collaboration with the lights from En Sof. The result of this refusal was
that the lowest seven vessels could no longer hold the divine light, so
that they broke. The upper three remained intact. This is what the
Lurianic Kabbalah means by "the breaking of the vessels" (*shevirath ha-
kelim*). The breaking of the vessels formed a dramatic catastrophe in
the divine plan of creation. Everything had now been shaken out of its
ideal connection and knocked from its true place within the divine
order. As a result the sefiroth too were no longer in their original
place. It is because of this state of imperfection that all the worlds that
were to appear after this catastrophe, including our creation, were no
longer in accordance with the ideal order intended by God.

After the breaking of the vessels a large portion of the divine sparks
fell, together with the fragments of the broken vessels, into the lowest
part of the primordial space. Another, smaller portion of the lights
returned to En Sof after the break. The fragments that had fallen down
subsequently formed an independent realm of evil powers called *kelippoth*, "shells". These are hard shells which had enclosed the kernels of
light and formed the roots of raw matter. The fallen divine sparks were
now imprisoned between these kelippoth and became intermingled
with them. In this event we find for the second time the aspect of
divine exile. Not only had the deity gone into exile within itself during tsimtsum, but now, after the breaking of the vessels, the divine
lights found themselves also in exile between the forces of evil. Since
everything had been driven from its original place, the whole cosmos
bore the mark of exile.

In the development of this second phase, too, Luria was inspired by
mystics before him. The idea of the primordial man is already found in
Merkavah mysticism (Chapter 2, § 4). In tractate *Shi'ur Qomah* (Measurement of the Divine Figure) we find a description of the form of
God as creator of the world, a form which contains all the mysteries of

creation. The kabbalists of the Castilian school and the Zohar were familiar with the motif that God tried several times to bring creation into being. When God was not successful in this, he destroyed the failed emanated worlds. From the left-overs of these lost worlds the left emanations, the forces of evil, then formed. In the breaking of the vessels Isaac Luria fell back on the symbolism of the distinction between divine lights and vessels, which Moses Cordovero had posited.

Although the *shevirath ha-kelim* unmistakably signified a cosmic catastrophe, the kabbalists supposed that this had all occurred in accordance with a divine plan. For in this catastrophe the goal of the whole creation also comes to the fore: to purge the cosmos of the powers of Din. The breaking of the vessels formed a necessary precondition for the following phase in Lurianic doctrine: the cosmic restoration. Israel ibn Sarug, one of the most important of Luria's disciples, compared the necessity of the breaking with seed, which must first burst before bringing forth fruit.

3.2.3 The cosmic restoration

After God's withdrawal and the catastrophe of the breaking of the vessels there follows the third and most important phase in the cosmic process in Lurianic teaching: the restoration (*tiqqun*) of the broken vessels. Everything that had been broken and scattered has to be restored and set back in its proper place within the divine order.

To this end God makes a renewed attempt to bring creation into being. From En Sof and from the forehead of the Adam Qadmon there emerges a stream of divine light, from which now for the second time the ten sefiroth emanate. By comparison with God's first attempt to bring creation into being, this is now a much more complicated and nuanced symbolism for describing the divine world. This second time it is not simply a matter of an unfolding of the ten separate sefiroth; the sefiroth can now be divided into five "countenances" (*partsufim*; singular: *partsuf*) of the deity, each of which represents a particular aspect of God. The first three sefiroth each form a partsuf of their own, the fourth to the ninth sefiroth together form the fourth countenance, while the tenth sefirah forms the fifth partsuf. The partsufim have their own symbolic names, which—with a radical shift of meaning—are borrowed from the Zohar. The first three are called *Arikh Anpin* ("the Longsuffering One"), *Abba* ("Father") and *Imma* ("Mother") respectively; the fourth is called *Ze'eir Anpin* ("the Impatient One") and the fifth partsuf has the name *Rachel*. Besides the fact that the ten sefiroth are divided into five partsufim, in each separate partsuf—and this makes the symbolism rather complicated—all ten sefiroth are present in ever new combinations ("configurations"). At the end of the emanation process the five countenances together form the total personality of the God of Israel.

Besides the symbolism of the ten sefiroth and the five countenances of the deity, Lurianic Kabbalah is also familiar with another system for describing the transition from the most spiritual part of the divine world to our material reality: the doctrine of the four worlds. The symbolic names of these four worlds—already known in early Kabbalah, but elaborated further by Luria—represent an increasing degree of condensation from above to below: the world of *Atsiluth* ("emanating"), *Beri'ah* ("creating"), *Yetsirah* ("forming") and *Asiyyah* ("making"). Everything that appears descends through these four worlds. In coming into being the human, too, has passed through this whole process.

For the earlier kabbalists redemption meant an individual inner process of return to the perfect state of before the fall of Adam (on this see above, § 1.4). At first sight the Lurianic view of tiqqun seems to have a lot in common with this. But the process of restoration is viewed in a more nuanced way in Lurianic Kabbalah. According to Luria no such state of absolute perfection, such as the earlier kabbalists longed for, ever really existed; God and the divine world were never a perfect unity, since the powers of Din were already present *within* En Sof. To be sure, God did create an ideal order, but this was ultimately destroyed because the powers of Din refused to collaborate further. Restoration in Lurianic Kabbalah is a repairing of the vessels, the reattainment of the state prior to the breaking of these vessels, but this involves the fact that the evil that is present has to be completely eliminated from all the worlds. Only in the future, at the redemption, does a true ideal order dawn, in which the vessels are repaired, but in which—unlike in the original state—no potential evil powers are present any longer.

In the Lurianic writings there is deep and extremely detailed discussion of the many dynamic processes and mutual relationships that lie hidden in the separate sefiroth, countenances and worlds. Since, as has been said, Lurianic symbolism is anything but systematic and coherent, many details of this whole process frequently remain obscure and unclarified. One has to remember that all this is a matter of mythic images and is not about real events in time.

Adam's task and the role of the human in creation. With the emanation of the sefiroth, which form the countenances of the deity, and the four worlds, the deity wants to arrive at the restoration of the original harmony. In this plan of restoration the human being also has a fundamental part to play. It is not only God but God and human together that are able to realize the restoration; it is the human who must complete the divine face. The human gradually descended through the four worlds to the one we know as Adam, from paradise. This Adam, who was still a spiritual being, formed the last link in the long process of tiqqun; with his coming, the original divine harmony was almost complete. The whole divine world as macrocosm was reflected in a single being: the human, as microcosm. Adam stood over against God as a perfect divine being; in him all worlds came together. There was only one thing missing from the definitive restoration: Adam had to connect his whole being to God. With this deed he and the deity would become a unity and the whole cosmos would be a manifestation of divine harmony, in which good and evil were definitively separated. Adam would then also be the Redeemer who had brought an end to the cosmic exile.

As a result of the Fall, however, none of this comes about. By failing in his assignment, Adam achieves precisely the opposite of the original harmony: what transpires is a repetition of the breaking of the vessels on another level. At the moment that Adam enters the Garden of Eden, the worlds are almost restored. But when he is driven out of paradise, a cosmic catastrophe again takes place, which moreover occasions an even more profound and irreparable break than the breaking of the vessels. In the Lurianic myth Adam's soul contains the sparks of the souls of all future human beings in a great harmonious unity. As a result of the Fall, this cohesion of souls is broken. All the soul sparks fall down and get mixed with the fragments of the broken vessels and the divine sparks that had found their way into the lowest parts of the primordial space after the breaking of the vessels. The human sparks then remain as it were incarcerated among the kelippoth.

With Adam's fall our world appears. From that moment Adam loses his link with the higher worlds and gets caught up in the powers of Din. He no longer has his original spiritual form but is surrounded by a material form or a physical body that is related in nature to the kelippoth. That is the reason why in our world and in the human being, good and evil are entangled with each other. The task of restoration is now given to the descendants of Adam. They now have to liberate all the divine sparks from imprisonment by the left-hand side. The restoration consists of the fact that each liberated spark ascends from the area of evil and returns to its proper place in the spiritual worlds. Only when all the sparks have re-ascended and the mystical body of Adam Qadmon has regained its original spiritual state, will the restoration be complete. By overcoming the evil in himself, the human makes a contribution to the mythical victory of good over evil in the cosmos. The whole course of human history here on earth is then to be taken as human attempts to fulfill this task. In particular it is the task of each Jew in this process to make a contribution to the eventual restoration. This contribution consists primarily in the study of Torah, the observance of the daily commandments and mystical prayer.

After Adam's fall the soul sparks became imprisoned between the fragments of the vessels which, separated from their center, the divine lights, had developed into an area of evil, formed by the powers of Din. These evil powers, depicted as the kelippoth, "shells", have no life of their own; they cannot sustain themselves. Their life power they thus have to derive from the sparks locked into their area. If these sparks were to be freed from the area of the kelippoth, evil would be deprived of the force of life and thus automatically be eliminated. For this reason the redemption of the sparks is a spiritual activity of the human being, which ultimately has the aim of keeping the vital energy from the satanic powers of Din.

Male and female powers in God. Like their predecessors, the Lurianic kabbalists proceeded from the idea that in the divine world male and female powers are engaged with each other in dynamic processes. In Lurianic doctrine, in this regard an important nuance is applied. The male powers are associated with the heart of something, the essence or the divine spark, while the female powers stand for the form, the envelopment in which something appears. The fact that a creation can come about is due to the female powers, which ensure that things have a form, a shape. Ideally these two principles are inseparably linked; the one cannot exist without the other. The imagery used for this is that a fruit cannot ripen if there is no peel around it. In the same way the divine lights of the sefiroth can only reveal something of the deity by virtue of the vessels. In a harmonious situation the two cosmic principles, male and female, are valued as positive. However, as soon as the harmonious balance between the male and female principle is broken, the surrounding form becomes an isolated, self-standing power. In Lurianic teaching this is a negative side of the female principle, which is associated with the demonic or with the forces of Din. The demonic or evil element in creation emerges where the outward side, the female, leads a life of its own without contact or harmony with the center, with the male principle: it is the form, without content. Restoration involves the restitution of the harmonious relationship between the male and the female principles.

One has to bear in mind that this opposition between male and female powers in Lurianic doctrine is not just referring to males and females in our world; it is exclusively a matter of cosmic principles in the divine world. So here we have to do with a more profound approach to this problem than we found in the Zohar. The Zohar made no clear distinction between a positive and negative side of the female cosmic power and, moreover, frequently equated the woman, as a person in our world, with the demonic.

Exile as a symbol for God, the world and the Jewish people. As we have seen above, the three basic ideas on which Lurianic Kabbalah is constructed—the withdrawal of God, the breaking of the vessels and the restoration of the original harmony—are based on the motif of the exile of the deity. Exile is thus a cosmic principle which underlies everything from the very beginnings. This Lurianic view of exile forms an extension and deepening of the traditional historical view of the exile of the people of Israel into a symbol of cosmic proportions. The whole universe, our world and the whole of humanity, find themselves in a state of exile. While in the traditional rabbinic view and in earlier Kabbalah the concept of exile is exclusively applied to the historical situation in which the Jews find themselves, it is now a matter of the state of the whole world, the nations and the Jews together. The exile of the Jewish people was no longer viewed by Luria and his disciples as something into which this people was unlucky enough to fall in the course of history, but as a feature of a determinative cosmic principle running from the hidden deity, through all the realms and on to our created world: life in our world is life in exile.

Within this universal exile the Jewish people did occupy a special place. Since the exile was seen by the Jews as a symbol of the exile of creation as a whole, it was their duty to restore the original ideal situation that pertained before the breaking of the vessels. The Jew thus had a responsibility towards humanity and the world: it was no longer just a matter of the redemption of the Jewish people from the diaspora, but of the redemption of the whole of creation. Alongside the earlier negative attention to suffering in exile, the concept of exile now also acquired a clearly positive aspect: exile is a commission to restore. In this collective commission each Jew was given an individual task.

The Messiah in Lurianic Kabbalah. Since humans play an active role in bringing about tiqqun, Lurianic Kabbalah views the redemption not as something that suddenly breaks into our world from another reality, but rather as a slow, gradual process in our reality. To the Lurianic kabbalists the perfection of the tiqqun also implies the redemption of this world: restoration is redemption. In the Lurianic writings one will thus seek in vain for speculations on the identity of the Messiah. According to Lurianic teaching, the Messiah is no longer a figure who brings about the redemption through his own efforts at the catastrophic end-times; he only appears at the moment that the restoration is complete. For the Messiah as a person no great task is reserved; his appearance is no more than a sign to indicate that the redemption has already come.

The circles around Isaac Luria were convinced that the redemption would occur in their day and that the process of restoration had reached a definitive stage. The redemption was expected in the year 1575, when Luria would reveal himself as the Messiah and constitute the living proof that the process of tiqqun was complete. However, when he died three years before this, and the redemption did not come about, this was interpreted as meaning that the generation of the time had not been found worthy of entering the World to Come. In retrospect, it had to be admitted, Isaac Luria had not been the victorious Messiah of the House of David, but the Messiah ben Joseph, who was to die in the struggle, as was predicted in the descriptions of the end-times in the Book of Zerubbabel (see § 1.3 above). The redemption had been postponed and it was now the Messiah ben David who was awaited for the real completion of the restoration.

3.2.4 Reincarnation

The idea that a person's soul is constantly re-embodied here on earth in accordance with particular laws is one of the pillars of Lurianic doctrine. The topic of reincarnation (*gilgul*) was not only important in Lurianic Kabbalah, but also exercised far-reaching influence on the Shabbetai Zevi movement and Hasidism. Our most important sources for the details of this teaching are an anonymous work from 1552, *Galya Raza* (Revealed Mystery), along with a book by Hayyim Vital which has come down to us in two versions: *Sefer Gilgulim* (Book of Reincarnation) and *Sha'arei Gilgul* (Gates of Reincarnation). After the death of Luria in particular the doctrine of reincarnation became widely known throughout the population. In due course many popularized views found their way into popular belief and folklore.

As we saw in the previous chapter, classical Kabbalah was also familiar with the idea of the transmigration of souls. Although opinions on reincarnation were divided and not all classical kabbalists were equally interested in this doctrine, in general rebirth was seen as a punishment, the consequence of previously committed transgression—in the sexual area in particular—which had to be paid for in a subsequent life. In Lurianic Kabbalah, however, a much more positive image of reincarnation developed, as a phenomenon that was valid for everyone and which was accepted by all kabbalists as a universal principle. According to Luria, the transmigration of souls had everything to do with the process of cosmic restoration; the prime way in which the tiqqun was to be brought about was through people contributing more and more to the process in a chain of many lives.

Like the universe as a whole, the soul also finds itself in exile. After the fall of Adam, each soul has come into contact with the kelippoth and must purge itself of evil in order to be able to assume its rightful place in an ideal cosmic order. Since Adam's fall human souls run through a chain of incarnations, a process that will not end until the tiqqun is perfected. Each soul has the task of working on its own restoration until a state of perfection has been reached. Although many still adhered to the earlier idea that in subsequent incarnations a person had to atone for mistakes and transgressions previously committed, the emphases began to be placed more on reincarnation as a challenge within the process of restoration. A person can try again at each new opportunity. In the course of a whole long chain of lives, each person contributes to the separation between good and evil, liberates himself or herself from evil and opts for good. The Messiah can only come at the moment that the very last soul has been freed from the area of the kelippoth.

In Lurianic doctrine all souls have their place within an enormous, hierarchical system. Before the Fall, Adam's soul contained all human souls of all peoples who would one day appear on earth. By analogy with the traditional view that both the human and the divine body consisted of 613 parts (see Chapter 3, § 1.6.4 on the commandments), this primordial soul of Adam too was composed of 613 spiritual original parts, also called "boughs". Each bough in turn consisted of 613 "branches" or "large souls", each of which in turn had an unspecified number of individual human souls ("leaves" or "sparks"). Between souls belonging to the same branch there is a relationship to which the kabbalists paid great attention. The individual process of tiqqun, the perfection of the soul and its liberation from the area of the shells, is partly determined by the state of the other souls in the branch to which the individual soul belongs. Thus a single individual can contribute by means of his positive deeds to the perfection of the other soul sparks within the group, but by the same token by negative actions he can damage the others, so that all the related souls actually sink deeper into the kelippoth. For the restoration each soul is dependent on the other souls of the branch; unrelated souls from another branch cannot contribute to someone's perfection. It can also happen that the soul of a just person, who already has the reincarnation process behind him, temporarily enters into a person to help him out in some matter or another. Another possibility is that a soul that has not previously had the opportunity in earlier incarnations to live up to any one of the 613 commandments, temporarily enters a person in order to see to that. Relations between souls and biological relationships, by the way, are two different things which do not necessarily overlap.

Between the various human souls there can be a great difference; some great souls or branches have their ultimate origin very high up in the world of Atsiluth, while others come from the lowest regions of the world of Asiyyah. The refinement of the individual human soul has a direct influence on the restoration of that part of the divine world from which the soul originates.

In the Zohar we already met the three parts of the human soul: *nefesh*, *ruah* and *neshamah*. Lurianic doctrine added two levels: *hayyah* and *yehidah*. These five parts—the terms are borrowed from an ancient midrash (*Genesis Rabbah* 14.9), which deals with five terms that can be used to describe the soul—together form a single individual soul spark. It is every person's task to bring all layers of the individual soul to perfection: the greater the perfection, the closer a person comes to his own Self. Each person is given a nefesh at birth. The other parts of the soul, which have not yet entered it, can be acquired as the soul becomes refined. Lurianic doctrine, then, sees the transmigration of souls as a positive process of self-realization. It is not the case that each person can attain all levels of the soul in a single earthly life. The two highest stages are of such a spiritual quality that only very special people like Abraham, king David and the Messiah himself reach this level.

There were various views regarding non-Jews in this process. On the one hand, some people felt that the transmigration of souls was valid for all humans but that non-Jews had neglected their task of restoring the cosmos. On the other hand, others found, in particular during and after the expulsion from Spain, that the souls of non-Jews came from the area of the kelippoth and not from the area of sanctity—a Jewish variant of the Christian principle that no salvation could be expected outside the Church. Later kabbalists softened these statements and assumed that non-Jewish soul sparks too had something holy in them that awaits restoration and redemption.

In the view of the Lurianic kabbalists, hidden behind historical events here on earth—which once again were themselves symbols of processes in the divine world—lay the tiqqun processes of soul sparks. Outwardly one sees wars, rivalry, collaboration and peace, but behind all these concrete things lie the connections between related souls embroiled in a lengthy process of reincarnation and restoration. That is what is really going on in the world and in the course of history.

3.2.5 Practical Kabbalah: mystical and magical techniques

In Lurianic Kabbalah an important place is occupied by the application of techniques for getting into a state of ecstasy and for receiving visions. The use of mystical or magical techniques—it is often very difficult to distinguish between them—goes back in Judaism to the period of apocalypticism. When Kabbalah appeared, in the twelfth century on the Iberian Peninsula, there was already a more than 1000-year-old tradition of such techniques.

We have seen above how Merkavah mysticism made use of various techniques to ascend through the heavenly realms to the throne of glory. We then saw how in the Rhineland the Ashkenazi Hasidim preserved, reinterpreted and extended the traditions about these techniques. The early kabbalists on the Iberian Peninsula resisted the application of ecstatic techniques alongside their theoretical doctrine of the sefiroth. So they adopted an adversarial position towards Abraham Abulafia and his teaching of ecstatic Kabbalah (for the opposition between theosophical-theurgic and ecstatic Kabbalah see the previous chapter, § 2.6.2). With Abulafia's departure from the Iberian Peninsula in 1280 ecstatic Kabbalah moved via Italy to the Middle East. There, a process emerged in which theoretical-theosophical Kabbalah (ideas about the structure of the divine world) gradually went along with ecstatic or practical Kabbalah (the use of techniques to gain direct access to the divine world), a process that was eventually to culminate in Safed.

The ascent to the heavenly realms was again given a new impulse by the Safed kabbalists. There were experiences of going up to heavenly academies, where famous deceased classical rabbis sat together. The mystic studied here, in their company, and received revelations of deep secrets about the Torah and Kabbalah. Isaac Luria himself was known as a very intensive heavenly traveler; each night, ascending in the company of ministering angels, he visited one of the many academies there were in the other worlds. Thus Luria studied with the ancient rabbis or with the prophet Elijah. After such heavenly journeys the revealed secrets and everything that had been learned were passed on to the other kabbalists. The ascents led not only to a euphoric experience of a vision, but also to a lively discussion and an enormous literary creativity, so that the content of what had been learned was written down during the day.

A technique much used in Safed is that of visualization. The mystic formed an internal picture of the sefiroth or the letters of the Tetragrammaton within circles and in various colors. These visualizations play an especially important role in prayer. In the previous chapter we mentioned mystical prayer in the case of the Gerona kabbalists and the Ashkenazi Hasidim. In his thoughts, and with a special concentration or intention (*kawwanah*), the mystic directs words and sentences from the traditional prayers to corresponding sefiroth; for the words of the liturgy are symbols referring to particular sefiroth (see Chapter 3, § 2.4). By mentally connecting the various sefiroth with each other in this way, the mystic contributes to the repair of the break that runs through all the worlds (see Chapter 3, § 1.2). Not only does he wish to behold the sefiroth in mystic contemplation, but at the same time he strives to influence them to such an extent that divine light flows from above to our world. The Safed kabbalists built further upon this tradition. In support of this activity a technique was used by which each separate sefirah was visualized as a particular color corresponding to the character of the sefirah. The sefirah's color was viewed as something that clothed the sefirah like a garment. Besides the sefiroth, the letters of the Tetragrammaton were also visualized. Sometimes this also occurred in colors, and sometimes the letters were seen within circles or in combination with constantly changing vowel signs. Exactly what the kabbalists saw and experienced during these visualizations and how the techniques worked, is by no means always clear, owing to the lack of material.

In addition, the traditions concerning the determination of a person's character on the basis of physical features (physiognomy) and by the shape and lines of the hand (chiromancy) form, as in Merkavah mysticism, an integral part of practical Kabbalah in Safed. While the

Hekhaloth literature nowhere draws a connection with the phenomenon of reincarnation, in Lurianic Kabbalah we regularly meet remarks on the interpretation of various aspects of previous incarnations on the basis of the lines of the forehead (metoposcopy) and the hand, as well as by reading the human aura. The kabbalists saw the aura as a book in which everything is recorded that a person has experienced and done in the chain of lives. It was said of Isaac Luria that he was very expert in perceiving previous incarnations in this way. Luria could see from what source a particular soul had sprung. Sometimes he showed extraordinary deference to relatively unknown persons because he recognized in them the reincarnation of famous rabbis from the Mishnah. Once he also recognized in a rabbi from his circle a spark of the soul of the prophet Jeremiah. Luria not only saw the past but also the future of a particular soul and gave advice as to the proper actions to correct faults and shortcomings from previous lives. If we are to believe Luria's hagiographer, Luria mastered all the sciences and also understood the language of trees, birds and angels.

In the mystical activities the Safed kabbalists applied another remarkable technique: weeping. By deliberately giving free reign to his tears the mystic could attain a state of trance in which he received visions or had hidden knowledge of the Torah revealed to him. In this the kabbalists were following a very ancient tradition; already in apocalyptic literature we find references to this form of shedding tears. A late midrash (*Midrash Hallel*) tells how in the second century of our era, the famous Rabbi Akiva was only able to gain his vision of the throne of glory by weeping fervently and how his contemporary Rabbi Ishmael used the weeping technique in the hope of learning the date of the redemption. Extensive information on mystical weeping is found in discussions by Rabbi Abraham ha-Levi Berukhim, a disciple of Isaac Luria. He relates that in mystical weeping the same physical posture is adopted as in the ascent through the heavenly realms—a sitting position with the head between the knees. After sitting thus for a certain length of time in dead silence, one begins to weep incessantly. At the moment that the crying has progressed to the stage that he loses, or is on the point of losing, consciousness of his surroundings, the hidden worlds open up to him. Lurianic literature contains testimonies in reference to the mystical weeping of well-known kabbalists. Thus Luria had once said to Berukhim that the latter would die if he did not hurry to the Wailing Wall in Jerusalem. On arrival at the Wailing Wall Berukhim began crying, lost consciousness and received a vision of the Shekhinah. It is known of Hayyim Vital that after vigorous weeping at his impotence and his lack of time to study Torah he fell asleep and received a visionary dream. Besides its purpose of gaining visions and revelations, the weeping technique could also be applied to influence processes within the divine world.

In the very broad scale of techniques—some of which were nothing short of magical in character—we find among other things the use of amulets and talismans, astrology, alchemy, automatic writing, magic spells and all kinds of divination. Many of these practical techniques are found not only in Safed but also in various mystical movements before and after Safed.

Though the use of practical techniques in Kabbalah may have accompanied a theoretical, theosophical approach, this does not mean that any technique could be practiced without further ado; the kabbalists often disagreed over which techniques were allowed and which were not. Although a distinction was made between the practice of techniques on the basis of pure and impersonal motives and on the basis of selfish objectives such as personal advantage and gain, the dividing line was certainly not always clear. Misuse of techniques could give rise to great physical and spiritual dangers. Some kabbalists thought that it was all right to have knowledge of these matters, but that they should never be put into practice. While certain kabbalists thought that the powers of evil, the powers of the left-hand side, should be countered with their own means—read: with the aid of demons, the use of unholy names, black magic, sorcery—, others were very much against this. Such a renowned Safed rabbi as Rabbi Joseph Taitatsak claimed that the wisdom of alchemy was identical to that of Kabbalah. Hayyim Vital, on the other hand, regretted in retrospect having devoted two years of his youth to the study of alchemy.

3.3 Isaac Luria's disciples

The most important of Isaac Luria's disciples was Hayyim Vital (1543-1620). Before Vital joined up with Luria and his circle, he was already a famous kabbalist with a number of works to his name. Initially he was stand-offish towards Luria, who had arrived in Safed only a short time before and had not yet earned his spurs in Kabbalah. Moreover, Vital, who was convinced of the extraordinary quality of his own soul, was not impressed that Luria did not immediately recognize him as an elevated soul. When Vital finally was present at one of Luria's lessons, Luria was very much impressed by him, which gave Vital cause to acknowledge Luria as his teacher. According to Vital's own account,

Luria maintained that Vital's soul was of a higher order than the highest angels and even that Luria had received visions in Egypt with the mission to go to Safed to meet and instruct him, Hayyim Vital. Since then Vital had a marked influence on the development of Lurianic doctrine. Vital's influence is particularly noticeable in such a central element as messianism.

After Luria's death, Vital saw himself as the absolute authority among the students of his great master. No one but himself, Hayyim Vital, was in a position really to understand the Lurianic teachings. He had a number of the most important students sign a declaration in which they acknowledged him as authority and promised under oath never to divulge any of the teaching to the outside, only to study the Kabbalah among themselves and then only in the presence of Vital himself. Vital's attempts to keep the teachings of Luria secret from the outside world were not entirely successful. Very much against the wishes of the other students he was the only one given charge of written versions of Lurianic teaching; so it was difficult for followers and other interested persons to gain material for study. But when in 1587 Vital lay very sick in bed, the opportunity was grasped to buy over his brother Moses and to extract the desired manuscripts secretly from the sick man's house, so that they could be copied and disseminated.

Vital's best-known work on Lurianic teaching is *Ets Hayyim* (Tree of Life), in which he more or less systematically describes the views of Luria in detail. The book consists of eight parts called the "gates (to the work)", hence the alternative title of the work: *Shemonah She'arim* (Eight Gates). Each gate (*sha'ar*) deals with one topic, such as theosophical teaching, the exposition of biblical passages, reincarnation, the commandments, and prayer mysticism. This work, which is known in various versions, is always seen as the authoritative representation of Lurianic Kabbalah. Another important work by Vital is *Sefer ha-Hezyonoth* (Book of the Visions). This is a sort of mystical diary that Vital kept through the whole of his life. Here he wrote down his own dreams and those of others, as well as revelations he received. A large part of the work consists of the statements made to Vital by Luria regarding the superiority of Vital's soul and regarding Vital's messianic mission in this world. Much of this information was revealed to Vital after the death of Luria. His teacher continued to appear to him and instruct him in dreams. Of the later Jewish mystics, Hayyim Vital was to become the most studied Lurianic kabbalist.

Rabbi Joseph ibn Tabul was another important disciple of Isaac Luria. He was one of those who refused to sign the declaration drawn up by Vital. After Luria's death he went his own way; he also taught Lurianic doctrine to students who had never themselves studied under Luria—something Vital had tried expressly to avoid. Although Ibn Tabul added genuinely new ideas to Lurianic doctrine at a number of points, he himself maintained that he did nothing other than to interpret what his master had taught him. Like Vital, he also ascribed his own mystical revelations to Luria. A notable difference between Ibn Tabul's account of Lurianic teachings and that of Vital is that for the former the mythical element is much more strongly represented than for Vital. This is particularly clear in relation to tsimtsum and the breaking of the vessels. Vital was not too concerned with the all-too dramatic events within the divine realm.

As the third important representative of Lurianic teaching one may name Rabbi Israel ibn Sarug. As a result of Gershom Scholem's influence it has long been assumed that Sarug cannot have been a direct disciple of Isaac Luria and that he must have borrowed all his knowledge from the manuscripts removed from the house of Hayyim Vital. More recent research, however, is inclined to regard Ibn Sarug, who himself was one of the most important of Luria's disciples, was indeed a direct disciple of Luria. His best-known work, in which Luria's ideas are expounded, is *Limmudei Atsiluth* (Doctrines on Emanation). Ibn Sarug was extremely interested in mystical techniques. Among the specifically innovative elements of Ibn Sarug's is the idea of the *malbush* ("garment") in which the Torah is viewed as a divine garment consisting of combinations of letters. While Hayyim Vital and Joseph ibn Tabul were active in the Middle East, Ibn Sarug turned up in Italy as a successful disseminator of Lurianic Kabbalah. The odd fact that Vital never refers to Ibn Sarug is probably due to his disappointment at the fact that Ibn Sarug was causing a stir as the great innovator and disseminator of Lurianic Kabbalah. Though Vital saw himself as the legitimate representative and interpreter of Lurianic teaching, he did not seem able—at least during his lifetime—to match the success of Ibn Sarug.

Some time after the death of Luria the circle of followers disbanded. Each went more or less his own way and the most influential disciples formed schools of their own. Each head of a school was of the opinion that he was the true representative of Isaac Luria. After 1610 Safed too began to decline as a kabbalistic center. Many kabbalists had left Safed; Hayyim Vital spent the last years of his life in Damascus, where he died in 1620. No one had so much evident authority that he was in a position to step into Luria's shoes and to form the bonding factor in the circle of Lurianic mystics.

3.4 The transmission of Lurianic Kabbalah

Since Luria himself scarcely wrote anything, for the reconstruction of his ideas we are dependent on descriptions of his teachings in the works of some of his disciples. In the presentations of Luria's Kabbalah, however, we encounter striking differences and contradictions. Gershom Scholem and many after him tried to explain these facts from the way in which Luria's followers had passed on his teaching. The question was to what extent the students had faithfully presented Luria's ideas; after all it was possible that some followers had not fully grasped the teaching or that they deliberately described certain elements of Lurianic Kabbalah differently because they differed from Luria in opinion. In that case the personality of the student in question would have colored Luria's teaching; for personal reasons some topics would have been omitted, altered or distorted.

More recent research, including that of R. Meroz, Y. Liebes and Y. Avivi, however, has shown that the differences in the transmission of Luria's teachings are not due to an unreliable transmission by his followers. First of all, on closer inspection it appears that Vital, Ibn Tabul or Ibn Sarug indicate precisely in their works what derives from Luria and what they themselves have added or interpreted. It is clear that they did all they could to be faithful to Luria in their presentation. Secondly, it seems from new manuscript material that after Scholem's research it has come to light that the differences and contradictions are not always to be ascribed to one particular disciple. Some elements of the teaching which for instance were not found in Vital's work—so that it was assumed that he deliberately did not adopt them—seem to have been described by him reasonably well after all. In other words: there are fewer differences and contradictions between the works of Luria's followers than was initially supposed. The differences that indisputably remain are not due to unreliable transmission by the disciples.

How, then, are the discrepancies to be explained? It has to be assumed that they come from a dynamic development of Lurianic doctrine. The remaining differences and contradictions are largely the result of the inner development Luria experienced in the time that he resided in Safed. Time and again he adjusted his ideas. The development of his insights can be followed fairly well; the various witnesses to Luria's teaching indicate various stages. It is therefore not a matter of internal contradictions in his ideas, but of the development of the content of the doctrine.

Further, it has become clear that the followers contributed actively, right from the beginning of the Lurianic school, to the emergence of what we now know as Lurianic Kabbalah. Luria was indeed the leader of the group—he received the most far-reaching divine revelations— so that his input in the emergence of the Lurianic system was certainly the most important, but some of his followers also received divine revelations which were recognized as such by Luria. The circle around Luria must have been the stage for very lively discussions, from which new views emerged. In consequence of revelations of disciples or discussions, Luria repeatedly adjusted his ideas. So throughout its existence the whole school brought numerous innovative elements into the Lurianic system which strictly speaking do not derive from Luria but which do form a fixed component of Lurianic Kabbalah. The central theme of messianism, for example, thus comes partly from Vital and not entirely from Luria himself.

The attempt to gain a picture of Lurianic teaching by distilling Luria's own ideas from the books of his followers, is thus actually not the right way to proceed. Anyone who wants to know precisely what Luria himself thought of something is asking only part of a question; we cannot speak of Lurianic Kabbalah as exclusively the teaching of Isaac Luria. Lurianic Kabbalah is a kabbalistic system which came into being through a dynamic process of development by Isaac Luria and the active input of his followers.

3.5 Lurianic Kabbalah up to Shabbetai Zevi

It is not the case that Isaac Luria and his kabbalistic doctrine enjoyed great fame in Safed and beyond right from the beginning, let alone that Lurianic Kabbalah was viewed as the only true Kabbalah. After all, at the same time that Luria and his group were active in Safed, there were other kabbalistic schools, including that of Cordovero. Luria and his followers were, however, convinced that their teaching represented a superior version of Kabbalah by comparison with all other approaches. Although, for instance, they recognized Cordovero's Kabbalah as an authentic tradition, they thought that the latter contained a lower or incomplete form of Kabbalah, suitable only for the first acquaintance with mysticism; it was Kabbalah for beginners. Deeper and true insight could only be gained through Luria's system.

It was not until around 1600 that kabbalists began increasingly to view Luria as the mystical leader of Safed par excellence. Contemporaries of Luria, however, would not have shared this view. Twenty years after Luria's death we see legends starting to form about his life. An important witness in this regard is formed by a few letters of Solomon Dresnitz, who had come to Safed from Moravia in 1602 to study Kabbalah. In these letters, addressed to kindred kabbalistic spirits in various countries, Dresnitz wrote down everything he heard about Luria. Besides factual descriptions of Luria as a person these documents also contain many hagiographic legends concerning Luria. Dresnitz's letters have contributed a great deal to the international fame of Luria and Lurianic Kabbalah.

Gradually Lurianic Kabbalah was almost completely to displace the earlier Kabbalah as we know it up to Moses Cordovero. From the beginning of the seventeenth century "Kabbalah" increasingly became synonymous with the Lurianic system, while Kabbalah became known far beyond the circles of the mystics. In simplified form Lurianic teaching also spoke strongly to the imagination of ordinary people. On the one hand this teaching gave answers to the questions that had arisen after the expulsion from Spain: it was not only the individual Jew who suffered in exile, the whole cosmos and even the deity were bowed under exile. On the other hand the individual Jew was aware of his not inconsiderable task as a person: each had his own contribution to make to the great process of tiqqun; the fate of the whole world was directly dependent on the behavior of the individual.

What impressed everyone particularly was the fact that each Jew was doing his bit towards the restoration, regardless of whether he was a mystic or an illiterate. Knowledge of the details of the doctrine, as was known to the intellectual mystical elite, was not necessary; everyone participated through his deeds in the restoration of a coming world. Lurianic doctrine had given an explanation for what the Jews had had to go through in history. The exile of the Jews stood as a symbol of the exile of the whole cosmos; the Jews were not only bringing about restoration for their own people but also for the world.

However complicated, detailed and innovative the teaching of Luria may be in many regards, the way in which each Jew could contribute to the cosmic restoration was simple and traditional: by observing the commandments. Lurianic Kabbalah did not introduce any change to the daily commandments but gave them a mythical depth so that they

were the means by which humanity, the world and divine realms
could be restored. Since Lurianic Kabbalah explained why it was precisely in the commandments that the purpose of creation lay, these
were observed with new zeal.

There seems to have been such an enormous radiance from Lurianic
teaching that for the first time in a very long period the whole Jewish
world was united as one, in one and the same belief, the same symbolism and the same theological system, in which exile and messianic
redemption had a central position. Practically all the kabbalistic and
popular works written before 1660 borrowed their inspiration from
Lurianic doctrine.

Lurianic Kabbalah thus constituted the background for the emergence in 1665 of the Kabbalah of Shabbetai Zevi, which we shall
consider more closely in the next chapter.

5

The Kabbalah of Shabbetai Zevi

With the emergence of the Kabbalah of Shabbetai Zevi one of the most controversial periods in the history of the Jewish religion dawns. The actions and influence of the remarkable figure of Shabbetai Zevi, who believed he was the long-awaited Messiah in the second half of the seventeenth century, still today give rise to heated debates in the study of Judaism. This "Messiah" was finally to convert to Islam and to occasion an enormous upheaval among his massive following.

Before we go into the theoretical and historical aspects of sabbatianism in detail, and into its influence and the controversies to which the movement has led, we shall first pay attention to the figure of Shabbetai Zevi himself.

1. The life of Shabbetai Zevi

Shabbetai Zevi was born in 1626 in Smyrna (Izmir), possibly on the ninth of the month of Av—that is, on the anniversary of the destruction of the Temple, which moreover fell on a sabbath in that year. This fact was to help determine his messianic self-consciousness in his later life. His father, Mordechai Zevi, had come from the Peloponnese, probably from a family of Ashkenazi origin. As a young man he had settled in Smyrna, were he later became an agent for German and English merchant houses. The economic rise of Smyrna at the time made him wealthy; Shabbetai's brothers Elijah and Joseph were rich merchants. Shabbetai received a traditional rabbinic education, became familiar with Talmud and Midrash and began to read kabbalistic works from the age of eighteen.

Certain traits in his personality gave an early indication of a psychological disorder, which Gershom Scholem has characterized as a manic-depressive psychosis. Although his state of mind varied from the euphoric to the depressive, he also experienced more stable periods in which he functioned in a more or less normal fashion. In the writings of Nathan of Gaza in particular, who was later to become Shabbetai's leading "prophet" (see § 2), mention is often made of the temptations which Shabbetai went through during his numerous periods of depression. We can deduce that they were demonic and erotic in nature. On the other hand, when in a state of exaltation he must have had a strong, suggestive attraction. The manic or euphoric moods which came in phases were accompanied by strange actions which had an antinomistic character and were performed by him evidently in a state of religious excitement, as holy, sacramental actions. The most striking feature was his continual inclination to pronounce the divine name, the Tetragrammaton, out loud and in public. When he was not in a state of depression, he impressed people by his worthy behavior and his considerable knowledge of the rabbinic and kabbalistic sources. He also gained respect on account of his good singing voice. Unfortunately none of his writings has been preserved. It seems his emotional life was very strongly developed. As a young man he married twice. However, because he did not fulfill his marital duties, these marriages ended in divorce.

A variety of bizarre and deliberate violations of the Jewish law led to his being banished from Smyrna by the rabbis in 1654. Several times already he had said that he believed he was the Messiah, though no one took him seriously. In the following ten years he traveled around Greece and Turkey and stayed for some time in Jerusalem. Shabbetai Zevi maintained that the commandments had been abolished and gave expression to this belief by, among other things, reversing Ps. 146.7: "the Lord liberates the captives" (*mattir asurim*) into the blasphemous "God permits what is forbidden" (*mattir issurim*). In order to free himself from the demonic forces which oppressed him, he made use of practical Kabbalah (read: magical techniques).

In 1663 he moved to Cairo, where he joined up with a kabbalistic circle to which the head of the Egyptian Jewish community, Raphael Joseph, also belonged. There he married a year later for the third time. In 1665 he traveled to Gaza in order to consult Nathan of Gaza on the healing of his manic-depressive attacks. On their meeting, Nathan announced that he had already seen Shabbetai Zevi as the Messiah in a vision. The young Nathan convinced Shabbetai that he was indeed the Messiah (see the following section). Soon after this, Shabbetai Zevi proclaimed in public that he was the Messiah, which led to an enormous upheaval. The real driving force behind Shabbetai Zevi was Nathan of Gaza, who with his propagandistic gifts foresaw the nascent movement of a kabbalistic-messianic theology. Nathan predicted that

Shabbetai Zevi would soon assume the crown of the Ottoman Sultan, after which the ultimate redemption would dawn. He spurred everyone on in the time left before the redemption to join in sincere repentance in the form of fasting and other ascetic practices.

During a stay in Jerusalem Shabbetai Zevi gathered together a great crowd who acknowledged him as the Messiah. Nonetheless the rabbinic authorities did not recognize him as such and banished him from the city. Shabbetai Zevi then moved via Aleppo to Smyrna. One sabbath he went to the synagogue of the Portuguese community, where his opponents congregated. When he was not admitted, he made his own way in by smashing down a door with an ax. He then proclaimed himself to be the "Messiah of the God of Jacob", announced the imminent dawning of the redemption and spurred the community on to proclaim the divine name together. Shabbetai Zevi's entourage had grown considerably in the meantime; both ordinary members and eminent rabbis were counted as "believers" (*ma'aminim*), a term which soon attracted the specific meaning of "sabbatian". "Unbelieving" opponents could no longer intervene on account of the massive, stormy protest of the adherents. Real terror was applied to "the unwilling", for instance by means of plundering their houses. Some fled from the messianic violence, while others kept anxiously quiet. From far and near, delegations were dispatched to acknowledge Shabbetai Zevi officially as the Messiah. He appeared regularly in royal apparel in the synagogue, divided up kingdoms of his future empire among his followers and surrounded himself with twelve men in accordance with the number of the tribes of Israel. Public life was disrupted to such an extent that even trade came practically to a stop. In the mass hysteria that followed, all sorts of people suddenly went into a state of trance and saw visions of Shabbetai Zevi as the king of Israel.

After his stay in Smyrna Shabbetai Zevi moved to Constantinople (Istanbul), where the Jewish community in the meantime was fully informed of what had been happening in Jerusalem and Smyrna, though the information in some cases was embellished with spontaneous legend-formation. It was not long before practically the whole of the Jewish population in the city was under the spell of the new Messiah. Some opponents, however, were able to convince the Turkish authorities of the necessity of arresting him. Both the massive excitement that Shabbetai Zevi caused and the prediction that he would dethrone the Sultan brought about his imprisonment in February 1666. Probably as a result of his personal charm and considerable bribes he enjoyed special privileges in prison, such as permission to entertain his followers. Soon after this he was transferred to the prison of Gallipoli (Gelibolu), where he also lived like a prince, receiving his subjects in audiences. Pilgrims came from all over to visit him and to take part in the messianic rites initiated by Shabbetai Zevi, which were clearly directed against the Jewish law (such as the eating of forbidden food, for example).

When the mass hysteria reached a climax in the summer of 1666, the movement had become too vigorous, as far as the Turkish authorities were concerned. The constant complaints from opponents in Jewish circles were also a reason for intervention. In September a government commission appeared in Gallipoli which took Shabbetai two days later to Adrianople (Edirne), where he was tried in the presence of the Sultan. Although Shabbetai denied any messianic claims there, he was finally placed before the choice of being executed or converting to Islam. He opted for the latter. On his conversion he assumed the name of Aziz Mehmet Efendi. He was then given the honorific title, "Guardian of the Palace Gates", and was granted a considerable state pension.

Shabbetai Zevi's conversion to Islam created an enormous shock. Apostasy from Judaism was the worst thing an orthodox Jew could imagine; but that the Messiah in person should swap the religion of his fathers for Islam was for many people incomprehensible and unimaginable. Opponents saw this as proof that Shabbetai Zevi was an imposter and a large section of the "believers" came to the same conclusion. Others, however, refused to give up their faith in the Messiah and refused to see that the redemption had evidently not dawned after all. They sought a mystical, theological explanation for what at first sight was the paradoxical behavior of the Messiah (see the next section).

Nathan of Gaza, who throughout all this time had maintained contact with Shabbetai Zevi by means of letters and messengers, continued to believe in the new Messiah even after his conversion to Islam and visited him a number of times. Shabbetai remained in contact with his adherents in various communities, especially in the Balkans, Turkey and Italy. Thereafter he led a double life: externally he presented himself as a Moslem, while secretly he remained the Messiah of the Jews. In this period he held firm to his remarkable antinomistic actions, which he encouraged his followers to engage in also. Until 1672 he lived in turn in Adrianople and Constantinople. In that year it became clear to the Turkish authorities that their most eminent convert had not really become a devout Moslem and that he was carrying on with his social subversiveness. Shabbetai Zevi was banished to Dulcigno

(Ulcinj) in Albania. There too his adherents continued to visit him, although Shabbetai withdrew increasingly from public life and reports of him became more and more scarce. On the Day of Atonement, 17 September in the year 1676, he died. In 1680 his "prophet", Nathan of Gaza, also passed away.

2. The role of Nathan of Gaza

Around the middle of the seventeenth century a large section of the Jewish world lived in the expectation that the restoration would be perfected at any moment, the Messiah would appear as proof that the tiqqun was complete and the redemption of this world would be realized. In this period of hopeful anticipation, around 1643/1644 a man was born in Jerusalem who was to have a decisive influence on the emergence of the later Kabbalah of Shabbetai Zevi: Nathan of Gaza. He must have been very intelligent and he was regarded from a young age as a great rabbinic scholar who studied Lurianic Kabbalah with dedication. He regularly received ecstatic visions of a prophetic nature. Nathan had a name for being able to see the earlier incarnations of each human soul and was able to determine in what way the personal tiqqun would have to be perfected. From various countries many people paid him a visit to consult him on the fate of their soul.

Shabbetai Zevi too heard tell of Nathan of Gaza's prophetic gift. In April 1665 he decided to consult him in the hope that he would be able to do something about his manic-depressive disposition and demonic possession. Shortly before their meeting, Nathan, who must already have heard of Shabbetai Zevi when they both lived in Jerusalem, received a prophetic vision, after vigorous weeping, in which the messianic mission of Shabbetai Zevi was revealed to him. During the consultation Nathan convinced Shabbetai Zevi that he really was the Messiah. A month later, Nathan again received a vision which once again confirmed the messianic mission of Shabbetai Zevi. Fully convinced now, Shabbetai Zevi proclaimed himself in Gaza as the Messiah. As the prophet of the new movement and the driving force behind Shabbetai Zevi, Nathan apprised the Jewish community by means of numerous letters and oral messages of the fact that the Messiah had arisen in Palestine in the person of Shabbetai Zevi. Within a few months all the Jewish communities in the diaspora had heard the intriguing news. It caused great consternation; the fact that the news of this Messiah and his prophet had evidently come from the Holy Land itself added a great deal to its plausibility.

In his description of Shabbetai Zevi as the Messiah, Nathan made keen use of motifs from the ancient apocalyptic myths, such as the Book of Zerubbabel for instance (see Chapter 4, § 1.3), and of generally known ideas on the redemption with which people had become acquainted from Lurianic Kabbalah. By appealing to these familiar motifs he brought about a very speedy spread and acceptance of his messianic ideas concerning Shabbetai Zevi. In order to lend further strength to Shabbetai's status as Messiah, Nathan wrote a work which he ascribed to a twelfth-century scholar in which the coming of Shabbetai Zevi as Messiah was "predicted" in considerable detail.

When Nathan's letters were followed by the (miracle) stories from Jerusalem, Smyrna and Constantinople, all hell broke loose in the Jewish communities. The reactions of the masses corresponded with those in Palestine and Turkey: "unbelievers" were terrorized, lengthy periods of fasting were observed, trade came almost entirely to a standstill and many sold all that they had to go to Palestine. Poets composed verses which were presented to Shabbetai Zevi, and the leaders of the Jewish communities informed Shabbetai Zevi officially that they recognized him as the Messiah.

The report of Shabbetai's arrest did not arouse any suspicion among believers with respect to his messianic claims; the fact that, contrary to Turkish custom, he was not immediately sentenced to death as a troublemaker, had the effect of reinforcing the messianic fervor. Moreover, Nathan of Gaza soon provided a theological explanation for Shabbetai's imprisonment in a tractate entitled *Derush ha-Tanninim* (Exposition on the Dragons). Building on the above-mentioned apocryphal motifs and Lurianic Kabbalah, Nathan expanded on the quality of the soul-spark of the Messiah. Even such a soul as that of the Messiah, in his view, had to arrive among the satanic powers of evil subsequent to the breaking of the vessels. From the beginning of creation the soul of the Messiah had been engaged in an incessant struggle with the demonic powers in the realm of the left side. Now that the time had dawned for tiqqun to be perfected, the Messiah freed himself from that area of evil and revealed himself in a human incarnation. The manic-depressive attacks from which Shabbetai Zevi suffered, Nathan interpreted as a symbolic reflection of the defeats and victories which the soul of the Messiah had suffered and won in the depths of the kelippoth. This also formed the explanation for the periodically occurring transgressions of the Jewish law committed by Shabbetai Zevi. His imprisonment in Turkey, too, was a symbol of the sojourn of the soul of the Messiah in the realm of evil. Shabbetai's arrest was thus a necessary phase which was to precede the ultimate redemption.

With the myth that the descent of the messianic soul spark to the forces of the left-hand side belongs to the mission of the Messiah, Nathan of Gaza comes up with an idea of which no trace is to be found in traditional or kabbalistic literature. In the teaching of Isaac Luria we find nothing about the origin of the soul of the Messiah— and moreover the Lurianic kabbalists, as we have learned, had no special interest in the personality of the Messiah.

Nathan's explanation was accepted without question by the sabbatians. Even the fact that Shabbetai Zevi self-confidently signed some of his letters with "I am the Lord Your God, Shabbetai Zevi" or "the firstborn son of God" did not seem to alienate many believers. In Yemen mystical commentaries were written in which the whole life of Shabbetai Zevi—interwoven with the most fantastic legendary tales that had come into circulation in the meantime—was interpreted symbolically.

In the following section we shall see that, contrary to what might have been expected, Shabbetai Zevi's apostasy did not mean the end of the messianic excitement, but on the contrary was precisely to give a boost to the rise of a movement that was to become known as sabbatianism.

3. The rise of the sabbatian movement and its teaching

The shock and consternation that followed Shabbetai Zevi's conversion to Islam caused a deep and serious internal crisis in the religious life of the "believers". Rabbis who had not let themselves be caught up by the mass messianic excitement and had remained skeptical towards Shabbetai Zevi, called upon everyone to turn back to traditional orthodoxy. A portion of Shabbetai Zevi's adherents, totally disillusioned, paid heed to this call. The orthodox authorities wished to return to what in their view was normal Jewish life and wanted as quickly as possible to forget this event which had so shamed Judaism. People pretended no such thing had happened.

Many kabbalists, meanwhile, shocked by the chaotic events surrounding Shabbetai Zevi, came to the conclusion that mysticism was not appropriate for the masses. Like the classical kabbalists of the time before Luria, they withdrew to study Kabbalah in small, closed and elitist groups. They were of the opinion that such matters were suitable only for a very scholarly upper class.

But others who had believed in Shabbetai Zevi refused to acknowledge that they had been mistaken. The inner belief in the coming of the Messiah and the imminent redemption had been experienced so intensively that even such a shocking event as a conversion of the Messiah was not able to shake their faith. This group of people, who would never conceive of giving up their messianic expectation, sought an answer to the paradoxical situation which had arisen after the conversion of Shabbetai Zevi. Their inner perception of the redemption was now at odds with the irrefutable concrete facts that had occurred: despite the appearance of the Messiah the outside world was still languishing in a state of exile and the redemption had not yet really set in, while furthermore the Messiah himself had become unfaithful to Judaism. According to Gershom Scholem the real beginnings of the sabbatian movement lie in the emergence of this specific body of ideas.

In the sections that follow (§§ 3.1 – 3.3) we shall see that a peculiar theology developed in sabbatianism, full of paradoxes and contradictions, which came from and was fed by serious kabbalistic ideas. In section 4 we shall, however, see how this body of ideas gradually split off into heresies that can no longer be taken seriously. Since these currents, the roots of which doubtless lie in Kabbalah, have had a considerable influence on the history of Judaism, they need to be described in this book.

3.1 Nathan of Gaza as the movement's theologian

Nathan of Gaza provided the answer to the religious crisis of those who wanted to continue to believe in Shabbetai Zevi. Immediately after it became known that Shabbetai had converted, he declared that this was a great mystery, the meaning of which would be revealed in the future. Isaac Luria had already taught that it was the task of the Jewish people to redeem the divine sparks of Jews and non-Jews. To this Nathan added that there were also sparks that could not be freed from their captivity merely by commandments and prayer. The liberation of these sparks belonged to the task of the Messiah himself. He would have to descend into the realm of darkness in order to overpower the devilish forces from the inside and to free the last sparks, with which the mission of the Messiah would be completed. In order to enter the area of the kelippoth the Messiah had to don the clothing appropriate for these areas: outwardly he had to become a Moslem.

Nathan's explanation followed seamlessly on from the declarations he had given earlier as regards the state of the soul spark of the Messiah, his antinomistic actions and his imprisonment. By entering into the kingdom of evil the Messiah was bringing himself into danger, but he would save the world. His constant transgressions of the Jewish law were continued in the extreme with *the* transgression par excellence: apostasy from Judaism. Though he would be reviled for it, his conversion to Islam was a sacred task which had to be fulfilled before Shabbetai Zevi would reveal himself to the world in his full glory as the Messiah.

In order to reinforce his defense and explanation of Shabbetai's apostasy, Nathan drew upon motifs from *Sefer ha-Temunah* (Book of the Figure) where there is talk of cosmic periods, each of which has its own corresponding Torah (see Chapter 3, § 2.6.1), as well as upon the ideas of the classical kabbalists, who believed in a spiritual and perfect Torah of Emanation (*Torah de-Atsiluth*), which in our concrete world, the post-Fall world, could only manifest itself to a very limited extent and necessarily adopted the form of the Torah of the Creation (*Torah de-Beri'ah*; see Chapter 4, § 1.4). According to Nathan, with the coming of the Messiah a period of transition had begun, in which the redemption had not yet fully been realized. In this transitional phase the present Torah would give way to the perfect Torah of the future redeemed world. Since the Messiah in the person of Shabbetai Zevi already moved on the level of the future spiritual Torah, he was no longer bound to the commandments and prohibitions of the Torah we know. The world was in a period of transition; the redemption was beginning to be sketched out in the highest spiritual realms, but had not yet become fully crystallized in our concrete reality. Nathan of Gaza emphasized that it was only Shabbetai Zevi, as the Messiah, who had the right to transgress the law and that every Jew must stick strictly to the observance of the commandments until the real redemption had dawned. Nonetheless with this sabbatian kabbalistic theology he laid the foundations for a heretical doctrine: the time of the old Torah is past.

Although antinomism was a danger that often threatened throughout the history of Judaism, it had never become a dominant or undermining factor of any significance. The classical rabbis had, it is true, speculated on the character of the Torah in the World to Come and had wondered hypothetically whether the commandments would still apply with the coming of the Messiah. And it is true that the kabbalists had developed the idea of a special spiritual Torah for the World to Come, but as long as the messianic time still lay in an unspecified distant future, the danger of antinomism was not acute. Jews who no longer felt comfortable with the religious regulations turned their back on their religion and left Judaism for what it was. There was never any question of an antinomism having threatened Judaism from within. With the sabbatian theology of Nathan of Gaza, however, this was indeed a genuine danger. Just one more step and there would be real anarchy and heresy in the heart of Judaism.

After the death of Shabbetai Zevi in 1676 Nathan announced a new aspect of the doctrine of the Messiah. He had not really died but had passed over into occultation; he was merely hidden in higher realms. The Messiah was invisible to ordinary people, while he was busy in other spheres with the fulfillment of his mission. Since the doctrine of reincarnation was generally accepted, no one saw anything odd in the idea that the Messiah had known many incarnations on earth from Adam onwards and that the process was still not over. Among the later radical and heretical followers of Shabbetai Zevi (see below, §§ 4.1 and 4.2) various leaders were to arise who regarded themselves as reincarnations of Shabbetai Zevi.

Besides the Exposition on the Dragons mentioned above, Nathan of Gaza wrote a few other works, the two most important of which merit mention: *Sefer ha-Beri'ah* (Book of Creation), in which he expounds his kabbalistic system, and *Zemir Aritsim* (Eradication of the Tyrants, after Isa 25.5), which goes into the character of the Torah in the messianic period and the antinomistic behavior of Shabbetai Zevi.

3.2 The contribution of Abraham Cardozo

Besides Nathan of Gaza there were others who contributed to the dissemination of sabbatian doctrine. The most important of them was Abraham Miguel Cardozo (1627-1706). Cardozo was the offspring of a Marrano family in Spain. (*Marranos* is the term for Jews who remained in Spain after the expulsion and who outwardly converted to Christianity under the coercion of the Inquisition, but secretly led a Jewish life.) Cardozo studied medicine and Christian theology at the university of Salamanca and led a nomadic life after that; among other places he lived in Tripoli, Cairo, Turkey and Italy, where he earned his keep as a doctor. In Italy he converted back to Judaism and occupied himself with the study of theological questions, with classical rabbinic literature and Lurianic Kabbalah.

The report of the existence of Shabbetai Zevi and Nathan of Gaza meant a great reversal for Cardozo. He immediately became a convinced follower of the new Messiah and enthusiastically spread the teachings of sabbatianism—even after the apostasy of Shabbetai Zevi—in all the places he stayed. Cardozo maintained correspondence with Shabbetai Zevi, Nathan of Gaza and other leading figures in the movement. He won over numerous adherents, but also provoked vigorous protests on the part of local rabbis; more than once he was banished or excommunicated. He regularly received messianic visions about the redemption. Initially he regarded himself as the Messiah ben Joseph (see Chapter 4, § 1.3), but later changed his mind.

The best known of his numerous writings is *Iggeret Magen Avraham me-Erets ha-Ma'arav* (Letter of the Shield of Abraham from the Maghreb, 1668). In this work Cardozo defends the apostasy of Shabbetai Zevi, which he does not see as a sinful act or a failure on Shabbetai's part, but precisely as a fulfilling of his messianic duty. It is inconceivable, according to Cardozo, that such a pious man as Shabbetai Zevi should have strayed from the right path, as many were claiming; the whole idea of God's justice would then come under question. The actions of the Messiah, whose soul originated from an unimaginably high level, constituted an unfathomable secret for ordinary people. Picking up on the Lurianic teaching of exile, tiqqun and redemption, Cardozo suggests that the Messiah simply has to travel puzzling paths in order to fulfill his mission in the process of restoration. In support of his view Cardozo refers to Bible stories in which there is also talk of apparently forbidden acts: Ruth, the matriarch of the Davidic royal house, from whom the Messiah would issue (see the previous chapter, § 1.1), comes, as a Moabite, from an incestuous relationship between Lot and his daughters (Gen 19); Tamar seduces her father-in-law Judah, from which union Perez is born, an ancestor of David (Gen 38); king David deliberately lets the husband of the desirable Bathsheba die and from their union comes king Solomon (2 Sam 11–12).

As an ex-Marrano Cardozo was struck by the parallels between the life of the Marrano Jews and Shabbetai and his followers who had converted to Islam: a double life by pretending to adhere to a particular religion while secretly one follows another religion. The fact that large communities from Spain, which had been Marranos for generations, saw in Shabbetai Zevi's conversion a religious justification for their own and their forefathers' "apostasy", contributed much to the popularity of sabbatianism.

3.3 Sabbatian exegesis

Following Nathan of Gaza and Abraham Cardozo, others too played a part in the development of a specifically sabbatian theology. If it was true that the antinomistic actions and the apostasy of Shabbetai Zevi formed part of the divine plan, then it must be possible to find this alluded to in the Bible, in traditional rabbinic literature and in mystical literature. In sabbatianism we see clearly how it is possible, by means of exegetical mental gymnastics on the basis of the tradition, to "prove" precisely the opposite of what Judaism had always stood for. It turned out to be possible to undergird and lend authority to sabbatian teaching by citing quite a number of ideas and motifs from the rich traditional literature.

An example of such radical reinterpretation of the tradition in support of sabbatian doctrine we have already seen above, in Nathan's apology for Shabbetai Zevi's antinomistic behavior and his conversion to Islam; the Messiah did not follow the Torah of the unredeemed world, the Torah of Creation, but a Torah of a higher order, the world of emanation. Cardozo too had already pointed out that the Bible is in fact full of "antinomistic" behavior. A further justification of Shabbetai Zevi's double life was found in the book of Esther, in which the Jewess Esther marries the non-Jewish king Ahasuerus, but remains secretly faithful to her Jewish identity. The Psalms were now taken as laments of the Messiah, who had to become apostate in fulfillment of his mission. Thus for instance the clause from Psalm 143.3, "The enemy causes me to dwell in darkness" was interpreted as the words of the Messiah speaking of his stay in the area of the kelippoth.

In justification of antinomism the motif of the Tree of Life and the Tree of the Knowledge of Good and Evil from the creation story could also be of service. Already in the Bible (Prov 3.18) we read that Wisdom—which was equated with the Torah in Jewish tradition—is really the Tree of Life. Because, since Adam's fall, the world is bowed under the domination of the Tree of Knowledge, the "real" Torah of the Tree of Life had always been hidden. The sabbatians saw the same thing in the story of the two pairs of stone tablets from Exodus 31–34. The first pair, which Moses smashed when he saw the people worshiping the golden calf, had contained the original Torah, while the second pair stood only for the Torah of the unredeemed world. The conclusion was clear: the fact that in a new, redeemed period a totally different Torah would apply, with totally different "laws", had been predicted all this time in the Torah! Moreover, did not every Jew know that other laws applied to the sabbath than to the six ordinary days? Well then, in the unredeemed world of the six days one had to keep the unredeemed laws of the Mishnah—and after all it was no coincidence that the Mishnah consisted of precisely six orders. But in the redeemed world, the world of the cosmic sabbath, all these laws would no longer be valid.

Although some aspects of this reasoning can be found earlier, for instance in the Talmud or the Zohar, here in sabbatianism they are given an entirely new meaning. For the rabbis and even for the kabbalists the messianic period was still far off, in a distant future. That in the messianic period other laws would apply, was then for them merely a statement of theoretical interest; for daily life it had no direct consequences if sometime, at the end of the world, some laws would be different from now. In the context of the acute messianism of the sabbatians, it was quite a different matter. For them, redemption had begun: the Messiah has *now* come, redemption has *now* begun, and therefore the time of the new Torah has dawned *now*. It is clear that such a conviction was potentially very undermining for the Jewish community.

4. Radical sects within sabbatianism

One of the most important problems in the formation of sabbatian teaching was the question of how one was to act in the transitional period between the coming of the Messiah and the definitive redemption of the world. Should one follow Shabbetai Zevi in his apostasy, or not? Had the old Torah come to an end or not? From the beginning there were great differences of opinion on these pressing questions among the followers of the new Messiah, which were to lead to a split into two groups—moderates and radicals.

The moderates—following Nathan of Gaza and Abraham Cardozo—thought that as long as redemption had not yet definitively and concretely arrived, the old Torah had not lost anything of its practical validity. Since the forces of evil, the kelippoth, were not yet completely defeated, until such time as they were, one should continue to keep rigidly to the traditional commandments. For the inner consciousness of these moderate sabbatians, however, the great reversal had already taken place: in the spiritual worlds the redemption was already a *fait accompli* and it would only be a matter of time before it was also realized in reality. To give expression to this inner conviction, people limited themselves to symbolic transgression of the Torah, such as secretly eating a fruit or even a piece of bacon (!) on the traditional days of fasting, in particular on the ninth day of the month of Av, which for sabbatians was regarded as the festival on which the birth of the Messiah was celebrated.

The radicals among the believers thought they should follow the Messiah in his apostasy from Judaism. Like him, they needed to descend into the area of evil to fight it from the inside and to stand by the Messiah in his sacred mission. In so doing they took the definitive step towards a heretical form of Judaism. By outwardly letting go of Judaism as a whole, they indicated that the old Torah had completely lost its validity and could—indeed *should*—be transgressed; the only Torah that mattered now was the Torah of Emanation. This principle was succinctly expressed in the paradoxical slogan: "The annulment of the Torah is its (true) fulfillment" (*Bittulah shel Torah zehu' qiyyumah*). Another much used term in this connection was *mitswah ha-ba'ah ba-averah*, "a commandment that is performed (precisely) by transgressing it". This term is already found in classical rabbinic literature, but there it refers to the disallowed observance of a commandment because it rests on the transgression of another commandment (such as the performance of a ritual using a stolen object). In sabbatian circles, however, this meaning was deliberately distorted into the heretical opposite: commandments are only kept by transgressing them.

On the one hand we therefore see a group which inwardly adhered to the new Messiah in the person of Shabbetai Zevi but outwardly remained Jewish, and on the other hand we see groups who gave a more radical expression to the same inward conviction by outwardly converting to Islam or Christianity. Both currents however continued to keep intensive and friendly contact with each other; what was important for the sabbatian was the inner conviction, the belief in his Messiah. Whether one lived externally as a Jew, as a Moslem or as a Christian, was of secondary importance.

We shall now pay closer attention to two radical and heretical groupings or sects which came from sabbatianism, but which had in the meantime gone their own way completely. One of these sects, the Dönme, was ultimately to convert to Islam, while the other, the Frankists of Jacob Frank, was to go over to Christianity.

4.1 The Dönme sect

Already at Shabbetai Zevi's conversion to Islam in 1666 about two hundred families had converted to Islam in discipleship to their Messiah. They regarded themselves as the warriors who must stand at the Messiah's side in the last and most difficult struggle against the powers of the left-hand side. In many cases these were leading families from Adrianople, Constantinople and Smyrna, among them scholars and kabbalists. Up to his death in 1676 this group maintained close contacts with Shabbetai Zevi in his place of exile, Dulcigno in Albania.

After Shabbetai Zevi's death, his fourth and last wife Jochebed (whose Turkish name was Aisha) moved to Saloniki (Thessalonica). There a group of sabbatians formed under the leadership of her father Joseph Filosof, Solomon Florentin and Jacob Querido, the brother of Jochebed. According to the latter her brother Jacob was a reincarnation of Shabbetai Zevi.

After a period of messianic excitement, in which many people received revelations and visions concerning Shabbetai Zevi, in 1683 there followed a mass conversion of some three hundred families to Islam, who wanted thereby to follow in Shabbetai Zevi's footsteps: outwardly Islamic and inwardly Jewish. The year 1683 is then seen as the real beginning of the *dönme* sect (Turkish for "apostate" or "convert"). Many converted families from outside Saloniki moved to this town, which then became the center of the sect. Besides Saloniki many members of the sect also lived in Adrianople, Smyrna, Constantinople and other places, especially in the Balkans, which belonged to the Ottoman empire.

The Dönme sabbatians formed a closed community and lived in certain areas of the city. Marriages were entered into only between members of the sect, marriage with other Moslems was strictly forbidden. Outwardly people lived as loyal Moslem citizens of the Ottoman empire—some even went on the pilgrimage to Mecca—but inwardly in secret they were sabbatian Jews. The sect maintained friendly contacts with sabbatians who had remained Jewish, as well as with Sufi and Dervish circles, mystical currents in Islam. Each had both a Hebrew and a Turkish name; in public life Turkish was spoken, while among themselves they used Ladino (Judeo-Spanish). As a sort of communal faith code they had a list of 18 commandments that served as guidelines for the Dönme members and were ascribed to Shabbetai Zevi himself.

Internal differences of opinion led to the break-up of the Dönme into various directions. It was not long before a group surrounding Jacob Querido separated from the original sect, who called themselves "Jacobites", unlike the original group, who were now known as "Izmirites". From the latter group, around 1700 an extremely radical group of sabbatians split off, under the leadership of Barukhya Russo (whose Turkish name was Osman Baba), who was regarded by his followers as the reincarnation of Shabbetai Zevi.

The radical character of the sect of Barukhya is evident in the fact that they taught that Shabbetai Zevi possessed a divine nature—and later the same divine status was to be attributed to Barukhya himself. But even more striking was the way in which the members of the sect made use of the concept of the Torah of Emanation. Moderate sabbatians thought that the time of the Torah of Emanation had in fact already dawned, and as a sign that the old Torah would soon be replaced, they symbolically transgressed the Halakhah by certain actions. Barukhya, however, went a significant and decisive step further: he claimed to have knowledge of the real content of the Torah of Emanation. According to him, it consisted of a reversal of all the commandments and prohibitions from the old Torah into their opposites. What is forbidden in the old Torah is in fact recommended in the Torah of Emanation, or even a commandment. This meant that the break with tradition was complete. Not only had the old Torah already been replaced by the new, but the transgression of the traditional law was elevated to the status of an ideal.

Throughout the rank and file of the sect this idea was applied in practice; scholars and rabbis with great knowledge of the tradition transgressed the daily commandments just as much as the lower social classes. Within Barukhya's group in particular, but also in the other currents of the Dönme—and to a lesser extent also among moderate sabbatians—people applied themselves to transgression of the law in the area of forbidden sexual relations (such as those in Leviticus 18, including incest). During sabbatian festivals bacchic and orgiastic rites were held, which included a religiously inspired form of "partner-swapping". To this end an idea of Cardozo's was used, who suggested that before the Fall Eve had lived in a state of promiscuity, in which she belonged to many men. According to Cardozo, after the redemption this state of promiscuity would be restored to honorable status. Since more radical sabbatians were, unlike Cardozo, of the opinion that the Torah of Emanation already applied, they put the intended situation straight into practice.

There are indications that such orgiastic rituals within the Dönme were held right into the twentieth century. Although from the end of the nineteenth century we see the beginnings of a tendency among the Dönme to assimilate with their Turkish environment, there are still families in Turkey who are known to be descendants of Dönme members. According to Scholem, descendants of Dönme families had important posts in Turkish public life, such as the minister of finance, Djavid Bey, after the revolution of the Young Turks in 1909. When the founder of the secular Turkish state, Mustafa Kemal (1881-1938), later called Ataturk, came to power, people in his birthplace, Saloniki, used to tell that this man was the offspring of a Dönme family. This rumor is either confirmed or denied according to political affiliation.

Since the Dönme members succeeded extremely well in keeping their beliefs hidden from the outside world and since the written witnesses from which their ideas derive have been lost in the course of time or have been destroyed by opponents, for a long time we knew very little about the Dönme sect. What we know today we owe to the fact that in the last decades material has occasionally come to light that derives, among other things, from assimilated ex-Dönme families who wanted to come to terms with their sabbatian past and wanted to divest themselves of the prayer books or manuscripts in their possession, so that this material became available for study.

As far as the number of adherents is concerned, the Dönme sect was still a rather small group by comparison with the second radical, heretical grouping which emerged out of sabbatianism: the sect of the Frankists.

4.2 Jacob Frank and Frankism

The founder of the Frankist movement was Jacob Frank (1726-1791), from Podolia, a region in the then Kingdom of Poland, where many sabbatians lived. As a merchant, he came into contact with the Dönme sect of Barukhya Russo in Saloniki in 1753. On his return to Podolia he quickly became the leader of the sabbatians and founded a sect with himself at the center. A considerable portion of its adherents was later ultimately to convert to Christianity. Jacob Frank's movement spread over large parts of central and eastern Europe.

4.2.1 The disputation of Kamieniec

In 1756 Frank and his followers were caught in the pursuit of the same sort of heretical orgiastic rituals practiced also by Barukhya's Dönme sect. This caused a great commotion in the Jewish community and in particular among rabbinic authorities, who since the upheaval of Shabbetai Zevi's conversion to Islam had done everything they could to forget what had happened as quickly as possible and tried to encourage the community to turn anew to an orthodox, traditional life-style. The subversive morality of these radical sabbatians was such a thorn in the side of the rabbinic authorities that they sought to root out the movement completely; anyone with real or imagined sympathies for Frank and his sect was banished. The direct legal consequence of the excommunication of Frankists from the Jewish community was that the sect members could be persecuted and killed with impunity.

The persecutions by the rabbis took such unpleasant and dangerous forms for the Frankists that the latter turned to the Catholic Church in Poland with a request for protection. In so doing they deliberately emphasized the religious views that seemed to be reconcilable with the Christian faith, and suggested that they were being persecuted precisely for these convictions by their "fellow-Jews". The Church agreed to the request of the Frankists, since it saw in this group a potential mass conversion to Christianity, while at the same time the Frankists could be a useful instrument in the Christian struggle against Judaism. Thus began a process of several years of tug-of-war between the Church and the sect, which was to end with the conversion of the Frankists.

Presumably on the insistence of a number of fanatical Catholic clerics, in 1757 a public disputation was organized between Frankists and rabbis in Kamieniec, in which the tenets of sabbatian faith were to be debated. Thus among other things the debate considered the sabbatian thesis that the Talmudic (i.e. rabbinic) interpretation of the Torah rested on a misapprehension. At the conclusion of the debate the bishop determined that the Frankists had won the dispute. The rabbinic Jews, who had right from the start participated in the debate only with the greatest reluctance, found severe punitive measures imposed on them: among other things huge quantities of religious literature, especially the Talmud, were publicly burned.

4.2.2   The teaching of Jacob Frank

In the meantime in the town of Iwanie a group of sabbatians had formed under the leadership of Jacob Frank, functioning more or less as a closed community. Here Frank formed his real Frankist-sabbatian doctrine, which in a number of respects was closely connected with Christian dogma. He realized that in the long run it would not be possible to avoid a definitive conversion to Christianity; with this doctrine he prepared his followers for the Christian life they would live outwardly, while in secret they would be living a Frankist sabbatianism.

Frank was not particularly learned and had only an elementary knowledge of rabbinic tradition. His theories in fact boil down to a few simple points. He saw in himself and in his "doctrine" the fulfillment of the mission of Shabbetai Zevi and Barukhya, but preached an antinomism that was much more extreme. What we find here is a strong nihilism which strives to break down all religion as superfluous nonsense: all forms of institutionalized religion are merely phases a person has to go through before experiencing the only true God, who has always remained hidden.

Although Jacob Rank viewed himself as an incarnation of Shabbetai Zevi and the successor of Barukhya Russo, the figure of Shabbetai Zevi was relegated to the background in Frankism. The Kabbalah of the Zohar and of Isaac Luria, too, no longer played any part. Frank came with a myth all his own, from which the customary kabbalistic terms and symbols were missing—although in content these still came down to a revision of earlier kabbalistic ideas. In part he built upon ideas of the Dönme sect, which included the notion that Shabbetai Zevi was an incarnation of God who came as Messiah to perfect tiqqun and to abolish the present Torah, and that Barukhya Russo himself was also of divine nature (see the previous section). According to Frank, God was incarnate for the first time in Shabbetai Zevi and he himself constituted the second incarnation; in the future He would be incarnate a third time as a woman.

In the time that remained to the world before the revelation of God as the Virgin, the true Jew (read: the Frankist) had to assume a completely new lifestyle, which Frank indicated by the phrase "the way to Esau". In rabbinic tradition Esau often stands for Christianity. Just as Christianity neither feels bound to nor keeps the Law, so for Jacob Frank "the way to Esau" meant a life of lawlessness and abandon, especially in the area of sexuality. By means of clever exegesis Frank was able to "show" that this heretical view had already been stated in the Bible. In Genesis 33.14 Jacob (!) promises his twin brother Esau that he will meet him in Seir. The Bible story does not, however, give any subsequent account of such a journey by Jacob to Esau. In this passage Frank read a reference to his own teaching and suggested that it was now up to him, Jacob Frank, finally to undertake this journey in fulfillment of the biblical text. "The way to Esau" thus meant a life in which the members of the sect lived outwardly as Christians, while they kept their true beliefs deeply hidden from the outside world. Frank also read this secrecy of "the way to Esau" in the Bible, by making skillful use of the dual meaning of two Hebrew words, *massa' dumah*, from Isaiah 21.11. In the context of that verse, *massa'* means "pronouncement, utterance of God" and *dumah* is the proper noun, Dumah, another name for Edom: "utterance of God concerning Dumah". *Massa'*, however, can also mean "burden" and the word *dumah* can additionally mean "keep silence". So in Isa 21.11 Jacob Frank read: "the burden of keeping silence". Moreover, the fact that Dumah is another name for Edom was not without significance, since according to Gen 36.8 Edom was the same as Esau. So the term in Isaiah could be seen in a sense as "the burden of Esau". Frank's conclusion was that the Bible itself already indicates that keeping secret the Frankist teaching, "the way to Esau", was a heavy burden for believers.

In Frankism the veneration of the "Lady" (*gevirah*) played an important part. This use was inspired by the biblical figure of the *gevirah*, an eminent woman at the court of the ancient Israelite kings (e.g. 1 Kgs 2.19). As *gevirah* among the women of the movement, Jacob Frank's own wife was the central focus of the ritual veneration of the woman. When she died in 1770, this status devolved to Frank's daughter Rachel, whose Christian name was Eve. Many Frankists had cameo portraits of her in their possession. All this arouses strong associations with the Christian idea of the Virgin. Similarly following the Christian model, Frank appointed twelve of his most important followers as apostles, and alongside them twelve female apostles, who also rendered service as his lovers.

4.2.3   *The Lvov disputation—the conversion to Christianity*

While Frank was developing his new teaching in Iwanie, preparations were underway for a second public disputation, this time in Lvov (Lemberg). The intention was that before the Frankists would definitively convert to Christianity, they would have to subscribe to the principles of Christian faith in a public debate. In order to mislead the church authorities their convictions were once again formulated in such a way that to Christians they appeared to confirm the truth of Christianity, while the Frankist in the know could draw his own conclusions. One of the motions debated ran: "All the biblical prophecies concerning the Messiah have already been fulfilled." This declaration could of course be greeted with agreement by Christians as a reference to the figure of Jesus as the Messiah. But Frankists, too, could agree with this motion, since they secretly saw the Messiah in Jacob Frank. For their part, the rabbinic Jews did all they could to convince the Church of the double and untrue character of the sect it was planning to accept in its midst. The Church remained deaf to these arguments, however. The most important aspect of the Lvov disputation, which was held in the summer of 1759, was actually the special wish of the

Church that the Frankists should confirm in public the Christian claim that Jews indulged in ritual murder by slaughtering Christian children so as to use their blood for religious purposes, such as the preparation of unleavened bread. This ineradicable Christian superstition, which raised its head time and again from the Middle Ages onwards, with all its horrendous consequences for Jews, had thus been falsely confirmed "by the Jews themselves".

The Polish Catholic Church saw its aims achieved: a week after the disputation, with much ado the ceremonial mass baptism of the Frankists took place, Jacob Frank included, whose Christian name from that point on was Joseph Frank. The news of the imminent mass conversion of the Frankists had, partly as a result of the efforts of the Church, spread through large parts of Europe and even beyond, with lightning speed. From the Protestant side in Germany, attempts were undertaken to convert the Frankists to the "only true" form of Christianity. Besides the Frankists who converted to Christianity, there were also large groups which did not take this step and ultimately remained within Judaism. This made no difference to the recognition of Frank's leadership; as in the case of the Dönme it was not too important what religion one belonged to outwardly.

4.2.4   The Frankist community and the end of the movement

After their conversion the Frankists were better off in a number of respects; economically they were able to develop and many Frankists revealed a talent for penetrating the higher echelons of society. Often Frankists ran independent businesses, occupied public office or became army officers. In Poland and Austria various families were even admitted to the aristocracy. There were also contacts between Frankists and Masonic circles. There are still controversies surrounding the Frankist background of eminent persons such as the most famous Polish poet, Adam Mickiewicz.

Although many Frankists had now officially become Catholics, great mistrust continued to exist in church circles towards the new converts. A number of Frankists were persuaded to divulge information on the secret lifestyle of fellow believers. The consequence was that Jacob Frank had to appear before a church court and was imprisoned for a period of thirteen years in the fort of Czestochowa. Like Shabbetai Zevi during his imprisonment, Frank also succeeded in maintaining contact with, and instructing, his followers; his prison, too, strongly resembled a royal court. Within the walls of the fort, secret sexual, orgiastic religious rites were held.

After Frank's release, he moved to Brno (Brünn) in Moravia, where he again held court. Frankist families sent their children from all over to Brno to serve at Frank's court. To his courtly personnel belonged uniformed soldiers who were to conquer a separate area for the Frankists in the end-time wars. Through a network of contacts which Frank maintained with persons in high position and influential government offices, in 1775 he and his daughter were granted an audience with the Empress of Austria. Presumably he promised her the help of his movement and that of the Dönme sect in the struggle against the Turks. In order to bolster the exclusive standing of his movement, Frank had circulated the story that his daughter Rachel (Eve) was an illegitimate child of the Russian Empress Catharina. This story was believed even in the highest circles; her whole life long—she died in 1816—Frank's daughter was to pass as a Russian princess of the House of Romanov.

In 1787 Frank and his court moved to Offenbach, which was to be the last center of the Frankists. When Frank died in 1791, there was no one with sufficient charisma to lead the Frankist movement. The community in Offenbach disintegrated quickly and many left. Nonetheless Frankism continued as a movement; families in various countries maintained contact, whether they had outwardly become Christians or had remained Jewish. They continued to marry within their ranks and regularly organized meetings in which religious rites were conducted.

As in the case of the Dönme movement, among the other sabbatian currents in the course of time large amounts of historical documents disappeared, were destroyed or deliberately suppressed. Thus a chronicle of the life of Jacob Frank written in Offenbach, which included a precise description of the sexual rituals, has unfortunately been lost. With the disappearance of the Frankists the last stage of the sabbatian movement came to an end.

5. Shabbetai Zevi: a controversy

Since the appearance of Shabbetai Zevi everything to do with sabbatianism has constantly given rise to bitter controversies and heated debate. It is clear that in the eighteenth century rabbinic Judaism was not only embarrassed by the confrontation with the sabbatian movement, its antinomism and acute messianic feelings, with the sects of the Dönme and Jacob Frank and with the Church, but it also got into serious difficulties as a result. In order to turn this tide, many orthodox rabbis set about unmasking sympathizers with the sabbatian movement—quite a number of whom were still found within Judaism—and exposing and excommunicating them. The primary targets were rabbis who had positions of leadership in their communities who were whispered to be secret sabbatians.

A well-known figure in such heretic-hunts was Rabbi Jacob Emden, a man who combined a fanatical religious zeal with a special talent for tracking down sabbatian heretics. He set up, for instance, an investigation into the possibly sabbatian sympathies of a respected and eminent scholar, Rabbi Jonathan Eybeschütz (ca. 1690–1764) of Prague. Emden showed that a number of amulets with sacred names made by Eybeschütz contained cryptic references to the name of Shabbetai Zevi. Furthermore, according to Emden, a book with a clearly sabbatian character, entitled *Wa-Avo' ha-Yom el ha-Ayin* (Today I Shall Come to the Source), was written by Jonathan Eybeschütz. With his accusations addressed to Eybeschütz—who by the way vehemently denied everything—Emden unleashed a controversy that dragged on and on in the East-European Judaism of the time, giving rise to great divisiveness.

Another personality who was to bring considerable disruption to the eighteenth-century Jewish world was Moses Hayyim Luzzatto (1707–1746). Already as a young learned kabbalist he developed original, strongly messianically tinted ideas, which were in part concerned with the way in which people could actively work towards the redemption of Israel. Although he was not a sabbatian, Luzzatto had a number of ideas in common with sabbatianism—such as the descent of the Messiah into the area of darkness. In so doing he awakened the distrust of antisabbatian heretic-hunters, which was reinforced by the fact that he regularly received revelations from a heavenly maggid (cf. Chapter 4, § 2.1). He was also continually bothered and opposed on account of his messianic ideas; ultimately he was prevented from speaking and writing about them.

In the nineteenth century, the time of the *Wissenschaft des Judentums*—the Jewish scholarship that undertook the first research into the history of Judaism—the figure of Shabbetai Zevi and the sabbatian movement continued to occupy minds. Most scholars of that time wanted to see Judaism primarily as a rational and abstract religion (for details see Chapter 1, § 1). Within this rational view there was no room for mysticism, which was viewed as a backward by-product on the periphery of Judaism. The *Wissenschaft* tried to trivialize Shabbetai

Zevi and the sabbatian movement and dismiss it as fraud and decep-
tion, without content and without any connection with serious
Judaism. That all this had taken place within Judaism was ascribed to
the stupidity of people who had been open to false influences. Now
that the period of enlightened thinking had dawned, the *Wissenschaft*
argued, such stupid religious excesses should be consigned entirely to
the past.

While many in our own day subscribe to this opinion of nineteenth-century scholars, even those who do not oppose mysticism in
principle find themselves confronted by a big problem: where, exactly,
is the boundary line between serious mysticism as appears in Kabbalah,
and a complete derailment from tradition? In the figure of Shabbetai
Zevi do we have an anomaly, a sudden and unique aberration, or can
one speak of an obvious and logical product of a historical development that took place within Jewish mysticism?

In order to be able to answer such questions and to determine the
right place of the Kabbalah of Shabbetai Zevi within the historical
development of Jewish mysticism and Judaism in general, the phenomenon must be approached without preconceived ideas. Gershom
Scholem, who wrote a monumental work on Shabbetai Zevi, was of
the opinion that the movement could not be dismissed as a hysterical
craze or a pathological excess, since—even if it were true—it would
not *explain* the movement as a whole. Sabbatianism must have had real
appeal and have met religious needs that were current among the Jews
of the time. The fact that the sabbatian movement had a truly enormous following, as well as the fact that a large number of great and
scholarly rabbis had associated themselves with the movement, indicates that there was much more going on than an outburst of religious
hysteria which should be forgotten as quickly as possible.

Other attempts to explain the movement from the perspective of a
single determinative factor have also failed to convince. Some have
claimed that it was primarily social and economic conditions that
formed the basis for sabbatianism: the messianic element in it would
only have been a banner under which the Jewish masses could rebel
against the social and economic elite. In view of the fact that sabbatianism had at least as many adherents in rich and elevated circles as
among ordinary people, however, such explanations do not seem
probable. Many nineteenth-century scholars tried to see sabbatianism
as what came "from outside" and emerged under the influence of
Christianity. There are, indeed, interesting parallels of content between Christianity and sabbatianism; one might think for instance of

the paradox that the Messiah has already come even though the world has not yet been redeemed, or of the emphasis on the faith in the Redeemer at the cost of the commandments. And one might also mention a number of points of possibly direct Christian influence on sabbatianism, such as the large proportion of Marranos or the Frankist doctrine of the Virgin. But it is once again the case that a tendentious explanation, such as that sabbatianism grew out of Christian influence, is inadequate.

According to Scholem sabbatianism was not only a consequence of external factors, but precisely the result of an inner religious crisis within Judaism. The phenomenon of Shabbetai Zevi was just as much part of the historical development of Judaism and Jewish mysticism as all other currents. Sabbatianism was the ultimate product of the whole historical development of Jewish mysticism, in particular that which developed from Lurianic Kabbalah. The movement would not have been possible without the preceding history of Judaism, a history marked by a continuing desire for the end of exile, suffering, persecution and oppression. As long as the exile continued, the Jewish people was merely "traveling through" in a world that was temporary and ephemeral in nature. The ultimate goal of existence was the promised World to Come. The figure of Shabbetai Zevi released latent forces which had been mounting up within the Jewish people for centuries. Messianism, however, contains a strange paradox: on the one hand the hope for another, better life forms the driving force and source of inspiration for life in an unredeemed world, and on the other hand the attempt to realize this hope in our world is quickly doomed to failure.

Not only is the movement of sabbatianism deeply rooted in Judaism and in the preceding mystical currents, but it is also a factor of significance in the further history of Judaism in the modern period. The Jewish Enlightenment (Haskalah) goes hand in hand with a crisis in religious tradition. Scholem was of the opinion that important elements in the Haskalah and Zionism are first found in sabbatianism. The mysticism of Shabbetai Zevi thus in a sense formed the basis for modern developments in Judaism. An important aspect of the Haskalah is the new, different attitude towards tradition, while Zionism in fact wants to put an end to exile in this world. Both elements are found in sabbatianism. In the hasidic movement too (see the next chapter) Scholem recognized elements of sabbatianism.

Scholem's thesis that sabbatianism was a marginal phenomenon in Jewish history but forms part of a continuous process, still today gives rise to heated and sometimes bitter differences of opinion. Both from the religious side and from the scholarly side this viewpoint has met with vigorous protests.

An example of such a conflict concerns the supposed sabbatian sympathies of the above-mentioned eighteenth-century Rabbi Jonathan Eybeschütz. Closer examination led Scholem to endorse Jacob Emden's "accusation" against Eybeschütz; the latter had indeed secretly been a sabbatian and also the author of the aforementioned sabbatian tractate. As a result he brought upon himself the fierce indignation and great wrath of rabbis in Jerusalem and became the target of ferocious attacks from the orthodox. Already put out at Scholem's claim that the Zohar was only written in the thirteenth century and not by the second-century Rabbi Simeon ben Yohai, the rabbis had had enough; for them it was inconceivable that a highly regarded rabbinic scholar such as Eybeschütz could have seen the Messiah in Shabbetai Zevi.

There has also been criticism on the part of present-day scholars. Such scholars as Eliezer Schweid, Moshe Idel and others dispute parts of Scholem's evaluation of the place of sabbatianism in the historical development of Judaism. According to them, first of all, the sabbatian movement cannot be regarded as a continuation of Judaism, but rather as a departure from it. Further, it is denied that sabbatianism had any positive influence on the content of the Haskalah, hasidism or Zionism. If there is any question of a connection, this is a negative one: the new movements took up a position precisely against sabbatianism. According to these scholars sabbatianism is thus not to be regarded as the first step towards modern Judaism. One may safely say that the debate is still very much alive.

6

Hasidism

Hasidism, which constitutes the most recent manifestation of Jewish mysticism, is perhaps the face of modern Judaism that is best known among the general public. For many people the term "hasidism"— which comes from *hasid*, "pious"—tends to conjure up images of the orthodox religious areas of Jerusalem, New York or Antwerp, where hasidim live and continue to wear their traditional garb. Particularly as a result of the work of the German Jewish philosopher Martin Buber and the literature of such authors as Isaac Bashevis Singer or Chaim Potok, hasidism is widely known.

Despite the correspondence in the name, hasidism should not be regarded as a direct continuation of the twelfth-century Ashkenazi Hasidim. The roots of the movement, which was not initially regarded as in the least orthodox, lie in the Eastern Europe of the eighteenth century. A description of hasidism, then, should begin with that time and place.

1. Introduction

At the beginning of the eighteenth century we see the emergence of hasidism in Podolia, part of the then Kingdom of Poland, which also comprised the Ukraine, Lithuania and Belorussia. The Jewish communities had suffered badly from the disruptive influence of the very unfavorable social, political and economic circumstances of the day.

In his book on hasidism, *Mysticism and Rationalism*, the cultural anthropologist Daniël Meijers presents a concise description of what he calls the "sociogenesis" of hasidism: the social background against which the movement arose. The leadership of the Jewish communities in Poland was traditionally in the hands of a small elite of rabbis and scholars, who occupied themselves largely with the study of Torah, tradition and Halakhah. Communal life relied on the respect it had for its leaders and on the acknowledgement of their religious authority. This elite group was also responsible for religious instruction and the education of religious officials, in relation, for example, to the copying of the Torah scrolls, the preparation of phylacteries, and ritual slaughter. The money needed for the upkeep of this educated elite and for the maintenance of religious institutions was provided by the members of the community.

As a result of internal political tensions, pogroms and wars, this social pattern became disrupted. The majority of the Jewish population fell into such poverty that the money needed for the smooth functioning of their society could no longer be found. Many parents did not have the financial means to have their children take religious education, so that religious knowledge in the community as a whole dwindled badly. Furthermore, any community was able only to maintain a small number of scholars, while the number of religious officials had to be drastically reduced. All the work that was previously done by these civil servants now had to be done by a very small number of people. Those who were still in a position to follow a course of religious education, found there was no longer any work for them, since there were no funds to pay for it.

This gave rise to a growing group of unlettered and uneducated poor people, contrasting with a very small elite of scholars and well-off members of the community. What often happened was that a few rich Jews in the community assumed important positions and developed as the real power-brokers, upon whom many people—in particular the scholars—were dependent. The few religious leaders who now bore responsibility for the community were too much in demand to pay attention to the needs of ordinary people. The growing social gulf between the unlettered poor, who had no funds to contribute, and the wealthy and scholarly elite was exacerbated by the contempt shown by the scholarly elite towards the unlettered masses, who were referred to pejoratively as *am ha-arets*, "the people of the land". In the eyes of rabbis and scholars, an illiterate Jew was not capable of true piety.

The social circumstances described here probably contributed significantly to the emergence of the new mystical movement of hasidism, in which, as we shall see, a distance from the ordinary, unlettered Jew is clearly preserved.

2. Early hasidism

2.1 The Ba'al Shem Tov and the first generation of hasidim

In hasidic tradition, Israel ben Eliezer (ca. 1700–1760) is regarded as the founder of the movement. Unfortunately we do not know anything of his life with certainty; none of his personal documents has come down to us from which we might have learned of his ideas. For information on the life of Israel ben Eliezer and the teaching he is supposed to have spread, we are entirely dependent on what hasidic tradition tells us, a tradition in which the historical facts that may be there have been colored very much by legendary influence.

According to the well-known tradition, Israel ben Eliezer was born in 1698 or 1700 in Okup in Podolia. His mother died in childbirth and his father also passed away while Israel was still very young. The Jewish community that was responsible for his maintenance and education sent him to the Jewish school (*heder*). Although he was a good student, he did not feel at home at school; he found instruction in the details of halakhah particularly difficult. So he grasped every opportunity to withdraw from lessons and to wander around in the open air. Later he earned his keep by bringing small boys to and from school and by helping out in the synagogue.

Israel ben Eliezer married a descendant of a rabbinic family from Brody, despite the resistance of the bride's erudite brother, Rabbi Abraham Gershon of Kutov. The latter was very much opposed to his sister's marriage to an illiterate, but in the end he had to give up his opposition. According to hasidic tradition, however, Israel ben Eliezer was anything but illiterate. From the age of fourteen he is said to have been a member of a secret society of mystics, the "hidden righteous" (*tsaddiqim nistarim*). Although he presented himself to the outside world as illiterate, after lengthy instruction by one of the "hidden righteous" in secret, he participated in the study and activities of these mystics. Other traditions speak of instruction in the secrets of practical Kabbalah (magic) and still others relate that after a regular study of Torah, Talmud and Kabbalah he gained his knowledge by supernatural means, through instruction by the Old Testament prophet Ahijah of Shiloh (1 Sam 14.3). During the wedding meal Israel ben Eliezer told his bride that he was really one of the "hidden righteous", but that he wanted to keep this secret for some time to come.

Since Rabbi Gershon of Kutov considered it inappropriate for his sister to marry an illiterate, he gave the newly married couple a horse and cart and asked them to settle elsewhere. Israel ben Eliezer left with his wife for the Carpathian mountains, where after many years in the quiet of nature he prepared for his coming task in the world. He provided for himself by digging clay, which his wife sold in the town.

When Israel ben Eliezer was thirty-six, he considered the time ripe to go to the outside world and to take on the task that God had prepared for him to do. After he had made himself known to those in his vicinity, he devoted himself to the healing of the sick. From his home in Medziborz he regularly journeyed through the land to heal people with the aid of magical spells and amulets and by driving out evil spirits. Israel ben Eliezer's miraculous healings occupy an important place in the legends about his life. He was known as Ba'al Shem, "Master of the Name", and more frequently as Ba'al Shem Tov, "Master of the Good Name". A *ba'al shem* was someone who was initiated into the secret knowledge of the Divine Name (the Tetragrammaton) and was capable of performing healings and miracles through the magical use of divine names or of their individual letters. In hasidic literature Israel ben Eliezer is also commonly referred to as the *Besht*, a word composed of the first letters of the title Ba'al Shem Tov.

Besides healing people, he also supported the Jewish community as a consultant and adviser in their practical daily problems. The Besht was described as an engaging and charismatic personality who cared very much for his simple, unschooled fellow human beings. It was not long before he acquired a fast-growing circle of followers. The Ba'al Shem Tov is also supposed to have laid the foundations for a mystical doctrine which was elaborated by a small circle of mystics around him and in due course further developed by their disciples. Since we have no personal writings of his, it is not easy to determine what the precise content of his teaching may have been; there continues to be much discussion about this. Presumably mystical prayer lay at its center. By means of this prayer a state of ecstasy was attained: *devequth*, "cleaving to God". Some traditions tell us that the Besht experienced moments of mystical transport. His first concern is said to have been to seek the direct, emotional experience of the deity, so that he did not pay so much attention to the intellectually demanding study of Torah and Talmud as practiced by rabbis at that time. So it is understandable that it was primarily ordinary, unlettered people who found themselves attracted to the new movement.

2.2 Views of the emergence of hasidism

So far we have followed the main lines of the life of the Besht as told by hasidic tradition. In light of the lack of reliable sources from the period, however, it is very uncertain whether this tradition can be reconciled with the historical facts. Scholarly research into the early period of hasidism is deeply divided on the true circumstances of the emergence of this new mystical movement.

There are scholars who, in line with hasidic tradition, are of the opinion that the Ba'al Shem Tov can indeed be regarded as the founder of the newly emerging hasidic movement. Others, on the other hand, subscribe to the view that the Besht was not the central and leading figure of hasidism from the beginning. They think, rather, that at the beginning of the eighteenth century there would have been various small, scattered groups of inspired people living on the margins of the established Judaism of the time. Most of these socially disadvantaged groups were led by charismatic personalities. We scarcely know anything with certainty of their religious ideals, ideas, behavior and prophetic activities. These various groups probably did have common ideas, although there may have been significant differences. In the first instance one might think of common views with regard to ecstatic prayer (*devequth*) and the awareness of the divine indwelling in all human beings and things. According to this view, the Besht would have played a role in just one of a number of such groups.

In the traditional view, such names as Nahman of Horodenka, Menahem of Przemyslan, Pinhas of Korzec, Mendel of Bar and Nahman of Kosov are mentioned, all of whom were among the Besht's first disciples. Those who assume that the Besht was not their leader or the most important of them, think rather that these people were not so much his disciples as his colleagues or rivals: charismatic personalities who were each the leader of a group of their own. It is not impossible that even the Besht was one of the less important leaders. As an exorcist, magician and seller of amulets he will certainly not have been held in high social regard.

Finally, there are also scholars who doubt whether the stories of the Ba'al Shem Tov really go back to a historical kernel, and who do not discount the possibility that the figure of the Besht may never really have existed.

2.3 Dov Baer and the second generation of hasidim

According to a hasidic tradition, just after his death in 1760 the Ba'al
Shem Tov appeared in a night vision to his son. He commissioned
him to inform his closest followers that he had appointed one of his
most devoted followers, Rabbi Dov Baer, as his successor and the
leader of the hasidim. Just like the Besht, Dov Baer was gifted with
charismatic and spiritual qualities. He became the heart and soul of the
incipient organization and enjoyed great respect, outside of hasidism as
well as within. His followers gave him the nickname, "the Great Maggid of Mezhirech".

For information on the life and work of this Dov Baer we are unfortunately dependent on hasidic traditions, as in the case of the
founder of the hasidic movement. Dov Baer was probably born in
1710 in Lukatz in the district of Volhynia, was given a traditional religious education and developed into a great scholar in classical
rabbinic literature and in Kabbalah. Initially he made a living as a
teacher and itinerant preacher (*maggid*). Since his health left something
to be desired, he turned to the Ba'al Shem Tov in the hope of healing.
After consideration of the teaching of the Besht he became a convinced adherent of the new movement.

During the Besht's lifetime there was scarcely any question of an
organized movement. Early hasidism really centered on one person:
the Ba'al Shem Tov. Dov Baer laid the foundation for hasidism as a
social organization. He systematized the ideas of his master and trained
up a body of leaders; after all, the spread of hasidic ideas had need of
people who could provide religious leadership. He moved the center
of hasidism from Medziborz in Podolia to Mezhirech in Volhynia, and
then sent out those he had trained to such areas as Galicia, the
Ukraine, Lithuania and Belorussia. Thus between 1760 (the death of
the Besht) and 1772 (when Dov Baer died), hasidism spread steadily
across large parts of eastern Europe.

Since no writings have come down to us from Dov Baer either, for
the reconstruction of his ideas we are dependent on his followers and
their disciples. Their works preserve a good deal of material that is
ascribed to him. Dov Baer is supposed to have further developed the
doctrinal points of his master the Ba'al Shem Tov. An important element of his thought is the great value he attached to everyday human
activity. Behind even the simplest act, according to Dov Baer, there
lies a hidden, deeper inner significance.

Among the most important of Dov Baer's followers, who were to
play a part in the further development of hasidism, were, among others,

Elimelekh of Lejask, Shneur Zalman of Liady, Nahum of Chernobyl, Levi Isaac of Berdichev, Menahem Mendel of Vitebsk, Jacob Isaac of Lublin, Israel of Kozienice and Solomon of Karlin. After Dov Baer's death in 1772 there came an end to the single-handed leadership of the hasidic movement. His followers, who had settled in various towns in the meantime, formed separate communities, in which as *tsaddik* (see § 3.5) they formed the spiritual center.

As we have seen, there are scholars who think that hasidism did not begin as a single movement under the leadership of the Ba'al Shem, but that it was a case of a variety of small independent groups existing beside one another. According to these scholars Dov Baer did not extend an existing, still immature movement, but his achievement was precisely to have been the first to manage to unite all these hasidic groupings into a single group under the authority of a single leader.

2.4 The third generation: the tsaddikim and their communities

The disciples of Rabbi Dov Baer assembled numerous new adherents around them and founded hasidic communities everywhere. Each disciple then gave leadership to his own community, himself forming the spiritual center as its *rebbe* or *tsaddik*. It was no longer really a matter of a central leadership of the movement as a whole, as had been the case under Dov Baer. A community of hasidim was named after the place where the members had settled with their tsaddik. Thus for example the community around Rebbe Aaron, which had its center in Karlin, was known by the name of Karlin hasidim, and the adherents of Shneur Zalman were called the Lubavitsch hasidim, after the Belorussian town of Lubavitsch. With the increase in the number of hasidic communities the need for religious specialists also grew, so that there was again work for young scholars. New schools and prayer-houses were founded and many people were trained for all kinds of religious functions.

Before going in more detail into the developments in hasidism from the third generation onwards (for this see § 4 below), we shall first pay attention to the fundamental aspects of hasidic teaching and the problems associated with them.

3. Hasidic doctrine

In scholarly research into hasidism there is a lively discussion on almost all aspects of the movement. As far as the content of the hasidic teachings is concerned, we are confronted with a number of problems. First of all there is the difficulty that we have no written sources available from the first decades of hasidism. Secondly, the question arises how the hasidic movement relates to other mystical currents in Judaism: what did hasidism take over from other movements and what are the new elements? Finally, there are a number of problems concerned with the interpretation of particular aspects of hasidic teaching. We shall deal in turn with these questions.

3.1 The sources

One of the biggest problems in the study of hasidism is the fact that there is no direct and original source available to us for the beginnings of the movement; the earliest hasidic writings that have come down to us date from the period between 1780 and 1811 and comprise exegetical sermons (homilies). The oldest material from which hasidic ideas can be derived was thus not committed to writing until twenty years after the death of the Besht—and as many as eight years after the death of his successor, the maggid of Mezhirech.

In 1780 Rabbi Jacob Joseph of Polonnoye, one of the most important of the Besht's followers, published the work *Toledoth Ya'akov Yosef* (Histories of Jacob Joseph). In this work the author recorded hundreds of the Besht's homilies and sayings from his own recollection. This work gave the nascent movement its first authoritative hasidic text, which was to become a source of inspiration in the further development of hasidic doctrine. The dissemination of this work meant that the ideas ascribed to the Besht could become known to a wider circle.

A need was felt for more literature containing material from the Besht. Many publications followed in short order. Before his death in 1782 Rabbi Jacob Joseph of Polonnoye published two more works, *Ben Porath Yosef* (A Young Fruit-tree is Joseph, 1781; referring to Gen 49.22) and *Tsafenath Pa'neah* (1782; referring to Gen 41.45). The followers of Dov Baer published two collections of homilies by their master, *Maggid Devaraw le-Ya'aqov* (Sermons to [the People of] Jacob) and *Liqqutei Amarim* (Collected Sayings). From the third generation such works as *No'am Elimelekh* (Delight of Elimelekh) by Rabbi Elimelekh of Lejask and the works *Tanya* (Doctrine), *Tsawwa'ath ha-Rivash* (Testament of Rabbi Israel Ba'al Shem) and *Kether Shem Tov* (Crown of [Rabbi Israel] Shem Tov) by Rabbi Shneur Zalman, became well known.

Followers of the Ba'al Shem Tov used to adopt material from the Besht in their own sermons, generally highlights which they could still remember. Many sermons by the Besht's followers were in turn writ ten down by their followers, so that various versions of a single sermon came into circulation. After a while the sayings ascribed to the Besht were again collected from various homiletic works by different authors, put together and published as independent works of the Ba'al Shem Tov.

A problem for the history of hasidism is thus that we know scarcely anything about the development of a hasidic doctrine prior to 1780. This means that we do not know for sure whether the basic elements of hasidic doctrine that formed later really do have their origins in the ideas of the Ba'al Shem Tov, the founder of the movement. Since even Dov Baer, one of the earliest of the Besht's disciples, rarely quotes his master, his work—which was very significant for the further development of the hasidic teachings—unfortunately does not answer the question of what ideas really formed the heart of the earliest hasidism and where they came from.

Those who think that hasidism arose from various groups that existed alongside one another, do not believe that the heart of later hasidic doctrine goes back to one man, the Besht. They are of the opinion that from the publications between 1780 and 1811 it can be deduced that, especially after the absorption of the various groupings into a single movement under Dov Baer, the memories of the earliest period became ever more vague, and gradually a somewhat distorted and legendary picture of the origins of the movement emerged. In this view, the notion of the Besht as the founder and central leader of the hasidic movement developed in the historical consciousness from the third generation onwards.

Closely related to the problem of the exact historical development of the teachings in early hasidism is the question when we can speak of the real beginning of the movement. Some see the beginning in the year 1736, when the Ba'al Shem Tov first went public. Others view 1760 as the beginning year, since that was when Dov Baer started out as the successor of the Besht and transformed incipient hasidism into an organized, mass social movement. Others again are of the opinion that one can only speak of a hasidic movement after the death of Dov Baer in 1772, when the phenomenon of the tsaddik arose, which is so typical of the movement. It has also been proposed that hasidic ideas only really became disseminated through the works that were written

on them; in that case, hasidism would have begun in 1780 with the
publication of the work by Rabbi Jacob Joseph mentioned above.

Apart from the collected exegetical sermons hasidism produced another literary genre: hasidic stories. Among the general public in our
day, hasidism has become familiar mainly as a result of these stories.
Much less well known, however, is the fact that the story collections
that enjoy such popularity, in hasidic circles too, begin to appear in
large numbers only from 1863 onwards, a full hundred years after the
death of the Ba'al Shem and eighty years after the appearance of the
first hasidic work, *Toledoth Ya'aqov Yosef*. Early hasidism was familiar
only with two narrative works: *Shivhei ha-Besht* (Praise of the Besht)
and *Sippurei Ma'asiyoth* (Tales of Rabbi Nahman of Bratzlav), both of
which were published in 1815.

From the above it will be clear that research into the nature and
significance of hasidism is concerned in the first instance with the collected sermons from the period between 1780 and 1811.

3.2 The relation between hasidism and earlier mystical currents

So far we have seen that each new mystical current that arose adopted
in one way or another more or less mystical ideas, motifs and notions
that were formulated in earlier periods. Hasidism is no exception to
this. We have to ask ourselves, therefore, what were the ideas that
hasidism built upon, and wherein lies the distinctive and original contribution of the movement. In other words: what is the precise
relationship between hasidism and previous mystical currents?

Opinion is rather divided on this question. Some people see Lurianic Kabbalah, the Kabbalah of Shabbetai Zevi and hasidism as three
different phases of one and the same broad process; with such themes
as restoration, redemption, messianism and evil, ideas would have
emerged in Isaac Luria's mysticism that sabbatianism and hasidism developed further, each in its own way. Others, however, deny any
direct connection between the three currents, while others again occupy positions between these two poles.

It is clear that in general the hasidim felt more at home with classical
Kabbalah. As far as their view of God and the Torah was concerned,
most of them preferred to derive their inspiration from the sefirotic
system as described in the Zohar and in Cordovero, rather than from
the extremely complicated cosmic speculations of Isaac Luria. Nonetheless it cannot be denied that the hasidic mystics also make extensive
use of terms known to us initially from Lurianic Kabbalah. Sometimes

the hasidic doctrine seems to center on such terms as tsimtsum, tiqqun and the redemption of the sparks. We shall see, however, that the use of these terms does not necessarily mean that hasidism must be viewed as a direct continuation of Lurianic Kabbalah; although the terms are borrowed from Lurianic Kabbalah, the ideas connected with it underwent a thorough transformation within hasidism and were given completely new content. In addition, the fact that the hasidim made use of Lurianic terminology does not tell us very much, since Lurianic theories had made their mark on much of Jewish thought. Whether they agreed with Luria or not, practically everyone made use of Lurianic terminology, which had come into fashion.

So it cannot be claimed that hasidism is a direct continuation of Lurianic Kabbalah; in addition to the sources mentioned above, hasidism also adopted elements—with some degree of adaptation—from various other currents. Thus ethical thinking forms an important element within hasidic teaching. In this regard people drew their inspiration from ideas that had developed since the days of the medieval Ashkenazi Hasidim (see Chapter 3, § 2.5.3) as well as from the genre of ethical literature known to us from Safed (see Chapter 4, § 2.2).

Although many people have difficulty with the claim, there are indeed indisputable links between hasidism and sabbatianism. Hasidism arose primarily in the provinces of Podolia and Wolhynia; there were not only important centers of sabbatians here, but this is also where the Frankists caused much commotion at the end of the life of the Besht. It is clear, for example, that hasidism originally was primarily disseminated by peripatetic, socially marginal preachers influenced by the ideas of sabbatianism.

There are indications that the Ba'al Shem Tov was very much impressed by a mystical work entitled *Sefer ha-Tsoref* (Book of the Goldsmith), which was ascribed to a certain Rabbi Adam Ba'al Shem. Lurking behind this uncommon name, however—at least according to Scholem—is the seventeenth-century crypto-sabbatian Rabbi Heshel Tsoref. It is not clear whether the Besht was aware of the sabbatian origins of this work. Besides this there circulated among the disciples of Dov Baer an introduction to Lurianic Kabbalah by another crypto-sabbatian author, Jacob Koppel Lifshitz, who according to tradition was the object of much praise on the part of the Besht. In addition there was another homiletic work from the eighteenth century, *Hemdat Yamim* (Most Precious of Days), which was much read by the early hasidim but was sometimes ascribed to the sabbatian "prophet" Nathan of Gaza.

Despite the above-mentioned links between hasidism and sabbatianism, it would not be right to regard hasidism as a direct continuation
of the Kabbalah of Shabbetai Zevi and sabbatianism. Sabbatianism may
well have contributed to the formation of some aspects in the body of
hasidic ideas, but the hasidic movement, unlike sabbatianism, is not
associated with antinomism, heresy or extreme forms of messianism.

Since hasidism clearly makes extensive use of older currents, it is
justifiable to ask what was hasidism's particular and original contribution to the historical development of Jewish mysticism. This question,
which is also frequently posed in scholarly studies, seems on closer
inspection to be rather difficult to answer. In almost every case, each
theme, idea or aspect in hasidism can be shown to have been known
already in an earlier phase of Jewish mysticism. Though it is clear that
hasidism, unlike the teaching of Isaac Luria, did not add a completely
new speculative mystical system to the Jewish mysticism that already
existed, it transformed all these earlier elements in such a distinctive
way and so filled them with its own ideas that the movement can be
seen as a new, creative phase in the history of Kabbalah.

3.3 The hasidic interpretation of Lurianic Kabbalah

In Lurianic Kabbalah we met the term tsimtsum, the beginning of the
process of creation. In order to create room for creation, a contraction
or withdrawal of the deity takes place, which thereby purges itself of
disharmonious or potentially evil forces (see Chapter 4, § 3.2.1). This
understanding of tsimtsum was dropped in hasidism. The hasidim did
not go along with the idea of a purging of evil forces in God or that of
making room for creation. They interpreted the creation process in
the first instance as a revelation of divine lights. These, however, were
of such an intensity that this divine light was imperceptible or unbearable by humans. In order to make his lights visible to humans, God
had radically to curtail their intensity until only a much weakened
form remained. For the hasidim, tsimtsum meant that God was acting
out of sheer love towards humans when he restricted and masked part
of his lights. By reducing the intensity of the lights, God enabled the
human being to perceive God's revelation in creation. In a process of
constantly increasing veiling of the divine lights our creation comes
into being, a world in which the divine can no longer be perceived
directly. In this transformation of the Lurianic concept of tsimtsum,
hasidism distanced itself from such ideas as a struggle within the deity
or the voluntary exile of God.

Closely linked with the reinterpretation of the Lurianic concept of tsimtsum there arose in hasidism another view of the origins and the nature of evil. Lurianic Kabbalah saw the origins of evil in En Sof. After the breaking of the vessels the divine sparks had become imprisoned among the kelippoth, the forces of evil. According to Luria the world could only be redeemed by liberating the divine sparks from evil—and out of the matter associated with it—by ignoring evil and as it were "starving" it, so that it would be deprived of the life force which it drew from the sparks. In Lurianic Kabbalah, then, the emphasis was on the redemption of the divine sparks by eliminating evil (for details see Chapter 4, §§ 3.2.2 and 3.2.3).

The hasidim on the other hand saw evil as not so fundamentally opposed to the divine as in Lurianic Kabbalah; evil after all originally came from En Sof and thus, however evil it was, it still contained a divine spark. For them, evil was rather the unavoidable consequence of the gradually increasing veiling of the divine lights, which decreased in intensity as the creation process advanced. For the hasidim evil was really a temporary state of good, which arose as a result of the divine light becoming weaker and weaker. While Luria's interest was in the liberation of the good spark from evil, in which process evil itself was annihilated, the hasidim thought that evil as a whole needed to be redeemed, since it also contained a divine spark. By redeeming evil it could be brought back, transformed or bent back into its original, good and harmonious state. For the hasidim it was not a matter of ignoring evil—as with Luria—but of a confrontation with it, so that it could be refined and reshaped.

Besides ideas on evil, the hasidim also reinterpreted Lurianic views in relation to the Messiah, restoration and redemption. For Luria the whole universe turned on the cosmic disaster of the breaking of the vessels and the restoration that had to be attained after it. In hasidic teaching such a disaster was no longer an issue; the breaking of the vessels was explained much more simply and less dramatically by drawing a comparison with a tailor who had first to cut up the roll of material into pieces in order to make a suit. In hasidism we thus no longer see the acute messianic tensions we meet in Lurianic Kabbalah and in Shabbetai Zevi. The hasidim still of course believed in the traditional ideas of the final redemption which would dawn for the whole world under the leadership of the Messiah, but these did not have so much contemporary significance; the redemption was once again, as in rabbinic literature, transferred into a distant future.

Emphasis now centered on the redemption of the individual, as had also been the case in the period before Lurianic Kabbalah (see also Chapter 4, § 1.4). While Lurianic Kabbalah focussed its attention on worlds in exile, hasidism oriented itself to the individual exile of each person; the Lurianic idea of tiqqun was seen in the much more limited context of human beings in their personal environment and daily life. Tiqqun became primarily the redemption of someone's own spark.

This hasidic reinterpretation of Lurianic ideas meant a demythologization of the creation process as seen by Luria; the greatest dramatic and cosmic elements of the process were weakened considerably, while the terms which Luria used for this occurrence (contraction, breaking of the vessels, restoration) were given a much more concrete meaning. By relating the elevation of the sparks exclusively to the individual rather than the universal redemption, the acute messianism of the Lurianic and sabbatian Kabbalah was neutralized in hasidism. In Kabbalah, by the way, this process of demythologization was already underway before hasidism; such kabbalists as Luzzatto had already begun to interpret Lurianic Kabbalah in less mythical terms. Such interpretations did, however, gain broad dissemination as a result of the activities of hasidism.

The neutralization of the acute messianic element in hasidism is also evident from the fact that concrete ideas concerning the Messiah and redemption became spiritualized. Such terms as the Promised Land or Zion were taken more as an inner condition within a person and thus not seen in the first instance as geographical pointers. Such ideas as exile or redemption were viewed as a condition in the inner person, without eschatological significance. Actually, each individual was a redeemer; each person individually redeemed his or her own personal world. Seen in this light, it is not surprising that—with a few marginal exceptions—there was little interest among the hasidim in settling in Palestine. They sought the redemption in the first instance in themselves and so they had no need to journey to another country.

3.4 Devequth

Regarding the techniques for attaining a state of ecstasy or devequth ("cleaving to God"), the hasidim were able to draw upon a long tradition (see Chapter 3, § 2.6.2). Absorbed in meditative prayer, by means of a special concentration or intent (*kawwanah*) the mystics of Gerona, the Ashkenazi hasidim and the Lurianic kabbalists directed the letters, words, names and sentences from the traditional prayers to the sefiroth to which they corresponded, in order to come into personal and intimate contact with the deity and its world.

In ecstatic prayer the way in which the Hebrew language was viewed also played an important role. In relation to language mysticism too, the hasidim could draw upon a long tradition, the basis for which Isaac the Blind had already laid in the late twelfth century. In the elaboration of their language mysticism the hasidim had derived their inspiration primarily from ideas that ultimately go back to Isaac's description of the emanation process, in which the term *davar*, which can mean "word" as well as "thing", occupied a central position. As we have seen, Isaac the Blind was familiar with two parallel processes of emanation: the "spiritual things", which stand for the world of the sefiroth, as well as the "spiritual words", which represent the Hebrew language (see Chapter 3, § 2.3). Both systems of symbolism, that of the sefiroth and that of language, were often used interchangeably by the earlier kabbalists. In order to arrive at the state of devequth, the hasidim could thus orient themselves to the sefiroth, to the Hebrew language or to the veiled lights that were discussed in the previous section. In all three cases it is a matter of a symbolic representation of the descent or the compacting process in creation.

Ecstatic prayer could be performed in two ways. On the one hand one could focus on the sefiroth or language in profound silence, sitting motionless, or it was possible during prayer to make vigorous rhythmic movements with the body. In order to reach a state of ecstasy, during prayer the hasidim directed their attention to the words of the prayers or to their separate letters. Their concern was not with the meaning but with the spiritual lights contained in the concretely visible letters and words. Each letter, each word and each sacred name was, after all, the result of increasingly veiled divine lights which originated in En Sof. Letters and words were viewed as vessels or wrappings which contained the divine light from En Sof. By means of contemplative techniques the mystic tried to connect with the hidden spiritual element (*pnimiyyuth*) in the language by divesting it of its wrappings. At the moment that he has contact with the spiritual core, he sees the connection between this core and its external form. The connection (*yihud*, "unification") between core and outer form is very important and is constituted at the moment that the mystic attains a state of highest ecstasy, in which he "cleaves" to God and is able to receive revelations.

Not only the Hebrew letters but also the Torah as a whole, or the commandments—which after all form a reflection of the world of the

sefiroth, see Chapter 3, § 1.6.4—could be the object of mystical contemplation. Since the whole of creation is the product of divine light
that is increasingly veiled, anything could in fact be the focus of meditative contemplation: a tree, an animal or an object. There is a divine
kernel to everything, which can unite the hasidic mystic with the external form in mystical prayer. During ecstasy the mystic arrives at a
state of I-lessness and is touched by the divine. This state is associated
with the highest sefirah, Kether, which, as we have seen, is also called
Ayin ("Nothing"). The hasidim saw the transition from "I" (*ani*, spelt
aleph–nun–yod) to I-lessness or the Nothing (*ayin*, spelt *aleph–yod–nun*)
reflected in the Hebrew language; both words are constructed from
the same language elements and indicate the relationship between two
sorts of consciousness: a consciousness of one's self and a consciousness
of God. Technical terms used for this process are *bittul ha-yesh* ("the
annihilation of being") and *hitpashtuth ha-gashmiyyuth* ("the divestment
of corporeality").

In hasidic teaching the idea of the Lurianic tiqqun, a restoration in
which everything is set back in its rightful place within the divine
order, was closely connected with devequth. A mystic who in a state
of ecstasy made a yihud between the spiritual heart and the external
form of something contributed to the ultimate restoration of the world
and to the unification of everything that was broken, separated or isolated by Adam's fall. In hasidic doctrine the redemption of the sparks
was thus identical with the making of a yihud in a state of devequth.
The individual character of redemption thus was given much greater
emphasis than the collective and universal aspects that so dominate
Lurianic Kabbalah. The mystic gave shape in a completely individual
way to the redemption of the sparks and the restoration. Although
ideas about the future collective redemption of humanity and the
world were still present in the background, in ecstatic prayer no part
was played by messianic notions of the World to Come (see also the
previous section). The Lurianic idea of reincarnation (*gilgul*) also, in
which an individual soul contributed to the universal process of tiqqun
in connection with other soul sparks of a group, was accorded a much
more modest and individual character in hasidism. Reincarnation was
now limited to only the personal sphere of life and one's own environment (see also Chapter 4, §§ 3.2.3 and 3.2.4).

The redemption of evil, which had to be brought back to its original harmonious state, was an important element of the tiqqun process
for the hasidic mystics. A hasid who tried to attain a state of devequth
could find himself frustrated by the interference of evil thoughts, of a

sexual or other nature. Since according to hasidic teaching evil should not be ignored but rather confronted head-on, the mystic had to come to terms with the evil thought; he looked towards its source or its core in order to transform the evil thought and thus to redeem it. This was obviously not without danger, since in the confrontation with evil there was the possibility that it would gain hold of the mystic after all.

As has been said, the hasidim could draw upon a very long tradition in relation to devequth. The concept of devequth, which occupies such an important position in hasidic thinking, can already be found in many spiritual traditions from the Middle Ages, although the term had quite a different content for the hasidim than the way it was understood by medieval philosophers and mystics. In the Middle Ages the term devequth, "cleaving", was used for the ultimate ideal towards which one strove; only someone who was thoroughly familiar with Torah and tradition, possessed very advanced knowledge and had spent much time in preparation, could hope at the end of a long and arduous path to be graced with the experience of direct contact with the divine. It is clear that the experience of devequth was thus reserved for only a select few.

In hasidism the term was given quite a different content. For the early hasidim the state of devequth was no longer the far distant ultimate destination on a long journey, but rather the beginning, the point of departure for anyone who yearned for God. Such a state lay within the reach of any hasid who had a desire to "cleave" to God; anyone who was deeply affected by God's omnipresence was in fact already in a state of devequth. The ideal was now—and herein lies the great difference from previous currents—that *every* hasid should find himself in a state of devequth, and, moreover, *permanently* so. (In this regard there was even a statement ascribed to the Besht that anyone who was not in devequth was really an idolater.)

The *joie de vivre* that the hasidim demonstrated, which was expressed in singing and dancing, among other things, went back to the idea that the creation was the result of a loving act of God towards humans. The background of the hasidic commandment to joy had everything to do with the realization of God's omnipresence and his presence in everything that exists and lives. The technical term for the realization that God is present in everything is *panentheism* (not to be confused with pantheism, in which everything that exists is regarded as divine). In brief: devequth was a form of joy about God's presence in the world.

The ideal of constant ecstasy meant that one should be able to sustain the state of devequth when participating in social life or performing one's daily work—something that was almost unthinkable and reserved only for the exceptionally far advanced. Daily life, everyday reality, did not necessarily pose any obstacle to a constantly ecstatic consciousness, a constant realization of the closeness of God; as long as one had the right spiritual attitude, sparks could be redeemed in practically any area of life. Even in an innocent conversation with a neighbor a divine spark was hidden. If this was liberated in the course of the conversation, the chat constituted a religious act in itself. According to this understanding of devequth, all physical acts (eating, drinking, sleeping, walking, reading, writing, speaking, singing etc.) offered the hasid the chance to honor God in the concrete world around him. The technical term for this was *avodah ba-gashmiyyuth* ("worship in the physical", "honoring God in corporeality"); a Bible verse frequently quoted in this connection was *In all your ways acknowledge him* (Prov 3.6).

Though the ideal may have been for the hasid to be in a constant state of devequth, in practice everyday life made demands on people that were at odds with this ideal. It stands to reason that people frequently had to undertake concrete actions which demanded their full attention, making total devequth impossible. But quite apart from this, experience taught that even the most advanced mystic was in no position to "cleave to" God constantly and without interruption. This led to the theory of *gadluth* (lit. "greatness") and *qatnuth* (lit. "smallness"). These terms, which originally came from Lurianic Kabbalah and stood for various circumstances in the deity, signified in hasidism the two different states in which a person, animal or thing finds itself by nature, in an up-and-down movement. Gadluth is the state of perfection and completeness, while qatnuth represents the incomplete, lesser state. This continuous alternation of state explains why the mystic cannot always be in devequth. After the degree of devequth has been perfected in a state of gadluth and communion with God is experienced in its full intensity, there follows immediately a "falling back" into qatnuth, in which this state of cleaving cannot be maintained. In this lesser state a person can recover from the demanding ecstatic experience and occupy himself with normal daily affairs. During the qatnuth phase the mystic continues to yearn for the perfected devequth and prepares with renewed effort for a return to the state of gadluth.

In hasidic doctrine a higher status was ascribed to the attainment of devequth than to the study of Torah, which had traditionally stood in such high regard. In earlier mystical currents study of the Torah was a means of eventually reaching the state of devequth. Since hasidism had taken "cleaving to God" as its point of departure, study of the Torah and tradition now seemed superfluous: why should one spend one's time on tedious study if one could experience the state of devequth by means of a simple awareness of God's nearness? Moreover, it was impossible to go through the emotional and intimate experience of cleaving to God and simultaneously give the same committed effort associated with the study of the often complex literary tradition. It is clear that the vast majority of the hasidim saw the attainment of devequth as of much greater importance than traditional study and that the ascent into spiritual worlds was very difficult to combine with concrete and intellectual occupation with Torah and the detailed rabbinic discussions in the traditional literature.

Although hasidism had many adherents who were primarily interested in achieving a "cleaving to God" and paid little attention to intellectual education, not everyone was in agreement with this preference; there were some who thought that devequth and study could indeed go together well. Though devequth was always given greater emphasis in hasidism than intellectual study, later hasidism from around 1800 did pay more attention to the study of the Torah and traditional literature than had previously been customary. In addition, hasidism attracted not only the unlettered but also many scholars and rabbis, who in their realization of a state of devequth attained precisely such a combination of emotional experience and intellect.

When the phenomenon of tsaddikism, the other pillar of hasidism, begins to emerge during the third generation of hasidim, a shift takes place in the experience of devequth. At this point we shall therefore look in more detail at the figure of the tsaddik.

3.5 The tsaddik

Inextricably linked with the modern picture of hasidism is the figure of the *tsaddik* (lit. "righteous", also called *rebbe*), the charismatic spiritual leader of a hasidic community. We nonetheless do not see ideas on the figure of the tsaddik and his leadership arise in an elaborate form until the third generation of hasidim. The first tsaddikim were disciples of Dov Baer, the Besht's successor (cf. §§ 2.3 and 2.4). We know only little with any certainty about such theories during the first two generations of hasidim. It is possible that they contain elements that formed the basis for the ultimate doctrine of the tsaddik, but we cannot say for certain.

In hasidism the tsaddik is a charismatic person who possesses unusual spiritual qualities. While traditionally the leadership in Jewish communities was reserved for scholars, and leaders enjoyed authority on the basis of their erudition, in hasidism leadership was linked with charismatic qualities. A tsaddik thus did not necessarily have to be a rabbi or a scholar; as long as the person in question possessed spiritual charisma and mystical insights, in principle anyone could be a tsaddik. Tsaddikim who were lacking a decent knowledge of the tradition had experts in this field available to advise and support them. From a material point of view each spiritual leader was maintained by the members of his community. The members were very much devoted to the tsaddik, placed intense confidence in his spiritual qualities and owed him absolute obedience.

In the hasidic ideas on the figure of the tsaddik there is a very noticeable influence of Lurianic teaching on reincarnation and the related process of cosmic restoration. The tsaddik and his community formed a group of people among whom there was a strong sense of spiritual unity. It was only within this limited circle of related souls that it was possible to work towards personal redemption and the restoration. The soul of the tsaddik came from the highest celestial world (*atsiluth*) within the hierarchy of human souls. The tsaddik was then also seen as a righteous person who was sent to earth to assist and lift up a community of related souls that was entrusted to him.

With the coming of tsaddikism a gradual shift developed in the experience of devequth and the redemption of the sparks. Although ideally each hasid had to be constantly in a state of devequth and although devequth was often represented as easy to realize, in everyday practice it turned out that not everyone, by a long chalk, was in fact capable of reaching a state of devequth. In the doctrine of the tsaddik we see too that the responsibility for devequth increasingly devolved on the person of the tsaddik; it was he who, on behalf of the whole community, went into a state of ecstasy, engaged in confrontation with evil and redeemed the sparks.

A tsaddik was regarded as possessing an exemplary piety and of being permanently in a state of devequth. Since, as spiritual leader, the tsaddik was responsible for the well-being of the members of his community, he had to descend frequently from his ecstatic state (*gadluth*) in order to be with people and to support them in their spiritual and material needs (*qatnuth*). Afterwards he would ascend once again to the state of devequth. Since the tsaddik found himself in a constant process of descending and ascending, for the members of his community he constituted a mediator between the divine and the human world.

After the tsaddik had consorted with his followers he took all the evil and all the committed sins with him in the form of evil thoughts when he re-ascended to the state of devequth. Not only the evil thoughts but also the remorse that followers showed for their deeds were transferred to the tsaddik, who took them up with him in prayer, where they were accepted thanks to his spiritual efforts. Instead of each hasid trying individually to ascend to a state of devequth, it was the tsaddik who took all his followers and their common daily affairs with him, lifting them up in spirit. The tsaddik could also draw strength from the unshakable belief in his spiritual qualities and his followers' devotion to him. With the help of this strength, during ecstatic prayer he was in a position to attract divine energy or light-power (*shefa'*, see Chapter 3, § 2.6.4), which was transferred to the community through him. As a result the community members were blessed with health, sufficient means, children etc., while this light-power also offered them protection against the forces of evil.

In the literature of early hasidism there is some uncertainty with regard to the question of who in fact was capable of redeeming the sparks. Often we find statements that clearly suggest that it was exclusively the tsaddik who was regarded as capable of coming to terms with evil and of redeeming the sparks, but with equal frequency it appears that ordinary hasidim too were able to do this. A definitive answer to this question is not given in early hasidism.

The doctrine of the tsaddik contains elements which suggest that sabbatianism may have contributed to its formation. The tsaddik's descent from a state of devequth to the human world of his community members is reminiscent of the descent of Shabbetai Zevi into the world of evil or the kelippoth; both the Messiah and the tsaddik are exposed to the dangers of evil, which they have to confront. The tsaddik, who had the task of exposing himself to evil thoughts in order to lift them up, always had to beware of the danger of falling victim to such thoughts, after which he would no longer be in a state to ascend. The idea of the descent into evil or the area of the kelippoth is unique to sabbatianism and is unknown in any other previous movement. That the hasidim must at least have taken over the core of this thinking from sabbatian sources is thus very probable. A fundamental difference from sabbatianism, however, is the fact that the doctrine of the tsaddik has no antinomistic aspect to it. In hasidism it is not a matter of the doing of evil acts but—and then only with regard to the tsaddik—of confrontation with evil thoughts in order to lift them. The descent of the tsaddik has primarily to do with his responsibility for the well-being of the members of his community.

As is the case with many other elements of hasidic doctrine, the term *tsaddiq* too is older than hasidism itself. In early Judaism the term is used in particular for someone who strictly keeps the laws and commandments. In the literature of early Kabbalah the tsaddik was a mystical symbol associated with the ninth sefirah, Yesod, which plays such an important role in the celestial world as the bridge between the divine and the material world. Hasidism adopted earlier ideas on the tsaddik and probably transformed them in phases into the figure of the hasidic spiritual leader as we know him from the third generation of hasidim onwards.

3.6 The role of magic in hasidism

As will have become clear in the course of this book, in varying degrees magic played a part in all the mystical movements. We have seen that a mystic who wanted a direct experience of the eternal divine reality could make use of magical techniques in his attempts. There have always been vigorous discussions among mystics on the question of what magical techniques are permitted and what are not, and on the question whether the use of magic as such was in fact permitted. On this point there was no unequivocal view (see also Chapter 4, § 3.2.5).

In hasidism too magical techniques had a part to play. It is difficult to tell the extent of the influence of magic in hasidic doctrine; as in the case of the previous mystical movements, there is no comprehensive study of the influence of magical aspects on hasidic mysticism. Remarkably enough, serious scholarly literature on hasidism unfortunately devotes little or no attention to the subject of magic in hasidism.

The only exception is Moshe Idel, an authority in the field of ecstatic Kabbalah. In various studies of the use of (magical) techniques in various Jewish mystical movements he establishes that the hasidic mystical literature—as also that from Safed—sometimes contains information on the ascent to heavenly realms or on the use of weeping techniques in order to obtain visions. The tsaddik attempted by means of "working the deity" (theurgy) to direct divine energy or light-powers (*shefaʿ*) to his followers, and was often famous for his magical powers, his second sight and the miracles he performed. In their healings of people the so-called "miracle rebbes" made use of letter magic, amulets and talismans, which were also implemented in the driving out of demons (exorcism).

Nonetheless Idel points out that we still know little about the exact techniques that were used in the process of kawwanah during ecstatic prayer. Hence we also know little about the various stages of spiritual consciousness that the mystic passes through in this process.

4. Opponents of hasidism: the mitnagdim

Hasidism today is rightly associated with Jewish orthodoxy. However, at the time of the rise of hasidism in the eighteenth century it was precisely its orthodox character that was subjected to serious doubts. Established Judaism, rabbis and scholars, for whom the study of Torah, the traditional rabbinic literature and the Halakhah were in central position, greeted the new religious movement with suspicion from the start. As long as hasidism did not exercise any actual influence and power within the Jewish communities of the day, the opposition by orthodox rabbinic circles was restricted largely to the more or less openly expressed contempt for hasidim. The orthodox opponents of the hasidic movement were called *mitnagdim* ("opponents").

One of the most important leaders who turned against the hasidim was Rabbi Elijah ben Solomon Zalman (1720-1797), nicknamed the Gaon of Vilna (Vilnius), who was regarded as one of the greatest scholars of his day. Besides numerous works in the field of Jewish tradition, the Vilna Gaon also had considerable knowledge of the natural sciences, mathematics and anatomy. Besides this he was known as a great connoisseur of both classical and Lurianic Kabbalah and as the author of many kabbalistic works.

But why were the mitnagdim so opposed to the newly emerging hasidic movement? A variety of factors may be mentioned. In the first place the mitnagdim felt threatened by the hasidim. As has been said, traditionally the leadership of the Jewish communities rested in the hands of rabbis and scholars who occupied themselves with the study of the Torah and of Jewish tradition. In the view of this intellectual elite the hasidim were undermining their authority by attaching greater value to prayer and emotional religious experience than to the intellectual study of Torah and traditional rabbinic literature. Spontaneous and enthusiastic religion was completely at odds with traditional norms, according to which knowledge of the Halakhah had pride of place and study of the Torah was the only way to come close to God. In the eyes of the opponents of the hasidim it was inconceivable that all these uneducated people could have been touched in any way by the Holy Spirit. The Vilna Gaon dismissed ecstasy during prayer and the revelations received as delusions and lies; he wanted nothing to do with the ostentatious movements the hasidim made in their prayer or with charismatic leaders who performed miracles. The joyous behavior of the hasidim—which came to expression in music, song and dance among other things—was unacceptably frivolous and also in conflict with these norms, as far as the mitnagdim were concerned.

Secondly, the mitnagdim also had practical objections against the hasidim. They opposed the prayer rite which the hasidim had introduced—they used Isaac Luria's prayerbook—which did not correspond with the traditional Ashkenazi rite. When these were prohibited, the hasidim had no choice but to pray in hasidic prayerhouses of their own. The result of this was, however, that the traditional synagogues were less well attended and the monetary income dependent on attendance fell short. Further, the hasidim had introduced a new slaughter-knife made of stronger metal than had been customary, which also met with fierce resistance from the mitnagdim. The latter were of the opinion that the use of such a knife was at odds with the strict rules for ritual slaughter. Although there was no clear halakhic rule for this, the hasidic method of slaughter was forbidden. Since in the orthodox view anything that had not been ritually slaughtered in the correct manner could not be eaten, orthodox Jews could no longer eat at the same table with hasidim. The result of this was that part of the tax levied by the Jewish authorities on ritually slaughtered meat now came to the hasidic community. It is self-evident that the drop in income was a very serious matter for the mitnagdim. The fact that hasidim and orthodox Jews were no longer able to pray or eat together extended the social gulf between the two groups. The mitnagdim took a dim view of the fact that more and more faithful Jews were leaving the orthodox community in favor of the hasidic.

Thirdly, the mitnagdim were extremely sensitive to anything that smacked of sabbatianism. They knew that the early hasidic preachers were influenced by sabbatian thinking and that books with sabbatian leanings circulated in these circles (see above, § 3.2). Their fear was that hasidism would go the same way as sabbatianism; Shabbetai Zevi had also begun, after all, with only minor alterations to the Halakhah. In the changes made by the hasidim with respect to ritual slaughter and liturgy, the mitnagdim thought they could recognize the beginnings of a new outburst of the same antinomistic chaos as the sabbatians had produced.

In hasidic doctrine too the mitnagdim thought they could see correspondences with sabbatianism. What particularly concerned them was the hasidic idea of the uplifting of evil. The mitnagdim thought they could see a correspondence between sabbatian ideas of the necessary descent into evil—the conscious transgression of the commandments—in order to advance the redemption and the way in which the hasidim wanted to transform evil into the original good (see above, §§ 3.3 and 3.4). Although on this point sabbatian influence on the hasidim is indeed a possibility, it is clear that hasidic doctrine has something quite different in mind than sabbatian doctrine. Unlike the sabbatian, a hasid would never deliberately commit evil; evil should categorically not be committed. If evil crossed his path, however, then he had to enter into a confrontation with this evil. The hasidim, moreover, were still concerned exclusively with evil thoughts and not with evil deeds.

The mitnagdim also had similar objections towards the figure of the tsaddik. As we have seen, the tsaddik made an ascent to God and a descent to the world and his community. In this fall the mitnagdim saw a variant of the sabbatian idea of the descent of the Messiah into the area of impurity.

In summary it may be stated that the mitnagdim were afraid of a quickly spreading hasidism that would undermine their traditional power and spiritual values and they feared that the efforts of the hasidim would bring about a new wave of antinomism. It follows from this that the conflict between hasidim and mitnagdim cannot be reduced to a dispute between rationalists and irrationalists, as has sometimes been suggested. The reality turns out to be more complicated than this. Among the mitnagdim there were also kabbalists, one of whom was the Vilna Gaon, and he would have no truck with the rational philosophy of Maimonides. Although among the hasidim direct religious experience had pride of place, Torah study was not neglected in the least, as we have seen.

Although the controversy between hasidim and their orthdodox opponents had been running for some time already, in the summer of 1772 it came to a veritable explosion in Lithuania under the leadership of the Gaon. This can be explained—though opinion is divided on this too—from the fact that Dov Baer, the successor of the Besht, had melded the various hasidic groups into a unity and the movement was beginning to gain mass support. The quickly growing hasidism was viewed in this period as an acute threat to the Jewish establishment. The hasidim were banned and their books were publicly burned, in front of the entrance to the synagogue of Vilna. In order to root out hasidism for good the Gaon sent letters to the leaders of various Jewish communities in which he called upon them to excommunicate the hasidim and to prevent them from forming their own communities and founding hasidic prayerhouses.

The conflict between hasidim and mitnagdim divided the Eastern European Judaism of the time into two camps and left deep wounds. In communities where the hasidim constituted only a minority, there were real persecutions and whole families were evicted from their homes and driven away. A prohibition was placed on marrying hasidim, giving them accommodation or doing business with them. Hasidic prayerhouses were closed and any form of hasidic community life was rendered impossible. Even in communities in which these parties were equally represented, great tensions arose. Insults and accusations flew to and fro, or people used physical violence, sometimes ending fatally, to settle things. The conflict situation did, however, vary considerably among the different Eastern European countries. In Lithuania, where the mitnagdim were in the majority, the hasidim suffered more from the persecutions, while in the Ukraine, where the hasidim were the main party, bans and rabbinic orders had scarcely any effect.

It was only when the Jewish Enlightenment (Haskalah) exerted its influence in the Jewish world that an end came to the bitter and fierce struggle between opponents and hasidim. The rising Haskalah was viewed by both mitnagdim and hasidim as a common enemy. Although both parties agreed to differ on many issues, they tried to present a united front against the rationally-minded adherents of the Jewish Enlightenment, who rejected out of hand any submissiveness of the Jew to religious tradition.

5. Third-generation hasidism

In the previous sections of this chapter we examined hasidic doctrine, and at this point we shall address the historical development of hasidism as a movement.

From the third generation—the period from 1772 or so—we see the rise of various hasidic communities forming around a charismatic leader. The number of independently functioning local communities grows quickly and hasidism develops into a spiritual factor in Eastern European Judaism that was there to stay. With the increase in the number of communities—and thus in the number of tsaddikim—an

ever greater multiformity arises in hasidic leadership. Initially the tsaddikim were often famous and very special personalities who led their
communities in a very individual way. Each tsaddik had his own views
of hasidism and often placed personal emphases on parts of the teaching and the way in which these were to be put into practice. This led
to the formation of traditions that were characteristic of a particular
group. So we should not, in fact, speak of hasidic doctrine as if it were
a monolithic entity.

Thus Levi Isaac of Berdichev (1740-1810) was famous for his piety
and philanthropy. In all his efforts with the members of his community sympathy came before righteousness and he displayed an
unshakable belief in human goodness. Nahman of Bratzlav (1772-
1810), unlike the other tsaddikim, placed strong emphasis on messianic
ideas. Naphtali of Ropczyce (1760-1827)) distinguished himself from
the majority of hasidic rebbes with his firm emphasis on the serious
study of Torah; one should study the Torah at least until the age of 25,
and only after that should one occupy oneself with hasidic doctrine.

The strong growth of the hasidic movement and its spread over
large parts of Eastern Europe gave rise to a need for more and more
new communities and leaders. The disciples of Dov Baer, who in the
meantime had become the founders of important hasidic communities,
could not of course meet this need. However, among their disciples
there were individuals who were aware of their charismatic qualities
and felt called to found communities of their own, with or without
the agreement of the older tsaddik. Between the various groups there
were often tensions and long-running conflicts.

Quite soon after the rise of tsaddikism the charismatic leadership became hereditary and dynasties—in the literal sense—of tsaddikim
arose, in which the spiritual qualities of a father were also passed on to
the son. Sometimes a younger son who felt called to be a tsaddik
founded a community of his own. Not only was the leadership of the
tsaddik based on inheritance, but also the disciples of a particular dynasty remained loyal to the dynasty generation after generation.

Many hasidic communities were reminiscent of mini-kingdoms.
The tsaddik ("the king") came very close to holding court as the charismatic center-point of his followers. Each hasid could gain an audience with the tsaddik and ask him for advice or support. The tsaddik
listened to all the problems, human cares, family matters and business
concerns and tried to lend support were possible. He could then plead
with God on behalf of his followers during his ecstatic prayer. There
were tsaddikim who gave their followers magical formulas on amulets

or parchment at the audience. According to legendary tales, these formulas on the basis of letter magic had a miraculous effect. Thus for example sick people recovered and childless women became fertile.

Alongside support for his community members, the tsaddik also taught his disciples, expounding his interpretation of hasidism. On the sabbath and feastdays the followers assembled in his residence to pray, eat, sing or dance with the tsaddik. The tsaddik, dressed completely in white, sat at the head of the table. Those who sat with him were usually his close family, important hasidim, rabbis, scholars or rich worthies. During the meal the tsaddik would preach in Yiddish, generally on a mystical or ethical interpretation of the week's passage from the Torah. The crowd sat or stood around the table. After the meal it was a special honor to get hold of the tsaddik's leftovers; everything the tsaddik touched possessed holiness.

From around the middle of the nineteenth century there were tsaddikim whose courts could compete with the European royal courts. Israel of Ruzhyn was famous for the regal standards he kept; he lived in a beautiful house, sat on his throne in clothing embroidered in gold and moved around in a coach drawn by four horses. Architects, painters and decorators came from Paris and Italy to embellish his house. According to the London *Jewish Chronicle* of 13 July 1886 "the apartments contain [the] most splendid Turkish and Persian carpets as well as the most heavy damask hangings". Despite this pomp and splendor Israel of Ruzhyn led a very ascetic and pious life. The dynasty of the rebbes in Sadgora lived in a beautiful palace in the Moorish style, as befitted—as they put it—direct descendants of the biblical king David.

In the book *Life is with People* by Zborowski and Herzog, a description is given of the courts of the tsaddikim: living chambers for the tsaddik and his family, the staff and their families, prayer rooms, halls, kitchens, storerooms, gardens, stables for horses and coaches and pieces of land on which the necessary food was cultivated. There were tsaddikim who possessed a golden chair to sit on, others had a menorah (a seven-arm chandelier), the candles of which were lighted by means of a silver staircase.

It goes without saying that it was by no means all tsaddikim who lived in such a regal fashion. There were also tsaddikim who lived very sober lives and were sometimes even poor, their following consisting not of thousands of people but of only a few hundred or less.

The hasidim cultivated an intense devotion to their tsaddik and had a firm belief in his spiritual qualities, which he applied to the advantage of his followers; what the tsaddik did was beyond all criticism. There was no greater wish than to be in the vicinity of the tsaddik and to participate in his religious life. Many hasidim who did not live in the direct vicinity of their tsaddik made an effort to spend time at the tsaddik's court at least once a year.

5.1 The hasidic story

In the second half of the nineteenth century, from 1863, hasidic stories begin to appear. It is mainly through these that people today have become acquainted with hasidism. Although opinions vary greatly as to the extent to which the narrative literature accurately reflects hasidism, there is no doubt that for the later period the hasidic story is a typical feature of the hasidic movement (see also §§ 3.1 and 6). A number of short examples of hasidic stories are given below; naturally they do not do justice to the extent and diversity of this literary form. The bibliography at the back of this book mentions a number of collections of hasidic stories.

A recurrent theme in many of the hasidic tales is the intense desire for intimate contact with God, with regard both to scholars and the unlettered. The first story is about a tsaddik; the second—one of the best-known of all the stories—is about an illiterate.

> While he was completely absorbed in his prayer, people heard the Rabbi of Liady say: "My Lord and God. I do not desire Thy Paradise, I do not desire the blessedness of the World to Come. I desire only Thee, Thee alone."

> A poor shepherd-boy who could neither read nor write wanted to pray to God. He put his fingers in his mouth and whistled as loud and shrill as he generally did when calling his sheepdog. Then he said to God: "Lord of the World, I cannot read or write. I do not even know the words of the prayers. But accept my whistling, because I love Thee."

The following story displays another frequently recurring motif in hasidic thinking: direct emotional experience ranks higher than intellectual knowledge.

> A hasid complained to Rabbi Bunam that after praying he was often troubled by severe headaches. "What does prayer have to do with your head?" exclaimed the Rabbi. "Prayer must come from the heart; it is not work that is performed by the head."

In the above we have seen that it is of great importance for hasidic doctrine to discern the divine reality behind everything one experiences; even daily occupations teach people something about God. This is clear from the following story.

Rabbi Barukh's grandson Yehiel was once playing hide-and-seek with other children. He hid himself well and waited for one of his friends to find him. When after a long time this did not happen, he emerged from his hiding-place and to his great disappointment he discovered that the boys had given up looking for him and gone home. In tears he came home to his grandfather and told him what had transpired. Then tears ran down Rabbi Barukh's cheeks and he said: "That is what God says too: I hide, but no one wants to seek me."

5.2 Developments in hasidism to the present day

The period between 1772 and 1815 was marked by vigorous growth in hasidism, in which the movement spread not only in Poland but among other places in Lithuania, the Ukraine, White Russia, Russia, Prussia, Austria and Hungary. It was in this period that the doctrine and ideas surrounding the charismatic leadership crystallized. From 1830 or so a degree of stabilization set in.

As a result of the rise of the Jewish Enlightenment polemics between hasidim and mitnagdim reduced in ferocity. The two groups now formed a common front of traditional, religious Judaism—hasidism had in the meantime become regarded as part of orthodoxy—over against the rational thinking of the Haskalah. The hasidim felt threatened by the enlightened views of a large section of the Jews who were not primarily interested in the continuation of tradition and the observance of the commandments. The adherents of the Enlightenment (*maskilim*) saw in hasidism mainly a form of primitive superstition by credulous, stupid people, which would soon disappear under the influence of enlightened ideas.

The hasidim's reaction to the challenge on the part of the Enlightenment was one of separation; the tsaddikim withdrew with their communities in order to avoid the secular Zeitgeist. The hasidim remained faithful to their lifestyle and maintained their own traditions. This tendency has persisted until the present day.

An unavoidable by-product of the enormous growth in the number of hasidim, the number of communities and thus also the number of tsaddikim was a certain leveling-out of the original spirituality. As a result of increasing externalization the lifestyle of many tsaddikim no longer had much in common with earlier ideas on charismatic leadership; by contrast with his earlier colleagues a tsaddik now lived almost constantly among his followers and no longer ascended to a state of devequth during prayer. Magic was accorded more attention, to the detriment of mystical depth. Often the standing of a tsaddik could only be measured by the luxuriousness of his court.

A debilitating factor for Eastern European Judaism was the fact that from the late nineteenth century large groups of hasidim were forced by anti-Semitism, pogroms, unfavorable socio-economic conditions and war to leave their land. Many tsaddikim emigrated with their followers to Western Europe, Palestine and especially the United States. The holocaust brought a definitive end to Eastern European hasidic life.

In illustration of the continuation of the hasidic dynasties one might mention the Karlin hasidim (named after the town of Karlin in Lithuania). The Karlin dynasty was founded by Aaron ben Jacob, one of the disciples of Dov Baer. This dynasty continued through to Rebbe Israel ("the miracle rebbe of Stolin", 1868-1921). Four of his five sons were killed by the Nazis. Initially the only surviving son lived incognito in Germany, but when the Karlin hasidim discovered that he was still alive, he was immediately proclaimed the spiritual leader of the dynasty. The present Karlin rebbe, the grandson of the one who survived the war, lives for half of the year in New York and the other half in Jerusalem. Hasidim still visit the grave of Rebbe Israel, in Frankfurt, to pray.

5.3 The Lubavitsch hasidim: the doctrine of habad

In the historical development of the various groups of hasidim and the pluriform character of the hasidic leadership a group has emerged that has developed so much a character of its own that it may be called a variant of hasidism: habad-hasidism.

The founder of this separate movement was Rabbi Shneur Zalman of Liady (1745-1813). He was one of the disciples of Dov Baer and, like many other disciples of the Maggid of Mezhirech, founded a group of his own and a dynasty of his own, in Liady. Shneur Zalman came from a line of scholarly rabbis—the famous Rabbi Löw of Prague (1520-1609) was one of his ancestors—and already as a young man he was known as a promising scholar, halakhist and kabbalist. He was also familiar with secular sciences like mathematics and astronomy. After spending a number of years being initiated into the doctrine of hasidism by Dov Baer, he moved to Lithuania and Belorussia in order to spread his view of hasidism, habad-hasidism, there.

The doctrine of habad—the term *habad* is an acronym of *hokhmah, binah* and *da'ath*, terms which stand for three different levels of the intellect—forms a combination of hasidic mysticism and traditional study of Torah, Tradition and Halakhah. The ideal is a combination of rational knowledge and constant intellectual effort with mystical insight; alongside daily study there is ecstatic prayer. A hasid who wanted to realize a state of devequth by means of prayer, needed to have at his disposal a certain knowledge of talmudic literature and the mystical teachings of hasidism. Among the habad-hasidim prayer often took place in silence and was not linked with rhythmic movements of the body. In habad-hasidism, then, rational knowledge of Jewish tradition and direct emotional religious experience of the divine were regarded as two essential and inseparable elements.

The character of charismatic leadership in habad-hasidism differed in an important regard from other hasidic groupings. Although the tsaddik was the undisputed leader of the community in habad-hasidism too, still great responsibility remained with the "ordinary" hasidim. In the first place each hasid had to help himself further by his own efforts and could not lay all responsibility for his physical and spiritual well-being on the tsaddik. Instead of resolving all problems by performing miracles, the habad-rebbe wanted everyone to try to develop his own insight by means of individual study, meditation or by some other means. It was only subsequently that the rebbe would lend support by way of advice, deeds or prayer. For these reasons Shneur Zalman developed an extensive doctrine surrounding the possibilities, tasks and responsibilities of the *benoni*, the "average person". There was little practical purpose in keeping the ideal picture of the tsaddik in view, since tsaddikim are simply a particular and rare sort of people; the ordinary person could get on better with a package of practical ideals and duties which, with the necessary effort, he could fulfill.

Shneur Zalman formulated his mystical doctrine among other things in one of the earliest writings of hasidism (see also § 3.1), which is known by the name of *Tanya* ("Doctrine"). By comparison with other early literature this work has a very systematic structure. Even today it is still regarded as one of the most important works for habad-hasidim. In the 1780s Shneur Zalman founded an academy for the study of the Torah and traditional literature in combination with the study of hasidic doctrine; only the most promising disciples were selected for this.

After Shneur Zalman's death in 1813, the charismatic leadership passed to his eldest son, who settled in the Belorussian village of Lubavitsch (near Smolensk)—hence the name Lubavitsch hasidim. Among the hasidim who emigrated to the United States, among other places, from the end of the nineteenth century, there were also Lubavitsch hasidim. In 1940 the incumbent rebbe of the Lubavitsch dynasty, Joseph

Isaac Shneersohn (1880-1950), also settled in New York, where he developed the habad movement further into an organization with its own schools, newspapers, publishing houses and charities, not only in the United States but also in Israel and elsewhere.

6. Controversies in scholarly research

Hasidism gained widespread recognition through the influence of the Jewish philosopher Martin Buber (1878-1965), who became fascinated from an early age with the lifestyle of the hasidim. As described in § 3.1, in 1815 two works were published with hasidic stories and from 1863 a large amount of books appeared with hasidic tales containing especially legends, miracle stories and sayings by various charismatic tsaddikim. Buber set himself the task of making hasidism and the message he saw contained in these hasidic stories accessible to the world. He achieved this in a large number of publications, among the best-known of which are *The Tales of Rabbi Nachman*, *The Legend of the Baal-Shem* and *Tales of the Hasidim*. According to Buber, the essence of hasidism is to be found in the stories; they display the soul of hasidism and form a mirror of true hasidic life. In the story, according to Buber, the hasid expresses his innermost feelings and the reader of the story thus comes into contact with the hasidic view of eternity and the meaning of life.

Although Buber gained great popularity with the image he presented of hasidism, from a scholarly point of view serious objections have been raised against his approach. Gershom Scholem in particular criticized Buber's views in the 1960s in a polemic that became known as the Buber-Scholem controversy.

Scholem's critique applies primarily to Buber's claim that the essence of hasidism is evident in hasidic narrative. His reproach to Buber is that he bases himself exclusively on the collections of stories which appeared especially from 1863 onwards, and overlooks the extensive homiletic literature written by the hasidim in the period 1780-1811. Unlike Buber, Scholem—who builds on studies by Rivka Schatz-Uffenheimer—thinks that the heart of hasidic doctrine must in the first instance be studied on the basis of these early exegetical sermons, and not on the basis of story collections which did not appear until much later. By neglecting the earlier literature of the hasidim, Buber does not, according to Scholem, give a reliable picture of hasidism. Buber was not a historian. He was not directly interested in the theoretical teachings of hasidism and certainly not in its historical development;

his concern was mainly with conveying the inner experience of the hasidim. Scholem acknowledges that Buber's books are literary masterpieces, engagingly and impressively written—but they tell us more about Buber's own world of experience than about that of the hasidim.

Buber had no time for magic, for example. Anyone who reads his studies on hasidism will get the impression that hasidim paid scarcely any attention to magical techniques; they were only a marginal phenomenon in the movement. The stories in which there is indeed talk of magic, Buber considered not to be essential to hasidism, so that he did not include them in his anthologies. Attentive study of the earlier sources, however, teaches us that the opposite is true: magic was an integral part of hasidic life. Scholem criticized Buber for selecting and judging his material on the basis of a hasidism that he personally fondly imagined.

Another point in Buber's view of hasidism is the relationship between divine life and daily life. The separation between God and the world—which Buber called the "primordial evil" of all religions—had been restored in hasidism; daily life *is* divine, concrete reality *is* holy. We have seen, however, that the hasidic sources as a whole did not speak of a *coincidence* of the two realities but rather suggest that the divine could only be experienced by looking *beyond* concrete reality; in contemplation the hasid tried to view God's unity and eternity in daily life, or in Scholem's words: to distil divine life *from* daily life (see § 3.4).

Buber's claim that hasidism should be viewed as a mysticism for the laity and the unlettered is disproved by the older homiletic material, as we have seen. In addition, Buber saw a radical break between hasidism and the early mystical movements, which he was wont to refer to simplistically in a pejorative way as "gnosticism" or "kabbalistic gnosticism". Hasidism, according to Buber, had liberated itself fully from what in his view was sinister gnosticism and transformed itself into a pure ethical system. We have already indicated that hasidism did indeed have its roots in earlier mystical currents (§§ 3.2 and 3.3) and that the relationship between Jewish mysticism and gnosticism is much more nuanced than Buber suggested (Chapter 3, § 2.2).

Scholem's critique of Buber can be briefly summarized as follows: many readers who expect to be able to get to know hasidism from Buber's work have no inkling of the existence of other sources than hasidic stories. The unsuspecting reader does not realize that from Buber's books he or she is only becoming acquainted with a personal interpretation by someone who feels strongly attracted to hasidism, namely the very personal view of Martin Buber.

Scholars accept the way in which Gershom Scholem studied and described hasidism as the standard method. In the controversy between Buber and Scholem in fact two totally different approaches collide. Buber's approach is that of an individual who has been deeply touched on a personal level by what hasidism has to say and who reports this in an impressive and engaging way in his literary work. Scholem on the other hand is the historian of religion who adopts a certain distance to the object of study and is primarily interested in the historical development of hasidism and the ideas found in it. It would not be too much to say that the two gentlemen to some degree were talking at cross-purposes; Scholem was not interested in Buber's personal experience, while Buber had little sympathy with Scholem's detached study. Moshe Idel saw very perceptively that it is remarkable that Scholem's liberal and multiform view of Judaism evidently left no room for Buber's perspective, while Buber—in whose work dialogue occupies a central position—was evidently unable to enter into a fruitful dialogue with Scholem.

Buber was not the only one, by the way, to look to hasidic legends as his main source for hasidism. Quite a number of scholars have neglected to study early hasidic literature in any detail. This is understandable, in view of its high degree of difficulty. To begin with, these hasidic homilies are so compact and so complex that they are untranslatable and thus not accessible in any modern language. The method of discussion used is so complicated that each passage in the original would require many pages of footnotes and explanations for the train of thought to be followable.

Although Scholem placed strong emphasis on the study of early sources, it is notable that he did not conduct any research into the phenomenon of the hasidic story. It cannot be denied, after all, that never before in the history of Judaism had so many religious stories been written and told as by the later hasidim. This fact at least calls for an explanation. The phenomenon of the story and its role in hasidism was first studied intensively by Joseph Dan. He came to the conclusion that in later hasidism the telling of stories was elevated to the status of a religious act in its own right; religious feelings could also be directly expressed by the telling of stories—which is itself a rather important development to be observed in hasidism. All this is not to say, however, that these many legends sketch a historically reliable picture of the hasidic movement. In more recent times G. Nigal discovered that the first steps in the telling of stories can already be found in the work of Jacob Joseph of Polonnoye.

Another important and controversial point in research into hasidism is the significance of messianic ideas in the movement. The question was whether early, pre-1800 hasidism was characterized by an acute messianic fervor, a direct expectation of the coming of the Messiah. Scholars like Simon Dubnow and Martin Buber were of the opinion that messianism had disappeared from hasidism, while according to Ben Zion Dinur, hasidism was in fact interlaced with strongly messianic ideas. The discussion reached its climax between Gershom Scholem and Isaiah Tishby. The latter deduced from various passages which mention the Messiah that messianism was one of the most important features of hasidic doctrine. Scholem interpreted the same quotations in quite a different way; according to him the passages in question were not concerned with an acute messianic fervor but rather used traditional standard formulas that are to be found in all layers of Judaism. For him such texts proved nothing other than that the hasidim, like all Jews, believed in the ultimate coming of the Messiah, without their thinking and actions being dominated by the idea of an imminent redemption. As we have seen (cf. § 3.3), Scholem supposed that messianic elements in particular were neutralized in hasidism.

7

Language Mysticism

In the course of this book we have become acquainted with Jewish mysticism from a historical point of view. All the currents have been dealt with in chronological order, and in the process the most important ideas of each separate current have been discussed and the developments from one idea to another have been presented.

Without wanting to neglect the historical aspect, in this chapter we want to look particularly at just one specific topic—language mysticism. We have referred a number of times to the Hebrew language, which was the object of speculation in all the mystical currents. However, we have not yet looked in detail at the basic thinking underlying the ideas of language mysticism.

1. Hebrew as a sacred language

When developing their view of language the Jewish mystics based themselves on the literature of the classical rabbis, who in turn, in shaping their own views of the Hebrew language, made use of linguistic features of the Hebrew Bible.

When we open up Genesis, the first book of the Bible, we read that God brings creation into being by speaking. Gen 1.3, for example, reads, *And God said, "Let there be light." And there was light*. In a tractate of the Mishnah (*Avoth* 5.1), we find the rabbinic view that God created the world by speaking ten times: the firmament, the domains of plants, animals and humans came into being by means of ten divine utterances of creation (*ma'amaroth*, derived from the verb *amar*, "speak"). The creative acts of God were thus in the first place a divine linguistic utterance. As an authoritative support for this view the rabbis quoted such Bible verses as Ps 33.6, *By the word of the Lord the heavens were made, and all their host by the breath of his mouth*.

To the rabbis, Hebrew was a sacred language. This view was so fundamental that in rabbinic literature the expression "the sacred language" (*leshon ha-qodesh*) is the most common way of referring to Hebrew. That Hebrew was a sacred language was not, however, self-evident. The Bible only very rarely refers to Hebrew as a language. What we do find in the Bible is the view that there was a primordial language that was in existence since the creation of the world. The story of the tower of Babel (Gen 11.1-9) teaches us that before the construction of the tower the whole world spoke "the same language and the same words". The Bible leaves us in some uncertainty, however, as to the identity of this language; nowhere does it say that it was Hebrew.

The rabbis, however, had no doubt that this primordial language was Hebrew; Adam and Eve spoke Hebrew, God had addressed them in that language and even the serpent had spoken to Eve in Hebrew. Since this idea is not explicitly mentioned in the Bible, the rabbis had to deduce it from the biblical text. Partly on the basis of the etymological explanation in Gen 2.23 of the word "woman" (*ishah*) from the word "man" (*ish*) they concluded that the Torah must originally have been given in Hebrew, since, according to them, it is only in Hebrew that the words "man" and "woman" are etymologically related; in any other language this explanation in the Bible would have been impossible.

Another well-known concept from rabbinic tradition is that of the preexistence of the Torah: the Torah existed already before God created the world. God looked into the Torah and then created the world. For the rabbis that meant that if the Torah was preexistent, Hebrew too must necessarily date from before the creation. It was of course the language in which the preexistent Torah was written (see also Chapter 3, § 1.4).

2. The connection between word and content

We have seen that in rabbinic tradition the creation of the world is in the first instance a linguistic act; God creates the world by uttering Hebrew words. In Gen 1.3 light is created when God speaks the Hebrew word for "light" (*or*). Light can come into being like this, because according to the rabbis there is a connection between the sound of the word *or* and light itself. The sound of the word *or* actually contains the formula, the blueprint, for light, while conversely all the light in the world bears the stamp of the word *or*. In fact God manufactures light by uttering precisely this combination of sounds. The word for "light" is not just a word, but a proper name for light, a fixed name which belongs to light. The word *or* is an expression of the nature of light.

Since the rabbis supposed that the sounds of the sacred Hebrew language were inextricably linked with the letters in which the language was written, they made no distinction between the sound of a word and the letters in which the word was spelt: sound and writing were identical. When God creates light by uttering the sound of the word *or*, at the same time he utters the letter combination *aleph–waw–resh*. In the name of "light", *aleph–waw–resh,* is a formula with the aid of which light can be formed. This specific letter combination represents the nature of light. Each of the ten divine acts of creation thus contains the uttering of letters in a particular sequence and combination. Everything we see around us in the world is thus the result of a combination of letters pronounced by God in a particular sequence—the whole world was created from letter combinations. An example of this view in rabbinic literature concerns Bezalel, the builder of the Tabernacle (Exod 31). It was a well-known rabbinic idea that the Tabernacle was built according to the same pattern as the whole cosmos. In rabbinic tradition it is related of Bezalel, who according to the Bible already was filled with *God's spirit, wisdom, insight and knowledge* (Exod 31.3), that he was familiar with "the letter combinations with which the heaven and the earth were created" (b *Berakhoth* 55a). The latter of course is strongly reminiscent of the ideas we encountered in *Sefer Yetsirah* (see Chapter 2, § 3.2).

According to the rabbis, as far as Hebrew was concerned there was a natural link between the sound of a word, its meaning and its spelling. Modern linguistics on the other hand states that there is no connection at all between sound, meaning and spelling. That the sound of a word does not correspond with its meaning is evident, from a modern point of view, in the fact that various languages use quite different sounds for the same thing: the Dutch word *boom*, Spanish *árbol* and German *Baum* sound different but have the very same meaning as the English word *tree*. The fact that in German the combination of the sounds *b*, *au* and *m* refers to a tree is not due to a *natural* connection between specifically this combination of sounds and the tree itself, but through the fact that this link has arisen as a result of common *agreement* (or rather, by *convention*). The same applies to the relationship between sound and spelling. Language, according to modern scholarship, is a systematic totality of sounds. The way that sounds are then set down in writing is arbitrary and is also based on convention. Until 1926, for example, Turkish was written in Arabic script. When it was decided to introduce the Latin alphabet, nothing changed in Turkish as a language; the sounds and the pronunciation remained the same, only the way in which they were set down in writing changed. In short, for modern linguistics there is no connection between the sound of a word, the meaning of that word and the letters with which the sound is written down.

The rabbis would probably have objected to these arguments that this link might not exist in all other languages, but that in the sacred Hebrew tongue there is indeed a link between sound, meaning and its written form. The question whether language arose by nature or by convention is, by the way, much older than rabbinic literature. Already in the fourth century BCE there is a debate on this question in Plato's dialogue, the *Cratylus*.

3.   From views of language to language mysticism

We have seen that the rabbis had a very specific understanding of language, in particular of the Hebrew language. It is a question of a view of language—or, if you like, a "linguistic theology"—which cannot, however, be regarded as a *mystical* view of language. In rabbinic literature we find no language mysticism as such, since after all mysticism has to do with the development of spiritual activity in order to come to a direct perception of the celestial world. As far as we know, that is not yet the case in rabbinic literature.

Jewish mystics share the view of language found in rabbinic literature but extend it considerably in a mystical direction. Language mystics believe that language has a numinous aspect alongside a communicative function. Through the voice, sound and melody "something" is conveyed that cannot be expressed in language, a message from another, hidden, secret dimension.

Various mystical currents, each in its own way, combined the rabbinic view of language with the numinous aspect of language. It is only at the point when a mystical current uses this thinking within its spiritual activity in order to come into contact with the celestial world, that we can speak of real language mysticism (see also Chapter 1, § 3).

4.   Language in Jewish mysticism

In ancient Jewish mysticism the Hebrew language served as an aid to the mystic during his visionary journey through the palaces of the seven heavens to reach the final goal of his journey: to view God as King on his throne of glory. The mystics of Merkavah mysticism in particular laid emphasis on the notion that the Hebrew language has an inherent power. Since there is a connection between the sound of a word and its letters, God brought creation about by speaking. From this it is clear that there is great latent power within sound and letter. Humans too, created in the image of God, can speak. By analogy with divine speech the Merkavah mystics applied the power of language in order to facilitate their ascent to the throne of glory.

The central place of language in the ascent through the heavenly palaces is expressed above all in the frequent use of names (divine and angelic names), as well as formulas and letter combinations in which the letters of the Hebrew alphabet were taken to be independent powers (for details see Chapter 2, especially § 5.4). In fact even an ordinary word is a name; Hebrew *or* is the name of what we refer to as "light". A divine name or an angel's name—which are often very difficult to tell apart in Merkavah mysticism—is, however, charged with a greater power than the appellation of an arbitrary concrete thing; such a name is a concentration of divine forces. According to the way in which the various letters constituting a divine or angelic name are arranged, the forces concentrated in them can perform different functions.

As we have seen, "angels" must be taken as divine powers, each with its own name. Since the name represents the divine qualities of the angel concerned, by knowing the name of a particular angel one gains real power over that angel. This understanding flows from the rabbinic view of the link between the sound of a word (or a name) and what that name indicates. If a link exists already in the concrete, earthly world between name and content—as in the word *or* and light—it must apply all the more to the spiritual world of the angels. In this world name and content indeed coincide; the name of an angel *is* the angel itself. By knowing the name one can manipulate that name—and thereby also the angel itself—since name and power are identical.

The combinations of Hebrew letters as individual powers also play a role in Merkavah mysticism. In the long lists of angelic names that we find in many Hekhaloth texts, all sorts of combinations of Hebrew letters can be distinguished. Some of them are constructed from new combinations of biblical divine names, while many other names or formulas are constructed as strange, unpronounceable and apparently meaningless combinations which do not occur in Hebrew. The mystics were definitely not concerned with conceptual and pronounceable mystical linguistic utterances in these cases, but merely with the combining of powers.

In an extensive analysis of the Hekhaloth tractate *Ma'aseh Merkavah*, Naomi Janowitz has concluded that the basis of the text is a view of language; it is language that brings about the ascent. The dialogues in the texts have to do with the ways in which language is used: what a heavenly traveler must say and what the mystic himself hears from the heavenly realms. Nowhere in the text do we find information about human activities. The text itself is a verbal act; the reading aloud of the text is the ascent itself. The ritual power of language is evident from the form of the text, and it has the desired effect: to speak is to ascend. So this whole Merkavah text is to be taken as one great linguistic action, while in turn language is the expression of the ascent itself. The frequent use of direct speech in the text reinforces the performative character of the language used: when something is spoken, it happens. While the structure of the text forms an exact mirror image of the structure of the various heavenly realms, the description of each realm corresponds in its linguistic usage with the character of that realm. In the lower regions, where the mystic is still close to the earth, rather ordinary language is used, while in the highest celestial realms abstract words occur which exceed human comprehension.

For a mystic, the ascent to the throne of glory was very closely connected with a precise knowledge of the powers that lay latent in the language. Not only did the mystics require this knowledge to be able to ascend, but it also accorded them the insight into the structure of the celestial areas, which they so desired.

The writings of the Ashkenazi hasidim of the Rhineland in the late twelfth and early thirteenth centuries are the first to speak of the creation of a *golem*, a person made of clay with the help of letter magic. The idea behind this is the rabbinic view explained above, that humanity and the world were created from letter combinations. The making of a golem thus relies on the imitation of the creation process by humans; in imitation of God, who created humans with letter combinations, a human creates a golem in the same way. Other aspects of views of language held by the Ashkenazi hasidim have been dealt with in Chapter 3, § 2.5.3.

The kabbalists too were inspired in the development of their mystical theory of language by the rabbinic view of language. Among the classical rabbis the history of creation was in fact imagined in quite a simple way: God spoke, and whatever he said came almost simultaneously into existence. Hidden behind the coming into being of creation through a divine linguistic utterance, however, the kabbalists saw a very extensive and complicated process. Between the moment that the linguistic utterance left the lips of God and the moment that what was spoken gained concrete form in creation, there was a whole area, according to the kabbalists, in which the language gradually unfolded. It was precisely the linguistic processes that took place in this area that were given special attention by the kabbalists.

The very beginnings lie in En Sof, from which still undifferentiated, soundless and formless spiritual linguistic elements gradually coarsened and materialized. These elements condensed more and more as they descended step by step, finally crystallizing in the concrete sounds of the language we use and in the concrete letters of the writing we use. Language and writing thus coincide. The writing, which for modern linguistics is a secondary and in fact an arbitrary reflection of real language, is to the kabbalists a veritable treasure-trove of the secrets of language. The twenty-two letters of the Hebrew alphabet form the deposit of powers or energies from the divine worlds. The form of each separate letter is the object of mystical contemplation; anyone who can see through these forms understands something of the emanation process. In the letter forms there are hidden references to all phases of the emanation process, from the stage where language is still the pure thought of the deity and where there is as yet no question of audible sound or word, through to the ultimate stage of concrete language, in which audible sounds and visible letters exist. The written letters were viewed by the kabbalists as symbols referring to processes in the celestial worlds.

In Chapter 3 we discussed the various details of the crystallization of language in the linguistic views of Isaac the Blind, while the mystical interpretation of the concrete forms of the letters was discussed in connection with the Castilian kabbalist Jacob ben Jacob ha-Cohen. The symbolic approach to language in general was dealt with in the section on symbolism.

The linguistic views of Kabbalah have a great deal, of course, to do with the mystical view of the Torah. The kabbalists were not primarily interested in the concrete meaning of the Torah text. What the Torah says in concrete human terms, they regarded as an outer shell—the significance of which, however, was not denied. But above all, the point was that each separate word of the biblical text had to be understood as a symbol. Since God is not directly perceptible by humans, the Torah and the divine language served as pointers to and as an expression of the dynamic processes in the celestial world, by means of which the kabbalists endeavored to get to know God and explain him.

In Kabbalah, however, a further interesting idea was added: the Torah itself is in fact nothing other than a succession of divine names. In the introduction to his commentary on the Torah, Nahmanides elaborates on this idea: the received text of the Torah contains concrete information. But by displacing the spaces between the words there emerges a long series of divine names—naturally very difficult to pronounce—all of which have symbolic meanings. Initially the Torah was written in uninterrupted form, without word divisions, so that to some extent the Torah could be read as the usual collection of commandments and prohibitions, while Moses was orally given the tradition according to which the Torah could be read as a succession of divine names. This connected with a note in the Talmud, according to which each separate letter in the Torah is of the utmost importance; one letter too many or too few would disturb the series of divine names and destroy the harmony of the cosmos.

Contemporaries of Nahmanides even went a step further: the Torah as a whole is one great divine name. Thus God makes his stamp on the whole Torah, while the Torah in turn as a blueprint makes its stamp on the whole of creation. In this view the deepest nature, the inner heart of the Torah is formed by the divine name itself, which appears in its highest concentration as the Tetragrammaton. The more concrete layers of meaning, which of course are also contained in the Torah, are waterings-down, expositions on a lower level, of the one Holy Name.

5. Gematria

In the preceding chapters reference has been made to the use of Hebrew letters as numbers. The mystics who made use of the numerical value of the letters were inspired in the elaboration of their systems by the way in which the classical rabbis dealt with the numerical value of the letters.

Use of letters as numbers is not specifically Jewish. The origins of this are lost in the distant past. The earliest known examples of the use of letter characters as numbers date from Akkadian texts from the early eighth century BCE, while comparable techniques occur already in Sumerian texts. An inscription by the Assyrian king Sargon II (722-705 BCE) tells us that this king had the walls of Khorsabad made with a length of 16,283 cubits, which corresponded with the numerical value of his name.

We also come across the use of the numerical value of letters among the Greeks. Neo-Platonists and neo-Pythagoreans were already familiar with the technique of adding up the letter values of a word in order to determine the character of that word. Thus the neo-Pythagorean Numenius (ca. 125 BCE) based his understanding of the creation of the soul among other things on the numerical value of the letters and their form. Already Pythagoras (ca. 570-500 BCE)—and later also Plato (ca. 429-347 BCE)—was convinced that the reality consisted of a harmonious whole of relationships, which he perceived, for example, in geometry, mathematics and music. Since these relationships could be expressed in numbers, for Pythagoras number was the basis of the material and the non-material world; through number one could learn something about the essence of reality.

The classical rabbis, similarly, were familiar with the use of the numerical values of letters, which they indicated by the term *gematria*. The origin of this term lies in the Greek *geometria*. The term, "geometrical number" (*geometrikos arithmos*) is already found in Plato, though he uses it still with the literal meaning of a geometrical relationship. Neo-Platonists and neo-Pythagoreans adapted this term to the technique of the addition of the letter values of a word in order to determine the character of that word.

The technique of gematria is also applied in rabbinic literature as an exegetical method, though to a limited degree. Words from the Bible or particular ideas from tradition could be interpreted by adding up the value of the letters and where possible linking it with other words of the same value. In his allegorical exegesis, Philo of Alexandria too (see Chapter 3, § 1.6) made extensive use of numerical interpretations. An example of the use of gematria in rabbinic literature is found in the Talmud (b *Yoma* 20a), where it is posited that the Satan has no hold on humans on the Day of Atonement. In support of this idea it is pointed out that the letter value of the word for "the Satan" (*ha-Satan; he(5)–sin(300)–teth(9)–nun(50)*) is exactly 364. From this the rabbis deduced that the Satan has power for 364 of the 365 days, but not on the one remaining day, the Day of Atonement.

There are a few other systems related to gematria, the most important of which are *atbash* and *notariqon*. The atbash system is based on the substitution of certain letters for others: the first letter of the alphabet (*aleph*) is replaced by the last (*taw*), the second (*beth*) by the penultimate (*shin*) and so on. Thus the expression "the king of Sheshach"

Letter	Name	Numerical value
א	aleph	1
ב	beth	2
ג	gimel	3
ד	daleth	4
ה	heh	5
ו	waw	6
ז	zayin	7
ח	heth	8
ט	teth	9
י	yod	10
כ , ך	kaf, final kaf	20
ל	lamed	30
מ , ם	mem, final mem	40
נ , ן	nun, final nun	50
ס	samekh	60
ע	ayin	70
פ , ף	peh, final peh	80
צ , ץ	tsade, final tsade	90
ק	qof	100
ר	resh	200
ש	shin	300
ת	taw	400

Figure 3
The Hebrew alphabet

in Jeremiah 25.26 in an Aramaic translation (Targum Jonathan) is translated as "the king of Babel", since according to the atbash system Sheshach (*shin–shin–kaf*) is the equivalent of Babel (*beth–beth–lamed*). The *notariqon* system—of which there were also variants—strictly speaking has nothing to do with numbers. It is a technique of seeing in each letter of a word the first letter of another word, with which associative links can easily be made. A clear example of this can also be found in the Talmud (b *Sotah* 5a): "Rabbi Yohanan said: 'Man' (*adam*, written as *aleph–daleth–mem*) stands for 'ash' (*efer*, the first letter of which is an *aleph*), 'blood' (*dam*, the first letter of which is a *daleth*) and 'gall' (*mara*, the first letter of which is a *mem*)."

The above examples of gematria and related forms in traditional rabbinic literature clearly show that here there is still no question of any mystical exegesis on the basis of gematria. The latter is the case only with the Ashkenazi hasidim. They were the first who discovered hidden layers of meaning in the Bible, Talmud and Midrash on the basis of the relation between the Hebrew alphabet and numbers. This mystical gematria influenced Kabbalah on the Iberian Peninsula in the second half of the thirteenth century in the persons of such kabbalists as Abraham Abulafia, the Cohen brothers and Moses of Burgos, of the Castilian school. We have no indication of any influence of the Ashkenazi hasidim on the earliest kabbalists in Provence and Gerona; the use of gematria scarcely, if ever, occurs among the latter. The kabbalists of the Castilian school reinterpreted the gematria systems of the Ashkenazi hasidim and partly through personal mystical visions about them the mystical gematria systems gradually spread further afield. In some medieval manuscripts we find expositions of more than seventy different gematria systems. In sabbatianism and eighteenth-century hasidism, mystical gematria once again occupied an important place.

Within the confines of this book it is impossible to give a description of all the sorts of gematria and the various applications that were used for mystical exegesis. In what follows we shall therefore give only examples of some of the most common, which we borrow from the kabbalist handbook by Moses Cordovero, *Pardes Rimmonim* (Garden of the Pomegranates; see Chapter 4, § 2.2). In that work Cordovero devotes a number of chapters to various methods using language and letters, including Abulafia's combinatory techniques.

The ordinary value of a word is calculated, as we have seen, by adding up all the numerical values of the letters of that word. The ordinary value of the word *adam*, "man", for example, which is spelt *aleph(1)–daleth(4)–mem(40)*, is in total 45.

Besides this words also have a full value (*milluy*), which is obtained by writing out the names of the letters of a word in full and then calculating their ordinary value. To calculate the full value of the word *adam*, we need to write out the names of its three (Hebrew) letters. The name *aleph* is spelt *aleph(1)–lamed(30)–peh(80)*, 111 in total; the name *daleth* is written *daleth(4)–lamed(30)–taw(400)*, 434 in total; and finally the name *mem* is spelt *mem(40)–mem(40)*, 80 in total. The full value of *adam* is thus 111 + 434 + 80 = 625.

The hidden value of a word (*ne'elam*) is calculated by subtracting the ordinary value from the full value. The hidden value of *adam* is therefore 625 − 45 = 580.

As an example of much more complicated ways of calculating we might mention one of Cordovero's methods, *merubba' kelali* ("general square"), which consists of the sum of the products of the ordinary value and the letter values of the separate letters. The word *adam* is built from the letter values 1–4–40, altogether 45. The general square arises as follows: 1 x 45 + 4 x 45 = 45 x 45 = 2025.

Unfortunately as yet there is still no comprehensive, historical study of language mysticism in Judaism and the techniques associated with it. There is still plenty of room for new insights. From recent research it appears, for example, that in thirteenth-century Castile there must have been various schools, to which Moses de León also originally belonged, which were extensively occupied with language and letter mysticism and were not oriented towards theosophical Kabbalah with its sefirotic doctrine. Manuscripts that have only recently been studied, some of them anonymous, make it clear that language mysticism probably played a more central role in medieval Jewish mysticism than has previously been supposed on the basis of available studies of theosophical Kabbalah.

8

Popular Literature on "Kabbalah"

In the course of reading this book the reader will have acquired an idea of the historical development of the various currents within Jewish mysticism, the ideas that emerged over the centuries and such topics as the sefiroth, language mysticism and messianism. Now, as indicated at the beginning of the book, we shall look into some of the popular literature on Jewish mysticism.

Despite the constant process of research into Jewish mysticism and the scholarly publications that are appearing all the time, there is no denying that the public commonly associates Jewish mysticism in general, and Kabbalah in particular, with occultism of a rather dubious kind. A number of clear causes can be pointed to for the emergence of that image of Jewish mysticism. We shall take a brief look at the background circumstances that gave rise to this persistent misperception.

From the fifteenth century on there has been great interest for Jewish mysticism in Christian circles, boosted by the conviction that Kabbalah—like Egyptian, hermetic and gnostic writings—contained very ancient, secret insights that are in agreement with Christian doctrine. Important in this respect was the learned Giovanni Pico della Mirandola (1463-1494), who began to study Kabbalah at the Platonic Academy of Florence and thought he could confirm the divinity of Christ and the truth of Christianity on the basis of this mystical teaching (see also Chapter 3, § 2.6.5). A characteristic feature of this Christian Kabbalah was a particular attention to practical-magical aspects. Jewish kabbalists wanted nothing to do with this current—if they were aware of it at all—being of the opinion that Christian Kabbalah gave a distorted picture of Jewish Kabbalah.

Initially some Christian kabbalists still had a considerable knowledge of kabbalistic teaching, though sometimes was acquired through Latin translations. Johann Reuchlin (1455-1522), who wrote the very

important work *De arte cabalistica* in 1517, is the prime example of this.
In the course of time, however, knowledge of Jewish mystical sources
generally diminished among Christian scholars. In particular after the
appearance of the work *De occulta philosophia* (1531) by Cornelius
Agrippa of Nettesheim (1487-1535), the misunderstanding became
established in Christian circles that Kabbalah primarily had to do with
magic, witchcraft and numerology. Slowly Christian Kabbalah developed into an independent system of Christian esoteric speculation,
which led a life of its own and no longer had much to do with the
original Jewish Kabbalah. From the end of the sixteenth century we
see for example that alchemical symbolism becomes a firm and important component of Christian Kabbalah, while in Jewish Kabbalah alchemy never played more than a marginal role. At the end of the
eighteenth century the teachings of Christian Kabbalah had an influence on the ideas of the Freemasons.

From the eighteenth century we see also that the literature of
Christian Kabbalah left its mark on various occult persons and groups
in western Europe. From the mixture of Christian-kabbalistic ideas
with those of occultism a great amount of literature emerged, which
firmly claimed to be based on Jewish Kabbalah but in reality constituted an amalgam of non-coherent, confused and sometimes simply
fanciful ideas of dreamers and charlatans. That such phenomena were
published on such a large scale, made their way into the public domain, and are taken seriously, is partly due to the fact that until the
twentieth century no counterbalance to this sort of literature was offered from the side of scholarship. Since there was no interest in Jewish mysticism in the nineteenth-century *Wissenschaft des Judentums*, no
attempt was made on the part of Jewish scholarship to counter the way
in which Kabbalah was distorted and misused.

It was only after serious scholarly research into Jewish mysticism had
been set in motion at the beginning of the twentieth century that reliable information on Jewish mysticism gradually became available, by
means of which the centuries-old distorted view of Jewish Kabbalah
could be set right.

Despite the results of almost a century of scholarly research we have to
state that the occult literature just mentioned shows no signs of losing
popularity. Since the large number of recent translations and reprints
of occult works on "Kabbalah" continue to appear, it will perhaps be
useful to offer some critical notes on a number of popular books on

the subject, which may be considered representative of the whole range of pseudo-kabbalistic literature.

Eliphas Lévi. In popular occult literature one regularly finds references to the works of the French occultist Alphonse-Louis Constant (1810-1875), who wrote under the pseudonym of Eliphas Lévi, a judaization of his two forenames. After his training as a priest, he immersed himself in the literature of Christian Kabbalah and occultism. His personal interpretation of this is described in a number of works, the best-known of which is probably *Dogme et rituel de la haute magie* (1856)—published in English as *Transcendental Magic: Its Doctrine and Ritual* (1910). In this thoroughly magical work, which deals in the main with incantations, spells, potions, fortune-telling and magical ceremonies for raising the dead, "Kabbalah" has a dominant position.

Entirely on the basis of his own inspiration Eliphas Lévi is in a position to tell us that Tarot cards derive from Kabbalah. He was the first person to bring the Tarot into connection with Jewish mysticism, without any concrete evidence. Unfortunately he was not the last to make such a claim; many authors have followed him uncritically in this, as if it were a matter of historical fact. In illustration, some of Lévi's absurd statements follow:

> The allegorical star of the magicians is none other than the mysterious pentagram; and those three kings, sons of Zoroaster, led by the flaming star to the cradle of the microcosmic king, would be sufficient to prove the totally kabbalistic and truly magical origin of the Christian doctrine.

> Behold the darknesses of the hellish sanctuary swept away, behold the sphinx of the horrors of the middle ages dissuaded and tipped from his throne: *quomodo cecidisti, Lucifer?* The terrible Baphomet is no more.

> Without the Tarot, the magic of the ancients is a closed book to us, and it is impossible to get through to one of the greatest mysteries of the Kabbalah.

Around the turn of the century another frequently cited French occultist, Gérard Enhausse (1868-1916), under the pseudonym of Dr. Papus, wrote a large number of occult works, in which Kabbalah and Tarot occupy an important place. The same criticism applies to these works as to that of Eliphas Lévi.

The Order of the Golden Dawn. A great influence on the distortion of the original Jewish Kabbalah is the occult and secret society of "The Order of the Golden Dawn", founded in 1888 by the British writers S.L. MacGregor Mathers and Dr. William Wynn Westcott. Among the members of this society was, among others, Edward Alexander

Crowley (1875-1947) who wrote under the name of Aleister Crowley or Frater Perdurabo and later formed a society of his own. The occult literature of the members of this society and their followers displays great influence from Christian-kabbalistic literature, a minimal knowledge of Jewish Kabbalah and the most fantastic ideas. What they claim about Kabbalah, as with Eliphas Lévi and Dr. Papus, can be regarded as pure charlatanism.

Some of the members of this group, especially MacGregor Mathers, were inspired by two works: *Clavicula Salomonis* (Key of Solomon) and *The Book of the Sacred Magic of Abra-Melin*. Although neither of the two works is of Jewish origin or has anything to do with Kabbalah, these books were regarded in European occult circles as classical texts of practical Kabbalah.

A.E. Waite. Arthur Edward Waite (1857-1942) is another author who continues to rouse great interest. His book, *The Holy Kabbalah* (1930), which incorporates his earlier work, *The Secret Doctrine in Israel* (1913), cannot withstand the test of criticism. Waite seems to have scarcely any knowledge of the kabbalistic sources and bases himself rather uncritically on unreliable secondary literature such as the abovementioned Eliphas Lévi, Wynn Westcott and Dr. Papus. He was thus absolutely convinced of the connection between Tarot and Kabbalah.

Dion Fortune. Very much cited as an authority and initiate in the world of secret kabbalistic teaching is Violet M. Firth (1891-1946). She was a member of the Order of the Golden Dawn and wrote a number of works under the pseudonym of Dion Fortune. The most important of these are *Psychic Self Defense* (1930) and *The Mystical Qabalah* (1935). The former, which has been translated into many languages, contains Fortune's personal ideas and experiences with regard to the defense against adversarial psychic powers, in which "kabbalistic" topics are also addressed. Since the second book is popular in modern pseudo-kabbalistic literature, it will be worthwhile looking at the content of this work in more detail.

In our historical overview of Jewish mysticism it was made very clear how Jewish thinking, both in Jewish philosophy and in mysticism, is rooted in the Hebrew Bible and its exposition in the tradition. Philosophers and mystics reinterpreted the spiritual heritage of classical rabbinic Judaism as we have shown in the various interpretations of the daily commandments and messianic thought in Judaism. Jewish philosophy and mysticism were thus inseparably linked with tradition and dependent on it. Anyone who wants to go in greater detail into Jewish mysticism, or the Kabbalah in particular, must first gain some insight into Jewish tradition and secondly become thoroughly acquainted with the ideas of Jewish mysticism.

However, Dion Fortune conveniently ignores this indisputable fact. Although she continually speaks of "the Holy Qabalah, the mystical system of Israel", she is not interested in its historical background. She thinks she can bypass the tradition, since there would have been an unwritten Kabbalah which was transmitted only to initiates as secret knowledge since time immemorial. As an initiate in that unwritten Kabbalah herself, she does not even need to know Hebrew, beyond familiarity with the alphabet. By appealing to the existence of an unwritten Kabbalah for initiates, Fortune makes it impossible for anyone to check her statements: even the most arrant nonsense is thereby spared any criticism *a priori*. The only justification she gives for her work is that in her book she makes use of "the system given by Crowley, to supplement the points on which MacGregor Mathers, Wynn Westcott and A.E. Waite, the prime modern authorities in this field in England, kept silent". In illustration of this a few quotations follow, from which the reader can gain an impression of the thinking of this initiate in the unwritten Kabbalah:

> The point of view from which I approach the Holy Qabalah in these pages differs, so far as I know, from that of all other writers on the subject, for to me it is a living system of spiritual development, and not a historical curiosity ...

> The interpretation of the Qabalah is not to be found, however, among the Rabbis of the Outer Israel, who are Hebrews after the flesh, but among those who are the Chosen People after the spirit—in other words, the initiates. Neither is the Qabalah, as I have learnt it, a purely Hebraic system, for it has been supplemented during mediaeval times by much alchemical lore and by the intimate association with it of that most marvellous system of symbolism, the Tarot ...

> Let it be clearly understood, therefore, that I do not say, This is the teaching of the ancient Rabbis; rather do I say, This is the practice of the modern Qabalists, and for us a much more vital matter, for it is a practical system of spiritual unfoldment; it is the Yoga of the West.

In what follows in *Mystical Qabalah* Dion Fortune makes extensive use of astrological symbols. The fact that astrology, like alchemy, plays only a marginal role in historical Jewish Kabbalah, will not have worried Fortune; as will have become clear, she does not feel tied in any way to the history of Jewish mysticism. For her the teaching of the sefiroth, astrology and the Tarot are not three separate systems, but three aspects of one and the same system, which cannot be understood in isolation from each other. (The Dutch translator of Fortune's book suggests in his preface that the Tarot must have been the Bible of the gypsies, the people who he says probably come from the ancient Atlantians.)

In her description of what she regards as Kabbalah, Fortune has no qualms at all in referring as the whim takes her to Priests of the Ancient Mysteries, the philosophy of European Magic, the Holy Wisdom, eastern religions, Tibetan magic, the literature of Christian Kabbalah and the books of the members of the Order of the Golden Dawn. In illustration of Fortune's fantastic and often incomprehensible interpretation of "kabbalistic" symbolism, we shall cite here a few passages:

> The Sahasrara *Chakra*, the Thousand-petalled Lotus, situated above the head, is referred by Crowley to Kether, and there can be little reason to quarrel with this attribution.

> In Binah we find the root of Form. It is said of Malkuth in the *Sepher Yetzirah* that it sitteth upon the throne of Binah—matter has its root in Binah–Saturn–Death; form is the destroyer of force. With this passive destroyer goes also the active destroyer, and we find Mars-Geburah [*Gevurah* is another name for the sefirah Din—JHL] immediately below it on the Pillar of Severity; thus is the force locked up in form set free by the destructive influence of Mars, the Siva aspect of the Godhead. Chokmah, the Zodiac, represents kinetic force; and Chesed, Jupiter, the benign king, represents organised force; and the two are synthesised in Tiphareth, the Christ-centre, the Redeemer and Equilibrator.

Fortune makes an appeal to a centuries-old, secret and orally transmitted wisdom. In reality, however, this "wisdom" constitutes a product of a fashion in the eighteenth and nineteenth century, which came from the uncritical and uninformed mixture of Christian Kabbalah with all things occult. It is regrettable that the *pseudologia fantastica* of this popular book has inspired many to think up even greater subjective nonsense, referring to Dion Fortune as their authority.

However interesting, exciting or enjoyable people may find such books as Dion Fortune's *The Mystical Qabalah*, they really have nothing at all to do with Jewish mysticism or Kabbalah.

Sefer Yetsirah in modern occult literature. The Book of Creation has attracted the special interest of many occult authors. In the course of time various editions of the book have appeared and it is regularly cited in much of the literature. Typical of the way in which the book is commonly presented is *The Book of Formation (Sepher Yetzirah) in-*

cluding: The 32 Paths of Wisdom, Their Correspondence with the Hebrew Alphabet and the Tarot Symbols.

Characteristic of many occult works is the stubborn misconception that *Sefer Yetsirah* belongs to kabbalistic literature. In our discussion of ancient Jewish mysticism we looked into the background of this book (see Chapter 2, § 3.2 and Chapter 3, § 2.2). There we saw that the Book of Creation is an anonymous work which belongs to the tradition of *Ma'aseh Bereshith* and was probably written between 300 and 600 CE. This is the first work to use the word *sefiroth*, a newly coined term which means something like "primordial numbers". However, it has to be emphatically stated that the Book of Creation is *not* a kabbalistic book, since Kabbalah arises as a mystical movement in the Provence only six to nine hundred years after the publication of the Book of Creation. The kabbalists of Provence and Gerona merely took over the term sefiroth from *Sefer Yetsirah*, but gave it quite a different meaning than we meet in the Book of Creation. In the latter book sefiroth stand for primeval numbers, while in Kabbalah the word refers to aspects or attributes emanating from God.

The Book of Creation contains a treatment of cosmology and cosmogony and hints at hidden knowledge of the creation of heaven and earth. This has inspired many modern authors to write fanciful commentaries which claim to make use of this hidden knowledge. Knut Stenring too repeatedly makes a connection between the Book of Creation and the Tarot. And, not for the first time, this creates a multiple misunderstanding: first, *Sefer Yetsirah* is not a kabbalistic work, secondly, neither *Sefer Yetsirah* nor Kabbalah has anything to do with the Tarot, and thirdly, what occult authors understand by "Kabbalah" in general has nothing to do with *Sefer Yetsirah* and the real Kabbalah. It is not surprising that in his commentary Stenring relies on, among others, Eliphas Lévi, Wynn Westcott and A.E. Waite and expresses the wish that his exposition "will not only awaken interest in the text itself but also in kabbalistic philosophy in general and will lead to a much-needed renaissance of occultism."

Charles Poncé. Another well-known book is *Kabbalah: An Introduction and Illumination for the World Today*, published in 1978. In the preface to the Dutch edition of this book, Prof. H. van Praag introduces Poncé as a phenomenologist of religion with "much interest in the universal aspect that characterizes all mysticism. As an orientalist … he draws parallels between Kabbalah and Yoga and Kabbalah and Tibetan mysticism." An important feature of this book—something we also meet in varying degrees among the other authors discussed—is that it takes pains to see as many connections as possible between all kinds of elements in Kabbalah and eastern religions and spiritual systems.

One is apt to wonder, however, whether a superficial comparison of different religions is so illuminating. The danger of "parallelomania" is that one too quickly assumes that one thing roughly corresponds with another. It cannot be denied that there are always agreements to be found between mystical systems—in an abstract sense, after all, all religions boil down to the same thing—but whether a comparison between the Tetragrammaton and the "Tantric seed-syllable", for example, really clarifies very much about Judaism or about Tantrism, is open to doubt. It is perhaps more useful and more instructive to point out the unique and characteristic features of each form of mysticism, with attention to the development of ideas and their place within a particular religious context.

Moreover, anyone who wants to draw a comparison between two religious systems must first engage in intensive study of both of them. As far the eastern parallels adduced by Poncé are concerned, we cannot express a judgment, but where it is a matter of Judaism, our conclusion has to be that this has not occurred. Although, alongside such occult authors as Waite, MacGregor Mathers, Wynn Westcott and Stenring, Poncé also includes studies by scholars like Scholem and Tishby in his bibliography, there is little evidence of influence of these scholarly works in his book. On Haggadah, for instance, he says: "Through the introduction of the Agadah (legend), the mystical experience of Judaism, kabbalism was the cause of great spiritual change in Jewish history." A glance at any reliable discussion of Judaism—of which Poncé cites a few—will show that this claim is well wide of the mark.

Furthermore, the book contains the mistaken notion that there is talk of emanations in *Sefer Yetsirah*, while this can only be said from the Book Bahir onwards. And—almost predictably—we find very many references to magical techniques as well as the supposed agreement between Kabbalah and the Tarot cards. Finally we must note that the book is replete with mistakes in Hebrew words and sentences and in the transcriptions or translations of them. The latter applies, by the way, to much of the other popular literature on "Kabbalah".

Erich Bischoff. In popular literature on "Kabbalah" we often meet references to Erich Bischoff (1865-1936). Although in Bischoff we encounter none of the confused fancies of such people as Dion Fortune, his work, which was written largely before the scholarly research of Gershom Scholem was underway, must be regarded today as completely out of date. His much-cited book, *Kabbala: An Introduction to Jewish Mysticism and its Secret Doctrine* (translation of the 1903 German edition; reprinted in 1991), aims to be a comprehensive survey of the history of the ideas of Kabbalah and is presented in the form of a catechism. At the time Bischoff was writing, he could not be familiar with the results of later scholarly research, in which the historical development of Jewish mysticism was set out. So it is not surprising that he comes to incorrect interpretations with regard to the dating of some works and currents, as well as to misleading descriptions. Thus for example he counts such books as *Sefer Yetsirah* or the magical work *Sefer ha-Razim* from ancient Jewish mysticism as Kabbalah. Isaac the Blind is called the "founder" of the sefirotic doctrine, and with regard to Lurianic mysticism Bischoff states that its most important idea is reincarnation.

Anyone looking for serious information on the history of Jewish mysticism will not really benefit from reading Bischoff's *Kabbala*. Nor can we agree with the anonymous author of the preface to the Dutch edition, which reads: "In short, after reading Bischoff's *Kabbala*, not only are all the fundamental questions of life re-addressed, but also unexpected horizons of spiritual experiences and possibilities open up, which will be able to inspire precisely the modern, often unorthodox, non-churchgoing seeker."

It should hopefully be clear that the very popularized literature on Jewish mysticism is apt to mislead the interested lay reader rather than sketching a reliable and accessible picture of Jewish mysticism. On the other hand the numerous scholarly surveys and detailed studies of Jewish mysticism are too specialized for the general interested reader.

This does not, however, necessarily present an insurmountable problem; anyone who wants to get to know Jewish mysticism and is willing to make the effort to go more deeply into its various aspects, can do so on the basis of the works mentioned in the bibliography of this book. The works of such authors as Ariel, Fine, Matt, Blumenthal and Hallamish are reliable and suitable as a starting point for further study. One can then proceed to extend the knowledge gained by consulting the literature mentioned in these books. Anyone who wants to become acquainted with the mystical texts themselves, is best served in the first instance by the anthology of Zoharic texts compiled by Gershom Scholem, *Zohar: The Book of Splendor* (1977) or Daniel Matt's anthology, *Zohar: The Book of Enlightenment* (1983).

To immerse oneself in Jewish mysticism is to immerse oneself in Jewish tradition. Fortunately the latter, too, need not be a problem; there is a host of good books on the market, in which various aspects of religious Jewish life and the history of Judaism are discussed in an accessible and informative way. In this literature we find such subjects as Torah and traditional literature, the commandments, the synagogue, liturgy, the Jewish calendar, sabbath and feast-days etc.

According to Jewish tradition a person's lifespan is one hundred twenty years. One should continue to study until one is eighty, and after than one may content oneself with the repetition of the knowledge gained. The reader is hereby invited to further study—or to the rereading of this book.

Bibliography

N.B. It should be borne in mind that much of the literature on Jewish mysticism is in Hebrew. Those who read Hebrew are referred to the bibliographies in the literature below.

INTRODUCTION

1.1 The Scholarly Study of Jewish Mysticism

Biale, David, *Gershom Scholem, Kabbalah and Counter-History* (Cambridge, MA/ London 1979).

Dan, Joseph, *Gershom Scholem and the Mystical Dimension of Judaism* (New York/ London 1987). [A detailed discussion of Scholem's views on all phases of Jewish mysticism.]

Scholem, Gershom, *Major Trends in Jewish Mysticism* (New York 1941). [Chapter 1 (pp. 1-39) discusses the view of the *Wissenschaft des Judentums* on Jewish mysticism.]

Schweid, Eliezer, *Judaism and Mysticism according to Gershom Scholem: A Critical Analysis and Programmatic Discussion* (Atlanta 1985). [A critique of the main lines of Scholem's work on the basis of the notion that Judaism is primarily a rational religion.]

Spector, Sheila E., *Jewish Mysticism. An Annotated Bibliography on the Kabbalah in English* (New York/London 1984).

1.2 Historical Background: The Jewish People and its Traditional Literature

Ahlström, Gösta, *The History of Ancient Palestine from the Palaeolithic Period to Alexander's Conquest* (Sheffield 1993).

Cohn-Sherbok, Dan, *Atlas of Jewish History* (London 1994).

Goldberg, David J. & John D. Rayner, *The Jewish People: Their History and Their Religion* (Harmondsworth 1989).

de Lange, N., *An Introduction to Judaism* (Cambridge 2000).

—— (ed.), *The Illustrated History of the Jewish People* (London 1997).

Lemche, Niels Peter, *Ancient Israel: A New History of Israelite Society* (Sheffield 1988).

Maier, Johann, *Geschichte der jüdischen Religion* (Berlin–New York 1972).

Strack, Hermann L., & G. Stemberger, *Introduction to the Talmud and Midrash* (trans. M. Bockmuehl; Edinburgh 1991)

Seltzer, Robert M., *Jewish People, Jewish Thought: The Jewish Experience in History* (New York/London 1980).

1.3 What is Jewish Mysticism? / General overviews

Ariel, David S., *The Mystic Quest. An Introduction to Jewish Mysticism* (New York 1988). [An elementary, topically arranged introduction.]

Dan, Joseph, *Three Types of Ancient Jewish Mysticism* (Cincinnati 1984).

—— *Gershom Scholem and the Mystical Dimension of Judaism* (New York/London 1987).

Fine, Lawrence, "Kabbalistic Texts", in: Barry W. Holtz, ed., *Back to the Sources: Reading the Classic Jewish Texts* (New York 1984), 305-95.

Jacobs, Louis, *Jewish Mystical Testimonies* (New York 1977). [Gives original texts by mystics from all currents of Jewish mysticism in translation, with a short introduction.]

Scholem, Gershom, *Major Trends in Jewish Mysticism* (New York 1941). [Chapter 1 (pp. 1-39) deals among other things with the question of what Jewish mysticism is.]

Schweid, Eliezer, *Judaism and Mysticism according to Gershom Scholem: A Critical Analysis and Programmatic Discussion* (Atlanta 1985).

ANCIENT JEWISH MYSTICISM

Alexander, P., "3 (Hebrew Apocalypse of) Enoch", in: J.H. Charlesworth, ed., *The Old Testament Pseudepigrapha* I (London 1983), 223-315. [Contains an introduction to and an English translation of *Sefer Hekhaloth* with commentary.]

Blau, Ludwig, *Das jüdische Zauberwesen* (Leipzig 1898; Darmstadt 1987).

Blumenthal, David R., *Understanding Jewish Mysticism. A Source Reader* I, *The Merkabah Tradition and the Zoharic Tradition* (New York 1978). [Contains a translation and commentary on *Sefer Yetsirah* and a *Ma'aseh Merkavah* text entitled *Pirqei Hekhaloth*.]

Chernus, Ira, *Mysticism in Rabbinic Judaism* (Berlin/New York 1982).

Cohen, Martin Samuel, *The Shi'ur Qomah: Liturgy and Theurgy in Pre-Kabbalistic Jewish Mysticism* (Lanham/New York/London 1983). [With English translation and commentary on the tractate of the Measurement of the Divine Figure.]

Dan, Joseph, *Three Types of Ancient Jewish Mysticism* (Cincinnati 1984). [One of the few works dealing with language mysticism.]

—— *Gershom Scholem and the Mystical Dimension of Judaism* (New York/London 1987).

—— "The Religious Experience of the Merkavah", in: Arthur Green, ed., *Jewish Spirituality* I: *From the Bible through the Middle Ages* (New York 1987), 289-307. [Goes more deeply into the transition from esoteric speculation to mystical activity.]

Daxelmüller, Christoph, *Zauberpraktiken: Eine Ideengeschichte der Magie* (Zürich 1993).

Gruenwald, Ithamar, *Apocalyptic and Merkabah Mysticism* (Leiden 1980). [Contains introductions and commentary on various Merkavah texts.]

Halperin, D.J., *The Faces of the Chariot: Early Jewish Responses to Ezekiel's Vision* (Tübingen 1988).

Horst, P.W. van der, "The Measurement of the Body. A Chapter in the History of Ancient Jewish Mysticism", in: Dirk van der Plas, ed., *Effigies Dei: Essays on the History of Religions* (Leiden 1987), 56-68. [Contains an English translation and commentary on the Measurement of the Divine Form.]

Janowitz, Naomi, *The Poetics of Ascent: Theories of Language in a Rabbinic Ascent Text* (New York 1989). [Translation and interpretation of the tractate *Ma'aseh Merkavah*.]

Jonas, Hans, *The Gnostic Religion* (2nd rev. edn, Boston 1963).

Kaplan, Aryeh, *Sefer Yetzirah: The Book of Creation* (York Beach, MN 1990).

Kuyt, Annelies, *The 'Descent' to the Chariot: Towards a Description of the Terminology, Place, Function, and Nature of the* Yeridah *in Hekhalot Literature* (Tübingen 1995).

Margalioth, Mordecai, ed., *Sepher ha-Razim: A Newly Recovered Book of Magic from the Talmudic Period. Collected from Genizah Fragments and Other Sources* (Jerusalem 1966).

Schäfer, Peter, *Übersetzung der Hekhalot-Literatur* (Tübingen 1987).

—— *Hekhalot-Studien* (Tübingen 1988).

—— *The Hidden and the Manifest God: Some Major Themes in Early Jewish Mysticism* (Albany, NY 1992).

Scholem, Gershom, *Major Trends in Jewish Mysticism* (New York 1941), 40-79.

—— *Jewish Gnosticism, Merkabah Mysticism, and Talmudic Tradition* (New York 1960).

—— *Kabbalah* (New York 1978), 8-35. [This work also contains articles on palmistry (pp. 317-19), Metatron (pp. 377-81), with bibliography.]

Trachtenberg, Joshua, *Jewish Magic and Superstition: A Study in Folk Religion* (1st edn 1939; New York 1987).

CLASSICAL KABBALAH

Ashtor, Eliyahu, *The Jews of Moslem Spain* (3 vols.; Philadelphia 1973-1984).

Azriel de Gérone, *Commentaire sur la liturgie quotidienne: Introduction, traduction annotée et glossaire des termes techniques par Gabrielle Sed-Rajna* (Leiden 1974).

Baer, Yitzhak, *A History of the Jews in Christian Spain* (2 vols.; Philadelphia 1961).

Biale, David, *Eros and the Jews: From Biblical Israel to Contemporary America* (New York 1992). [Chapters 4 and 5 deal with philosophical and kabbalistic views of sexuality.]

Blumenthal, David R., *Understanding Jewish Mysticism: A Source Reader* I, *The Merkabah Tradition and the Zoharic Tradition* (New York 1978) [Contains a translation and commentary on various fragments of the Zohar.]

—— *Understanding Jewish Mysticism: A Source Reader* II, *The Philosophic-Mystical Tradition and the Hasidic Tradition* (New York 1982). [Contains commentary on Abulafia.]

Dan, Joseph, "The Emergence of Mystical Prayer", in: Joseph Dan and Frank Talmage, eds., *Studies in Jewish Mysticism* (Cambridge, MA 1982), 85-120.

—— *Jewish Mysticism and Jewish Ethics* (Seattle/London/Philadelphia 1986).

—— *Gershom Scholem and the Mystical Dimension of Judaism* (New York/London 1987), 92-229

—— "Ashkenzai Hasidim, 1941-1991: Was There Really a Hasidic Movement in Medieval Germany?", in: Peter Schäfer and Joseph Dan, eds., *Gershom Scholem's* Major Trends in Jewish Mysticism—*50 Years After: Proceedings of the Sixth International Conference on the History of Jewish Mysticism* (Tubingen 1993), 87-101.

Dan, Joseph and Ronald C. Kiener, eds., *The Early Kabbalah* (New York/Mahwah/Toronto 1986). [Contains translated fragments from the Iyyun circle, the Book Bahir, Isaac the Blind, the Gerona group and the Cohen brothers.]

Giller, Pinchas, *The Enlightened Will Shine. Symbolization and Theurgy in the Later Strata of the Zohar* (Albany, NY 1993). [Deals with *Ra'ya Mehemna* and *Tiqqunei ha-Zohar*.]

Hallamish, Moshe, *An Introduction to the Kabbalah* (New York 1999).

Heide, Albert van der, "PARDES: Methodological Reflections on the Theory of the Four Senses", *Journal of Jewish Studies* 34 (1983) 147-59.

Idel, Moshe, "'We Have No Kabbalistic Tradition on This'", in: Isadore Twersky, ed., *Rabbi Moses Nahmanides (Ramban): Explorations in His Religious and Literary Virtuosity* (Cambridge, MA 1983), 51-73.

—— *Kabbalah: New Perspectives* (New Haven/London 1988). [Idel is a specialist in ecstatic Kabbalah. Here he gives his own original view of Jewish mysticism as a whole.]

—— *Studies in Ecstatic Kabbalah* (New York 1988).

—— *The Mystical Experience in Abraham Abulafia* (New York 1988).

—— *Language, Torah, and Hermeneutics in Abraham Abulafia* (New York 1989).

—— "The Contribution of Abraham Abulafia's Kabbalah to the Understanding of Jewish Mysticism", in: Peter Schäfer & Joseph Dan, eds., *Gershom Scholem's* Major Trends in Jewish Mysticism—*50 Years After: Proceedings of the Sixth International Conference on the History of Jewish Mysticism* (Tübingen 1993), 117-43.

Jaffé, Aniela, *The Myth of Meaning* (New York 1975).

Jung, C.G., *The Archetypes and the Collective Unconscious* (London 1968).

Kiener, Ronald, "From *Ba'al ha-Zohar* to Prophet to Ecstatic: The Vicissitudes of Abulafia in Contemporary Scholarship", in: Peter Schäfer & Joseph Dan, eds., *Gershom Scholem's* Major Trends in Jewish Mysticism—*50 Years After: Proceedings of the Sixth International Conference on the History of Jewish Mysticism* (Tübingen 1993), 145-59.

Liebes, Yehuda, *Studies in the Zohar* (Albany, NY 1993).

—— *Studies in Jewish Myth and Jewish Messianism* (Albany, NY 1993).

Maier, Johann, *Die Kabbalah: Einführung—Klassische Texte—Erläuterungen* (München 1995). [An extensive and solid introduction, with translated fragments from many of the mystics.]

Marcus, Ivan G., "The Devotional Ideals of Ashkenazic Pietism", in: Arthur Green, ed., *Jewish Spirituality* I, *From the Bible through the Middles Ages* (New York 1987), 356-66.

—— "The Historical Meaning of Hasidei Ashkenaz: Fact, Fiction or Cultural Self-Image?", in: Peter Schäfer & Joseph Dan, eds., *Gershom Scholem's* Major Trends in Jewish Mysticism—*50 Years After. Proceedings of the Sixth International Conference on the History of Jewish Mysticism* (Tübingen 1993), 103-14.

Matt, Daniel, ed., *Zohar: The Book of Enlightenment* (London 1983). [An anthology of translated fragments from the Zohar.]

—— "The Mystic and the *mizwot*", in: Arthur Green, ed., *Jewish Spirituality* I, *From the Bible through the Middles Ages* (New York 1987), 367-404. [A comparison of the significance of the commandments for mystics and philosophers.]

—— "'New-ancient Words': The Aura of Secrecy in the Zohar", in: Peter Schäfer & Joseph Dan, eds., *Gershom Scholem's* Major Trends in Jewish Mysticism—*50 Years After: Proceedings of the Sixth International Conference on the History of Jewish Mysticism* (Tübingen 1993), 181-207.

—— *The Essential Kabbalah: The Heart of Jewish Mysticism* (San Francisco 1995). [A collection of loose fragments from Zohar texts.]

Scholem, Gershom, *Major Trends in Jewish Mysticism* (New York 1941). [Pp. 80-118 on the German Hasidim; pp. 119-55 on Abraham Abulafia; pp. 156-243 on the Zohar.]

—— *Das Buch Bahir: Ein Schriftdenkmal aus der Frühzeit der Kabbala auf Grund der kritischen Neuausgabe* (Leipzig 1923; repr. Darmstadt 1970).

—— "Das Ringen zwischen dem biblischen Gott und dem Gott Plotins in der alten Kabbala", in: *idem, Über einige Grundbegriffe des Judentums* (Frankfurt a.M. 1970), 9-52.

—— "*Sitra achra*; Gut und Böse in der Kabbala", in: *idem, Von der mystischen Gestalt der Gottheit* (Frankfurt a.M. 1977), 49-82.

—— "*Schechina*; das passiv-weibliche Moment in der Gottheit", in: *idem, Von der mystischen Gestalt der Gottheit* (Frankfurt a.M. 1977), 135-91.

—— *Zohar: The Book of Splendor* (New York 1977).

—— *Kabbalah* (New York 1978).

—— *Origins of the Kabbalah* (ed. R.J. Zwi Werblowsky, trans. Allan Arkush; Princeton 1987). [Still the standard work on Kabbalah up to Gerona.]

Schweid, Eliezer, *Judaism and Mysticism according to Gershom Scholem: A Critical Analysis and Programmatic Discussion* (Atlanta 1985).

Sendor, Mark B., "The Emergence of Provençal Kabbalah: Rabbi Isaac the Blind's Commentary on *Sefer Yezirah* I-II" (Diss. Harvard University, 1994).

Talmage, F., "Apples of Gold: the Inner Meaning of Sacred Texts in Medieval Judaism", in: Arthur Green, ed., *Jewish Spirituality* I, *From the Bible through the Middles Ages* (New York 1987), 313-55.

Tishby, Isaiah & Fischel Lachover, eds., *The Wisdom of the Zohar: An Anthology of Texts* (3 vols.; Oxford 1989). [A standard work. Contains an extensive collection of texts from the Zohar with detailed introduction and commentary.]

Twerksy, I., *Rabad of Posquières: A Twelfth-Century Talmudist* (2nd rev. edn; Philadelphia 1980).

Vajda, Georges, *Le commentaire d'Ezra de Gérone sur le Cantique des Cantiques* (Paris 1969). [Translation and very extensive, but not easy, exposition.]

Verman, Mark, "The Development of *yihudim* in Spanish Kabbalah", *Proceedings of the Third International Conference on the History of Jewish Mysticism: The Age of the Zohar*. Jerusalem Studies in Jewish Thought 8 (Jerusalem 1989), 25-41.

—— "Classifying the *hug ha-'iyyun*", *Proceedings of the Tenth World Congress of Jewish Studies*, Division C, vol. 1, Jewish Thought and Literature (Jerusalem 1990), 57-64.

—— *The Books of Contemplation: Medieval Jewish Mystical Sources* (Albany, NY 1992).

—— "The Evolution of the Circle of Contemplation", in: Peter Schäfer & Joseph Dan, eds., *Gershom Scholem's* Major Trends in Jewish Mysticism—*50 Years After. Proceedings of the Sixth International Conference on the History of Jewish Mysticism* (Tübingen 1993), 163-77.

Wolfson, Elliot R., "Forms of Visionary Ascent as Ecstatic Experience in the Zoharic Literature", in: Peter Schäfer & Joseph Dan, eds., *Gershom Scholem's* Major Trends in Jewish Mysticism—*50 Years After: Proceedings of the Sixth International Conference on the History of Jewish Mysticism* (Tübingen 1993), 209-35.

The Zohar (trans. Harry Sperling and Maurice Simon; 5 vols; London/New York 1984). [A translation of more or less the whole of the Zohar.]

Zuckerman, Arthur J., *A Jewish Princedom in Feudal France, 768-900*. Columbia University Studies in Jewish History 2 (New York 1972).

LURIANIC KABBALAH

1. Messianism

Ben-Sasson, H.H., "Messianic Movements", *Encyclopaedia Judaica* 11 (1971), 1417-27.

Collins, John J., *Apocalypse: The Morphology of a Genre* (Missoula, MT 1979).
—— "Apocalypse, an Overview", in: Mircea Eliade, ed., *The Encyclopaedia of Religion* (New York/London 1987-), 334-36.
—— *The Scepter and the Star: The Messiahs of the Dead Sea Scrolls and Other Ancient Literature*. The Anchor Bible Reference Library (New York 1995).
—— *Apocalypticism in the Dead Sea Scrolls* (London 1997).
Fine, Lawrence, "Medieval Jewish Apocalyptic Literature", in: Mircea Eliade, ed., *The Encyclopaedia of Religion* (New York/London 1987-), 342-44.
García Martínez, F., "Apocalypticism in the Dead Sea Scrolls", in: Bernard McGinn, John J. Collins & Stephen Stein, eds., *The Encyclopedia of Apocalypticism* I (3 vols.; New York 1998) 162-92.
Gaster, T., "Resurrection", *The Interpreter's Dictionary of the Bible* (New York/Nashville 1962-1976), 39a-43b.
Gruenwald, Ithamar, "Jewish Apocalypticism to the Rabbinic Period", in: Mircea Eliade, ed., *The Encyclopaedia of Religion* (New York/London 1987-), 336-42.
Idel, Moshe, "Jewish Apocalypticism: 670-1670", in: Bernard McGinn, John J. Collins & Stephen Stein, eds., *The Encyclopedia of Apocalypticism* II (3 vols.; New York 1998) 204-37.
Jenni, E., "Eschatology of the Old Testament", *The Interpreter's Dictionary of the Bible* (New York/Nashville 1962-1976), 126b-133a.
—— "Messiah, Jewish", *The Interpreter's Dictionary of the Bible* (New York/Nashville 1962-1976), 360a-65b.
Klausner, J., "Eschatology", *Encylopaedia Judaica* 6 (1971), 860-83.
Mach, Michael, "From Apocalypticism to Early Jewish Mysticism?", in: Bernard McGinn, John J. Collins & Stephen Stein, eds., *The Encyclopedia of Apocalypticism* I (3 vols.; New York 1998), 229-64.
Ringgren, Helmer, "Messianism, an Overview", in: Mircea Eliade, ed., *The Encyclopaedia of Religion* (New York/London 1987-), 469-72.
Rist, M., "Eschatology of Apocrypha and Pseudepigrapha", *The Interpreter's Dictionary of the Bible* (New York/Nashville 1962-1976), 133a-135b.
Scholem, Gershom, "Zum Verständnis der messianischen Idee im Judentum", in: *idem, Über einige Grundbegriffe des Judentums* (Frankfurt a.M. 1970), 121-67.
—— "The Messianic Idea in Kabbalism", in: *idem, The Messianic Idea in Judaism and Other Essays on Jewish Spirituality* (New York 1971), 37-48.
VanderKam, James C. & W. Adler, eds., *The Jewish Apocalyptic Heritage in Early Christianity* (Assen/Minneapolis 1996).
VanderKam, James C., "Messianism and Apocalypticism", in: Bernard McGinn, John J. Collins & Stephen Stein, eds., *The Encyclopedia of Apocalypticism* I (3 vols.; New York 1998) 229-64.
Werblowsky, R.J. Zwi, "Jewish Messianism", in: Mircea Eliade, ed., *The Encyclopaedia of Religion* (New York/London 1987-), 472-77.

2. Lurianic Kabbalah

Cordovero, Moses, *The Palm Tree of Deborah: Translated from the Hebrew with an Introduction and Notes by Louis Jacobs* (London 1960).

Dan, Joseph, *Gershom Scholem and the Mystical Dimension of Judaism* (New York/London 1987) [Chapter 10, 244-85.]

Fine, L., *Safed Spirituality: Rules of Mystical Piety, the Beginning of Wisdom* (New York 1984).

Idel, Moshe, *Kabbalah: New Perspectives* (New Haven/London 1988).

Jacobson, Yoram, "The Aspect of the 'Feminine' in the Lurianic Kabbalah", in: Peter Schäfer & Joseph Dan, eds., *Gershom Scholem's* Major Trends in Jewish Mysticism—*50 Years After: Proceedings of the Sixth International Conference on the History of Jewish Mysticism* (Tübingen 1993), 239-55.

Meroz, Ronit, "Faithful Transmission versus Innovation: Luria and His Disciples", in: Peter Schäfer & Joseph Dan, eds., *Gershom Scholem's* Major Trends in Jewish Mysticism—*50 Years After: Proceedings of the Sixth International Conference on the History of Jewish Mysticism* (Tübingen 1993), 257-74. [An important study with new insights.]

Schechter, S., "Safed in the Sixteenth Century", in: *idem, Studies in Judaism*, second series (1908; repr. Philadelphia 1977), 202-328.

Scholem, Gershom, *Major Trends in Jewish Mysticism* (New York 1941). [Chapter 7 (pp. 244-86) on Isaac Luria and his school.

—— "Gilgul; Seelenwanderung und Sympathie der Seelen", in: *idem, Von der mystischen Gestalt der Gottheit* (Frankfurt a.M. 1977), 193-247.

—— *Kabbalah* (New York 1974). [Pp. 67-79 on Kabbalah after 1492 and the Safed school; pp. 420-28 on Isaac Luria.]

Schweid, Eliezer, *Judaism and Mysticism according to Gershom Scholem: A Critical Analysis and Programmatic Discussion* (Atlanta 1985).

Werblowsky, R.J. Zwi, *Joseph Karo. Lawyer and Mystic* (Oxford 1962).

THE KABBALAH OF SHABBETAI ZEVI

Dan, Joseph, *Gershom Scholem and the Mystical Dimension of Judaism* (New York/London 1987). [Chapter 11: "The Sabbatian Upheaval", pp. 286-312.]

Levine, Hillel, "Frankism as Worldly Messianism", in: Peter Schäfer & Joseph Dan, eds., *Gershom Scholem's* Major Trends in Jewish Mysticism—*50 Years After: Proceedings of the Sixth International Conference on the History of Jewish Mysticism* (Tübingen 1993), 283-300.

Scholem, Gershom, *Major Trends in Jewish Mysticism* (New York 1941).

—— *Kabbalah* (New York 1974). [Pp. 244-86 on Shabbetai Zevi; pp. 287-309 on Jacob Frank and the Frankists; pp. 327-32 on the Dönme; pp. 362-68 on *Magen Dawid*; pp. 396-400 on Abraham Cardozo; pp. 435-40 on Nathan of Gaza.]

—— "The Crisis of Tradition in Jewish Messianism", in: *idem, The Messianic Idea in Judaism and Other Essays on Jewish Spirituality* (New York 1971), 49-77.

—— "Redemption through Sin", in: *idem, The Messianic Idea in Judaism and Other Essays on Jewish Spirituality* (New York 1971), 78-141.

—— "The Crypto-Jewish Sect of the Dönmeh (Sabbatians) in Turkey", in: *idem, The Messianic Idea in Judaism and Other Essays on Jewish Spirituality* (New York 1971), 142-66.

—— "A Sabbatian Will from New York", in: *idem, The Messianic Idea in Judaism and Other Essays on Jewish Spirituality* (New York 1971), 167-75.

—— *Sabbatai Sevi: The Mystical Messiah.* Bollingen Series 93 (Princeton 1975).

Schweid, Eliezer, *Judaism and Mysticism according to Gershom Scholem: A Critical Analysis and Programmatic Discussion* (Atlanta 1985). [Pp. 133-40: "The role of Sabbatianism".]

Werblowsky, R.J. Zwi, "Novum Pascha Novae Legis Phase Vetus Terminat", in: Peter Schäfer & Joseph Dan, eds., *Gershom Scholem's* Major Trends in Jewish Mysticism—*50 Years After: Proceedings of the Sixth International Conference on the History of Jewish Mysticism* (Tübingen 1993), 277-81.

Yerushalmi, Y., *From Spanish Court to Italian Ghetto. Isaac Cardoso: A Study in Seventeenth-Century Marranism and Jewish Apologetics* (New York 1971).

HASIDISM

Ben-Amos, Dan & Jerome R. Mintz, eds., *In Praise of the Baal Shem Tov (Shivhei ha-Besht). The Earliest Collection of Legends about the Founder of Hasidism* (1970; repr. Northvale, NJ/London 1993). [An important translation of an important source for the history of Hasidism.]

Blumenthal, David R., *Understanding Jewish Mysticism: A Source Reader II, The Philosophic-Mystical Tradition and the Hasidic Tradition* (New York 1982). [Pp. 87-196.]

Buber, Martin, *I and Thou* (Edinburgh 1958).

—— *The Origin and Meaning of Hasidism* (Atlantic Highlands, NJ 1988).

—— *The Tales of Rabbi Nachman* (Atlantic Highlands, NJ 1988).

—— *Tales of the Hasidim* (New York 1991).

—— *The Legend of the Baal Shem* (Princeton 1995).

Dan, Joseph, *The Teachings of Hasidism* (West Orange, NJ 1983). [Mainly an anthology of Hasidic texts, but with a useful introduction.]

—— *Gershom Scholem and the Mystical Dimension of Judaism* (New York/London 1987). [Chapter 12: "Hasidism and the Modern Period", pp. 313-28.]

Elior, Rachel, "Hasidism—Historical Continuity and Spiritual Change", in: Peter Schäfer & Joseph Dan, eds., *Gershom Scholem's* Major Trends in Jewish Mysticism—*50 Years After: Proceedings of the Sixth International Conference on the History of Jewish Mysticism* (Tübingen 1993), 303-24. [Reactions by M. Hallamish and K. Grözinger on pp. 325-36.]

Foxbrunner, Roman A., *Habad: The Hasidism of R. Shneur Zalman of Lyady* (Northvale, NJ/London 1993).

Green, Arthur, *Tormented Master: A Life of Rabbi Nahman of Bratslav* (Judaic Studies series, 9; University of Alabama 1979).

Gries, Zeev, "Hasidism: The Present State of Research and Some Desirable Priorities", *Numen* 34 (1987), 97-108, 179-213.

Hammer, Harry J., "Resolving the Buber–Scholem Controversy in Hasidism", *Journal of Jewish Studies* 47 (1996), 102-27.

Heschel, Abraham J., *The Circle of the Baal Shem Tov. Studies in Hasidism*. Ed. by Samuel H. Dresner (Chicago/London 1985).

Idel, Moshe, *Hasidism between Ecstasy and Magic* (New York 1995).

Jacobs, Louis, *Hasidic Prayer* (New York 1972). [With a general introduction to Hasidism.]

Mahler, Raphael, *Hasidism and the Jewish Enlightenment: Their Confrontation in Galicia and Poland in the First Half of the Nineteenth Century* (Philadelphia/New York/Jerusalem 5745/1985).

Meijers, Daniël, *Revolutie der Vromen. Ontstaan en ontwikkeling van het chassidisme* (Hilversum 1989). [Accessible description of the development of the movement, with special regard for the social background and habad-hasidism. To be published in English as *Mysticism and Rationalism: the Sociogenesis of the Hasidic Movement.*]

Rabinowicz, Harry M., *The World of Hasidism* (London 1970).

Rabinowicz, Tzvi M., ed., *The Encyclopedia of Hasidism* (Northvale, NJ/London 1996).

Safran, Bezalel, ed., *Hasidism: Continuity or Innovation?* Harvard Judaic Texts and Monographs V (Cambridge, MA/London 1988). [Includes E. Etkes, "Hasidism as a Movement—The First Stage", pp. 1-26 and Y. Hasdai, "The Origins of the Conflict between Hasidim and Mitnagdim", pp. 27-45.]

Schatz-Uffenheimer, Rivka, *Hasidism as Mysticism: Quietistic Elements in Eighteenth Century Hasidic Thought* (Princeton, NJ/Jerusalem 1993). [Theoretical work for specialists.]

Scholem, Gershom, *Major Trends in Jewish Mysticism* (New York 1941). [Pp. 325-50 on Hasidism.]

—— "*Zaddik*; der Gerechte", in: *idem, Von der mystischen Gestalt der Gottheit* (Frankfurt a.M. 1977), 83-134.

—— *Kabbalah* (New York 1974). [Pp. 310-11 on the Ba'al Shem.]

—— "The Neutralisation of the Messianic Element in Early Hasidism", in: *idem, The Messianic Idea in Judaism and Other Essays on Jewish Spirituality* (New York 1971), 176-202.

—— "*Devekut*, or Communion with God", in: *idem, The Messianic Idea in Judaism and Other Essays on Jewish Spirituality* (New York 1971), 203-26.

—— "Martin Buber's Interpretation of Hasidism", in: *idem, The Messianic Idea in Judaism and Other Essays on Jewish Spirituality* (New York 1971), 227-50.

Shulman, Y. David, *The Chambers of the Palace: Teachings of Rabbi Nachman of Bratslav* (Northvale, NJ/London 1993).

Weiss, Joseph, *Studies in Eastern European Jewish Mysticism*. Ed. by David Goldstein (Oxford 1985).
Zborowski, Mark & Elizabeth Herzog, *Life is with People: The Culture of the Shtetl* (Introduction by Margaret Mead; New York 1952).

LANGUAGE MYSTICISM

Abrams, Daniel, "From Germany to Spain: Numerology as a Mystical Technique", *Journal of Jewish Studies* 47 (1996), 85-101.
Arndt, O., "Zahlenmystik bei Philo, Spielerei oder Schriftauslegung?", *Zeitschrift für Religions- und Geistesgeschichte* 19 (1967), 167-71.
Blau, Ludwig, *Das jüdische Zauberwesen* (Leipzig 1898; repr. Darmstadt 1987).
Dan, Joseph, *Three Types of Ancient Jewish Mysticism* (Cincinnati 1984).
—— "The Ashkenazic Hasidic Concept of Language", in: Lewis Glinert, ed., *Hebrew in Ashkenaz. A Language in Exile* (New York/Oxford 1993), 11-25.
—— "The Name of God, the Name of the Rose, and the Concept of Language in Jewish Mysticism", *Medieval Encounters* 2 (1996), 228-48.
Derbolav, Josef, *Platons Sprachphilosophie im Kratylos und in den späteren Schriften* (Darmstadt 1972).
Dornseiff, Franz, *Das Alphabet in Mystik und Magie*. Stoicheia. Studien zur Geschichte des antiken Weltbildes und der griechischen Wissenschaft, 7 (Leipzig/Berlin 1925).
Eco, Umberto, *The Search for the Perfect Language* (Oxford 1985).
Guthrie, W.K.C., *A History of Greek Philosophy* V (Cambridge 1978).
Idel, Moshe, "Reification of Language in Jewish Mysticism", in: Steven T. Katz, ed., *Mysticism and Language* (New York/Oxford 1992), 42-79.
Janowitz, Naomi, *The Poetics of Ascent. Theories of Language in a Rabbinic Ascent Text* (New York 1989).
Lieberman, Stephen J., "A Mesopotamian Background for the So-called Aggadic 'Measures' of Biblical Hermeneutics?", *Hebrew Union College Annual* 58 (1987), 157-225.
Munk, Michael L. & N. Scherman, *The Wisdom in the Hebrew Alphabet: The Sacred Letters as a Guide to Jewish Deed and Thought*. ArtScroll Mesorah Series (New York 1983). [A collection of rabbinic traditions on the Hebrew letters.]
Otte, Klaus, *Das Sprachverständnis bei Philo von Alexandrien: Sprache als Mittel der Hermeneutik* (Tübingen 1968).
Pohlenz, Max, *Die Stoa. Geschichte einer geistigen Bewegung* (Göttingen 1964).
Sambursky, S., "On the Origin and Significance of the Term Gematria", *Journal of Jewish Studies* 29 (1978), 35-38.
Scholem, Gershom, "The Meaning of the Torah in Jewish Mysticism", in: idem, *On the Kabbalah and its Symbolism* (New York 1969), 32-86.
—— "The Name of God and the Linguistic Theory of the Kabbala", *Diogenes* 79 (Fall 1972), 59-80; 80 (Winter 1972), 164-94.

—— *Kabbalah* (New York 1974). ["Gematria", pp. 337–43.]

Trachtenberg, Joshua, *Jewish Magic and Superstition: A Study in Folk Religion* (1939; repr. New York 1987).

Wald, Stephen G., *The Doctrine of the Divine Name: An Introduction to Classical Kabbalistic Theology.* Brown Judaic Studies 149 (Atlanta, GA 1988).

Zwiep, Irene, *The Mother of Reason and Revelation: A Short History of Medieval Jewish Linguistic Thought* (Amsterdam 1997).

POPULAR LITERATURE ON "KABBALAH"

Rabbi Akiba ben Joseph, *The Book of Formation (Sepher Yetzirah) including: The 32 Paths of Wisdom, Their Correspondence with the Hebrew Alphabet and the Tarot Symbols* (New York 1970).

Bischoff, Erich, *Kabbala: An Introduction to Jewish Mysticism and its Secret Doctrine* (York Beach, ME 1985)

Fortune, Dion, *Psychic Self Defense* (London 1930)

—— *The Mystical Qabalah* (London 1935).

Lévi, Eliphas, *Transcendental Magic: Its Doctrine and Ritual* (Chicago 1946)

Poncé, Charles, *Kabbalah: An Introduction and Illumination for the World Today* (London 1974)

Scholem, Gershom, *Zohar: The Book of Splendor* (New York 1977).

Index